Divorce in Psychosocial Perspective: Theory and Research

Divorce in Psychosocial Perspective: Theory and Research

by
Joseph Guttmann
University of Haifa

IEA
LAWRENCE ERLBAUM ASSOCIATES, PUBLISHERS
1993   Hillsdale, New Jersey   Hove and London

Lawrence Erlbaum Associates, Inc., Publishers
365 Broadway
Hillsdale, New Jersey 07642

Library of Congress Cataloging-in-Publication Data

Guttmann, Joseph
    Divorce in Psychosocial Perspective : Theory and Research / by Joseph Guttmann.
      p. cm.
    Includes bibliographical references and indexes.
    ISBN 0-8058-0347-5
    1.   Divorce — Psychological aspects. I. Title.
HQ814.G94 1993
  306.89 — dc20   92-33412
                                      CIP

Books published by Lawrence Erlbaum Associates are printed on acid-free paper, and their
bindings are chosen for strength and durability.

Printed in the United States of America
10 9 8 7 6 5 4 3 2 1

To Sarit, Dan and Barak, for successfully surviving my fatherhood.
To Yvonne for sharing with me respect for and love of parenting.
To Michal for standing by me and letting me stand by her.

Contents

Preface   ix

1 Divorce in Its Social Context   1

2 Theoretical Models of the Divorce Process   31

3 The Psychosocial Model of the Divorce Process   51

4 Divorced Mothers   82

5 Divorced Fathers   111

6 Children of Divorced Parents: Theoretical
       and Research Considerations   141

7 Parental Divorce and the Reaction of Children   168

References   202

Author Index   233

Subject Index   245

Preface

There are many books that deal with divorce and its aftermath. Some deal with the single-parent family in general, others focus more specifically on the impact of divorce on children and mothers, and still others examine the legal and/or sociological aspects of divorce. The recent renaissance of interest in fatherhood has also triggered some publications that examine the father's role in the divorce drama. Many books on divorce are characterized by their practical orientation toward the issues and problems posed by divorce.

None, however, has attempted to offer an integrated view of the massive theoretical and research literature about divorced adults and their children. And none has presented a comprehensive analysis of divorce as a psychological process within the larger social context. This book intends to fill that void. The purpose of the present volume is threefold: (a) to offer a comprehensive view of divorce as a social, interpersonal, and psychological phenomenon; (b) to review the theory and research about divorce in that literature focuses on the major protagonists of the divorce drama: the mother, the father, and the children; and (c) to introduce a new psychosocial theory of the divorce process.

This book is intended primarily for people whose interest in the subject of divorce is academic and/or clinical. In academia, it may serve students of family dynamics, divorce, and family therapy. Researchers may find this volume useful as it presents a broad framework from which research questions may be deduced and in light of which research results can be explained. In the clinical field, the book may serve psychiatrists, psychologists, social workers, counselors, divorce mediators, and other professionals who have a deep interest in divorce.

The organization of the book is intended to facilitate its use by the various professionals, given their different perspectives.

Chapter 1 presents the social and cultural context in which divorce occurs. It provides a descriptive analysis of divorce in a historical perspective and its present legal, social, and cultural context. The chapter reviews the social changes as factors contributing to the destabilization of the institution of marriage. It also reviews the social factors found to be related to the rate of divorce.

Although divorce is always a unique, personal, and subjective experience, there are common denominators within the process of most divorces. Chapter 2 presents several theoretical models through which some of these common denominators can be understood. The critical discussion of these models provides the reader not only with a theoretical spectrum from which to consider the proposed psychosocial theory of divorce but also with the necessary background for understanding the need for, and the conceptual assumptions of, the theory.

Chapter 3 presents a new psychosocial theory of the divorce process. This theory derives some of its content from other theories of the divorce process and from the writer's own clinical observations and research. But much of its assumptions and conceptual framework relies on the principles of the social exchange theory, cognitive consistency theory, and attribution theory. Others have already applied the social exchange theory to explain the process of marital breakdown; but its application was limited to the divorce crisis and was not applied to form a comprehensive model of the whole divorce process and a person's adjustment to it. The main purpose of the psychosocial theory is to show how, by adopting the principles of the social exchange theory together with some cognitive theories, one can achieve a more comprehensive understanding of divorce as a psychological process taking place within a social context.

Chapter 4 deals with the plight of divorced mothers. It examines the factors that contribute to their adjustment and provides an extensive review of relevant theoretical and research literature. Three central issues are faced by most divorced mothers who have custody of their children: (a) a significant decline in their social and economic standing; (b) a significant change in their relationship with their children, ex-husbands, other adults, and society at large; and (c) the managerial difficulties of heading a single-parent household. These issues as they relate to custodial and noncustodial divorced mothers are discussed in detail.

For approximately 90% of the fathers, divorce means life without the children. This is not accidental, and many factors contribute to this lopsided statistic. The purpose of chapter 5 is to provide the reader with a critical review of (a) the popular myths, stereotypes, and misunderstandings surrounding fatherhood as they relate to divorced fathers; (b) the father's influence on his children's cognitive, social, and emotional well-being; (c) the "absent father" literature and its underlying assumptions; and (d) the unique difficulties facing both a custodial and a noncustodial father.

The main purpose of chapter 6 is to offer the reader a conceptualized framework within which much of the "children of divorce" research studies can be viewed. The fact that the divorce process relates to a complex network of social and psychological variables makes it difficult to determine the real net influence of parental separation on children. Also, the interactions among the many variables included in the process complicate research designs and the interpretation of research results. In order to better consider and interpret the detailed review of the "children of divorce" research, presented in chapter 7, a developmental framework is proposed.

Social scientists have been increasingly aware of the great variety in both quality and intensity of children's reactions to divorce. Some of these variations can be accounted for by situational variables (i.e., socioeconomics, support system, parenting, family relationships) and some by the children's characteristics (i.e., age, sex, temperament). The purpose of chapter 7 is to review and reexamine some of the research literature's major findings and to organize these into children's developmental framework.

Although there is an extensive review of the divorce literature throughout the book, this review is by no means exhaustive. The virtual explosion of the literature on divorce (research and otherwise) since the 1970s forces selectivity in citation and reference. Three main criteria determined the selection process and the inclusion of bibliographical items in our discussion: (a) representativeness—that is, a bibliographical item that was judged to represent others well in its approach and/or conclusions about a particular issue; (b) uniqueness—that is, a bibliographical item that was judged as different, original and broadening the perspective on a particular issue; and (c) relevance—for instance, there are many theories of the divorce process. The four reviewed in chapter 2 were chosen because of their different theoretical orientations and because it was believed that, put together, they can provide a broad enough sense of the different approaches and issues in the divorce process. The same basic rationale dictated the reference to factors and variables that research studies found relevant to divorce. The shortcomings resulting from the need to be selective is acknowledged.

It is also acknowledged that the psychosocial theory of divorce, presented in chapter 3, is drawn in broad strokes and much of it needs to stand the test of research and clinical experience. The theory is limited to the psychological process of divorce as it occurs within a social context. As such, it does not serve as a conceptual umbrella for some of the other chapters in the book. It is hoped that further development of the theory will result in refinement of its conceptual assumptions and operational definitions. For the meantime, it is presented here with the hope that it will trigger the necessary discussion and research for it to be what it is meant to be: a framework for understanding the divorce process.

ACKNOWLEDGMENTS

Writing, for me, is often a lonely affair associated with swings from excitement to frustration. I could not have managed these without the encouragements of two very special friends and colleagues, Danny Bar-Tal and Arie Kruglanski, and of course that of my wife, Michal. Special thanks are also due to Kattie Claman-Sachs for helping me with the difficult task of checking, verifying, and typing the references. Finally, I wish to express my gratitude to Judi Amsel for her patience, understanding, and thoughtful input regarding the earlier drafts of this manuscript and to Debbie Ruel for her conscientious and careful editorial assistance.

1   Divorce in Its Social Context

Much of this book deals with divorce as a personal experience within a social context. This chapter, however, discusses divorce from the social perspective. The assumption is that in order to understand the etiology and consequences of divorce we must view divorce as a personal matter that is greatly affected by the social and cultural environment in which it occurs. It is the knowledge of the particular interaction between personal and social factors that gives us a better comprehension of the divorce phenomenon.

Even a cursory look at the divorce rate and trend in past decades shows the susceptibility of the divorce rate to short- and long-term fluctuations. For example, the rate of divorce dropped during the Great Depression of the 1930s, and quickly returned to its earlier level afterward. Then, toward the end of World War II and immediately after, it increased dramatically and reached a peak in 1946. The rate then decreased very rapidly, reaching almost its prewar level, only to mount again to record heights in the early 1970s. The aim of this chapter is to present the principal social factors that may account for these fluctuations in the frequency and trend of divorce. The chapter begins with a consideration of the difference, indeed the tension, between individualistic and social explanations of divorce. It then reviews the relevant statistics, and discusses the legal, social, cultural, and economic contexts that affect the divorce rate and are affected by divorce.

INDIVIDUALISTIC VERSUS SOCIAL EXPLANATIONS OF DIVORCE

The United States has among the highest divorce rate among the industrialized countries, but it also has among the highest marriage and remarriage

1

rates. These rates are not independent of each other, but are part of the same phenomenon. Common ideological and social factors lead to marriage, divorce, and remarriage.

Divorce was for decades perceived not only as an indication of pathology in divorcing individuals, but also as a social disease. The implicit and explicit prevailing belief was that divorce was harmful to the individuals involved and to society, and was an offense against God (Popenoe, 1988). Therefore, a remedy had to be found. The problem was at first believed to be the immorality of those involved; and the appropriate response was therefore censure and punishment. Later, as social scientists looked at the broader picture, they assumed that social ills were also to blame for the breakdown of families. They called on lawmakers to solve at least some of these social defects, and to protect the victims by raising high legal barriers against divorce. The psychological approach offered yet another view: Marital dissolution stems from the difficulties experienced by individuals. Therefore, divorce had to be eradicated by psychotherapeutic means and by providing support to families in crises (Halem, 1989).

More recently, the U.S. ideology of the family has emphasized personal fulfillment as the main reason for maintaining family relationships, and love as the basis for marriage (Theodorson, 1965). Most people do marry, probably expecting that the promises of this ideology will be fulfilled. But they find themselves pressured into organizing their family life along other (less romantic but more dominant) dimensions. Internal family responsibilities, the demands of formal organizations, gender role stereotypes, social restrictions, and societal prescription regarding family life complicate, and may even preclude, finding personal satisfaction within the family setting (Yorburg, 1973).

Divorce is often the consequence. But people rarely view their divorce in these terms. Social and structural factors are largely invisible to people who must cope with the personal consequences of these factors on a daily basis.

So long as divorce remained a relatively rare phenomenon, affecting only a small proportion of the population, it was accounted for in highly individualistic terms. Having learned that marriage results from being in love with the right person, divorcing people consider themselves or their partners as responsible for marital breakdown. Divorce came to be viewed primarily as a matter of mistaken choice, as only a personal, not a social structural, failure. The language of guilt and innocence, blame and vindication has thus been used as an explanatory framework by the divorcing individuals. The community views divorce similarly, reinforcing the perception that both happy marriages and divorces are functions of mate selection. Therefore, it encourages divorced persons to try again, and to embark on a search for new and more compatible partners (Feldberg & Kohen, 1980).

It was only when divorce became more frequent and visible, and its aftermath affected the lives of a substantial number of children and adults, that people began to appreciate marital breakdown as a social phenomenon, arising out of a particular social context, and affecting the fabric and structure of society. By now it has become abundantly clear to all students of family dissolution that in order to understand the etiology and conse- quences of divorce, one must keep an open eye and an open mind to divorce as a matter that is both personal and part of a much broader social trend. No individualistic reasons alone and no social reasons alone will provide the complete picture. An understanding of the interaction of these two sets of reasons now seems to be crucial for obtaining a better understanding of the phenomenon of divorce.

DIVORCE STATISTICS

In appraising the extent and trend of divorce we must rely on statistics from governmental agencies such as the National Office of Vital Statistics and the Census Bureau. But these statistics can be misleading. For one, they are incomplete. Only about half of the 50 states submit complete information to the federal government on the numbers and characteristics of the divorces granted within their jurisdictions (e.g., U.S. Bureau of the Census, 1990). Divorce statistics can also be difficult to interpret because the rates are calculated in different ways. The most common way of reporting the divorce rate is by calculating the ratio of the number of marriage licenses granted in a given year and the number of divorce decrees. Although this is a very simple and straightforward technique, it is somewhat deceptive. In 1988, for example, there were approximately 2.4 million marriages and 1.2 million divorces. Does this mean that U.S. citizens were almost twice as likely to marry as to divorce in that year? Or does it mean that half of all marriages end in divorce? Although many have assumed that these figures indicate that one in two marriages will end in divorce, we know that most of the divorces in 1988 involved marriages contracted in prior years. Thus, the ratio of number of marriages to number of divorces compares two very different populations. Furthermore, if for whatever reason many people decide not to marry legally, then the calculated divorce rate will show an artificial increase because it is compared to a lower rate of marriages. Finally, this measure may not give a good estimate of the likelihood of first marriages to end in a divorce. Some of the divorce decrees may likely have been issued to people who have been divorced before, and such persons are accounted for in the divorce statistics each time (Sweet & Bumpass, 1988).

A better way to calculate the divorce rate is by the crude rate (i.e., the number of divorces per 1,000 population). The problem with this is that included in "population" are children and adults who are not "divorce potential," either because they have decided never to marry or cannot divorce, for example because of religious reasons. Another somewhat more refined measure is the number of divorces per 1,000 married women. But the best way to determine the likelihood of a marriage in a given year ending in divorce would be to take a national sample of all marriages in that year, and then to follow them through life until the marriages are dissolved either by divorce or by death. The problem with this approach is that, although it would provide a very accurate statistic, by the time we have it, the statistic may no longer be a good predictor for current marriages.

Following these words of caution, the best statistic available is the crude rate. In 1989, the divorce rate was 4.8 per 1,000 population in the United States (National Center for Health Statistics, 1989). This is slightly less than 4.9 in 1984, which was the same in 1983 and 1982. From the turn of the century until 1964 the divorce rate had been 2.0 or less. In 1946 it more than doubled to 4.3 per 1,000 people, and then sharply declined to prewar rates. From 1958 there was a slow increase, until a rapid surge began in the late 1960s. Divorce rates peaked in 1979 and 1981 at 5.3 per 1,000 population. The 1989 divorce rate was the lowest since 1975 (Hernandez, 1988).

These numbers, however, give only a partial picture of the extent and trend of divorce in the United States. As noted by Leslie and Korman (1985), the reported rates are influenced by the following factors:

1. Divorced people are far more likely to be found in urban than in rural areas. This is partially so because there are fewer divorces in rural areas and because divorced people from rural areas tend to migrate to the city after the divorce.
2. As Glenn and Shelton (1985) reported, divorce rates are highest in the western part of the country and lowest in the northeast. This is partially owing to differences between the regions in people's average age (lower in the West) and religious beliefs (higher concentration of Catholics in the Northeast).
3. There is an inverse relationship between divorce rates and social class. That is, when education or income are used as indicators for social class, people from lower social classes tend to divorce more than do people from higher social classes.
4. In comparison to the divorce rate of people in their first marriage, the divorce rate among those of previously divorced is twice as high. For those who are married three or more times the rate is even higher. The divorce rate is lowest for remarried widows and widowers.
5. The divorce rate for men who marry in their teens is twice as high as for men who marry in their 20s. The same proportion holds for

women who marry at the age of 18 or 19. For women who marry at an even younger age the divorce rate is three times as high as for women who marry in their 20s.

6. The divorce rate is higher in the early years of marriage. Although the first year of marriage is also the peak year of separation, the third year of marriage is the peak year for the number of divorces being granted: "4.4 percent of the divorcing couples had been married less than one year. One-third of divorcing couples (33.7 percent) were married one to four years, and about one-fourth (27.8 percent) were married five to nine years. The remaining third of the divorcing couples had been married ten years or more with 15 percent married ten to fourteen years and 19 percent married fifteen years or more" (Eshleman, 1985, p. 584).

7. Booth, Johnson, and Edwards (1983) reported that people who attend religious services are less likely to divorce, and people who are undergoing very stressful experiences—such as unemployment or death of a child—are more likely to divorce.

But although these points tell us something about whose marriages are more likely to end in divorce, they do no more than give a clue as to why these marriages tend to dissolve. They also tell little about why the overall divorce rate in the early 1990s is so much higher than a few decades ago, and why the overall divorce trend is as described earlier. In order to find some answers to these questions we need to consider a number of broad social structures and trends. We have to examine what has happened to the barriers—legal, economic, religious, and cultural—that have in the past kept many people from dissolving their marriages.

DIVORCE AND THE LAW

No area in which society touches family life has changed as rapidly and dramatically since the 1970s as the legal procedure for dissolving a marriage.

Until 1970, there were legal restrictions and specified grounds for divorce. The legally accepted reasons for breaking up a marriage were adultery, desertion, cruelty, and nonsupport, and these were whether they were true or false. The basic rationale for this was, as noted by Clark (1968):

> that marital happiness is best secured by making marriage indissoluble except for very few causes. When the parties know that they are bound together for life, the argument runs, they will resolve their differences and disagreements

and make an effort to get along with each other. If they are able to separate legally upon less serious grounds, they will make no such effort, and immorality will result. (pp. 242–243)

In accordance with this rationale, under the old legal system, the legal proceeding needed to be, and indeed was, adversarial. It required that one party should be found guilty of wrongdoing and responsible for the family breakdown. That person was to be punished by the court vis-à-vis the postdivorce financial settlement. This traditional law reflected the social norms and accepted beliefs of the time: Marriage should be a lifelong commitment and that a man and a woman should devote themselves to each other, to their children, and to their home. In time, these assumptions about marriage, divorce, and gender-based division of roles and responsibilities came to be questioned. The public's growing awareness of the gap between these assumptions and reality brought pressure to bear on lawmakers to reform the divorce laws.

The "divorce revolution" (Weitzman, 1985) began in 1970 when California's state legislature enacted the no-fault divorce law. The no-fault law conditioned divorce only upon one partner's assertion that "irreconcilable differences have caused the irremediable breakdown of the marriage" (Weitzman & Dixon, 1986 p. 345). The underlying assumption reflected in this law was that bad marriages should be dissolved, that economic circumstances should determine alimony and the division of family assets, and that children, where possible, should maintain contact with both parents.

There is no uniform code of divorce law that is applied in all 50 states. However, as of 1988, all states except for South Dakota adopted some variation of no-fault divorce laws (Mintz & Kellogg, 1988). In some states, the divorcing couple must live apart for a certain period of time (from 6 months to 3 years) in order to obtain a legal divorce. In other less conservative states, "incompatibility" or "irreconcilable differences" must be shown by one partner if the other objects to the divorce. In most of these cases the fact that one partner chooses to leave the marriage is considered a sufficient proof of the need to divorce. Moreover, in some states, a divorce decree will be granted if one partner decides, for whatever reasons, that the marriage has reached a point of "irretrievable breakdown" (Halem, 1989; Mintz & Kellogg, 1988).

These reforms in family law appear to have emanated from changes in the larger fabric of society. Social trends and changes such as the women's movement, women's greater participation in the labor force, greater sexual freedom, the self-actualization theme of the 1960s and 1970s, and of course the increase in divorce rate, put the pressure on the lawmakers to change divorce statutes so that they might better reflect these social realities. A small part of these realities, which may nevertheless have been a strong motive for liberalizing the divorce law, was the fact that some lawmakers had themselves experienced painful divorces.

However, no-fault is not only a change in a legal code, it represents a cognitive scheme. Not only did it eliminate the need to prove a spouse's misconduct, but "it eliminated the concept of fault itself" (Weitzman & Dixon, 1986, p. 345). The new law was connected with the trend that took moral issues out of the hands of social and governmental institutions, and promoted individual freedom and equality between men and women. It was also compatible with the rejection of the traditional patriarchal pattern of the family, and with the demand that adult men and women be treated as autonomous and equally responsible for breakdowns in their marriage and for their life after divorce.

Several purposes were to be served by the reform of the divorce law: (a) the elimination of the need for hypocrisy, perjury, and collusion often required by the fault system, (b) the reduction of the levels of bitterness and suffering that are part of the divorce process, and (c) assistance given to reach a fairer and more rational financial settlement.

Weitzman and Dixon (1986) offered the following analysis of the four most important characteristics of the no-fault law:

1. The new law eliminates the "fault-based grounds for divorce."

No longer does one partner need to file suit against the spouse on grounds such as adultery, mental cruelty, physical abuse, desertion, or other such marital misconduct. The basic premise for "fault" divorces was that there was one "right" and/or "innocent" party and one "wrong" and/or "guilty" party that needed to be punished. By replacing the old system with a single new standard of "irreconcilable differences" there is no longer a need to invent false reasons for divorce. More importantly, the new system recognizes that in marital breakdown, there is no guilty or innocent party. Now as far as the personal relationship between spouses is concerned, the legal process of divorce begins and ends with a "petition for dissolution," where no justification need be given.

2. The new law removes adversarial confrontation from divorce proceedings.

The proponents of the reformed law realized that the fault-based law that is founded on antagonism aggravated the emotional trauma of dissolving a marriage. The language that is used under the new system reflects this nonadversarial approach to the legal process. Thus, "divorce" became "dissolution"; "plaintiffs" and "defendants" became "petitioners" and "respondents"; "alimony" became "spousal support"; and the court records read "in re the marriage of Doe" instead of "Doe vs. Doe" (p. 346).

3. Under the reformed law, the division of property and the financial settlement are based on equity, equality, and the economic needs of the former partners.

Although the rationale underlying the old divorce law was protection, that of the new law is equality. In the past, it was assumed, and generally accepted that the state had a legitimate role in protecting the family and its members in the case of one partner's gross misconduct. If that partner was physically abusing or committed adultery, he or she would be severely penalized by the court when financial arrangements were considered (Weitzman & Dixon, 1986). The reformers sought to grant financial settlement based on the prevailing social norms; that is, personal freedom and the principle of equality between the genders. No more were property and alimony to be granted on the basis of either fault or gender-based role assignments. Each spouse has equal right to the accumulated wealth of the family.

Some states (e.g., California) have taken this idea to its logical conclusion, so that judges decide on postdivorce property settlement by simply splitting the family's assets into two equal parts (Foster & Freed, 1974). But in most other states, judges continue to take each particular family's circumstances into account (Halem, 1989). They may (or may not) consider the length of the marriage, the number and age of the children, and the earning power of each spouse. Although this leads to a wide variety of judgments within and between states, it allows for individual differences in needs to be taken into account within a family and between families.

With regard to alimony, the trend is toward "no alimony at all or short-term alimony for 'rehabilitative' purposes, as opposed to the long-term or lifelong alimony in pre-no-fault days" (Mintz & Kellogg, 1988, p. 1708).

The push toward equality between the sexes on other fronts forced aside the view of the wife as dependent on and in need of the protection of her husband. The legislators of the no-fault law took note of the growing social recognition of women's changing social status, education, ability to be self-supporting, and of their demand to be treated equally. As a result no more financial support is awarded to a woman merely because she had been a wife and a mother. Generally, she is expected to be able to support herself by work as is her husband. This of course ignores the fact that women employed full time earn, on the average, far less than do men with full-time jobs. And although in most states judges are instructed to consider, in the matter of alimony, the length of the marriage and the earning power of the woman, alimony is often restricted by conditions and time (Weitzman, 1985).

The cutback in alimony is accompanied by a significant cutback in child support as well. Grants for child support have been reduced significantly since the enactment of the no-fault law. Child support grants following divorce decreased from 1978 to 1985 by 28.4%. Furthermore, in the 50% of the cases in which any alimony is paid at all, the amount received is far less than the actual cost of raising a child (Popenoe, 1988).

4. The no-fault divorce law redefined the traditional gender-based family and parental responsibilities.

Under the new system, the husband is not solely responsible for financial support, nor is the wife solely responsible for caring for the children. The new standards for property division and alimony reflect the legislators' belief in the responsibility and ability of each spouse to achieve self-supporting status. In addition, the "child's best interest" guideline assumes no inherent advantage for mothers in custody hearings. Not only are fathers and mothers equally responsible for the financial welfare of their children, they are also equally responsible for their children's overall well-being.

In summary, the most dramatic social change with regard to divorce other than its increased rate has been the widespread acceptance and implementation of no-fault statutes. In its social philosophy and rationales, the no-fault reform represented a further step in the separation of church and state, and reflected the immense appeal for many of the egalitarian approach to social issues. Indeed, as many writers argued (e.g., Kessler, 1975; Popenoe, 1988; Thornton, 1985), the law reformers did not lead but rather followed the public's changing attitudes about what was fair, just, and desirable. It was to this general sentiment that legal activists, together with behavioral and social scientists and policymakers, responded by formally challenging the mores and operational norms of domestic law. Halem (1989) argued that "overall the change [following the no-fault reform] has not been as radical as current reformers would like us to believe. In actuality, the 'new' reforms may be little more than reaffirmation of courtroom practices and philosophy on divorce" (p. 287).

Still, one cannot deny or ignore the change that the legal system has made and helped to create in divorce policies and practices. One of the obvious impacts was the lowering of the barriers to divorce. Did that contribute to the increase in divorce rate? Research shows that it did not. Comparing the divorce rate in reform states with those in "fault" states, Wright and Stetson (1978) concluded that "Whatever the effects of no-fault reforms on the life of individual couples, they do not seem to have contributed to the nation's rising divorce rates" (p. 580). But it did contribute significantly, and often disastrously, to the financial burden of divorced mothers (Weitzman, 1985). As of 1986, over one third (34%) of divorced female-headed families were below the federal government's poverty line, as compared to 13% of all households (U.S. Bureau of the Census, 1986). This is apparently the result of the fact that under the new system men are often required to pay alimony and child support payments that are unsubstantial. On the other hand, in about 90% of cases it is usually the woman who asks for and is given custody of the children. Thus, although the no-fault law has on the whole been successful in reducing the hostility promoted by the old system and in supporting the egalitarian approach to social issues, economically it dealt women a bad hand.

A brief look at the international scene shows that in recent years countries have increasingly tended to make divorce legal. In Argentina, divorce became legal in 1954. In Spain and Italy the tension between public demand for legal divorce and the religious law institutions is very high, and some form of legal separation has been made available. The change in the legality of divorce occurs mainly in Catholic and Islamic countries. For Catholicism is the dominant religion in countries where divorce is illegal, and the fundamental legal code of Islam allows men to have a far-reaching advantage over women.

Some Islamic countries, too, have changed divorce laws, and made divorce more difficult for men and easier for women. This was done in order to equalize the conditions under which divorce could be obtained. In Tunisia, for example, men have lost the right to divorce their wives by the traditional practice of pronouncing "I divorce thee" three times; men now have to plead their case before a court, and women are allowed to do the same (Nimkoff, 1965).

But when the rate of divorce is judged to be excessive by those in power, they may make divorce more difficult to obtain. This happened in the Soviet Union in 1954. But all in all, there does not seem to be a country where the general trend is reversed (i.e., where divorce was legal and later prohibited).

DIVORCE AND ECONOMIC CONDITIONS

There is little doubt about the nature of the relationship between changing the divorce law in the United States and the economic situations of divorced women (Halem, 1982; Weitzman, 1985). There are, however, conflicting opinions concerning both the nature of and reasons for the relationship between the changes in the economic conditions of a society and the fluctuation in the divorce rate.

The Industrialization–Divorce Connection

Several authors have investigated the effect of industrialization on family dissolution, and have examined whether and how the divorce rate changes with economic prosperity and recession. Generally, trends in divorce have corresponded with trends in both industrialization (Kitson, Babri, & Roach, 1985) and urbanization (Reiss & Lee, 1988). This trend is found both when the divorce rate is compared over time in a given country, and when the divorce rates in urban and rural areas are compared within a particular society. In the United States, for instance, during the 50 years between the Civil War and World War I, when the United States experienced rapid industrial growth, the divorce rate increased from 1 to 8 per 1,000 married women, although in the course of the next 50 years the divorce rate increased only from 8 to 9 per 1,000 married women. In other societies that underwent rapid industrialization during the same period, the divorce rate increased proportionately much more (Reiss & Lee, 1988).

Noteworthy exceptions are Japan and Islamic countries, where high divorce rates actually declined during the early stages of modernization (Goode, 1963; Trent & South, 1989). A suggested explanation for this is that the high divorce rate was associated with the very common practice of arranged marriages that was characteristic of these societies. When people were allowed free choice in selecting a mate, the divorce rate declined (Vogel, 1968). Another explanation points to the fact that kin support for a divorced woman with children was far more readily available before industrialization than it was following industrialization. Moreover, in the case of Japan, as people attempted to raise their standard of living and the family system changed, much of the individual's freedom of choice was reduced rather than increased (Goode, 1963).

But the general trend is clear both in the United States and on the international scene. In comparing the divorce rate in 1963 with that of 1981, in only 2 countries (Romania and Yugoslavia) out of 29, did the divorce rate decrease (United Nations, 1984).

Increasing industrialization and urbanization are correlated with the rising divorce rate because of their influence on the family as a unit and on its members as individuals. There are several possible reasons for this effect.

Economic Independence.   The industrial-urban complex has resulted in a reduction of the interdependency of marriage partners, who need each other less in order to survive than they did in the preindustrial rural society. Women's increased potential for employment and economic independence (Cherlin, 1981; Degler, 1980; Kitson, Holmes, & Sussman, 1983; Reiss & Lee, 1988), and men's ability to find alternative sources to satisfy their domestic needs, make both partners more likely to dissolve an unhappy marriage than otherwise.

Several studies have shown that married women who are employed are more likely not only to contemplate divorce (Huber & Spitze, 1980) but to go through with it as well (Ross & Sawhill, 1975). Most studies on the subject show that the probability of divorce increases as the wife's income rises, and that divorce is higher among couples where the wife has an independent source of income (Booth & White, 1980; Cherlin, 1979; Hannan, Tuma, & Groenevold, 1977, 1978).

Given these findings, women's earning power must be taken into account in our efforts to understand and predict the frequency and trend of divorce. Reiss and Lee (1988) made the point that if this interpretation of the statistics is valid, then we may not see much change in the divorce rate in the United States in the near future. If women most probably continue to take part in the labor force, and even increase their earning power, the divorce rate may not decline significantly. On the other hand, the fact that the divorce rate has leveled off and even decreased somewhat since the early 1980s, may only suggest that much of the effect of women's employment on family dissolution has already taken place.

There are studies that have shown different relationships to be obtained between the wife's financial independence and the probability of divorce (Hanson & Tuch, 1984; Mott & Moore, 1979; Smith & Meitz, 1983). But these seemingly conflicting results may be owing to the wife's financial independence affecting the probability of divorce differently under different circumstances (Riess & Lee 1988).

Some research results have shown that divorce is more likely only when wives' earnings are high relative to that of their husbands (Cherlin, 1979; Mott & Moore, 1979). Studies by Hiller and Philliber (1980, 1982; Philliber & Hiller, 1983) indicate that a wife's employment increases the probability of divorce only when she is working in a "nontraditional" job, and especially if her professional achievements are higher than those of her husband. Furthermore, a study by Spitze and South (1985) showed that divorce is more likely when the husband disapproves of his wife's employment, and the probability increases with the number of hours the wife works outside the home.

Mate Selection.   Another possible factor that may be contributing to the association between level of industrialization and divorce rate is the practice of mate selection. Industrialization promotes autonomy in the selection of marriage partners (Reiss & Lee, 1988), a practice correlated with an increase in the divorce rate (Kitson et al., 1985). The reason for this is that in an autonomous courtship system, sentimental rather than practical reasons are the bases for mate selection (Kitson et al., 1985). In addition, as observed by Nimkoff (1965), "sentiment is more ephemeral than survival, and a marriage based on love is more vulnerable than one based on economic needs" (p. 355). Thus, if urban-industrial growth promotes love-based marriages, and if in turn love-based marriage promotes a higher divorce rate, then it follows that as urban-industrial development proceeds, the rate of divorce will increase. To include the exceptional case of Japan, Riess and Lee (1988) qualified this factor and concluded that in a society wherein husband–wife stability is highly valued, the higher the emphasis on the importance of the affectionate tie between husband and wife, the higher will be the divorce rate.

Economic Prosperity, Depression, and Divorce

Economic conditions are also associated with the divorce rate as regards periodic fluctuations of economic prosperity and depression. It has been generally agreed among theorists and investigators that the divorce rate increases with prosperity, whereas during recession it decreases (Cherlin, 1981; Glick & Lin, 1986; Goode, 1980; Norton & Glick, 1976). Others, most notably South (1985), argued that in a review of the available statistics "it seems at least as likely [to conclude] that economic prosperity will reduce the divorce rate as raise it" (p. 33), and that the economics–divorce relationship is more complicated than previously thought.

For those who argue for the positive economics–divorce correlation, the reason for the drop in the divorce rate during economic depression is quite clear. Increased financial strain caused by scarce money and high levels of unemployment is undoubtedly very stressful for many families. Yet it is very difficult to think realistically of either supporting two households, or leaving one of the households in an untenable financial position.

Some statistics seem to support this hypothesis. Ogburn and Thomas (1922) and Ogburn and Nimkoff (1955) examined the relationship between the divorce rate and an index of the economic cycle during the years 1867–1906 and 1907–1950. They found a high positive correlation between the two variables. Vigderhous and Fishman (1978) examined the relationship between the divorce rate and unemployment during the years 1920–1943. Holding other variables constant, they reported a negative correlation.

Although a positive relationship between divorce rate and the societal economic conditions is often cited or assumed, South (1985) pointed to four possible faults in this claim: (a) Many of the statistics on which this claim is based are "outdated." That is, by the time these statistics are available they may be irrelevant. (b) By simply "eyeballing" the two trends and noting the similarity between them, one misses other factors that may contribute to divorce rate. (c) We cannot escape the fact that, on the microlevel of the single-family, many research studies show the opposite relationship: The higher the husband's earnings and family's socioeconomic level, the lower the likelihood of divorce (Cherlin, 1979; Cutright, 1971; Mott & Moore, 1979; Udry, 1966, 1974). Although there is not necessarily a correspondence in the economics–divorce relationship on the micro- and the macrolevels, the contradiction is nevertheless noteworthy. (d) There is at least one study (Preston & McDonald, 1979) showing that the higher the unemployment level, the greater is the divorce rate.

In a time-series regression analysis of data available in the United States after World War II, South (1985) found a different kind of economics–divorce relationship. His results show that although economic conditions have a small effect on divorce rate, "it tends to rise during economic contraction and fall (or at least rise more slowly) during periods of economic expansion" (p. 38).

One possible way to resolve these conflicting results is to recall, as South did, Ogburn and Nimkoff's (1955) distinction between two sets of factors, one of which affects the desire or motivation to divorce and the other the opportunity to divorce. Economic conditions can affect both sets of factors in different ways. During economic depression, the desire to dissolve marriage may be higher than during economic boom, but divorce may be less affordable. During economic prosperity, the motivation may be lower but the opportunity is greater. Which of these effects will prove to be more powerful depends on the social and economic context in which divorce occurs. As South (1985) wrote:

> In social contexts characterized by comparatively low average income and high divorce cost, as in the prewar U.S., economic expansion provides unhappy couples the financial means to obtain a divorce. In addition, low rates of women's labor-force participation probably deter wives from obtaining a divorce even though economic contraction may have depressed husbands' earning and couples' standard of living. (p. 38)

Thus, under conditions of economic prosperity, when divorce is more affordable, the motivational factor will determine the behavior. Whereas during economic depression, the cost of the divorce will be the dominating factor.

The following analysis of the divorce rate and economic fluctuation in the United States may well illustrate South's point. During the Great Depression, as noted earlier, the divorce rate dropped despite the strain on marital relationships caused by financial difficulties. The price tag on divorce was apparently greater than the motivation. After the divorce rate returned to the pre-depression level, it peaked in 1946. The large number of marriages contracted during the early years of World War II and the long separations due to the war, as well as seemingly bright prospects for the future, were apparently all factors that contributed to the record high divorce rate. By the beginning of 1960s the divorce rate started to increase dramatically from the low level of the 1950s. The economic slowdown forced many women to enter the job market even if only to maintain the family's standard of living. It is possible that wive's employment placed new and difficult strains on marriage. Possibly, as well, some women sought employment as a planned step toward leaving the marriage. There is no research to support either of these plausible explanations. However, it is evident that for many women, experiencing economic independence meant being able to dissolve an unhappy marriage (Ross & Sawhill, 1975; Strube & Barbour, 1983). The same may have been true of men. Realizing that their wives could be economically independent, and that divorce might now be as affordable for them as for their wives, more men sought divorce as a solution for unhappy marriages.

Socioeconomic Levels and Divorce

Notwithstanding the widespread belief that divorce is more frequent in our society among wealthier couples, the data consistently show that this is untrue. The research findings indicate a clear negative correlation between various measures of socioeconomic status and the frequency of divorce (Cutright, 1971; Fergusson, Horwood, & Shannon, 1984; Glenn & Supancic, 1984; Greenstein, 1985; Hampton, 1975; Martin & Bumpass, 1989; Norton, 1983; South & Spitze, 1986).

Income, occupation, and education are the three factors most frequently combined to indicate socioeconomic level. Although these three factors tend to positively correlate, they are not perfectly correlated. Furthermore, because these factors can have different effects on the divorce rate, we would do well to consider them separately here.

Income.   The explanation most frequently given for the negative relationship between income level and the divorce rate has to do with the cost of divorce. High-income couples have much more to lose from divorce than do low-income couples. The more a couple has, the further proportionately is the drop in each spouse's standard of living following divorce (Pett & Vaughan-Cole, 1986; Weiss, 1984). From the wife's perspective, the higher her husband's income, the more difficult it will be for her to replace it and maintain her socioeconomic level. From the husband's perspective, the higher his income, the less proportionately he will have left after the divorce. It should also be noted that the lower the income, the more difficult it is to meet the financial challenges of married life that may cause marital strain and lead to divorce.

It has been proposed that income level serves more as a barrier to divorce than as a source of happiness in the marriage (Cutright, 1971). Recent evidence suggests, however, that the relationship between income level and the divorce rate is more complicated. Some studies have found no relationship between income and marital stability (Mott & Moore, 1979; Ross & Sawhill, 1975), at least not when the level of family assets is considered (Booth, Johnson, White, & Edwards, 1986; Galligan & Bahr, 1978). Cherlin (1979) found that when the wife's income exceeds that of her husband, the likelihood of divorce increases. But when her income is lower than her husband's, the likelihood of divorce is actually reduced. The results of Hannan et al. (1977, 1978) show that it is not the level of income that predicts divorce but the stability of that income. Low-income couples with a stable income apparently escape the strain caused by financial insecurity, and their marriages have been found to be more stable (Cherlin, 1979). These studies suggest that more investigation is needed before the effect of income on marital stability is completely known and understood. They also suggest that the effect of the differences in the total family income on the divorce rate is less profound than was originally thought.

Occupation. Although earlier investigations (e.g., Goode, 1956a) showed occupational status to be a good and strong predictor of divorce, more recent studies report a much less clear relationship. This is true especially when level of education and other variables are considered. Locksley (1982) and Greenstein (1985), for example, reported that the negative effect of occupational status on the likelihood of divorce disappeared when the level of education was held constant. Rosow and Daniel (1972) reported that among professionals they found differences in divorce rates depended on the type of job that men held. Glenn and Supancic (1984) found lower divorce rates among professionals and people holding clerical jobs. Higher rates were found among people with laboring and service occupations and among women in more prestigious positions, such as in management and administration. Again, these differences were reduced substantially when education and income were accounted for.

Thus, although the divorce rate appears to be related to occupational status, the effects of intervening variables apparently account for much of this relationship. It is somewhat surprising that despite the increased number of women employed in various occupations, very little is known about the effect that women's occupational status has on divorce rates.

Education. Three different types of relationships between education and divorce rate have been found by investigators: (a) For men there is a negative correlation between the two variables (i.e., Kitson et al., 1985). (b) For women the correlation tends to be positive (Houseeknecht & Spanier,

1980). (c) there is a third effect—the "Glick effect" (Glick, 1957), whereby the likelihood of divorce for those who drop out of high school or college is higher than for those who never start.

Research shows that the higher the level of men's education the lower the probability of divorce (Bumpass, 1984; Kitson et al., 1985; Price-Bonham & Balswick, 1980). This is true with the exception of the Glick effect for those with 9 to 11 years of schooling and with 1 to 3 years of college. The Glick effect is explained in terms of the difficulty of these individuals to commit themselves to difficult tasks. Glenn and Supancic (1984), however, revealed data suggesting that at least for high school dropouts the high divorce rate may be explained by their younger age at marriage and lower socioeconomic level.

For women, divorce rates are lower among those with 8 or fewer years of schooling, and higher among those with postgraduate education (Carter & Glick, 1976; Houseeknecht & Spanier, 1980). Although the education–divorce relationship for women is not as clear as it is for men, the overall trend probably reflects the influence of women's economic independence on the divorce rate.

Income, occupation, and education are the most obvious factors associated with social class, and singularly or in unison they affect the likelihood of divorce. But there are more subtle ways in which socioeconomic levels can affect the divorce rate. In order to understand this relationship more fully, one must consider how belonging to a particular social class either exposes a marriage to, or insulates it from, intervening factors that increase the likelihood of divorce. One such factor is age at the time of marriage. Studies have consistently shown that early marriages are more frequent among people at the lower socioeconomic level, and that they increase the likelihood of divorce (South & Spitze, 1986). In fact, age at marriage was found to be the best predictor of divorce during the first 5 years of marriage (Martin & Bumpass, 1989). Other such factors are premarital pregnancy, which often creates the pressure in early marriage and generates family disapproval; difficulties in obtaining independent accommodation; lack of job security; and absence of material and emotional support from one or both sets of parents (Burgoyne, Ormrod, & Richards, 1987). This background exacerbates marital difficulties at the early stages of the marriage, before much partnership is established, and may therefore lead to an early divorce. For those marriages in which marital problems emerge later, the effect of factors that might deter divorce—such as joint ownership of property and shared personal experiences and history—may be much stronger.

As discussed in chapter 4, a person contemplating divorce weighs the cost against the benefits of dissolving the marriage. What this means economically is that one weighs one's present standard of living against one's hopes for the future. There is data (Marsden, 1969; Weitzman, 1985) to show that some separated and divorced women coming from the lower socioeconomic levels were actually better off financially after breaking up with their spouse. So, for these women there was at least a strong financial incentive to dissolve an unhappy marriage. Among wealthy couples, material comfort and security may deter wives from seeking a divorce. Furthermore, given enough money, estranged couples may be able to lead separate lives to a point that formal divorce becomes unnecessary, unless one wants to remarry.

Middle-class people also have more to lose by divorce than those of the lower class. Although they may not have much in the way of shared property and financial assets, they still have more as a couple than they would have as divorced singles.

In summary, the effect of economic conditions on divorce appears to be more complicated and less straightforward the closer this relationship is investigated. Although trends in divorce generally follow the trends in industrialization and urbanization, there are exceptions to the rule. The explanations of the exceptions reveal intervening cultural variables that reduce the effect of industrialization on divorce. The same is apparently true for the effect of other economic factors (Breault & Kposowa, 1987). Prosperity, depression, and socioeconomic levels relate to divorce rates vis-à-vis job opportunities, women's employment, levels of income and education, as well as to the more silent cultural variables such as mate selection practices, systems of social support, and the like. In a recent study, for example, Trent and South (1989) found a curvilinear (U-shaped) relationship of socioeconomic development and women's participation in the labor force with the divorce rate. The conclusion is therefore that because divorce occurs within a particular socioeconomic context, investigation of the subject must be continued in order to discover the more subtle web of the interactions between economic conditions in their various aspects and divorce.

RELIGION AND DIVORCE

Throughout history, religion has been one of the strongest factors in determining human conduct. The norms, values, beliefs, and behaviors that were reinforced by religion and that have assumed a religious significance, have tended to survive longer than those that have not been so sanctioned. Religion has been one of the conserving forces in society, and has tended to hold changes in the social order in check. Thus, although economic development and social progress increase the likelihood of divorce, religion has acted to repress and set effective brakes on this trend.

The major modern religions take definite positions on i⸍ premarital sexual behavior, mate selection, family size, ai regard to divorce, these positions range from a complete t of the Roman Catholic Church, to far more liberal policies, a. and Islam.

According to the Jewish and Muslim traditions, only men have the power to enforce their wish to divorce. In both traditions it is the man only who can grant a divorce to his wife, and not the other way around. Thus, a Muslim man can divorce his wife by repeating the statement "I divorce thee" three times. A Jewish man can request a divorce, and under certain conditions a rabbinical court can compel his wife to accept it, if she is unwilling. In both traditions, as well, women too have the right under certain circumstances to request a divorce (e.g., if her husband is sterile); but even a religious court cannot force an unwilling husband to grant it. Among Jews, the court may choose to punish an unwilling husband until he gives his consent. In Israel, marriage and divorce are sanctioned by religious authorities. In the United States and other countries where there is a strong Reformed Judaism movement, Jewish religious authorities recognize the civil court's jurisdiction over matters of divorce.

The Protestant churches also accept the divorce rulings of the civil court. Protestant ecclesiastical authorities discourage divorce, but in general place no restrictions on divorce, and favor neither gender in granting the decree. The Orthodox Church in Greece, on the other hand, has made a compromise and now limits divorce to three per person.

There are three possible effects of religion on the propensity to divorce (Reiss & Lee, 1988): (a) the effect of religious affiliation, (b) the effect of the degree of religious involvement (i.e., going to and taking part in religious services and activities), and (c) the effect of the difference in religious beliefs in interfaith marriages.

Religious Affiliation. Several studies have investigated possible differences in the divorce rate among people with different religious affiliations. Results generally show that Catholics, Jews, and Mormons tend to divorce significantly less than do Protestants (Albrecht, Bahr, & Goodman, 1983; Bahr, 1982; Coombs & Zumeta, 1970; Glenn & Shelton, 1983). Glenn and Supancic (1984) found that divorce is most frequent among those who claim "no religion."

When investigators have attempted to go beyond the broad religion classifications, they found great differences within each religion category. Thus, Bumpass and Sweet (1972) and Thornton (1978) found that Baptists and other fundamentalist Protestants had higher divorce rates than did nonfundamentalist Protestants. Presbyterians were found to have the lowest rate (17.3%) among the Protestant groups, followed by Lutherans

(18.7%), Episcopalians (20.5), Methodists (23.4%), and Baptists (24.5; Glenn & Supancic, 1984).

In a more recent study, Chan and Heaton (1989) reported that, in comparison to mainstream Protestant couples (who after 20 years of marriage have a 77.3% chance of remaining married), the marriages of Baptists, Christian fundamentalists, and Jews are less likely to survive (68.7%; 67.3%; and 65.4%, respectively). Only the marriages of Catholic couples have a better chance (87.9%) of survival after 20 years of marriage. After 25 years of marriage, the percentages are about the same for all.

Only a part of these results can be explained by the different religious attitudes toward divorce. Couples with a strong religiously based moral objection to divorce (e.g., Catholics) will tend to refrain from dissolving their marriages, although the absence of religious objection apparently does not by itself lead to a high divorce rate. Evidence of this is the low divorce rate among Jewish couples, as reported by most investigators. This may be accounted for by the very high values that Jews place on the family, as well as by the strong cohesiveness of the extended Jewish family and community, which may furnish a powerful supportive network for the nuclear family.

Degree of Religious Involvement. Religious involvement is strongly associated with and a source of traditional family values. The findings of studies have indicated that there is a distinctly negative relationship between the degree of involvement in religious activities and the frequency of divorce. That is, in the case of both men and women, the greater their attendance at religious services, the less likely they are to divorce (Fergusson et al., 1984; McCarthy, 1979). In their detailed analysis of seven large surveys, Glenn and Supancic (1984) showed that the divorce rate among those who "never" go to religious services (approximately 35%) is almost three times those who attend services "several times a week" (approximately 13%).

It is not clear why a high degree of religious involvement should reduce the likelihood of divorce. If a high level of religious involvement also indicates a high degree of religiosity, then because divorce is discouraged by all the major religions, we can assume that this would raise the cost of divorce among believers. Another possible explanation is that participation in organized religious life enhances "couple identity," and gives support to the family (Reiss & Lee, 1988). Glenn and Supancic (1984) also noted the need to determine whether this relationship is explained by the degree of people's religiosity or by the support obtained through social participation. A high degree of religiosity and strong reluctance to divorce may also be associated through a high degree of conservatism.

There is some data to show that religious involvement is positively associated with marital satisfaction (Glenn & Weaver, 1977; Heaton, 1984). Religious activities were also found to be strongly related to a range of indicators of marital happiness, such as a professed willingness to marry the same person again and a high level of agreement regarding marital roles (Kunz & Albrecht, 1977). These results may also explain the lower divorce rate among those who are more involved than others in religious activities.

Interfaith Marriages.   Glenn (1982) showed that the rate of interfaith marriages has significantly increased since the 1950s. The number of religiously heterogamous (mixed) marriages may be even higher than Glenn (1982) reported, because in many cases one of the spouses has converted to the religion of the other soon after the marriage (Thornton & Freedman, 1983).

The divorce rate in interfaith marriages has consistently revealed itself to be higher than in religiously homogamous marriages (Bumpass & Sweet, 1972; Burr, 1973; Chan & Heaton, 1989; Nye & Berardo, 1973). Marriages of Catholic–Mormon, Protestant–Mormon (Bahr, 1982), Jewish–Gentile (Maneker & Rankin, 1991), and Catholic–Protestant (Bumpass & Sweet, 1972) couples have all been found to be less stable than marriages between people sharing the same religious affiliation. The least stable marriages are those in which one spouse is Mormon (Bahr, 1982). Furthermore, when one of the partners in the marriage has no religious affiliation and the other does, the probability of divorce also increases (Goode, 1956a). Bahr (1982) found that the chance of divorce in interfaith marriage not only depends on the specific religions involved but also on which spouse has which religious affiliation.

Some studies show that part of the effect of religious heterogamy may be accounted for by extraneous factors such as age at marriage and social class differences (Bumpass & Sweet, 1972; Burchinal & Chancellor, 1962). Some of the effect may be due to there being more points of conflict over children's socialization and differences in values, traditions, and relevant habits and practices.

In summary, most research appears to present a clear picture as to the nature of the religion–divorce relationship (Maneker & Rankin, 1991). The studies have often found a linear relationship between religious variables and the divorce rate, despite theoretical reasons to suspect otherwise (Glenn & Supancic, 1984; Reiss & Lee, 1988). One notable exception is furnished by the results of the study of Trent and South (1989). Using a regression analysis, Trent and South could find no effect of religion on the divorce rate. Therefore, they argued that other researchers may have "overemphasized the effect of religion" (p. 402).

CULTURAL VALUES AND ATTITUDE TOWARD DIVORCE

Sociologists and other students of the family system have often referred to the effect of a society's family ideology on the family's structure and stability (e.g., Aries, 1962; Burgess & Locke, 1953; Goode, 1963; Roussel & Thery, 1988; Singer, 1975).

The growing emphasis on self-fulfillment, emerging from the culture of the 1960s, affected people's conception of and expectations from a marriage (Bellah, Madsen, Sullivan, Swidler, & Tipton, 1985; Rice & Rice, 1986). Current American culture and ideology of the family put a high premium on romantic love and self-fulfillment as a basis for marriage. They are the main reasons for maintaining a marriage, and one of the reasons for dissolving marriages (Burgess & Locke, 1953; Matusow, 1984). These motivations for embarking on marriage or divorce reflect hedonistic rather than committal cultural values. In a book entitled *Habits of the Heart: Individualism and Commitment in American life* (Bellah et al., 1985), the authors referred to such cultural values as "expressive individualism" and the "therapeutic attitude." Others have used terms such as *hedonism* (Glenn, 1987) and *narcissistic withdrawal* (Brodbar-Nemzer, 1986) to describe the *flight from commitment*. When such are the prevailing cultural values and norms, their contribution to a higher divorce rate is only to be expected.

Assumptions about family life and about expectations from the marital relationship are integral to the cultural ideology of the family. When the ideology changes so do these assumptions and expectations. When neither romantic love nor a spouse's support in the partner's self-realization was expected, neither could be a reason for divorce.

Now, with a more egalitarian and androgynous value system in effect, most people tend to view the family as an emotional rather than economic unit, and therefore they marry for affective reasons. But affective criteria for marital success are more difficult to meet (Weitzman, 1985) so that they are a potential source of frustration and dissatisfaction. Cultural values in contemporary America do not reinforce perseverance and long-term investment. Immediate gratification, adaptability, mobility, and replacement are the rules of the times (Rice & Rice, 1986). These values make affective bonding, as in an emotional unit, even more fragile and probationary.

Dissolving a marriage is now within the cultural consensus, as has been the concern over the consequences of divorce. Yet, divorced families are still often referred to in popular and professional literature as "partial" or "broken" families (e.g., Farnworth, 1984; Free, 1991; Vanderlinden & Vandereycken, 1991; Wilkinson, 1974). These characterizations reflect the general attitude of society and the stigma that the public attaches to single-parent families (Popenoe, 1988). The stigma is motivated by a concern over the growing threat to the traditional two-parent family and to the stability of society as a whole (Thompson & Gonzola, 1983). Before being "politically correct" became an important cultural value, social critics spoke of the single-parent family as a deviant form of family system. Although the judgmental tone may have disappeared, many have continued to assume that such families were detrimental to the well-being of children and of society, and even to the economy (Bernard, 1979; Levitan & Belous, 1981; Schorr & Moen, 1979). Based on these assumptions, some family policies were changed (Senate bills 1070 and 1378, 97th Congress) in order to reinforce traditional two-parent families. The concerns over the fate of the single-parent still remained high on the social agenda; the stigma, however, slowly disappeared and the normative climate has changed accordingly (Mintz & Kellogg, 1988).

It was this change in the normative climate, and in attitudes toward marriage and family, that was felt by many to have caused, or at least to have contributed significantly, to the current high divorce rate. But in examining this assumption, Cherlin (1981) showed that the change in attitudes had in fact only followed the already existing facts. That is, the more liberal attitudes toward divorce came in a big way only in the early 1970s, after the divorce rate was already high. With regard to the timing of the change in attitudes, Thornton's (1985) results are somewhat conflicting. He analyzed an intergenerational panel study of children and mothers, and concluded that "a definite trend toward approval of marital dissolution is observed between 1962 and 1980" (p. 856). But he also found that although the experience of divorce had a strong effect on subsequent attitudes, the liberal view of family dissolution did not have much influence on subsequent divorce.

One social movement that surfaced during the 1960s and changed social attitudes, cultural values, and ideology regarding the family was the women's liberation movement. The term *women's liberation movement* is an umbrella name for a broad spectrum of women's groups, all dedicated to improving the position of women in the society. The basic rational and motivation for change as regards the ideology of the family was stated in 1970 in an editorial in *Women: A Journal of Liberation:* "traditionally, women have been most oppressed by the institution of the family. . . . To be free, women must understand the source of their oppression and how to control it" (Staff, 1970, p. 1).

The literature dealing with the family contains some reference to the relationship between the family structure and the change in women's roles. As this topic is dealt with in other sections of this book, it is only briefly considered here. In general, these references in the literature have to do with the effect of the role conflict of women on wives and families. The role conflict itself is depicted as a consequence of the tension between women's needs and desires on the one hand, and culturally prescribed expectations of women on the other (Bird, 1971; Dager, 1967; Nye, 1967). The women's movement encouraged women to change these expectations by changing their perceptions of themselves and their traditional roles. Betty Friedman (1971), the "godmother of the modern women's movement" stated it very clearly in *The Feminine Mystique*. Being a wife and mother, she said, is not a sufficient career for most women. Women were encouraged to remain single, or to divorce if they had to, in order to pursue careers and self-actualizing callings. As Caroline Bird (1971) explained in her book, just as men do not have to marry or remain married for sex, neither do women have to marry for economic security or support: "The old deal of sex-for-support has long been a dead letter" (p. 39).

This movement had enormous impact on the acceptance of change and growth as important values (e.g., Bardwick, 1979; Lenz & Myerhoff, 1985). The family had to restructure itself to allow more room for both men and women to grow and to fulfill themselves. In order for this change to occur within a marriage, men had to adjust. As this was for many a difficult task, and given the social climate, divorce was a viable alternative.

DIVORCE AND OTHER SOCIAL FACTORS

Race and Ethnicity

Studies have repeatedly shown that Blacks have a higher divorce rate than do Whites and other minority groups (e.g., Frisbie, 1986; Martin & Bumpass, 1989; Moynihan, 1986; Teachman, 1986). Chan and Heaton (1989) analyzed 1,595 interviews of women who were married for minimum of 10 years. The interviews had been collected in the 1982 National Survey of Family Growth. Chan and Heaton reported that Blacks were more than 30% more likely to be divorced than Whites, and after 20 years of marriage, 17% fewer Black than White women were still married.

Because of the complicated interactions between race and other predictors of divorce, Martin and Bumpass (1989) suggested examining racial differences in divorce rate by expected rates. They estimated the combined risk of divorce for women with the highest and lowest risk characteristics. Their results show that, in the lowest risk group, the expected rate of divorce for Blacks is 38% and for Whites it is 18%. For the highest risk group, the percentages are 92% and 78%, respectively. In addition, Glenn and Supancic (1984) presented results showing that between 1973 and 1980 there were 68% more Black males divorced than White males, and 42% more than males in other minorities. The same study showed that during this period there were 75% more Black females divorced than White females, and 90% more than females in other minorities.

Although the results of the studies are in agreement, the explanations for the racial differences vary. One explanation that is often cited attributes the higher divorce rate among Blacks to their distinctive historical experience (Cherlin, 1981; Moynihan, 1965). In particular, the lingering effects of slavery are mentioned in this regard (Frazier, 1939). All members of a slave family could be sold separately, a situation that made the maintenance of an intact family very difficult. As a result, the Black subculture came to foster and make considerable allowance for marital dissolution. However, there is abundant evidence against the subculture explanation as well (Kitson et al., 1985). For one, when socioeconomic factors such as income, family size, and unemployment are controlled, the racial differences in divorce rate are greatly reduced (Chan & Heaton, 1989); Black families may even be less likely to separate than White families (Hampton, 1975). Second, there are data that show that Blacks do in fact have a very strong commitment to the family (Cherlin, 1981; Stack, 1974). Glick and Norton (1973), for instance, showed that although Blacks divorce more, they also wait longer before doing so. Finally, Cherlin (1981) showed that the difference in divorce rates between Blacks and Whites has been increasing over the past few decades, so that this historical explanation is not very plausible.

Another explanation attributes the higher divorce rate among Blacks to the closer ties maintained among the members of extended families (Cherlin, 1981; Stack, 1974). Divorce becomes a more plausible solution to marital difficulties when the support of an extended family is available.

The welfare system and its family social policy have also been blamed for encouraging divorce among Black families. But the results of some studies contradict this hypothesis (Bahr, 1979; Murray, 1986). Darity and Myers (1984), however, found no relationship between Black female-headed families and welfare attractiveness, suggesting that the high divorce rate among Blacks may be accounted for by a low gender-ratio—in other words, an undersupply of Black males.

For the present, the best explanation seems to reside in socioeconomic factors. That is, Blacks divorce more than Whites because, on the average, they are less educated, more often unemployed than Whites, and earn less than Whites when they are employed (Becker, 1981; Bishop, 1980). Nonetheless, although this explanation seems to be supported by research results, much remains to be learned about why and how these factors affect the propensity to divorce. They may affect Blacks and Whites differently. As Cherlin (1981) showed, the greatest differences between the races is actually found on the lowest socioeconomic level. As-yet-unknown factors make Black families less stable than White families when socioeconomic factors are the most potent.

Gender-Ratio

One of the recent and more interesting explanations of the divorce rate across time and societies is the gender-ratio theory (Guttentag & Secord, 1983). This theory assumes that women are more interested than men in stability, and that the relative availability of either gender determines division of gender roles, sexual morality, mate selection practices, and divorce rates. More specifically, Guttentag and Secord argued that when the gender-ratio is high (i.e., there is oversupply of men), women gain a sense of power and control. This would be translated not into sexual and economic independence, but rather into a deeper commitment to the family, and the traditional gender role division within society and the family. Because of the relative lack of alternative partners, men would tend to make a long-term commitment to a single woman, and use their political, economic, and legal power to reduce women's motivation and opportunities to dissolve a marriage. As a result, in high gender-ratio societies the divorce rate would be low.

By contrast, when the gender-ratio is low (i.e., there is an oversupply of women), women would tend to feel devalued and powerless in their relationship with men. Some women would react by intensifying their effort to attract and keep a man. Others would independently try to achieve economic mobility. Various forms of feminism would flourish and be used as vehicles for changing the balance of power.

When women are in surplus, men would gain a sense of power. They would be less willing to commit themselves to a single partner, and would tend to take advantage of the opportunity for multiple relationships. Those who marry would be more apt to get divorced. Thus, Guttentag and Secord (1983) predicted that in a society with a low gender-ratio, the divorce rate would be high.

In order to support their theory, Guttentag and Second analyzed different cultures at different times in history. Being in high surplus, women in ancient Athens had very few rights, whereas during the same period, Spartan women living in a low gender-ratio society, enjoyed considerable power and freedom. For more evidence, the authors cited examples from medieval Spain, the Jewish shtetl in eastern Europe, and the United States during the 19th and 20th centuries.

There are other sources supporting the gender-ratio theory. Trent and South (1989) reported that in their study of 66 societies, the divorce rate was found to be higher in societies with a low gender-ratio. Gender-ratio was also found to be highly correlated with the divorce rate in the Heer and Grossbard-Shechtman (1981) analysis of the U.S. population during the 1960–1975 period.

Although the relative number of men in a society as a whole may affect the divorce rate, the gender-ratio within a cohort or a specific cultural and socioeconomic context may have an even greater effect. This was found to be the case among the upper class in Muslim Spain during medieval times (Secord, 1983), and among Black Americans in the present period (Guttentag & Secord, 1983). The gender-ratio among Blacks in the United States is far lower than among Whites. Thus, the chances for Black women to be married is limited, and their ability to maintain their marriages is reduced. Consequently, Black women have a lower marriage rate and a higher divorce rate than White women, and more often bear children out of wedlock.

Investigators have only recently begun to examine the extent of the ramifications and validity of the gender-ratio theory. It is clear that gender-ratio interacts with other social variables. Secord (1983) attempted to account for male–female relationships and family structure in extreme gender-ratio situations by introducing concepts such as distribution of structural power and social control.

In light of these interesting and promising results, it is surprising that so few investigators have invested effort in exploring the gender-ratio theory. For insofar as the social level of analysis of marriage and divorce rates are concerned, the gender-ratio factor would appear to have a powerful effect.

Premarital Pregnancy and Birth

It is estimated that one in every seven first marriages involve a bride who is already a mother (Sweet & Bumpass, 1988); and it was estimated that by the early 1970s, one in every four women across social and socioeconomic groups, was pregnant at the time of her marriage (Hetzel & Capetta, 1973). Research results have repeatedly shown that premarital pregnancy and premarital birth are associated with a higher divorce rate (Bahr & Galligan, 1984; Billy, Landale, & McLaughlin, 1986; Bolton, Laner, & Kane, 1980; Bumpass & Sweet, 1972; Teachman, 1983). Coombs and Zumeta (1970) reported that 41% of the women who were married when pregnant were divorced 5 years later, in comparison to the 18% of divorced women who were not pregnant when they married. Furstenberg (1976a) found that more than 50% of his premaritally pregnant women were divorced after only 4 years of marriage.

The most important factors explaining these results were found to be economic difficulties, short periods of courtship, and lack of preparation for family life. Opposition by the couple's parents to the marriage, serious premarital difficulties in the relationship, and larger families of origin were also found to be important intervening variables (Thornes & Collard 1979).

These and other early studies (Christensen, 1963; Christensen & Meissner, 1953; Monahan, 1960b) failed, however, to distinguish between the effect of premarital pregnancy and premarital birth. More recent studies found that premarital conception alone does not increase the probability of divorce but premarital childbirth does (Bumpass & Sweet, 1972; Martin & Bumpass, 1989; Morgan & Rindfuss, 1985; Wineberg, 1988). But this may be the case for Whites only. Furstenberg (1976a, 1976b) made the same distinction and found that for Blacks both premarital birth and premarital pregnancy significantly increase the probability of separation and divorce.

With better methodology, Teachman (1983) analyzed data of the 1973 National Survey of Family Growth. He reported that for both Black and White women who married between 1950 and 1970, only premarital births and not premarital pregnancies were related to a higher divorce rate. For White women, the effect of premarital birth on marital instability seems, however, to be much stronger than for Blacks. Martin and Bumpass' (1989) study showed that among Whites the chance for divorce is 71% higher with than without premarital birth, whereas among Blacks the chance is only 16% higher in a parallel comparison.

In a comprehensive study of "Recent Trends in Marital Disruption," Morgan and Rindfuss (1985) analyzed data from the 1986 U.S. Bureau of the Census. They suggested that in studying the effect of premarital births three "interrelated dimensions" need to be considered: occurrence, sequence, and timing. Their results show that occurrence has a strong effect that shifts dramatically depending on sequence of the three events: marriage, pregnancy, and childbirth. They found that the effect of premarital pregnancy greatly depends on what follows next; marriage or childbirth. If it is marriage that follows, it has a strong negative effect early in the marriage, but a negligible effect later. They also found that "premarital conception" may actually decrease the probability of separation.

One explanation for the strong relationship found between premarital parenthood and a higher divorce rate may have to do with the heterogeneity of the samples. Statistics on the marital stability of marriages involving premarital birth include those instances in which the mother married a man who was not the child's father. Such marriages are even less stable than those in which the husband is the child's father (Furstenberg, 1976a; Teachman, 1983, 1986). This may account for some of the effect. Another reason may have to do with the possibility that a woman who is already a mother may enter a marital contract more hastily than she might otherwise. Some of the effect of premarital birth may be accounted for by the heavy burden that raising a child can place on marital relationships. Although Morgan and Rindfuss (1985) found that children do serve as barriers to divorce, and that a delay in childbearing may actually increase the probability of divorce, it is possible to argue within their own conceptual framework that the birth of a child may also take place too early in a marriage. Teachman (1983) and others (e.g., Ford, 1981; Rindfuss &

MacDonald, 1980; Spanier & Glick, 1980) introduced the concept of the life cycle in order to explain the effect of premarital birth on the probability of divorce.

In principle, premarital birth is a deviation from the expected sequencing of life-cycle events in the current U.S. culture. As a consequence, it causes a chain of negative effects, such as limited career possibilities, lower socioeconomic levels, and less family support, all of which ultimately lead to a marital disillusion.

The difference between Blacks and Whites may have to do with the degree to which premarital birth is regarded as a deviation from the expected life cycle. In White U.S. culture, premarital birth may represent a greater degree of deviation from the expected life cycle of events, hence less acceptance of it and its greater effect.

However, in order to find the net effect of premarital childbirth, many associated variables still need to be controlled in concert. Age at marriage, economic conditions, support from the families of origin, and the sequence and timing of significant events in the couple's relationship are a few of the variables found to affect divorce rate, and there may be intervening variables for the effect of premarital childbirth.

It must be clear by now that the interaction between social and personal factors determines the reasons for divorce and the consequences of marital dissolution. There are countless such interactions. In this chapter we discussed the most important of these. Thus, we pointed out that the change to the no-fault divorce law did not contribute to the increase in the rate of divorce, although it did foster change in the social climate and the policies and practices related to divorce. However, increasing industrialization and urbanization were found to correlate with a rising divorce rate because of their influence on the family as a unit and on its members as individuals.

Research findings have also shown a clear negative correlation between various measures of socioeconomic status and the frequency of divorce. Income, occupation, and education are the most obvious factors associated with social class, and singularly or in concert they affect the likelihood of divorce. But there are more subtle ways in which socioeconomic levels can affect both the tendency to divorce and the consequences thereof. Affiliation with a particular social class exposes or insulates a marriage in varying degrees from many intervening factors, such as age at marriage, premarital pregnancy and childbirth, job opportunities, wife's employment, and even silent cultural variables such as practices in mate selection, systems of social support, and family ideology.

These factors influence the tendency to divorce on two distinct levels: the desire or motivation to divorce, and the opportunity to divorce. Economic, social, and personal factors can have an effect on both these levels, and in different ways. So, for example, during periods of economic depression, the desire to divorce may be higher than in economic booms, although also less affordable. It is the interaction between these sets of factors that determines the reasons for divorce and the consequences of divorce, on both the personal and the social levels. During times of economic prosperity, the motivation for divorce may be lower, but the opportunity is greater. Which of these effects will prove to be more powerful depends on the social and economic context in which divorce occurs. We must therefore conclude that because divorce occurs within a particular socioeconomic context, investigation has to focus on revealing the complexity of interaction between individual psychological variables and the relevant sociocultural factors.

2 Theoretical Models of the Divorce Process

Divorce, like marriage, is as much a complex personal phenomenon as it is a multidimensional social one. Divorce is a drawn-out psychological and social process that occurs over a long period. Although the course each individual divorce takes is unique, there are common factors that justify a generalized approach over the individual situations. The path this common denominator follows is the theme of this chapter. The psychological subjective experiences present throughout the divorce process are analyzed in detail. Divorce is described as a process in which a couple experiences a personal crisis, with unique characterizations and exclusive opportunities for growth and development. This process begins with the first serious and consistent thoughts of divorce, it encompasses the formal proceedings leading to permanent separation, and it ends with the possibility of rebuilding a productive and comfortable life.

Viewing the divorce as a process rather than as an event points not only to the time factor, but also to its multidimensionality and complexity (see Spanier & Thompson's, 1984, comprehensive study). Theoreticians and researchers have developed various models (the crisis theory; Erikson's psychosocial developmental theory; the process of mourning; and others founded in case analysis, clinical experience, and insight) in order to explain the process of divorce. Some of these models originally addressed the problem of divorce. Other have attempted to apply an existing psychological model to the problem of divorce. All, however, view divorce as a process composed of different stages. These stages depict qualitative differences in the themes and the degrees of coping.

Although the stages are typically described as being of a linear structure, with an individual moving from one stage to another until the end of the process, the psychosocial model views the stages as stations on a loop. The perspective is such that movement among the stages may not flow just from one to the next, but may in fact be free-flowing and intermingled.

Different models differ in the content and number of stages attributed to the process, but all agree that divorce is not only a family crisis but also, and maybe even more so, a personal one. A situation is perceived as a crisis when previously effective problem-solving mechanisms are found to be inadequate in attempting to return to an equilibrium (Rapoport, 1965). The crisis may basically be perceived as either a threat or a challenge. The response to it depends on the person's subjective perception of his or her situation within the relationship. If the situation is perceived as a threat to one's basic needs, status, or identity, then anxiety might be aroused. On the other hand, if the crisis is perceived as a challenge, it may bring about reorganization or the utilization of strengths to search for new solutions. Both types of perceptions and corresponding responses may be found in a single individual throughout the crisis period (Wiseman, 1975). Any attempt to understand these responses and to discuss the process of divorce must take into account both the risks and the changes the divorcee experiences throughout the entire process. The different models do just that; they differ only in their estimation of the points of beginning and end, and in the importance given to a particular event or experience.

Four models are described here. They were chosen because of the differences in their theoretical orientation and in the levels of analysis of the psychological, social, and practical dimensions derived from them. Discussion of these models allows a broader understanding of the divorce process and forms a background for understanding the psychosocial model presented later.

MODEL 1: DIVORCE AS A PROCESS OF MOURNING

A model put forward by Wiseman (1975) is based on the application of crisis theory to the divorce process. The model assumes that divorce may bring about a psychological crisis similar to that following the death of a family member (Kubler-Ross, 1969). Divorce, however, has two unique characteristics: rejection and the need of both individuals to build a new life, separately, while at the same time being able to acknowledge each other. The chances to grow and mature are present in the divorce process, just as they are present in the mourning process. The five stages suggested by Wiseman are denial, loss and depression, anger and ambivalence, reorientation of lifestyle and identity, and acceptance and a new level of functioning.

Denial

The divorce process can be identified long before the appearance of the acknowledged stress factor that eventually causes the marriage to disintegrate. At this point, the marriage maintains itself only within a narrow range of pressures and stress. Denial is a frequently used mechanism that enables the marriage to continue.

Two kinds of denial mechanisms can be identified; both fulfill the same function. In the first, the partners typically state that their adaptation to married life, and indeed to one another, is satisfactory, despite their problems and difficulties. In the second, the couple might admit to having serious problems and difficulties, but attribute them to external factors (such as economics or children) in order to avoid earnest consideration of divorce. At this level, the marriage can function and last for a long time.

Some couples attempt to deal with their difficulties and may even improve their functioning as a family unit. However, this attempt might be aborted when faced with a stress situation that overturns the fragile balance of the family's functioning and its relationships. The couple will then react with responses typical of those elicited by crisis. To the outsider the cause may seem almost trivial. Yet even the most trivial factor can cause a crisis when the marital relationship is too rigid. At this stage, denial is no longer possible and divorce is considered as a viable option.

Loss and Depression

Whether or not the source of stress is internal or external, it makes the partners cognizant that "something is seriously wrong" with their marriage. They are faced with their inability to deal with the problem separately or together; realization that the "together" is the problem begins to seep in. This stage is characterized by the first awareness as to the seriousness of the matter and the urgent need to deal with it. The typical reaction to this awareness is similar to that following a meaningful loss: grief, depression, a sense of loneliness, and the inability to communicate with others. If at this point the partners are unable to openly and frankly discuss these feelings with each other, the marriage may well be lost already.

Anger and Ambivalence

As divorce becomes a more realistic option, feelings of anger, which are at the source of the depression, become stronger. This anger often occurs around the time when decisions regarding custody of the children, alimony payments, visitation rights, and other practical matters have to be made. It is usual for each side to be represented by lawyers, few of whom try to moderate their client's position in order to minimize frictions. Disputes over major and minor matters add to the frustration and anger in a spiral fashion, and serve as an outlet for feelings of injustice and pain. If these feelings are not openly expressed, they might manifest themselves directly or indirectly at later stages, in a less controlled and less constructive manner.

The more the partners manage to work through their anger and ambivalence toward each other and the divorce in general, the better they can plan coping strategies and not "look back with anger." If acceptance of the divorce does not occur in this stage, it will be increasingly difficult for the partners to confront the challenge of the following stages. It is during this third stage that ambivalent feelings and attitudes toward the whole process may creep in. Each partner may contemplate if he or she indeed did all they could to save the marriage. Also at this stage, thoughts of one more final attempt at reconciliation are formulated and sometimes even tried. Although these attempts are often doomed from the onset, they are often important in that they enhance the feeling that all has been attempted. This final effort increases the sense of internal justification.

Reorientation of Lifestyle and Identity

At this point, divorce is an actuality, and as such each person must find the best and most efficient way of managing this new reality. The central task facing the divorcee is to develop a new identity in those areas most affected by the marriage, personal, professional, sexual, and social. Both partners may be able to learn and develop new ways to achieve a higher level of functioning in these areas. The most prominent feature of this stage, however, is the reopening and redeveloping of old, unresolved issues of identity, which were pushed aside or only partially dealt with during the marriage.

For both partners, marriage was a major component of their self-identities. But many wives, especially those who married at a young age, do not develop a professional and social identity separate from their mates. They, therefore, lack points of reference that might allow them to promote self-esteem outside the framework of marriage. The marriage was so much a part of this woman's identity that she often has justifiable fears of being unable to replace the old behavioral patterns with new ones.

The issue of identity as a personal problem develops early in the divorce process. The need of "finding oneself" rises anew and demands an answer before a change in status and role can be fully accepted. As part of revising of one's self-image, there is a reevaluation of professional, social, and sexual identity. Not only do financial considerations lead divorced women to seek outside work, but also their desire to build a new identity and to boost their self-esteem.

For those who married at a young age or who had limited premarital sexual experience, the need to discover different types of interpersonal and sexual relationships is very real. Many divorced people enter sexual relations with partners to whom they have no emotional attachments and with whom chances of a long meaningful relationship are bleak. This "candy store experience" satisfies the need to repair a damaged self-image and helps foster positive feelings regarding sexual relationships. A secondary gain from such encounters is the avoidance of an emotional relationship that carries a commitment.

Some divorcees, however, may not allow themselves new experiences because of inner and social conflicts surrounding sex. Others, because of their fears and insecurities, confine themselves to shallow liaisons, unable to integrate and transfer new experiences into long-term relationships. Nevertheless, most divorced people overcome the distortions caused by pain and anger; they manage to reorient their lifestyles and identities, and to view the marriage and their former spouses in a realistic fashion.

Acceptance and a New Level of Functioning

"Acceptance comes about gradually as the divorced person begins to get some feelings for himself as an adequate person socially, sexually, and vocationally" (Wiseman, 1975, p. 211). At this stage, a willingness to invest in another long-term relationship consolidates; the ability to accept others, as well as to be accepted by others, is achieved. This is the basis on which a new identity and level of functioning is built. When feelings of anger toward the former spouse give way to understanding and cooperation (about children, etc.), this acceptance signifies the stage of letting go of the past and opening oneself to opportunities in the future.

At this stage, the newly developed coping mechanism is firmly established. The fears and apprehensions of new relationships subside; a second marriage, based on a more solid foundation, is possible. The success of a second marriage, however, depends on the degree of the successful resolution of those problems posed in each previous stage.

Wiseman's model of the divorce process is derived from two theoretical, psychological sources: crisis theory and Kubler-Ross' description of the mourning process. Wiseman's model describes the gradual progression of the psychological resolution of the divorce crisis. But, because of its exclusive concern with the emotional–psychological dimension of the individual divorcee, the model neglects to address the significance of the relationship between the couple during the crisis and the social framework within which the divorce occurs. Its focus on the individual psychological responses, without reflecting on the numerous intertwining social and relational factors, narrows its scope.

MODEL 2: THE SIX STATIONS OF DIVORCE

Bohannan (1968) viewed the divorce process as comprising six parallel processes. Because these experiences occur simultaneously, a distinction must be made among them to achieve a clearer understanding of divorce as a process. Despite the simultaneous nature of these experiences, the difficulties and potency of each can occur at various times and on different levels. The six experiences or "stations" are the emotional divorce, the legal divorce, the economic divorce, the co-parental divorce, the community divorce, and the psychic divorce.

The Emotional Divorce

Emotional divorce is the process of the marriage's disintegration. In this first stage at least one partner reduces his or her emotional investment in the relationship. The family unit continues to function in much the same way as before, but the quality of the relationship is now different. The family may even seem to function better, in a calmer more relaxing fashion. Yet a retrospective analysis will reveal that the serenity was misleading; it stemmed from a conscious or unconscious withdrawal of one partner from the marriage and from ignoring rather than confronting problems. In marital relationships, overlooking difficulties usually leads to more difficulties and to more overlooking, which allows the downward trend to gain momentum.

"Married people, like any other people, must continue to grow as individuals if they are not to stagnate" (Bohannan, 1968, p. 36). Only by experiencing new challenges can people fully participate in society, in a professional life, and in personal relationships. Western culture promotes tremendous competition for the time and energy of each one of us. If these different pressures are organized in such a way that marital life takes second place (not in spite of but because of the degree of importance one attributes to the marital relationship), then the basis for an emotional divorce is formed.

The Legal Divorce

"Until very recently, no country granted its citizens the clear right to divorce, as they have the clear right to marry" (Bohannan, 1968, p. 38). The state has always proclaimed its right of interest in divorce by keeping the sole right of rendering the official cachet to terminate the marriage. The state also determines the frame within which new family relationships may be carried on.

Most legal systems in the West have proven insensitive to the needs of the divorcing family and do not provide the right structure for "orderly and socially approved discharge of emotions that are elicited during the emotional divorce" (Bohannan, 1968, p. 42). As Bohannan viewed it, the legal system should. Bohannan singled out lawyers as those outsiders who have the most to do with the process of divorce and yet are the most untrained to do so. They are often the cause of intensifying enmity rather than lessening it. Although the legal process of divorce is simple indeed today, the frequent mishandling of the legal procedure causes the divorce to be "messy" and "dirty."

The Economic Divorce

The family is an economic unit, most of the estate being the joint property of both husband and wife. In divorce settlements, decisions are rendered on the premise that without the wife's "moral assistance and domestic services" the husband would not have been able to work and support his family. Therefore, every financial gain, even if not resulting directly from the husband's or wife's job (gain from investments or royalties) is considered joint property. As such, it is subject to division according to the settlement agreed upon or decreed.

Two basic assumptions that carry much weight in the final settlement decision should be noted. The first, is that the man is responsible for fulfilling the needs of his wife and children. The second, although more implicit, is that the division of property should in some way reflect the division of responsibility (i.e., blame) for the divorce. The financial arrangement is usually divided into alimony and child support payments. The husband is obligated to support his wife for as long as they are married, even if they are no longer living together. The obligation ends when the legal divorce becomes final. The husband must also financially support his children until they reach the age of 18. Violation of a court order in this respect entails legal repercussions.

The Co-Parental Divorce

"The most enduring pain of divorce is likely to come from the co-parental divorce" (Bohannan, 1968, p. 45). The term *co-parental divorce* reflects the notion that parents divorce each other but not their children, even though only one of them will be granted the right of custody. A century ago, fathers were automatically granted custody. Today, the courts prefer the mother as the custodial parent. The mother is thought to have the "natural" qualities required for the proper upbringing of children. Only if she is proven "seriously delinquent in her behavior as a mother" will she be denied custody rights or will the children be taken away from her at a later time. The courts view the rights and needs of children as paramount.

The rights of the custodial parent are more encompassing than those of the noncustodial former spouse, whose rights are usually limited to prearranged visits. This considerable difference in the parents' ability to affect the upbringing and education of their children is a primal source of pain and friction between the couple. The father often feels that the mother raises the children to grow apart from him and that she discourages any exhibited resemblance to the father. The mother, on the other hand, often feels that the father attempts to undermine her authority, while she is the one responsible for making and carrying out decision. Many divorced mothers would like to share the responsibility with someone who would not criticize them but would strengthen and advise them. When differences of opinion about the children's education existed during the marriage, there was at least the possibility of discussion. Divorce and custody arrangements, however, bring an unequal division of parents' rights. Feelings of suspicion and mistrust of one parent by the other, and hence difficulties in the relationship of each parent with the children, are often a source of much friction and pain.

The Community Divorce

Major changes in our lives, such as those related to enlisting in the army or going away to college, bring about changes of social reference. Divorce, too, triggers these changes. Many divorcees express a bitter disappointment in the relationships and friendships formed during their married lives. They feel that these friends abandoned them and failed to stand by their side during their hardest trials. Divorced people often feel uncomfortable when around old friends and blame them for making them feel uneasy. Because of the divorce, people feel forced to leave their old, secure community environment and search for another. Many will earnestly join some sort of social organizations. The new community often serves not only as a new social environment, but also as a strong supportive system. In the United States, divorce is an almost universal experience. Here divorcees are well versed in the experience of community divorce. But of all the formal and informal social modes of dealing with divorce this is "probably the aspect of divorce that Americans handle best" (Bohannan, 1968, p. 52).

The Psychic Divorce

"Psychic divorce means the separation of self from the personality and the influence of the ex-spouse" (p. 53). It is the process whereby divorced people gain back their autonomy; they become whole and independent once again. For all divorcees, but particularly for those who "marry to their weaknesses," the psychic divorce, although the most difficult part of the process, serves as the greatest challenge for personal growth and development. Psychic divorce may be regarded as the most important and potentially constructive element of the divorce process. It is here that the now-separated partners strive to develop stability, completeness, and independence. They learn to live alone without the support of and dependence on each other, without someone to blame for mistakes and failures, and without someone to arrest personal development. Dependence ·on the self has to be learned anew along with the faith and ability to deal positively with the environment, people, thoughts, and feelings.

"Divorcees," Bohannan wrote, "are people who have not achieved a good marriage — they are also people who would not settle for a bad one" (p. 54). For some, marriage serves as a haven for not having to mature and struggle for independence. All people bring to marriage their family of origin's lifestyle and ways of coping with old solutions to new problems. Life after divorce offers ample opportunities to try and find new solutions to familiar problems.

Bohannan's analysis of the divorce process is the most cited and referred to model in divorce literature. By describing each "stage" of this multidimensional drama, he helps to sort out a complex whole into manageable and understandable segments. His six stages represent the major sources of difficulties faced by the divorced. With the noteworthy exception of the last stage and with the allowance that it may be more applicable in some stages than in others, his unit of analysis is the divorcing family and the social ways relevant to the divorce process. The psychological lot and struggle of the individual throughout the divorce are briefly mentioned only as part of psychic divorce. The model, therefore, is of only limited help to those who wish a closer look and an in-depth understanding of the emotional turbulence and confusion inbred in divorce for each divorcee. The following model presents such an analysis.

MODEL 3: DIVORCE AS A PSYCHOLOGICAL PROCESS

The third model discussed here is probably the most detailed psychological analysis of divorce. Kessler's (1975) analysis, based on her years of clinical work with adults at various stages in the course of divorce, divides the psychological process into seven emotional stages: disillusionment, erosion, detachment, physical separation, mourning, second adolescence, and exploration and hard work. Kessler stressed that different people experience these emotions in a different order, that the start and end points of this process are unclear, and that the duration of these experiences differ according to the person's psychological makeup.

Disillusionment

The emotional divorce begins when the relationship's honeymoon is over. Disillusionment occurs when the early romantic blindness wears off and when differences and difficulties are discovered. The unwillingness to deal with these problems causes partners to focus and dwell on the negative aspects of the relationship. Disillusionment is an integral part of any long-lasting relationship. Just as it may be the starting point for the disintegration of a relationship, disillusionment may be the key to deepening and strengthening the relationship. It is often the process in which partners accommodate their expectations from one another to suit reality. Differences come out into the open, and the mutual psychological exposure allows the couple to distinguish between reality and an idealistic perception of their partner. Such a perception minimizes the occurrence of future disappointments and allows a feeling of tranquility and assurance to emerge. This feeling is based on the knowledge that people are loved for their strengths and in spite of their weaknesses.

Letting thoughts linger on disagreements, if they persist, is distracting. At first the disillusionment is inconsistent; it disappears from consciousness with the same ease that it appeared. But with time, awareness and focus on the negative becomes more concentrated. The person vacillates between idealization of the partner and total disappointment. In time, more and more energies are invested in negative aspects of the relationship. At this stage, it may seem to an outside observer, as well as to the partners themselves, that the family unit is still on solid foundations. If they recognized the significance behind their intensified need for crowds to enhance their indirect communication, they might have a chance to overcome their problems. But without the willingness and maturity they need to deal with the disillusionment, the relationship will continue to decline to the next stage.

Erosion

Because few people have the experience or ability necessary to steer successfully out of disillusionment, erosion commonly follows. The pain, frustration, and anger repressed in the preceding phase is now expressed outwardly. Although awareness of disappointment and dissatisfaction with the mate is more acute, the origins of those feeling are yet to become conscious.

At this stage the partners are still very much involved with each other, although their communication is negatively based. "Hurts are deep because the two people still care for each other" (Kessler, 1975, p. 26).

Even with all these problems, the marriage and the relationship may still be salvageable, but with increasing difficulty. The new style of communication between the couple is the main obstacle because it becomes habitual. Verbal and nonverbal overt or covert behavior are common ways to hurt, ignore, and avoid one another.

These and other habits and behaviors are reinforced by secondary gains; because they allow avoidance and satisfy needs, these habits are hard to give up. The refusal and denial that "something is wrong" are also signs of the relationship's disintegration.

"The concentration is on taking rather than giving," and the balance between the two is scrutinized with a most sensitive scale. The need for emotional satisfaction is sometimes fulfilled through an extramarital intimate relationship that become more meaningful as the marital relationship becomes less satisfying. A vicious circle develops that strangles the marriage.

Detachment

Detachment means a significant reduction of investment in the marriage. The dominant sense is of not caring. This stage is characterized more by a growing disinterest in the continuing conflicts than by their intensity. The joy of life, the excitement, the patience, and the will to give and share that were once a part of the couple's life are now repressed or channeled into work, hobbies, or other substitutes. Rarely do both spouses experience detachment from the marriage at the same time. But once one of them experiences such feelings, the chance that divorce will ensue is high.

The signs of psychological detachment are easy to identify: the stressful quiet, the arrested verbal communication, and the consistent avoidance of intimate situations. The detachment process is characterized by the gradual change of orientation from past to future. The detached partner begins to think about a life after divorce. Ideas and fantasies about living alone take place alongside concrete financial planning, occasional testing of the attraction one still has to the opposite sex, and mentally rehearsing the separation so as to prepare for life without a partner. Thoughts of divorce are not necessarily formed into a decision at this point and may not even be that dominant. The inner confusion and struggle with the appealing and appalling aspects of marriage are still at their peak. Most of these thoughts, however, center around the negatives.

Physical Separation

"Physical separation is the most traumatic aspect of the whole emotional divorce process" (Kessler, 1975, p. 28). It is here that the two individuals face their feelings of loneliness, anxiety, and confusion and their need to build a new identity. Kessler differentiated between the partner who initiated the separation and his or her spouse. In spite of the many similarities in the quality of difficulties each faces, there are differences. It is safe to assume that partners who initiate the separation have already detached themselves from the relationship and are therefore better equipped for living alone. It is also easier for them to keep their dignity, because they are not the rejected one. But initiating the divorce often brings about feelings of guilt and failure, feelings that easily transform to anger. Guilt is based on a sense of responsibility for the hurt and pain the separation inflicts on the spouse and children, although the sense of failure results from a sense of surrender to difficulties and failure of the marriage.

If the loneliness was hard to take in the hollow family shell, it is even more difficult in the first stages of physical separation. The partners have not only foregone the social charade of togetherness, but also their frame of reference and belonging. Yet it is the loneliness that constitutes the foundation for a new completeness, sensitivity, and openness to other interpersonal relationships. "Out of loneliness comes creativity, strong determination, courage, and deep commitment" (Kessler, 1975, p. 32). To promote these positive aspects, the person must face and deal with the anxiety created by fear of the unknown. Kessler divided the sources of this anxiety into three aspects: (a) the uncertainty of society's reaction and the ability to handle single life, (b) the anxiety created by breaking away from old habits and routines, and (c) the anxiety resulting from the need to redefine oneself as one experiences a new life. Experiencing these anxieties is potentially constructive in that they are the impetus for adaptive changes.

Mourning

"Mourning is a web of anger, hurt, loneliness and helplessness" (Kessler, 1975, p. 36). Mourning is the process by which a loss is psychologically worked through and in which both spouses try to free themselves from the psychological presence of one another. Memories of the previous relationship threaten to flood the beginning of the new independence. It seems as though every personal item evokes longing and pain. Memories, pleasant and unpleasant, the contents of which are not important, shake the confidence. Only the mental existence of the spouse and of the relationship is significant.

Anger and depression are essential components of the mourning process. If the anger is based on the repetitious bitterness that piled up during the marriage, if it is the outcome of energy invested in seeking for the spouse's faults in the marriage, or if it is even the release of repressed childhood feelings, then it is destructive anger. But if the anger stems from the present reality, from the attempt to build a new independence, or from the frustration caused by striving to build a new relationship with the ex-spouse, children, or others, then it is constructive anger.

Depression, too, is an integral part of the mourning process. It is the other side of anger. Both express guilt. But although anger is externalized guilt, depression is an internalization of it. Once the separation is fully registered, "frantic grief" turns into depression and then into sadness. Although depression does not enable any action, sadness does. The transition from destructive to constructive anger, from depression to sadness, is necessary because it is the continuation of psychologically working through the divorce and moving to the next stage of the process.

Second Adolescence

At this stage one might observe the largest leap in self-rehabilitation. There is an ability and readiness to accept the sense of relief and freedom associated with divorce. There is an inner joy associated with the realization of "making it." And there is an ability not to look back in anger but with a sense of objectivity. After all, divorce reduces the level of conflict and pain caused by an unhappy marriage. The release from pressures and stress that were a part of daily marital life, along with the divorce proceedings, enable the now-divorced individuals to view the future more clearly and perhaps more optimistically. The excitement and enchantment felt about future opportunities are similar to those experienced in adolescence. Repressed wishes and desires are now open to discovery and conquest, but with the risk also of overreacting to the new freedom. Overreaction is a natural and constructive element of the process of experiencing life afresh. But it is destructive if it becomes institutionalized as a mode of reaction that assists the person in escaping the reality of postdivorce difficulties. Those who are aware of this danger will find their own balance, after a time, between the wish to compensate for past deprivations and the fear of losing harmony with the self.

Exploration and Hard Work

During this stage the locus of control becomes internal again. "New insights into self and others encourage additional investigation and inquiry"

(Kessler, 1975, p. 43). There is a feeling of a free choice of goals and confidence in attaining them. Goals that were formerly defined in general and diffused terms now gain a specific and realistic translation. The ability to give and share personally and intimately consolidates. The ability and readiness to develop relationships not out of weakness but out of strength, not passively but with active participation, is experienced. The need to experience for the sake of experience lessens, and the ability to censure and consider the need for meaningful experiences increases. People who reach this stage of development can look back with satisfaction and discover the distance they have traveled and the changes they have made in themselves — changes that transpired in spite of, and maybe even because of, the divorce.

Although Kessler's model presents the most inclusive account of the psychological experience during divorce, it ignores the breadth of divorce as a social phenomenon. Kessler chose to write on the psychological effects of divorce; viewed in those terms, her work is comprehensive indeed. However, by not addressing the legal and economical framework in which divorce takes place, the model delineates only one dimension of the divorce process.

MODEL 4: DIVORCE AND ERIKSON'S DEVELOPMENT THEORY

The fourth model outlined here was developed by Smart in 1977. She proposed a model where the process of recovering from divorce could be viewed in the context of Erikson's theory of personality development. Erikson (1963) viewed the child's personality development as being sequential: Each stage is characterized by a crisis that the child must resolve in order to continue to develop a healthy personality. Individuals differ with respect to the level of solution at each specific stage and of the overall process. However, because Erikson assumed no boundaries for personal development, it is impossible to resolve completely any of the crises. In effect, then, this means that there is room for limitless improvement. Later life crises often cause a regression to earlier developmental stages that were never resolved successfully and that are relevant to the current crisis. Through these regressions emerge opportunities to reach higher levels of solutions and, in this way, further personality development. The deeper and more encompassing the current crisis, the more intense is the regression. Divorce, according to Smart, involves such a crisis. It causes a regression and shakes the foundations of the resolutions reached earlier in life, as described in Erikson's eight developmental stages.

Trust Versus Mistrust

A basic sense of trust or mistrust is the first polarizing conflict facing the very young child. The child's relationship with the mother constitutes the frame within which this conflict is felt and solved. The quality of the mother–child relationship determines the individual's place on the continuum in which a basic trust in people (a sense of security derived from close intimate relationships) is at one end, and mistrust and insecurity are at the other. Divorce, which involves a breakdown in a person's most intimate and significant adult relationship, means that the individual once again faces the trust–mistrust conflict. Dealing with this conflict successfully is crucial to the divorcee's ability to build trustworthy and intimate relationships in the future.

Autonomy Versus Shame and Doubt

Autonomy is developed from the freedom given the child to choose between different alternatives. When this freedom is prevented, the result is self-doubt and shame. The feeling of being in control results from making free choices; it is the basis for cooperation and satisfaction in doing and creating anything. Dependency, lack of self-restraint, and a sense of external control are the basis for feelings of doubt and shame. An intimate relationship, such as marriage, calls for concessions regarding autonomy and free choice. Some married people never develop the sense of real independence; they transfer to their spouse the childhood dependency on their parents. Others who have developed a sense of autonomy before marriage, feel trapped and restrained in their new relationship. And yet others manage to maintain their sense of internal control even in such an unremitting intimacy as marriage.

Following divorce, the needs of dealing with a newly found freedom, of rebuilding life, and of facing numerous choices and practical difficulties bring about the return of the old conflict. A clash is stirred up between feelings of trust in one's ability to manage one's affair and feelings of helplessness, doubt, and shame. If the divorce is to be a constructive personal experience, the divorcee must not avoid this dilemma but must use it to reach a more mature and higher level of autonomy.

Initiative Versus Guilt

In childhood, the resolution of this conflict is considered to be most crucial for the child's adequate social development. At this stage children try to discover the quality of their interaction with their human and physical environment. They test their strength by physical feats and personal relationships, and by exploring new territories and creating new opportunities. Initiative adds the purpose dimension to behavior. It implies having goals and plans to fulfill the newly achieved autonomy. To define the boundaries of the self, much of the child's activity is "anti" and demonstrative. The focus then changes to cooperation and relationships as means of widening social horizons. Guilt, in the form of inwardly directed anger, originates from those initiatives that are blocked or failed.

One of the main aspects of the divorce crisis (and the most important to adjust to) is the social void and the need to have it filled. The measure of initiative (vs. guilt) derived from former conflict resolutions marks the success the divorced person has in enlarging his or her social circle and supporting groups. In spite of past failures and present insecurities, an initiator will risk and invest the energy required to achieve needs. Where guilt is dominant, the person may abstain from searching for and widening social circles, and may thus retain the guilt that has risen anew following divorce.

Industry Versus Inferiority

The school is the stage upon which a battle is waged between the child's basic trust in his or her ability to overcome difficulties and to achieve by hard work, and the child's sense of basic inferiority and self-fulfilling failures. According to Smart, divorce reactivates this basic conflict by challenging the person with many practical, as well as personal, predicaments. The sense of failure, the shaken self-confidence, and the uncertainties following divorce bring about regression, along with the need to face again the challenge of industry and of faith in just rewards versus the beliefs in one's inability to achieve success.

Identity Versus Role Confusion

One of the most serious challenges facing the divorced person is redefinition of the self. Erikson's theoretical model views the first attempts to define a clear identity, which corresponds and unifies past experiences with one's own and others' expectations, as occurring during childhood. The crisis of divorce, along with the drastic changes in lifestyle that follow, often undermines the validity of previously held self-concepts and thus stimulates the need for new definitions. The danger exists that the divorcee will continue to function on the basis of old self-concepts, which are no longer appropriate for the new reality, and will, therefore, cause role confusion. Despite the danger, it is possible that the ordeal and the previously held level of resolution of the conflict will lead to new and more accurate evaluations of one's personal, social, sexual, and perhaps even professional identities.

Intimacy Versus Isolation

> The young adult . . . is ready for intimacy . . . the capacity to commit himself to concrete affiliations and partnerships and to develop the ethical strength to abide by such commitments, even though they may call for significant sacrifices and compromises. . . . The counterpart of intimacy is distantation: the readiness to isolate and, if necessary, to destroy those forces and people whose essence seems dangerous to one's own "territory" seems to encroach on the extent of one's intimate relations. (Erikson, cited in Smart, 1977, p. 76)

The sense of isolation begins with emotional detachment from the spouse and reaches a peak at the time of physical separation, when the construction and quality of social relationships often change drastically. Some friends drift away; others begin to criticize. The relation of the divorced person to his or her surroundings comes, as in adolescence, to a crossroads where one of two basic attitudes may be adopted: One attitude progressively leads to formation of acquaintances, friendships, and new intimate relationships; the other attitude progressively leads to an instrumental approach to people and relationships and, hence, causes social isolation. Thus, the adjustment of the divorced person to the new reality depends on both the attitude toward others that he or she developed as a young adult and the outcome of the new, postdivorce struggle with the old intimacy versus isolation conflict.

Generativity Versus Stagnation

Every couple, whether they have children or not, must decide if generativity, in Erikson's terms, is a part of their self-actualization and their intimate relationship. The focus of this conflict is between the universal need to procreate and the person's giving in to fears, frustrations, and risks that are inherent in the process of realizing this need. Smart maintained that this conflict is similar to the one parents face in reestablishing their relationship with their children following divorce.

The parent receiving custody of the children can derive from them happiness, satisfaction, and a sense of continuity. But children can also be perceived as being a source of frustration, as limiting new experiences, and as curbing the parent's ability to achieve self-actualization in other areas.

A new definition of parenthood is forced on the parent who is not given custody. This parent's relationship with the children can still be a source of satisfaction and self-actualization, even though the conditions are now quite different. However, children (just as they are for the custodial parent) can be viewed and treated as an arresting factor in personal development, as a continuous reminder of guilt, and as an unwanted obligation requiring time and energy.

Ego Integrity Versus Despair

Ego integrity pertains to the strength to fight and the courage to make use of life's opportunities in order to reach a higher level of self-actualization. Despair is perceived by Erikson (cited in Smart, 1977) as "the feeling that the time is now short, too short for the attempt to start another life and to try out alternate roads to integrity" (p. 77). Attaining a sense of integrity vis-à-vis the divorce is a sign of good adjustment.

Two of Waller's (1958) criteria mentioned by Smart seem especially relevant. One is that the emotions that arise throughout the divorce experience are now less dominant. Hurt and anger are reduced not by their denial or repression, but by working these feelings through, thus allowing awareness and openness to new experiences along with opportunity for ego integrity. The second criterion concerns the ability to reorganize life to suit the new circumstance. According to Waller, the danger is that instead of readjusting to the new conditions, adjustment is to the problems, in this way turning despair into the focus of life and experience.

Using Erikson's epigenesis approach enables Smart to highlight the essence of the inner psychological conflicts facing divorcees. Although this approach does not provide a comprehensive and integrative picture of the emotional process during the crisis, it does help to focus the central psychological conflicts and to tie their resolution to early development.

CONCLUDING REMARKS

The four models presented here do not represent all the attempts to understand and present the divorce crisis as a psychological process. Although Froiland and Hozman (1977), Weiss (1976), Federico (1979), Rice and Rice (1986), Krantzler (1975), and some others have also put forth models, the four addressed here cover much of the content of the others. Despite the differences between the various models in the number of stages, in the points of focus, and even in the depth of analysis, their content seems to form a wide common denominator.

To date, there has been no thorough attempt to integrate the ideas and concepts put forward in these four models into an integrative theoretical model. Nor has there been any attempt to propose a psychosocial analysis of the divorce process that would view the individual psychological adjustment in the wider context of divorce as a social phenomenon. Salts (1979) and McPhee (1984), however, have done some related work.

Salts compared seven different models. He defined the therapeutic objectives appropriate to the various levels of adjustment described by the different models. A latent assumption inherent in Salts' work was that not every theoretical distinction among different stages in a particular model has a therapeutic counterpoint. He searched for, and discovered, four stages across models. These stages, which present distinct differences in their corresponding therapeutic objectives, encompass different levels of adjustment, which are derived from different models that suggest the same therapeutic goals. For instance, in Kessler's first two stages (disillusionment and erosion) and in Wiseman's first stage (denial), the therapist must work with the couple to improve the interactions between them. "Improving interactions," therefore, is Salts' first stage. Another example follows from the common therapeutic denominator that Salts found in Kessler's physical separation and mourning stages and in Bohannan's legal divorce, economic divorce, and co-parental divorce stages. Salts viewed the common denominator as being the therapists' need to assist the couple during these stages in coping with the crisis and the changes that it causes.

The work of McPhee (1984) is different in scope and objectives. His goal was to formulate a model that would allow an empirical investigation of the variables affecting the process of adjustment to divorce. His theoretical starting point was role transitions theory. On the basis of this theory, and in relation to the reviewed divorce models, McPhee defined the variables that influence the process in operational terms. He suggested three research hypotheses, the empirical investigation of which would validate or invalidate his theoretical model. For example, one assumption is that the larger the amount of normative role transitions perceived as needed for the adjustment, the more difficult will be the transition from a predivorce to a postdivorce state. Another assumption McPhee deemed worthy of investigation concerns the relation between the divorcing couple's financial stability and the ease of adjustment to the divorce.

Creating an integrative model based on other models was not McPhee's objective, and indeed he did not suggest this. The relevance of his analysis to the present work is that in building a research model and in deriving from it empirical assumptions, McPhee drew together divorce crisis themes addressed by the four models presented in this chapter.

Apart from these types of attempts to incorporate data from other models, no other attempt to deal with a common denominator among the models has been reported in the literature. Further, the models presented here (and they are not unique from this point of view) suffer either from inconsistency in their level of analysis (Bohannan, 1968, and Kessler's, 1975, models) or from disregarding important dimensions of the divorce process because of their consistency (Wiseman's, 1975, and Smart's, 1977, models). For instance, Bohannan's model is not consistent regarding the unit of analysis presented in the "stations" nor in the source and consequence of the various psychological and practical difficulties. In the stage of "emotional divorce," for instance, the individual divorcee is the unit of analysis. Bohannan focused almost exclusively on the psychological dimension; he does not mention the practical or behavioral aspects (other than that they are a consequence of the psychological). In "legal divorce," on the other hand, the unit of analysis is the society's legal system, but the accent is on external events that might promote psychological difficulties (the lawyer–client interaction). There is no mention of those. By these different accentuations, Bohannan might be trying to stress the multidimensionality of the process, but if so it would seem important and necessary to maintain a consistent unit of analysis in each of the "stations."

Those models favoring the psychological aspect of the divorce process are loyal to the dimension they chose to present, but are, as a consequence, unfaithful to the multidimensionality of the phenomenon. Smart (1977), for instance, presented an interesting view of the psychological process of divorce, but she ignored the behavioral and social dimension of the process. Her model does not address itself to the unique aspects of divorce, and it may, therefore, be applied to any personal crisis.

Any theoretical model attempting to cover the whole process of divorce from its many dimensions and aspects must be based on the current data available and on an integration of existing theoretical models. It must deal with the psychological and social dimensions inherent in each stage.

The psychosocial model of the divorce process presented in chapter 3 derives some of its content from the four models described here. The objective of the psychosocial model is to achieve a more encompassing and profound understanding of the divorce process. The chapter attempts to integrate ideas, perceptions, and distinctions of various authors and theories, along with this author's own clinical observations and research findings.

3 The Psychosocial Model of the Divorce Process

Like marriage, divorce is as much a complex personal event as it is a multidimensional social phenomenon. Divorce is a drawn-out psychological and social process; although each particular divorce follows a unique course, certain common denominators justify the adoption of a generalized approach that would subsume individual situations. These common denominators have been used by researchers to set out various models of the divorce process (Ahrons & Rodgers, 1987; Bohannan, 1968; Federico, 1979; Kessler, 1975; Krantzler, 1975; Rice & Rice, 1986; Smart, 1977; Weiss, 1976; Wiseman, 1975). Some models were originally designed to deal expressly with the problem of divorce (Bohannan, 1968; Federico, 1979). In other cases, existing psychological models were adopted for the purpose (Rice & Rice, 1986; Smart, 1977; Wiseman, 1975).

All of these models agree on a number of assumptions – namely that divorce is a family crisis as well as a personal one, that it is a process that entails psychological risks as well as opportunities for development, and that this process unfolds in distinct stages that are characterized by qualitative differences of themes and of degree of coping. The models differ, however, on where they locate the points at which the process begins and ends, in the importance they assign to a particular event or experience, in the units of analysis that they employ and the consistency with which these units are used, and in the number and content of stages that they associate with the process.

The psychosocial model of the divorce process that is presented in this chapter derives some content from the models previously mentioned. It also draws on my own clinical observations and research findings. But most of all, the psychosocial model relies on the principles of social exchange theory (Nye, 1979; Thibaut & Kelly, 1959), cognitive consistency theory (Aronson, 1968; Festinger, 1957), and attribution theory (Heider, 1958; Weiner, Russel, & Lerman 1978).

Other writers have applied the social exchange theory to explain the process of marital breakdown (Albrecht & Kunz, 1980; Dixon & Weitzman, 1982; Kitson et al., 1983; Levinger, 1979a). But its application was limited mostly to the divorce crisis and was not applied to form a comprehensive model of the whole divorce process and a person's adjustment to it. The purpose of the psychosocial model is to show how by adopting the principles of the social exchange theory together with the cognitive theories, we can achieve a more encompassing and profound understanding of divorce as a psychological process taking place in a social context.

THEORETICAL ORIENTATION AND PRINCIPLES

The dominating theoretical models used in divorce research are currently based on the principles of social exchange theory (Wright, 1988). In general terms, this model suggests that the form and quality of social interactions are based on the individual's level of satisfaction from the relationship. The level of a person's satisfaction is determined by the ongoing rational evaluations of the outcome of his or her costs and benefits from the relationship. People seek a relationship in which their personal and social costs are minimum, whereas their benefits are maximum. The relation between costs and benefits is assumed to determine many aspects of the relationships and of each individual's behavior in them.

Thibaut and Kelly (1959) described two comparison levels used in this evaluation process. One is the level of outcomes that an individual believes he or she deserves. The less favorable the actual outcome is in comparison to the level that is believed to be deserved, the less is the person's attraction to the relationship. The source of dissatisfaction may, of course, not reside in the relationship itself, but may rather be derived from the second level of comparison — that of the level of outcome the individual believes he or she can and will get from an alternative relationship. The higher this level, the less attractive the current relationship. But even if the level of attractions within the marriage is low and the barriers offer minimal restraint, a relationship will not be terminated unless an alternative seems more attractive (Levinger, 1979b).

Levinger (1965), in his analysis of marital cohesiveness and dissolutions, considered some of these aspects in a relationship and, by blending them with Lewinian field theory, proposed an exchange model. In the model,

Levinger suggested that a person stays in a relationship because attractions to that relationship are more than attractions to alternative relationships and because the level of barriers prevents the person from leaving. The attraction is directly associated with its perceived rewards. "Rewards are derived from positive outcomes associated with membership in the relationship" (Levinger, 1979b, p. 40). These rewards may include receiving resources such as love, income, property, social similarity, companionship, sexual enjoyment, services, support, and security.

Barriers, as adopted by Levinger from the Lewin (1951) personality theory, are restraining forces that affect a person only when he or she approaches the psychological boundary. "Barriers lessen the effect of temporary fluctuations in interpersonal attractions" (Levinger, 1979a, p. 41). Financial burdens associated with divorce, social pressures exerted by primary groups, religious constraints, norms and values that militate against divorce, and obligations toward one's spouse and children are the kinds of barriers Levinger (1976) identified. Some attractions that favor the alternative course, dissolving the marriage, are the freedom and independence associated with single life, the prospect of having a new sex partner, and the belief that release from marriage offers a greater potential for self-actualization. In conclusion, Levinger (1976) stated: "Essentially, pair cohesiveness pertains to the net sum of the attractions and barriers inside a relationship minus the net attractions to and barriers around the most salient outside alternative" (p. 28).

Clearly, all the attractions and barriers that are associated with either marriage or divorce have only a subjective value. As regards meaningfulness, they are inversely related. That is, as long as the rewards are valued highly, the barriers are unmeaningful and, therefore, unfelt (Levinger, 1976). If, however, a person is dissatisfied with the relationship and attempts or even contemplates withdrawal from it, then social pressure (real or imagined) for instance, acts as a restraining force. Thus, the determining variables in an individual's behavior in a relationship lie in the resolution of the approach–avoidance conflict inherent not only in the relationship and in the perceived alternatives but also in the social context within which this relationship exists.

The social exchange theory assumes that the partners in the relationship accurately perceive their outcome and alternatives and rationally weigh the costs and benefits (Wright, 1988). But perceptions are not always accurate. They are biased by one's cognitive schema (Kruglanski, 1989), the adopted pattern of attribution (Heider, 1958), and the social and cultural context in which one lives (Bond, 1983); they are altered as the individual acquires new information (Thibaut & Kelley, 1959). Thus, a model of the divorce process and a person's adjustment to divorce should take into account the dynamic nature of the reciprocal effects that exists between the individual's perceptions of the net sum of the cost and benefits in the relationship and the changing life circumstances.

Festinger's (1957) theory of cognitive dissonance and Doherty's (1978, 1981, 1982) attribution model can add to our understanding of these reciprocal effects. The cognitive dissonance theory proposes that knowledge and meaning develop in a process in which individuals attempt to create internal consistency. When a discrepancy is perceived (but only then), either the perception or the attitudes and beliefs that generated it must be reexamined (Festinger, 1957; Kruglanski, Baldwin, & Shelagh, 1983). In this process of reexamination, individuals are often rationalizing rather than rational (Aronson, 1968).

Particularly during marital crisis, partners are likely to perceive a discrepancy between their original expectation and their present marital life. Inconsistencies between one's expectations of his or her partner and the actual behavior of the partner continue to be a source of conflict throughout the divorce. People's attempts to regain a sense of consistency about their lives (Bohannan, 1968; Wiseman, 1975) propel them into a pattern of attribution and behavior that is cognitively consistent with their attitudes and beliefs about themselves, their spouse, and the world (Alloy, 1982; Baucom, 1986; Fincham, Beach, & Baucom, 1987).

Patterns of attribution in the context of intimate conflicts are analyzed in Doherty's (1978) theory in terms of several causal dimensions. One of the most important dimensions is the locus of the cause to which a conflict is attributed. Doherty (1978, 1981) identified six potential causal loci: self, other, relationship, social, theological causes, and either luck, chance, or fate. A pattern of attribution is what emerges when we consider all these causes and their believed levels of responsibility. Heider (1958) cited the other important causal dimension that determines the pattern of attribution: The individual's perception of the nature of the cause, its stability, and its origin (internal vs. external), and the extent to which that cause reflects voluntary behavior (effort vs. luck). The pattern of attribution affects the individual's perception of an event and his or her reaction to it (Holtzworth-Munroe & Jacobson, 1985; Shaver, 1975).

Another aspect of attribution relevant to marital and postdivorce relationship is its orientation toward the past. Briefly stated, judgment of causation involves establishing what produced an event or outcome and thus involves analysis of past events (Weiner, 1986). This orientation and the need for cognitive consistency create the linkage between the couple's behavior and each partner's behavior in marriage and then in divorce.

The processes of cognitive consistency affect the process of causal attribution in that a person tends to infer causes that are consistent with his or her perception of self. Cognitive inconsistencies may be resolved by attributing the inconsistency to one's ability, effort, task difficulty, and luck (Heider, 1958). Thus, for instance, to resolve the tension caused by the conflict of receiving fewer than expected social rewards, a person may attribute the lack of social success to personal inability, to his or her investing too little effort in developing a good social relationship, to the high level of difficulty in establishing good relationships, or to bad luck. Discrepancies, dilemmas, and conflicts that developed during the marriage, during each step of the divorce, and during the adjustment process, and, more specifically, the way these problems are solved will determine the succeeding steps and the final outcome (Wright, 1988).

This theoretical approach proposes that the process of divorce can be better understood if the partners' behavior is viewed as a function of (a) their ongoing evaluation of the costs and benefits of their actions and relationship with others, (b) their striving for cognitive consistency, and (c) their patterns of attribution.

THE PROCESS OF DIVORCE

The Boundaries of the Psychosocial Model

No operational definition (as opposed to an indistinct description) of the psychological boundaries of the divorce crisis has previously been proposed. Adjustment to divorce, on the other hand, has been defined both conceptually and operationally. Probably the most common approach to the definition of adjustment has been to define it by how it is measured. The measures most commonly encountered in research include assessing the extent of experienced distress in terms of physical and emotional symptoms, and/or using measures of self-perceived adequacy of functioning (e.g., Spanier & Hanson, 1981; White & Mika, 1983).

The psychosocial model of divorce assumes that the process begins with a family crisis that eventually leads to divorce, and that the process ends when negative feelings related to the failing marriage and the divorce have subsided to a point where they no longer determine behavior and where the divorcee seizes the change for personal growth.

To clarify the boundaries of the proposed model, we define the *divorce crisis* as a process in which at least one partner becomes conscious of being dissatisfied with the marriage and begins seriously to contemplate divorce. In other words, the divorce crisis occurs (a) when at least one partner perceives that his or her cost in maintaining the relationship is higher than the benefits (within comparison), (b) when he or she expects higher benefits outside the marriage (outside comparison), (c) when he or she attributes the crisis to stable and lasting reasons, and (d) when, for the purpose of cognitive consistencies, he or she needs to consider a divorce. Divorce crisis need not lead to divorce. From the point of crisis, the couple may consciously or unconsciously (Federico, 1979) choose several paths of action, only one of which is to go through with the divorce. Another path may lead the couple to negotiate between themselves new and more satisfying ways of interacting or of creating a more fulfilling lifestyle. They may seek individual or marital therapy to help them survive the crisis. But if divorce is the road they choose to take, then they are said to be well adjusted at the stage in which they perceive themselves as fulfilling their obligations toward their children and former spouse without being dominated by feelings of resentment, anger, guilt, or pain, and when they function socially and professionally on levels that are satisfactory to them. In other words, divorced people are well adjusted (a) when they perceive the benefits of the postdivorce life to be higher than its costs (within comparison), (b) when they attribute their satisfaction to stable and lasting reasons, and (c) when their actions toward their children and former spouse are perceived to be cognitively consistent with their expectations of themselves.

This proposed definition of the divorce process offers both the framework within which the divorce crisis may be considered, and a point of departure for appraising the level of adjustment to and winning over the divorce crisis. Underlying the definition is the assumption that appraising deeds and feelings is important, but so is inquiring into their reasons.

The following psychosocial model of the divorce process consists of four stages: deciding, separating, struggling, and winning. Moreover, these stages are not viewed as following a linear structure, but rather as representing stations in a loop; thus movement between them, progression as well as regression, may intermingle.

Deciding

To Be or Not To Be.   When two people marry, they each bring to the relationship different sets of experiences and different personal histories from which they formed their attitudes, beliefs, and expectations concerning life and marriage. Accordingly, their views may differ regarding the many aspects of marital life, such as the roles of husband and wife, the practices and responsibilities of childrearing, and the like. These differences are not of equal significance to the quality and outcome of the marriage. The most important task facing couples throughout their married life is, however, dealing with significant differences and facilitating each partner's personal growth in the context of marriage.

A couple's failure to work together often leads to a divorce crisis even early in the marriage. After the couple's initial romantic idealism has faded, a process of "psychological undressing" sets in (Kessler, 1975), and the couple soon starts to discover the differences between their dreams and expectations and the actual turn of events. Conflicts arising from such differences are quite common during most marriages and may even act as a catalyst in strengthening the relationship and establishing the couple on a different, yet firmer footing. To do so, the couple needs to reduce or eliminate the tension caused by these differences. They may use rationalization and denial (Froiland & Hozman, 1977; Kraus, 1979; Wiseman, 1975). Or the couple may change their relationship so that each partner may feel a more favorable outcome when they compare the costs and benefits entailed in the marriage.

If the marriage partners are unable to work out either of these strategies and if at least one partner becomes preoccupied with the unfavorable discrepancies of the two sets of comparisons (within and outside), then the stride toward divorce gains momentum. The pace of this momentum and the final decision depends on (a) the psychological and social values of the resources each partner is perceived to have (Scanzoni & Szincovacz, 1980), and (b) the values attributed by each individual to both the psychological and social attraction and the barriers associated with remaining married or divorcing (Levinger, 1979a).

Personal and Social Resources.   Resources, as noted by Scanzoni and Szincovacz (1980), are the characteristics and properties of an individual. Resources refer to the broad range of reserves and aids that are potentially available to a person in times of need (George, 1980). When people have sufficient appropriate resources, they are less likely to view a stressful situation as problematic. Personal resources are drawn from an individual's four basic attributes: financial (economic well-being), educational (contributing to cognitive ability that facilitates realistic perception of the difficulties and problem-solving skills), physical health (well-being), and psychological resources (personality characteristics; George, 1980). Social resources are drawn from friends, neighborhoods, kin, and immediate family (McCubbin et al., 1980). For a resource to be a meaningful term in the context of interpersonal relationship, it must be considered with the value the individual attaches to it as a source of strength. Resources such as education, income, properties, self-esteem, social status, friends, and so forth may have different values to different people, and different values for the same person at different times.

The difference between partners' level of resources becomes especially important when they are deciding about divorce (Wright, 1988). The partner who feels that he or she has more resources will fear less the decision to divorce. Because of the numerous resources, their effect on the decision to divorce is a complex one. Thus, for instance, a partner may not fear the economic consequences of divorce because of his or her high level of income but may fear the social consequences because of low self-image. The process of cognitive consistency affects the perceived value of resources. Under certain circumstances when people receive less than they feel they deserve, then, for the sake of internal consistency, they will tend to lower the value of the relevant resource. For instance, if people receive significantly fewer assurances from a spouse than they feel their actions in the relationship warrant, they may either devalue the importance of the partner's praises as a source for building self-esteem or they may devalue their self-esteem.

Often it is only when the marriage is under threat that the differences in the levels of resources are fully exposed. Then the partner with the most resources usually has more power in the relationship, more ability to shape the relationship (Zartman, 1979), and therefore more latitude in the divorce decision. But an extreme difference in resources between partners may constitute a greater threat to the partner with fewer resources and thus may increase the possibility that that partner will take the first action in order to secure as many resources as possible. Steps such as secretly putting away extra cash or secretly preparing to move out of the house with the children and furniture have been taken by the partner with fewer resources (Scanzoni & Szincovacz, 1980). But these behaviors under these circumstances seem to be reactions to a threat or actual decision made by the partner with more resources.

Psychological and Social Attractions and Barriers.   The decisions to divorce not only depend on the partners' perceived levels of resources but also on the conclusion they reach when weighing the attractions and the barriers associated with the marriage and the alternatives. When the cost outweighs the attractions in the relationship, and/or when the attractions outweigh the costs in the alternative, there is an increased likelihood of a divorce decision.

Depending on individual and social circumstances, people may change their valuation of the attractions and barriers they associate with their marriage and divorce; thus, the outcome may be altered. People's perception of the attractions associated with divorce (e.g., expectations of personal freedom, sexual relations, spending money, and enjoyment from friends) and their perceptions of the barriers associated with marriage (e.g., strength of religious beliefs; obligation to spouse and children; financial costs of divorce; and social pressure from neighbors, relatives, and friends) were found to relate to the decision to divorce (Green & Sporakowski, 1983). Also related to the decision to divorce are the reduction of the legal and economic barriers to divorce (Lenthall, 1977; Weitzman, 1985); the change in our cultural values and attitudes toward marriage and divorce (Norton & Glic, 1976; Rice & Rice, 1986); and women's growing economic independence and pursuit of self-development (Bernard, 1971; Kaslow & Schwartz, 1987).

During the divorce crisis, an approach–avoidance conflict develops. The conflict is between the attractions and barriers reinforcing the marriage on the one hand and the attractions associated with divorce on the other. If the forces that work against preserving marriage are stronger, then a decision to dissolve the marriage is cognitively consistent and, therefore, is more easily made. But as the forces pulling in both directions even out, it becomes increasingly difficult to reach a decision that will enhance the sense of cognitive consistency. This may result in an unhappy, yet stable, marriage despite the heightened cognitive dissonance, because the decision to dissolve the marriage could not be reached.

To resolve the cognitive dissonance, the individual may devalue the pulling forces on either side of the equation. If people cannot do that by themselves, they can enlist or manipulate others to help them. Federico (1979) described two strategies that are often employed to terminate a relationship. Both strategies are used by those who want to dissolve the marriage yet stay in it. To resolve this internal inconsistency, they manipulate their spouses.

In the first strategy, the partner behaves in a way that is (consciously or unconsciously) calculated to have a devastating effect on the relationship causing the spouse to demand a divorce. The spouse's demand tilts away the responsibility for the divorce and leaves the partner with "no choice."

The second strategy is similar to the first except that the spouse's responses are just as provocative as the conduct of the other partner. For instance, if the wife divulges the existence of her affair with another man, the husband responds by becoming involved with another woman. Each time the wife acts to put a greater distance between herself and her husband, the husband responds in kind with a similar behavior. This process can continue until the wife demands a divorce on the basis of her husband's conduct. In this case, the person who set in motion the process of undermining the marriage is the one who demands a divorce. The pretext, however, is the behavior of the other partner. Both strategies help the partners who first wanted the divorce to attribute the reasons for it to their spouses. Thus, they keep their perceptions of themselves consistent with their attributions about the disintegrating relationship.

Most people, however, feel more comfortable rejecting than being rejected. Hill, Rubin, and Peplau (1976) reported that partners showed a systematic bias with respect to the question of who wanted to break up. There was a general tendency for respondents to say that they themselves were the ones who wanted to break up. Furthermore, former partners exhibited little attributional agreement on the contribution of factors internal to the relationship (e.g., differences in interest and background) and moderate to high agreement on external factors (e.g., interest in other persons). More women than men tended to attribute the decision to divorce to problem areas in the relationship; and more women than men were likely to compare the attraction in the relationship to the attraction of alternatives, whether potential or actual. Hill et al. (1976) and Kaslow and Schwartz (1987) found that women terminate relationships more readily than men.

Albrecht and Kunz (1980) conducted a unique study in that they actually tested the social exchange hypothesis at the deciding stage. They analyzed 1,265 questionnaires of people who reported that they or their spouse were or had been divorced. Their findings support the social exchange premise as presented here. The most important barriers for the decision to divorce were "financial concerns (especially for women), concerns for the children (especially for men), and the implications of such an action on personal religious beliefs" (p. 336). The most important costs in maintaining the marriage were reported to be the hurt in being betrayed, being physically abused (especially wives), loss of love, financial insecurity, and emotional difficulties. The cost–benefit balance was further tipped off by the following important expected benefits: alternative financial support (especially for women), alternative love relationship, and alternative sources for emotional and sexual gratifications.

Once the decision to divorce has been made and at least one of the partners has passed the point of no return (Federico, 1979), the psychological attractions associated with the marriage are further depreciated (Federico, 1979; Weiss, 1975). One's obligations to the relationship and the effort invested in it decrease as well. The behavior of one or both partners, at this point, is often designed to ensure that the net sum of the costs and benefits within the relationship remains less than that of the real or believed rewards offered by the alternative. A common behavioral expression of this behavior is a spouse's refusal to deal seriously with the difficulties of the marriage or to see a therapist (Kaslow & Schwartz, 1987). Triggering controversies or fights also helps a partner retain cognitive consistency with the decision.

For the reluctant partner, the net sum of the costs and benefits within the relationship may still be higher than the real or believed rewards offered by the alternative. If this is the case, he or she may try to reverse the process and act in a way that is designed to tip the balance in the other partner's mind in favor of the attractions and barriers associated with the marriage. But the reluctant partner may still be struggling with pro and con forces that are similar in strength and may be making up his or her own approach–avoidance conflict. If that is the case, a spouse's bickering behavior will help partners solve the conflict and more often than not will carry them over the point of no return.

Seldom does a couple reach the point of no return together. Usually, when one partner passes the point of no return and finally decides on divorce, that partner will try to bring the other to the same juncture. Professional counseling, at this point, is of almost no help (Albrecht & Kunz, 1980). Emotional and practical measures will be taken to end the relationship, at which time the second phase of the process begins.

Separating

The Impact.   Once the decision to divorce has been made, the couple must decide when to separate. Given the deteriorating ability of most couples to negotiate anything at this point, few are able to reach an agreement on the best time to part (Wallerstein & Kelly, 1980b). Although women more than men initiate divorce (Kaslow & Schwartz, 1987), in most divorcing families it is the husband who leaves home (Ahrons, 1980a) and, therefore, the actual separation depends more on his moves than on his wife's.

Although most physical separation follows soon after the decision to divorce is made, the time that elapses from the decision to the separation, as well as the ways that the separation occurs, varies a great deal (Melichar & Chiriboga, 1988). The separation may, for example, be the result of lengthy deliberation and detailed planning or it may be an unpremeditated response, such as following a major argument, of one spouse hastily moving out. These two extreme examples may still not be mutually exclusive because it is also possible that one partner has been planning for a long time to leave home but needed the anger (or the excuse) associated with a major fight to push him or her past the hesitation to leave (Kraus, 1979; Wiesman, 1975).

Review of the literature on transition reveals that the speed of passage through the stages of the divorce process is an important factor in the divorcing person's adjustment. A long and careful deliberation before the actual separation has been associated with somewhat less trauma in the aftermath of separation (Goode, 1956a; Krantzler, 1975; Weiss, 1975). Melichar and Chiriboga (1988) examined in detail these implications for women and found that those who spend more time between the decision to divorce and separation were "less likely to feel they could not get going, more excited and interested in things, and less likely to show signs of agitated depression. They also tended to manifest fewer signs of stress responses, and reported more feelings of pride" (p. 225). When the decision to part is reached slowly, it is also more likely to be accompanied by the kind of rows and heated arguments that, although painful at the time, allow the expression of strong feelings and provide a source of conflict resolution through some sort of understanding about what went wrong.

But regardless of the time and the ways, a separation still represents the most dramatic step in the process, and often the most stressful (Crosby, Gage, & Raymond, 1983; Goode, 1956a; Kessler, 1975). Although for some the separation causes feelings of relief or elation, these are rarely more than transitory feelings (Rice & Rice, 1986). More often than not, physical separation intensifies and gives new meaning to the sense of loneliness, fear, and pain that are aroused by the experience of loss (Bloom, Asher, & White, 1978; Pearlin & Johnson, 1977). Trafford (1982) compared the disorientation immediately following separation to the confusion and pain of adolescents leaving home for the first time.

Many people with whom I have worked, especially the instigators of their divorce, reported that before the separation they mentally rehearsed living alone. But even these rehearsals did not spare them the initial shock of being on their own. Their reaction to the disruption of comforting old habits and routines (Goode, 1956a) and to the fear of an unknown future took the form of an anxiety reaction. For some people the anxiety is so immense that they try either to deny or to turn back the clock. But such attempts are often doomed to failure, because they follow from and result in the same pattern that fell short numerous times in the past (Ahrons, 1980a; Kressel & Deutsch, 1977). As a consequence, the partners continue to battle but in the end are forced to accept the new reality (Crosby et al., 1983). The task of separating emotionally from a former partner lies at the heart of this acceptance. What complicates the process even more is the partner's need to separate and yet to cooperate. People need to redefine their relationship, not to terminate it, so they can negotiate their way from a nuclear family system to a binuclear system (Ahrons, 1980c). And they need to do so even though there comes a point when people feel so wounded, threatened, or frightened that escape and termination are all that are seem to be possible.

The process of emotional separation is greatly affected by the circumstances in which the marriage ended. In particular, these circumstances include the individual's understanding and portrayal of his or her own role as either the active (initiator) or the passive (recipient) agent in the decision to end the partnership (Burgoyne, 1984; Burgoyne & Clark, 1984).

The Active and the Passive Spouse.   A unique element of the divorce situation is the fact that there is an active spouse or "provoker" of the divorce process (whether or not the active spouse is the "decider" or the "filer" is beside the point), whereas in bereavement, for instance, most often there is not. The choice factor in divorce underlines the reversibility of the process and makes it more difficult for both active and passive spouses to accept and cope with the finality of separation. The way back, which remains open to the active spouse until the end and, theoretically even after the formal divorce, represents an ever-present temptation for an easy solution to the emotional and practical difficulties that arise as a result of separation. For the passive spouse, the mere possibility (however tenuous) that the process could be reversed may delay the conscious realization that the change is irrevocable, may encourage that spouse's harboring unfounded hopes for reconciliation, and may result in a misguided investment of energy in a false direction. As a result of these delays, the passive spouse recovers more slowly and later than the active spouse (Crosby et al., 1983; Kelly, 1982). This is probably because the active spouse, after the anxiety of making the decision, had a head start as a result of earlier cognitive acceptance (Crosby et al., 1986) and has more sense of control in the situation (Kelly, 1982). Active spouses tend to feel guilty (Brown, 1976) and have more fear (Crosby et al., 1983). But these emotions seem to hinder their progress toward adjustment less than the anger, traumatic sense of rejection, loss of respect from others (Weiss, 1975), and hurt (Crosby et al., 1986) that are expressed by passive spouses (Weiss, 1975).

The difference in the levels of desire for divorce may also give a wrong impression to outsiders and may reinforce each partner's belief about who is "guilty" of dissolving the marriage and who is *victim* (Hunt & Hunt, 1977). This sort of cognitive differentiation makes it easier for each partner to deal with the situation, because it gives direction to the partners' feelings and actions in a situation that is ambiguous and elicits confused and conflicting reactions. By now the quarreling couple has all but stamped paid on reciprocal responsibilities in the relationship. Each partner's recriminations and mutual apportionment of blame cause further disagreements, adding even greater strain to a relationship already heavily charged with ill feeling.

Even those who summon up the courage to leave violent, diminishing, or otherwise empty marriages find it hard to understand the sense of loss they experience when they are finally alone (Weiss, 1975, 1976). Hancock (1980) noted that basic to all losses sustained in divorce is the loss of a sense of meaning and belonging. But what makes it difficult to realize and deal with the persistent attachment is the fact that attachment is inconsistent with the unfolding reality and with the intense feelings of hurt and pain. To resolve this dissonance people may try to either reconcile or negotiate their way through the process of "psychic divorce" (Bohannan, 1968). But much of how they resolve this dissonance depends on their psychological and social resources.

Personal and Social Resources. While married and living together, people share many resources with their spouses. Wealth, household goods, friends, relatives, and even relationships with children are all part of what made up their togetherness. Severing these shared resources not only is the main task of the divorcing couple but is also the focal point of many conflicts. Each person fights to take as much as possible. Each tries to retain the material and social supports of the former life to reduce his or her losses, and each tries to make the (chosen or forced) alternative as highly attractive as possible. But at the time of separation, before any contract was signed, the division of the resources has, often, not been made and is therefore unclear. This uncertainty as to how much of what a person has, on whom and how much a person can rely for support, adds significantly to feelings of disorientation and anxiety (Weiss, 1975).

Initiating the separation may be part of a bargaining process. It may be a means to gain power, especially if the initiator has a low level of resources (Scanzoni & Szincovacz, 1980). By initiating separation and by withdrawing one's (tangible and intangible) share, one decreases the value of the other partner's rewards while lowering one's own costs. Life without the spouse may, however, intensify or create new inconsistencies. Difficulties encountered in single life may change people's perception of the level of resources they thought they had and could maintain as singles. Examples are when they discover their smaller-than-expected portion of the shared economic resources, their less-than-expected attractiveness to the opposite sex, or more-than-expected social disapproval. To deal with these inconsistencies, people may change their perception of their marriage to the worse, may devalue the particular resources, or may hope that their current plight is a transitional stage to a better future.

Many complexities and uncertainties engendered by becoming single again relate to the fact that once physical separation has taken place, the process of the family's disintegration moves from the private to the social domain. Despite the current divorce level, lifelong marriage remains a significant ideal for many (Skolnick & Skolnick, 1986). Separation also includes facing the effects of losing the status attached to being married. In societies such as ours, being married is an important social resource because it is a sign of adulthood and respectability (Cherlin, 1981). Being separated or divorced diminishes this status for both men (Blackburn & Mann, 1979) and women (L'Hommedieu, 1984). One symbol of social devaluation of the single-again status is the lower credit ratings that companies give divorced people (L'Hommedieu, 1984). As a result, divorced people inevitably experience pain and confusion that are all too frequently compounded by shame and embarrassment (Rice & Rice, 1986). Moreover, despite prevailing knowledge about "divorce-crazy America," which conveys the impression that there is no longer any social disapproval attached to being divorced, the experience of divorcees suggest differently (Albrecht et al., 1983). Although family and friends may be important supporting resources, there are few social conventions and little established etiquette to guide them in dealing with a formerly married couple who now present themselves as two separate, often hostile, individuals. Furthermore, the dynamics involved in dissolving a family often provide a ready source of potential conflict so that outside individuals are easily led into taking sides, adding fuel to an already explosive situation. It is, therefore, not surprising that many newly separated people describe changes involving some loss of contact with family and friends (Kaslow & Schwartz, 1987).

Many practical issues concerning the division of family resources demand immediate attention and cannot wait for the slow process of agreed-upon arrangements. This is especially true for mothers who are often confronted with the difficult situation in which they must assume the role of sole breadwinner and primary parent. Their most immediate and important concern is economic resources. Custodial mothers must face the need to deal, on an everyday basis, not only with their own emotional, social, and practical difficulties, but also with those of their children. The mother must reallocate her time and energy, reorganize life at home, and redistribute responsibilities—all in an atmosphere of uncertainty about the division of responsibilities and resources between her and her spouse. And she is often uncertain even about the separation itself.

Most spouses separate without a final decision as to whether the separation is temporary or permanent (Ahrons & Rodgers, 1987). This lack of finality casts a further burden on people because they may fear that their search for new and independent resources will be construed by their partners as a sign of permanent separation when such a decision has not yet been made. In addition to their own doubts, the newly separated individuals are faced with society's uncharted expectations of their behavior and roles (Goode, 1956a; Halem, 1989). Thus, society makes transition to the new role even more difficult (Burr, 1973). When we add a lack of clear expectations and an ambiguous family status to a lack of clarity about the resources that one has to negotiate these difficulties, what results is a living situation lacking in structure and consistencies. To combat these problems, the individual may plunge into dealing differently with the social and psychological attractions and with the barriers associated with both the marriage and the alternative.

Social and Psychological Attractions and Barriers.   Uncertainties about the psychological and social resources often change a person's perceptions of the attractions and barriers associated with marriage and divorce. When the decision to divorce was made, the partner assumed that his or her resources would be sufficient to realize the more-attractive alternative with more benefits and fewer costs (Levinger, 1979a). Upon separation, both partners may discover that the reality of single life is not as appealing as they had hoped or imagined. When they encounter the difficulties of living without a spouse, the approach–avoidance conflict may reemerge and become a dominant factor in determining one's feelings and behavior (Wright, 1988). Questions such as "Is this better?" are expressions of ambivalence and doubt about the rightness of the decision to divorce. Difficulties raise these doubts because they are the cognitive translation of more costs and fewer benefits, of higher social and/or psychological barriers associated with being married, and/or of fewer attractions associated with being single again.

While still living together, the couple may have exaggerated some of the attractions attached to the alternative and may have devalued those attached to the marriage. They may also have devalued barriers. For example, a woman may have overestimated the personal freedom she would gain by the separation, only to find herself later locked into the "children world" (Rose & Price-Bonham, 1973). And a man may have underestimated the barrier created by the children's reaction to the separation, only to find his part-time parent role so unsatisfying and painful that he feels he must terminate his relationship with his children (Kaslow & Schwartz, 1987). Thus, when the separation ceases being merely an idea, when it becomes an impending reality, and when one's resources are stretched far and depleting, then attractions and barriers may take on different values and create inconsistencies different from those expected.

One way to deal with these inconsistencies and to maintain the preseparation expectation of the cost–benefit comparison is by reinforcing one's negative perception of the marriage and/or of the spouse. Fights, bickerings, remembrances, and exaggerations of the unpleasant experiences while married; blaming others; and feeling hurt might be ways to help one focus on information supporting the decision to separate. There are no studies to directly confirm the use of this process, but there are studies that suggest it. For instance, women more than men experience the hardships associated with a single-parent home (Espenshade, 1985; Weitzman, 1985), and women more than men remember their marriages more negatively (Green, 1983; Laws, 1975).

The other way to regain cognitive consistency in the face of mounting difficulties is by changing one's expectations regarding the barriers associated with the marriage and the attractions associated with the alternative. Numerous investigations have demonstrated the effect that expectations have on feelings and behavior. Applying the results of these investigations to our topic of discussion means that reducing people's expectations lowers their subjective sense of costs and increases the value they assign to benefits. If that is what happens, then the person is able to feel better about the price of being separated and to take pleasure in having less. Either subjective approach will help to restore cognitive consistency — if these feelings match in their intensity the difficulties that are experienced. If neither of these ways work and if, because of difficulties, the person is unable to keep a favorable and large enough costs–benefits outcome, then a reconciliation will probably be considered (Ahrons & Rodgers, 1987; Wright, 1988). Low levels of resources (e.g., income, social support), which most likely result in a negative cost–benefit comparison outcome, were found to be significant in determining the likelihood of an attempt at reconciliation (Pearlin & Johnson, 1977; Spanier & Casto, 1979). Many couples not only consider reconciliation but actually retract their steps and reunit permanently or temporarily. Weiss (1975) estimated that "almost certainly not more than half of all separations go on to divorce" (p. 11). In their survey, Bloom, Hodges, and Caldwell (1977) found 162 separations for every 100 divorces. Although most couples consider reconciliation (Kitson et al., 1985) when the stresses of separation become too difficult, many will not reach the point of reuniting. To them, reconciliation may seem even more costly than continuing to deal with the separation. A brief reconciliation may actually make the next step easier and can be a way of one's resolving the approach–avoidance conflict by convincing oneself that the marriage is indeed worse than the separation. These individuals are still prepared to continue the struggle with the personal, social, economic, and legal consequences of the decision to end the marriage.

Struggling

The Emotional Stress.   Even families that have successfully negotiated the earlier transition find the attempt to reorganize their lives into two separate households a difficult struggle (Ashenhurst, 1984). After the initial shock of living alone has receded, feelings of anger and betrayal resurface with renewed intensity (DeFazio & Klenbort, 1975; Kessler, 1975). Attempts to adjust are often frustrating and painful (Albrecht et al., 1983). The circumstances are still new and so are many difficulties associated with them. Many old problem-solving strategies are no longer adequate and new ones have as yet to be devised and practiced. At times, the frustration and emotional upheaval connected with separation may even be manifested by a variety of physical and mental health symptoms (Briscoe & Smith, 1973; Radloff, 1975; Redick & Johnson, 1974; Warheit, Holzer, Bell, & Orey, 1976).

The literature debates the question of separation's comparative stress on women and men. For example, Bernard (1979) argued that the psychological costs are greater for men. Most men lose not only their homes and daily contact with their children but a structured lifestyle or a way of living. Others found contradicting results (e.g., Albrecht, et al., 1983; Glenn, 1981).

Women, even those who were members of middle- and upper middle-class and who were found to function well 1 to 4 years postseparation, reported feelings of depression, anger, vulnerability, low self-esteem, preoccupation with loss, fear of loneliness and aging, awareness of loss of status, fear about financial security and lack of support, difficulties coping with parenting pressure, and reconciliation fantasies (Wise, 1980).

The question of comparative stress of divorce on men and women pertains to the question of comparative resources and differences in the rewards exchanged in marriage. Men and women rely on marriage for material and psychosocial rewards to different extent. Women more than men gain in material terms—in particular economically—through marriage (Brandwein, Brown, & Fox, 1974; Cherlin, 1981; Sawhill, 1976) and rely less exclusively on marriage for emotional support (Bell & Newby, 1976; Lowenthal & Haven, 1968; Rossi, 1980). Men, more than women, rely on their spouse for emotional support and on the marital bond for the maintenance of other social ties and supportive social relations.

The issue of resources is confronted most forcefully during this postseparation time when most divorcing men and women are faced with decisions concerning the four main aspects of formal divorce: legal transition (filing for divorce), economic transition (property settlement), social transition, and co-parental transition (parental role, custody, and visitation). Dealing with these aspects of the divorce in effect defines anew the boundaries (rules that determine the parameters of the relationship and functions in the family) for people's lives in the binuclear family (Ahrons, 1979). In the earlier transition, the absence of clear boundaries created much of the confusion and stress; in this transition, the attempt to clarify boundaries generates the difficulties (Ahrons, 1980a). The courts will decide much of the clarification.

The Legal Transition.   Since 1970 when California adopted the no-fault divorce policy, almost all states have followed suit. This policy has reduced the need to engage in recrimination, connivance, or collusion (Perlman, 1982). No-fault legislation removed the issue of blame or fault from the legal arena. It is concordant with the system's view of marriage, because it takes into account circular causality and recognizes that both partners have contributed to the disintegration of their relationship. On the critical side of the no-fault divorce, two issues are most often raised: The first is its effect as a barrier to marriage (i.e., its effect on the divorce rate); the second, its effect on the parties' emotional adjustment. A number of studies cited by Bahr (1986) indicate that the change to no-fault divorce has had no discernible effect on the divorce rates. Bahr also argued that a long, drawn-out adversarial divorce may be beneficial and may even speed up the emotional separation because it allows each party's side to be heard and feelings to be ventilated.

Although no-fault divorce legislation reflects some change in the courts' attitudes, the legal system still operates in an adversarial model (Hancock, 1981). On the basis of a win–lose contest and the perceived finality of the courts' decisions, this process often escalates the spousal struggle for resources, adding stress to the already burdened system (Kay, 1970; Kurdek & Blisk, 1983). But although the legal process provides clarity to the boundaries of the postdivorced family relationship, it does not provide "an orderly and socially approved discharge of emotions that are elicited during . . . the preparation for the formal divorce (Bohannan, 1968, p. 48).

Lawyers often help their divorcing clients to negotiate the entire journey from initial marital problems to the final divorce (Murch, 1980). Parties who are concerned about financial and custody arrangements must rely on their lawyers' explanation and interpretation of the law and procedures of divorce (Hancock, 1981). As a result, lawyers become powerful figures in their clients' lives and important sources of information and support. Clients' dependency on their lawyers renders many divorcing individuals with uncharacteristic powerlessness, passivity, and frustration (Burgoyne & Clark, 1984). Often, lawyers are required to reaffirm their clients' attitudes and beliefs about their own and their spouses' responsibilities for the failing marriage and the crisis afterward. This helps the divorcing individuals to sustain cognitive consistency. Giving the lawyer instructions on what and how forcefully to fight is another way for a person to achieve cognitive congruency.

But the significance of the legal transition that gives divorced people "their freedom" lies not so much in the legal divorce itself as in the resolution of disputes about so-called "ancillary matters," which are more closely related to the economic and social aspects of divorce.

The Economic Transition.   Economics and its related services constitute some of both the attractions to a relationship and the most important barriers to divorce (Levinger, 1979a). As is the rule for barriers, the economic and material exchanges on which the partnership is based are fully exposed and realized only when a marriage is dissolving. Then, besieged by change and uncertainties, people often express fears about whether they will be able to manage on their own (Rice & Rice, 1986). They fight to retain the material supports of their former life and for the kind of financial arrangements that will enable them to start again without a drastic reduction in their accustomed standard of domestic comfort. That is, they fight to retain the cost-benefit and the attraction-barrier comparisons, which they expected to retain when the decision to divorce was made by the active spouse or accepted by the passive spouse.

Economics, being the basis and the result of many related resources, generates the most conflict in the divorce settlement (Burgoyne et al., 1987) and is the most frequently mentioned primary source of stress for a one-parent family (Brandwein et al., 1974; Hetherington, Cox, & Cox, 1976; Kurdek & Blisk, 1983). This conflict arises because the way economic issues are settled relates directly to the availability of other resources and to the probability for a quick recovery (Daniels-Mohring & Berger, 1984; Kitson & Raschke, 1981; Weitzman, 1985). This holds true particularly, but not only, because women are most often the custodial parent and because men reportedly retain 75% of their postdivorce income and are more financially upwardly mobile than women (Weitzman, 1985). Because of the significance that economics has on postdivorce adjustment, issues relating to economic transition may reawaken questions concerning the levels of attractiveness of the marriage and of the divorce. The seriousness of the economic questions, however, depends on people's expectations before the settlement.

The economic settlement may meet people's expectations. If so, cognitive consistency is maintained and no doubts regarding the divorce creep in. If it does not, it may affect people's attitudes toward the divorce. The partner who was awarded less than expected may find the divorce less attractive and vice versa. Being awarded more (or less) than is deemed fair by significant others can affect the level of other resources available to the divorcing couple. For example, the one who was awarded more than his or her share may lose the children's, family's, and/or friends' sympathy (Rasmussen & Ferraro, 1979), whereas the spouse can gain these. Nevertheless, after a financial settlement has been reached and the financial uncertainties are removed, a sense of cognitive consistency follows. Most (70%) of the 464 divorcees sampled in the study by Albrecht et al., (1983) felt "good" or "very good" about the final property settlement, even though the majority felt that they had lost more than they expected. To reinforce their sense of cognitive consistency, partners are also likely to attribute their gains and losses to reasons that match their beliefs about their spouses and themselves. But gains or losses in one sphere of the process do not make up the total outcome of costs–benefits comparison for the divorce process as a whole. For that, one needs to consider also the results of the parental and social transitions.

The Social Transition.   Social transition refers to the changing aspects of the divorcing person's relationship with family, former in-laws, old friends, and the community in what Bohannan (1968) called "community divorce." When the divorce was only considered, these groups' expected reactions to the divorce determined, at the time, the level of the social barrier to the divorce. Following the separation, the nature and quality of the separated individual's relationship with these groups change (Daniels-Mohring & Berger, 1984; Weiss, 1975). Separation results not only in the loss of a spouse but also in "social abandonment" making the separated individual, all too often, a social pariah (Gerstel, Riessman, & Rosenfield, 1985; Lewis, 1983). The process of uncoupling includes letting go of the emotional security and safety provided by the spouse and the social network associated with marriage. This loss makes many people feel anxious and fearful and gives them a very real sense of having lost an important, and at the same time phenomenologically essential, segment of their identity (Spanier & Casto, 1979).

Following the separation is a time when the separating person most needs the support of kin, friends, of significant others in the community (e.g., clergyman, the children's teachers). Yet it is also the time that such a relationship may be too difficult for everyone. Because the family's new boundaries are yet to be defined, others' interaction with members of the divorcing family is confusing and difficult. In-laws may not yet know the appropriate approach, friends may fear to take sides prematurely, and teachers may await the final agreement to find out their proper relationships with the divorcing parents.

Whether the social network is supportive or not is of a significant consequence to the chances for adjustment to divorce (e.g., Colletta, 1979a; Goode, 1956a; Kaslow, 1983; McCubbin et al., 1980). Generally, members of the family of origin are supportive of the divorcing person and, in many cases, provide significant services (Colletta, 1979a; Spanier & Casto, 1979).

Researchers, suspecting the significance of friendship on the adjustment to divorce, have investigated this issue repeatedly. For the most part, friends are supportive during the first phases of the separation, and this support has definite positive effect on the pace of recovery from the divorce crisis (Hetherington et al., 1976; Raschke, 1977; Spanier & Hanson, 1981). Weiss (1975) described three phases in the process of change in friendships. The first, "rallying around" is a period in which friends move to support the divorcing individuals immediately after separation. As time passes, each friend moves into a stage of "idiosyncratic reaction." The last stage is one of "mutual withdrawal." Both the divorcing individuals and the friends slowly distance themselves and allow the friendship to fade.

With the loss of many existing friendships, the divorcing individuals are faced with a social vacuum and the urgent task of building new relationships. But finding new friendships is often cited as one of the most difficult and frustrating experiences (Kohen, Brown, & Feldberg, 1979). In forming new relationships, especially heterosexual relationships, one needs to move from a couple-oriented to a single-oriented social life. Newly divorced individuals have often been away from the single-life milieu for some time and therefore are not aware of and have no working experience with the underlying rules and idiosyncrasies of moving around the single-life sub-culture. Males more frequently than females, who are often locked into the children's world, reported an easier time with it (Hetherington et al., 1976).

In this regard, noncustodial males may feel that they are actualizing one of the attractions they expected to be associated with their single lives. Where this is not the case (although establishing new and satisfying heterosexual relationships was a highly valued attraction when divorce was considered), doubts regarding the wisdom of divorce may arise again.

Social transition in divorce includes changes in lifestyle and roles and redevelopment of a satisfying social network. For the social network of single-again people to be satisfying, most people need the network to be in accordance with the social and cultural norms. Given that one's social reference group is an important potential resource of support, the public life of the divorced person must be conducted in a manner that will elicit approval rather than recrimination (Rasmussen & Ferraro, 1979). Trying to benefit from a fulfilling social life, but not at the cost of losing social approval, would have been easier if the person had provided a cultural chart of behavioral norms.

Not only is divorce regarded somewhat negatively in our culture (Lewis, 1983), but society affords no clear definition as to the proper relationship between itself and the divorced individual (Johnson, 1977). Hence, much of this relationship is characterized by uneasiness and suspicion. One's reputation in the community is based on one's status (Skolnick & Skolnick, 1986). The ambiguous status of divorced people raises new questions about their character and "when divorce takes place, the character of both spouses is up for review" (Rasmussen & Ferraro, 1979, p. 454). In no other aspect of the divorce process is the review more scrutinizing than in the co-parental transition of the divorce.

The Parental Transition.   The relationship between former spouses who continue to share childrearing responsibilities has in the last decade emerged as a critical variable in understanding postdivorce family adjustment (Buehler, Hogan, Robinson, & Levy, 1985/1986; Hetherington et al., 1976; Wallerstein & Kelly, 1980b). This new focus may be accounted for by changes in the conceptualization of postdivorced families. The substitution of the term *single-parent family* represents a significant change in public attitudes and understanding of what used to be called a *broken home* (Morawetz & Walker, 1983). With increased recognition of shared parenting in postseparation families, the paradigm is further altered to accommodate the noncustodial parent (most often, the father) and the father–child, father–mother dyads. Indication of this trend is the increased use of terms such as *double single-parent family* (Sager et al., 1983) or *binuclear family* (Ahrons, 1980c) to substitute for *single-parent family*.

Following the separation, each parent must reestablish an independent relationship with the children. To pass or accomplish this transition successfully, each child–parent relationship unit requires the continued relationship between the parents. To negotiate this very complex process successfully, parents must agree on clarification of roles and boundaries between parental and spousal relationship, redefining the former and terminating the latter (Ahrons, 1980c). The lack of role models and the absence of societal norms for continuing relationships between divorced parents complicates this transition.

Although some clinical reports suggest that healthy adjustment to divorce entails termination of relationship between former spouses (Kressel & Deutsch, 1977), more recent evidence suggests differently (i.e., the more exclusively "single" the family, the more dysfunctional stress is experienced by noncustodial fathers; Greif, 1984; Keshet & Rosenthal, 1978; Mendes, 1976), custodial mothers (Brandwein et al., 1974; Hetherington et al., 1976), and the children (Hetherington, Cox, & Cox, 1979a; Wallerstein & Kelly, 1980b; Weiss, 1980).

The structural change in the family because of divorce demands that parents change their parental roles and behavior. They have to add new ones and lose certain aspects of their old ones. Much of the parameters of parental and co-parental relationships are captured in the legal discussion and settlement of custody and visiting rights. Custody and visiting arrangements are the formal redefinitions of the continuing roles, rights, and responsibilities of each parent. But other issues (e.g., division of property, financial obligations) are often entangled with the custody issue. Furthermore, it is very difficult to keep custody consideration from being "contaminated" by issues stemming from the emotional and economic transitions of the divorce process (Ahrons & Rodgers, 1987). The struggle for specific custody arrangements is also the struggle to make the changes cognitively consistent with one's understanding of children's needs and expectations of him or herself as parent. A significant gap between custody arrangements and the desired provisions or between one's expectations and reality will result in psychological tension that most likely will spill over the whole family system.

Although having children increases the cost of divorce, constituting probably the most formidable barrier to divorce, it also may increase the level of intangible resources for the custodial parent. The presence of children appears to be a stabilizing force in the adjustment of the custodial parent, lessening detrimental effects of the separation. Custodial fathers find their parental role richly rewarding (Greif, 1982, 1985; Keshet & Rosenthal, 1978). Custodial mothers rated their children second only to friends as a source of support in adjusting to the divorce (Kurdek & Blisk, 1983).

Still, adjusting to single parenthood for women is not an easy task. Divorce causes a disruption in the regular childrearing practices and mother–child communication (Kressel & Deutsch, 1977). Furthermore, predivorce parent's competence does not carry over to single parenthood (Hetherington, Cox, & Cox, 1978). Custodial mothers were reported to have particular difficulties handling their children immediately after the separation (Hetherington et al., 1978), with much improvement over time (Wedemeyer & Johnson, 1982). The role shift from shared marital parenting to custodial parenting requires the mother to take on almost all the functions previously held by the father (Weiss, 1979). This role overload was found to take a severe emotional toll on the mother. Weiss (1980) confirmed Hetherington et al.'s (1979a) findings that custodial mothers "were experiencing considerable psychological distress: depression, anger, feelings of vulnerability, low self-esteem, . . . and difficulties with parenting pressure" (p. 151). These problems, however, may be attributed less to the divorce itself than to the absence of social support that constitutes one of the major sources of distress for custodial mothers (Brandwein et al., 1974). Indeed, a number of writers contend that single mothers are more vulnerable than others to stressful life events and common everyday family life strains simply because they have fewer social resources with which to cope with the effect of stress (Guttentag, Salasin, & Belle, 1980; McLanahan, Wedemeyer, & Adelberg, 1981). Fathers, as perceived by the custodial mothers, are of very little support and help (Weitzman, 1985). The reason for that may lie in the struggle the fathers themselves have in redefining their own role and place in their children's lives.

In their book *Part-Time Father* Atkin and Rubin (1976) commented that soon after the separation many men begin to feel that they are no longer fathers, that they are no longer needed by their children, and that their authority as a parent has been taken away from them. Divorced noncustodial fathers, especially in the transition period, appear to suffer from a pervasive sense of loss (Buehler et al., 1985/1986; Hetherington et al., 1976; Woolley, 1979), increased depression (Grief, 1979, 1985), lower self-esteem (Wallerstein & Kelly, 1980b), and increased anxiety (Keshet & Rosenthal, 1978; Weiss, 1976). Fathers also expressed fear that their ex-spouses might attempt to turn the children against them, further undermining their relationship with the children (Dominic & Schlesinger, 1980).

During visits, both father and children struggle to develop new ways of relating to one another. The father struggles to negotiate his way between maintaining his father role (which, at times, includes unpleasant interaction) and his wish to encourage and inspire his children to visit with him. Finding that very difficult, many fathers deal with this inconsistency by devaluing their parental self-esteem, feeling inadequate about their role as an effective parent (Stewart, Schwebel, & Fine, 1986). Others attempt to feel better by making it up to the children and to themselves by becoming a "Disney World" father, providing the children with gifts and constant entertainment (Dominic & Schlesinger, 1980).

Much of the difficulty in the parental transition stems from the fact that the boundaries of the parental role and co-parental relationship are neither clear nor firmly set until much later. Only after much of the antagonism "contaminating" the co-parental power issue is resolved can the co-parental boundaries become clear and manageable without many conflicts. Meantime, both parents attempt to establish the kind of relationship with each other, and individually with the children, that (a) helps them bring down to the minimum the cost of the divorce (e.g., doing most for the children), (b) maintains the alternative at a maximum level of attractiveness (e.g., doing most for oneself), and (c) maintains cognitive consistency (e.g., balancing (a) and (b) with one's attitudes, beliefs, and expectations). Achieving this goal is a difficult task, but it is the road to winning.

Winning

Adjustment and Winning. The measures of adjustment most commonly encountered in the divorce literature include assessment of the extent of experienced distress in terms of physical and emotional symptoms, and/or the use of measures of self-perceived adequacy of functioning (e.g., Nelson, 1981; Pett, 1982; Propst, Pardington, Ostrom, & Watkins 1986; Thomas, 1982). From this perspective, the measures that investigators have been using to assess adjustment can be viewed as measures of the outcome or of the result of adjustment. Adjustment is viewed as the intervening process or set of processes.

The psychosocial model suggests that there are four intervening processes:

1. The process in which one is reaffirming old and establishing new and autonomous personal and social resources and rewards;
2. The process in which one is achieving internal consistencies between one's thinking, feelings, and actions;
3. The process in which one attributional pattern enhances the sense of control over one's life; and
4. The process of self-affirmation and personal growth.

Crises can provide opportunities for personal growth. Divorce, according to Wiseman (1975), is such an opportunity. Such a radical upheaval of one's entire lifestyle may create the need to reexamine many aspects of one's habits and identity. Smart (1977) suggested that each of Erikson's developmental tasks is reactivated by the trauma of divorce, with unresolved matters from each stage requiring resolution in terms of the new crises and opportunities.

Winning, as perceived here, depends on the divorced person's advancing along the adjustment processes, which are the cornerstones to winning; winning takes adjustment a step further. Winning in the context of the divorce process means that the divorced person has seized the change for achieving a higher level of personal growth and self-actualization. This is different from the commonly used term *adjustment* that means "a change so as to fit, conform" (Webster's New World Dictionary, 1984), whereas *winning* means "to succeed in reaching or achieving a specific condition . . . by effort, labor, struggle, etc." (Webster's New World Dictionary, 1984). The proposed change is not merely a change in terminology. It suggests a higher "ceiling" in the conception of what constitutes such a resolution. It also suggests that one can more than reorganize his or her lifestyle "so as to fit or conform" better; one can actually be able to take advantage of the opportunity and come out of the divorce experience "reaching or achieving" a sense of being stronger and better. The notion of winning is capsulated in the divorcee's realization that in divorce one always gets custody of oneself; given that, one can take this opportunity for enhancing personal development.

The psychosocial model proposes that the degree of winning be assessed by the degree that divorced people (a) are able to mobilize old and new resources, (b) perceive the rewards of the postdivorce life as being higher than its cost, (c) attribute their resources and rewards to stable and lasting reasons, and (d) see their actions toward their children and former spouse as being cognitively consistent with their own wishes and sense of responsibility.

Personal and Social Resources.   Obviously the more resources one has, is improving, or is developing, the higher are the actually obtained rewards and the more positive is the cost–benefit comparison outcome. The results of studies that investigated the effects that personal resources have on adjustment to divorce underscore this point.

The presence of economic resources, particularly in terms of income, seems to be directly related to adjustment. A review of the literature suggests that, across studies, the more economically independent one is and the higher the actual amount of income, the better is the adjustment (e.g., Kitson & Raschke, 1981; Weitzman, 1985).

Education, as measured by the number of years of formal schooling, appears to have little correlation with measures of adjustment (Chiriboga, Coho, Stein, & Roberts, 1979; Kitson & Raschke, 1981). However, education as an intervening variable (contributing to cognitive ability that facilitates realistic perception of the difficulties and problem-solving skills) seems to contribute to adjustment. For example, having a higher education was found to relate to less stress and to easier role transition from being married to being divorced (Everly, 1978). Education is also one of the most important variables predicting women's attitudes toward gender roles and the women's movement (Mason, Czajka, & Arber, 1976; Rice & Anderson, 1982). Education also correlates with the readiness to engage in psychotherapy (Cantor & Drake, 1983; Wallerstein & Kelly, 1980b) and, hence, to increase the likelihood of adjustment and of winning.

Health as a personal resource refers to the individual's physical well-being. The presence and absence of physical symptoms were interpreted by some researchers as an indication of the divorcee's level of adjustment (Bloom et al., 1978; Bloom & Hodges, 1981). Pointing to the obvious difficulties in using mere physical health in the assessment of adjustment, Kaslow and Schwartz (1987) suggested referring to the physical "metamorphoses that occur in and by some people postdivorce" (p. 246) as a better indication of adjustment. They give examples of people who chose to have plastic surgery, others who changed hairstyles, and yet others who made other changes in their appearance. "In six months to a year, the divorced individual may look and feel substantially more attractive and physically healthier and more vibrant" (p. 246). Taking these kind of steps is a good example of improving on one's resources.

The results of studies investigating personality characteristics that associate with higher levels of adjustment do not directly answer the question pertaining to the importance of psychological resources for winning. That is because one cannot tell whether the personality characteristics that were found to be associated with adjustment were actually the intervening variables or the results of better adjustment. For instance, Thomas (1982) reported that people who seem to make the best adjustment to divorce score significantly higher on measures of dominance, assertiveness, self-assurance, intelligence, social boldness, liberalism, self-sufficiency, ego strength, and tranquility than those who adjust less well. A long-term, follow-up investigation needs to be carried out, beginning at the deciding stage, if we are to assess the importance of personal resources on a person's ability to come out of the divorce crisis a winner. It is, however, reasonable to expect that some basic and stable personality characteristics are important resources for one to build on and use the divorce crisis for personal growth.

Social resources refer to the individual people, groups, and/or organizations with whom the divorcee is involved and from whom he or she may gain support. The major sources of the social support network studied were neighborhoods, family and kinship, and mutual self-help groups. A growing body of literature suggests that social support protects individuals against the potentially harmful effects on mental health of a wide range of life events (for review, see Israel, 1982; Kaplan, 1977; Thoits, 1982). Research on divorce suggests that characteristics of social networks may be critical factors in adjustment to marital dissolution (Colletta, 1979a; McLanahan et al., 1981; Wilcox, 1981). Raschke (1977), for example, studying members of Parents Without Partners, found that the most strongly supported of her hypotheses was that "the more social interaction and/or involvement outside the home role relationship of the separated or divorced individual, with relatives, friends in organizations and so on, the lower will be the stress associated with separation and/or divorce" (p. 131). But the question of whether social involvement is an intervening variable for better adjustment or is a result of better adjustment can be raised here, too. Nevertheless, the importance of developing new and maintaining old social networks to one's personal growth is not in question. The opportunities to learn, experience, and practice new ways of relating are as important as the support provided by the network.

The road to winning leads divorcees through the search for objects and experiences that will help them find their social and personal boundaries, and will help them formulate a new identity and lifestyle. This end can be served by transitional networks and relationships (Taibbi, 1979). These interim experiences can serve as a mechanism for playing out the unfinished business of the past (Napier, 1978) or for corrective experiences. The danger lies in confusing a stepping stone with the ultimate objective. Yet few divorced people could manage to amend their social and interpersonal relationship without relying on transitional social resources.

The processes of cognitive consistency and causal attribution affect one's ability to make the better use of available resources. Under certain circumstances one may be receiving less or more than was expected. Then, depending on one's attributional pattern, one can reach a cognitive consistency solution. For instance, to resolve the tension caused by receiving fewer social rewards than expected, one may attribute the lack of social success to his or her own inability, to the too-little effort invested in developing good social relationship, to the high level of difficulty in establishing good social relationships, or to bad luck. Different patterns of attributes produce different feelings and different behaviors (Weiner, 1980). A winner's solution to the discrepancy would be one in which the emphases are on (developing) ability and (investing more) effort, regardless of the perceived level of task difficulty.

The vast majority of research studies, which deal with the issue of adjustment to divorce, have focused on either single or multivariate indications or predictions of adjustment. Few, if any, have focused on the interacting processes contributing to adjustment. Therefore, because the following discussion refers to a complex of such processes, it is mostly speculative.

Psychological and Social Attractions and Barriers.   For this last stage of the divorce process, attractions and barriers refer to a set of circumstances different than before. During the previous stages, attractions and barriers were references to the forces pulling toward maintaining the marital relationship. Now that the divorce is final, attractions and barriers are the forces pulling to maintain the new single status: attractions by considering the attained rewards and barriers by considering the tangible and intangible costs involved with a change in the new marital status. For instance, one of the attractions potentially associated with single lifestyle is the reward gained by feelings of freedom and independence. While before the separation and divorce these were the attractions associated with the alternative, now they could be associated with the present situation.

The dynamics underlying these are the same ones, suggested by Levinger (1979b), that operate during marriage. That is, both attractions and barriers reinforce the status quo. Barriers, however, are felt only when an alternative is considered.

Considering possible alternatives (e.g., reconciliation, or second marriage) at this stage, assumes to be negatively correlated with the level of achieved rewards and perceived barriers. That is, the fewer rewards one attains in being single, the more likely the divorcee is to consider the alternatives. Berman and Turk's (1981) findings confirm this pattern of correlation. They found that those with minor children, who tended not to want the divorce and who had lower status jobs and less education, had more difficulty completing the psychic divorce and would contemplate reconciliation. The direction of causality, however, is not clear. Low level of resources can contribute to lingering attachment, just as the other way around. During marriage, a high level of attraction to the alternative (divorce) is indicative of low levels of rewards and satisfactions within the marital relationship. In divorce, a persistent high level of attraction to an ex-spouse is also indicative of a low level of obtained rewards and satisfaction from single life, hence, poor adjustment (Crosby et al., 1983; Kitson, 1982; Weiss, 1975).

But after divorce there is another possibility: a high level of attraction to remarriage as the new alternative. The high level of attraction to this alternative may or may not be (and all the measures in between) indicative of poor adjustment to divorce. It can be an indication of poor adjustment if the attraction to remarriage results from the divorcee's inability to achieve a satisfactory level of rewards, and the remarriage is considered only as the best means for postdivorce adjustment. If, however, high levels of satisfaction and rewards achieved while being single are the results of the process of personal development, then the wish to remarry may be just another result of the same process. The difference is not in the behavior but in the motivation behind it. Hunt (1966) reported that even the divorced people who consider themselves successfully divorced "will not consider themselves wholly successful until they remarry" (p. 285). This statement may still reflect the great need of the divorced to resolve their socially ambiguous status. But it may also reflect the difference between remarriage as a means for adjustment and as a means for winning.

No winning can be achieved without divorced people understanding their contribution to the dysfunctional behavior pattern that led to the failure of the marriage (Napier, 1978). Just as essential for these people is learning about their reasons for choice of mate so they are not drawn into a similar pattern of relationship. A change in the pattern of attribution of the reasons for the failing marriage is necessary for most divorced people to become winners.

Attributions and Cognitive Consistency.   Hunt (1966) suggested that "it is what the formally married sees or believes about his own case that most affects his . . . adjustment or maladjustment to his new status" (p. 25). This suggestion implies that one of the more sensitive indicators of the quality of a person's transition through the divorce process is the change in the kind and pattern of that individual's attributions. A pattern of attributions is created in response to people's need to understand the world and make sense of their experiences of it (Weiner, 1986) in a cognitively consistent way. Divorce as crisis often shakes one's perceptions of oneself and one's understanding of relationships (Goode, 1956a; Kelly, 1982), thus creating the need to reformulate an attributional pattern. In it, one needs to account for the events leading to the divorce in a way that one can deal with and live with.

Throughout the preceding stages one would expect the attributions of both spouses to be quite different because each needs a different (often contradicting) set of attributions to maintain a cognitive consistency. Indeed, divorcing spouses were found to give different reasons and/or different weights to similar reasons (Hurowitz, 1981; Kitson & Sussman, 1982). But as the spouses move along the process and learn about what went wrong and why, their attribution may change, from an attribution characterized by prejudice and blame to one characterized by mutual responsibility and from external loci to an internal locus. For such changes to transpire, one needs to feel that this pattern of attribution is consistent with one's sense of well-being. If people are able to seize the opportunity set before them by the divorce crisis as described here, then such a change is possible.

To summarize the perception of a winner in the divorce context, I cite from Fromm (1974) who contrasted the narcissistic need to control, to retain, and to have with the self-affirming willingness to be. He said:

> If I am what I have and if what I have is lost, who am I? . . . The anxiety and insecurity engendered by the danger of losing what one has are absent in the being mode. If I am who I am and not what I have, nobody can deprive me

or threaten my security and my sense of identity. My center is within myself; my capacity for being and for expressing my essential powers is part of my character structure and depends on me. (pp. 109–110)

The trust involved in being, as opposed to having, springs from the act of self-affirmation. Having learned to affirm oneself through loss, rejection, and failure, one can experience life more deeply than before. With self-affirmation comes a diminished need to protect oneself against possible hurt (Davenport, 1981); one can behave proactively instead of reactively. We can love others and commit ourselves with increased confidence. For acknowledging the worth of our own love is, after all, the core of self-affirmation. The loss through divorce of someone we love or loved becomes less a deprivation, and it can be viewed as a challenge to personal growth.

4 Divorced Mothers

Between 1900 and 1965 the crude rate of divorce (i.e., divorce per 1,000 population) rose from 0.7 to 2.5 (Plateris, 1969), and by 1981 stood at 5.3 (U.S. Bureau of the Census, 1985). Using a more refined index, the number of divorces per 1,000 married women 15 years old and over reveals a similar situation. This rate increased from 9.2 in 1960 to 14.9 in 1970 and to nearly 23 in 1981 (U.S. Bureau of the Census, 1987). The annual number of divorces passed the 1 million mark for the first time in 1975, and reached an all time high of 1.2 million in 1981 (U.S. Bureau of the Census, 1985).

According to Norton and Glick (1976), divorce is primarily responsible for the fact that the single-parent family is the fastest growing form in the United States. Along with the growth of the divorce rate, the percentage (based on 1,000) of single parents with children under the age of 18 dramatically grew annually from 11.8 in 1970 to 22.5 in 1987 (U.S. Bureau of the Census, 1988). Consider the following statistics taken from U.S. Bureau of Census (1987):

- There were a record 9.4 million single-parent families in 1988 — 32% of the 27.7 million families with children under the age of 18 at home.
- By 1987, 15.6 million children under age 18 (29%) lived with only one parent, compared with 9% in 1960 and 12% in 1970.
- Between 1960 and 1986 the fraction of Black children under the age of 3 who were not living with both parents rose from 30%–60%.
- Nine out of 10 children in single-parent families reside in households headed by their mothers.

- The largest proportion of single-parent families headed by mothers arises from divorce (33% vs. 17% who have never married, 21% who are married with the husband absent, and 29% who widowed).

Stripped to its bare essentials, divorce is a major change. Most divorcing women change from living in a relationship where their husband is head of household, to becoming heads of their own households with their children. This chapter focuses on the divorcing woman (with or without custody of her children), rather than on her childless counterpart who can easily slip back into the status and lifestyle of the never-married woman.

Changes in a person's life create challenge, opportunity, and vulnerability. New strategies for daily living must be learned; old attitudes and patterns must be shed. Relationships change inside and outside the family and the meaning of one's existence must be reexamined. This process of relearning takes time. Although the pace may be most rapid during the first year or two following the divorce, relearning continues as other life changes occur. Despite individual and demographic differences among women, it is possible to examine the impact of divorce on all women through the prism of time.

CUSTODIAL MOTHERS (OR SINGLE-PARENT FAMILIES)

The most significant commonality across mother-headed single-parent families is the structural characteristic that only one parent lives with the children. Because the other parent is "absent," and perhaps because nearly 90% of single-parent families have been headed by women for over a century (Seward, 1978), single-parent families have long been thought to be in trouble. Whether trouble is defined as mothers managing a family alone and unattached, or as father absence depriving children of the necessary experiences and role models for satisfactory adult moral behavior, public interest in single-parent families has manifested itself as a concern. The common belief is that these families are "broken" and "disorganized" (Burgess, 1970), and that the presence of both a mother and a father are prerequisites for a child's normal development (Blechman, 1982; Levitan, 1979). Benson's (1909) article, entitled "Alarming Changes in American Homes" called attention to the turn-of-the-century "social problems" (cited in Blechman & Manning, 1976, p. 62), and Malinowski's (1930/1974) proposed sociological law that "no child should be brought into the world without a man—and one man at that—assuming the role of sociological father" underscored the professional community's concern with father absence.

Characteristics of Single-Parent Families

Single-parent families are frequently viewed as alike. The assumption is made that following divorce mother-headed single-parent families are more similar to one another than to other family types, and that they share a common lifestyle and common problems (Billingsley & Giovannoni, 1971). In some aspects of everyday life these families may share certain experiences. For example, they commonly experience a major reduction in family income (Weitzman, 1985), a sense of isolation and loneliness (Greenberg, 1979; Katz, 1979; Nock, 1981; Smith, 1980), role overload (Glasser & Navarre, 1965; Weiss, 1979), and unequal access to the material and social resources more easily available to two-parent families (Cherlin, 1981; Schorr & Moen, 1979).

Nonetheless, it is misleading to discuss "the single-parent family" because the concept covers a wide variety of types of families. One must distinguish between the paths along which the family system evolved, the extent to which the father is involved in child care, manner and level of functioning, patterns of interaction, and subjective well-being. Furthermore, they differ in economic lifestyles, opportunities and resources, social class, racial and ethnic background, and age of parents. The conclusion to be drawn is deceptively simple: Custodial-mother single-parent families are not a homogeneous group. Failure to see the diversity among families, however, has been a frequent conceptual error and, until recently, has hindered our understanding of these families. To paraphrase Billingsley and Giovannoni (1971) and Sprey (1967), understanding the diversity across single-parent families may be more important theoretically, clinically, and politically than the search for the common denominators of single-parent family life.

Several attempts have been made to develop typologies that capture the diversity among the families (Ahrons, 1979; Boss, 1977; Mendes, 1979; Rosenfeld, Rosenstein, & Raab, 1973), primarily using the precipitating cause or the absent father's degree of presence as the basis of classification. But it is yet impossible to say how many types of single-parent families exist or what proportion of families fall within each category. Equally uncharted are three spheres of single-parent family life that have important bearing on how these families manage, sometimes even thrive: the extent to which the noncustodial father is involved in the family, the nature of the mother–child boundary, and the home environment.

Society and Single-Parent Families

Early public and professional interest in single-parent families focused on the children growing up in these "partial" families. Although the single parent was usually widowed, at worst deserted, and also a "victim," public sympathies and worries focused almost exclusively on the children.

By 1980, however, death of a parent had become the least frequent factor in the establishment of single-parent families. Separation and divorce are now the most common causes of single-parent families, although since the 1970s, there has been a major increase in the number of families created by single women having babies. In effect, Americans are increasingly choosing single parenthood over unhappy marriages (Brown, Feldberg, Fox, & Kohen, 1976; Staples, 1985; Weiss, 1979). This choice can probably be attributed to a variety of factors, among them the diminished moral stigma associated with divorce and parenting alone. However, despite the diminished stigma attached to individuals, public concern with single-parent families has not diminished. Indeed, as the number of single-parent families increases, so does public alarm (e.g., Goldstein, Freud, & Solnit, 1973; Lynn, 1974). There is still concern that single-parent families are partial and broken and thus are harming children (Anthony, 1974). In addition there is now widespread alarm about the future of the traditional nuclear family. Social critics suggest that the choice to single parent is threatening the legitimacy of the traditional two-parent family and thus the stability of society. Rather than viewing the single-parent family as one type of family in the society, these families are defined as deviant family systems (Bernard, 1975; Levitan & Belous, 1981; Schorr & Moen, 1979). Social policymakers are often encouraged to reform existing family policy on the assumption that the single-parent family system is detrimental to the welfare of both the children and the economy (e.g., Senate bills 1070 and 1378, 97th Congress).

The interface between single-parent families and the larger society has largely gone undiagnosed. Reviewing titles listed in the Inventory of Marriage and Family Literature, it is as if single-parent families exist in a vacuum, unattached to and unaffected by major social institutions and service organizations.

Policymakers who consult family specialists for more comprehensive information regarding single-parent families vis-à-vis other institutions discover little systematic research. One finds only scattered references, indicating that the flow of influence and control between single-parent families and major social institutions in unidirectional, from institutions to families, but little systematic data exist to support this contention. It is therefore difficult to describe with any certainty the present societal status of single-parent families. With this in mind, what can be said about the linkages between the single-parent families and their environment? Are these families viewed as within the mainstream by the major social institutions, such as education, government, religion, and medicine?

Burgess (1970) and Schorr and Moen (1979) contended that many organizations and their programs view single parenthood as a temporary condition and transitional phase in a family career. The conventional wisdom is that the single-parent family will "go away" when the single parent remarries. With marriage, divorced families will be reconstituted or blended. In this sense, then, single-parent families are not recognized as "real" families. The conventional standard that a marriage is necessary before a social group will be defined as a legitimate family system (Sprey, 1979) may inhibit major social institutions from seeing a family nucleus when a father is absent.

This assumption, like most common sense assumptions, is in part justified. The reality is that the median interval between divorce and the second marriage is 3 years for those aged 35 to 54 (Glick, 1980). In recent years, the interval has been increasing, and the remarriage rate for divorced people has been dropping (U.S. National Center for Health Statistics, 1980). When the unit of analysis is shifted from each to all single-parent families, however, the common sense assumption is not justified. The reality is that by the time remarriage ends the single-parenting experience for one family, another has taken its place. Single-parent families are one family type in U.S. society. The view that single parenthood is temporary can thus become a powerful although tacit policy where a lack of accommodation to and recognition of these families is acceptable (Blechman & Manning, 1976; Hawkins, 1979; Hulme, 1976; Moroney, 1980; Schorr & Moen, 1979; Wilk, 1979). "When the plurality of organizations in a society tacitly defines a group as being outside the mainstream, members of that group will fare badly. With the plurality of institutions believing that the two parents are better than one, single-parent families face not only discrimination but attendant feelings of humiliation as well (Wolff, 1950, pp. 224–265).

Cogswell and Sussman (1972) noted that the interface between single-parent families and institutional systems was as Simmel would predict: dictated by institutions failing to support or acknowledge single-parent family systems as legitimate or viable families. Instead, institutional systems

> make certain assumptions about the family. They gear their services toward an ideal of what a family ought to be, namely, a nuclear traditional one . . . Because agencies idealize the traditional family, their programs are aimed at restoring this form and, thus, are ill-equipped to provide relevant supportive services to variant family forms. (p. 513)

Lindahl's (1979) analysis of the interface between local churches and single-parent families, for instance, concludes with such a restorative approach: "The church . . . must provide message and an experience of reconciliation and redemption to its members who suffer the anguish of broken human relationship" (p. 1708). Horowitz and Perdue (1977) found that when health professionals come into contact with single-parent families, the institutional approach often ignores their unique group composition and indiscriminately offers solutions designed for two-parent families, or it recognizes the one-parent family structure as "abnormal" and provides treatment aimed at helping the family members accept a regrettable situation (see Blechman & Manning, 1976; Wilk, 1979). Discussing single mothers who may have problems with external social service agencies and schools, Moroney (1980) pointed out: "She may have a problem, but, if so, it often is with a system which tends to be rigid" (p. 49).

Although individual family members may benefit from their contact with specific organizations and their programs, organizations continue to provide a rather inimical climate for single-parent families as families (Blechman & Manning, 1976; Hawkins, 1979). Given the slow rate of change in large-scale organizations, it is not surprising that there have been few accommodations to single-parent families since Cogswell and Sussman (1972) wrote the aforementioned quote. For example, they noted that health-care services for children are organized for the convenience of the medical care professionals and not around the availability of adults to accompany children to the agency. Some years later, clients were still supposed to adjust to the schedules of the health-care agencies (Hulme, 1976; Moroney, 1980; Wilk, 1979). Yet, the single parent may lose income and even jeopardize a job by having to accommodate the health organization's schedule (Brandwein et al., 1974).

Thus, institutions actually discriminate against one-parent families in two ways: by indiscriminately treating them as similar to two-parent families (Hawkins, 1979; Horowitz & Perdue, 1977) and by viewing the one-parent structure as "abnormal" (Blechman & Manning, 1976). Both approaches are dysfunctional for single-parent families. In the first case, they are obliged to fulfill the same functions and conditions as two-parent families, yet the limitations on their ability to do so are ignored (Brandwein et al., 1974; Horowitz & Perdue, 1977; Schorr & Moen, 1979). In the second case, the institutionalized view of the single-parent family as both temporary and deviant generates a daily barrage of subtle discrimination, for example, banks demanding co-signers for loans, landlords unwilling to rent housing (Brandwein et al., 1974), lack of easily available and affordable child-care options (Rossi, 1984; Sawhill, 1976; Woolsey, 1977) and reduction in employment opportunities (Bane & Weiss, 1980; Bradbury et al., 1979).

There is a sociopsychological analogue to the subtle, albeit formal, discrimination that single-parent families encounter. Because many families are treated as "nonfamilies" or are stigmatized as deviant, and a social distance is erected between "normal" and "abnormal" families, a self-fulfilling prophecy is put into effect. Schorr and Moen (1979) stated that all single-parent family members suffer from public images of the ideal and the single-parent family: "The most moving effect of misrepresentation is that many single parents believe what is said of them and add belief to the problems they face . . . The stereotypes involved are about as legitimate as most that are involved in discriminatory behavior — and as destructive" (p. 18).

Father's Involvement in Single-Parent Family's Life

The everyday reality of single-parent families suggests a wide variety of interaction patterns and family boundaries, ranging from the noncustodial father being minimally present as in the "sole executive" family system (Mendes, 1979) to being maximally involved as in the "binuclear" family system (Ahrons, 1979). The extent to which the noncustodial father is psychologically and interactively present in the family system depends to a large extent on the person's availability and freedom of access (Abarbanel, 1979; Boss, 1977, 1980; Fulton, 1979; Wallerstein & Kelly, 1980b), and on the extent to which the noncustodial father was "inside the family system" prior to the separation (Kantor & Lehr, 1975; Kelly & Wallerstein, 1977; Minuchin, 1974; Rosenthal & Keshet, 1981).

A number of studies suggest that parents living apart from their children may still be interactive inside the single-parent family boundary for some time (Earls & Siegel, 1980; Fischer & Cardea, 1981; Furstenberg & Talvitie, 1980). The father may frequently visit the children and share the responsibility in decision making. Mendes (1979) identified this father as an "auxiliary parent," and several authors have previously addressed this phenomenon within their discussion of the part-time father (Atkin & Rubin, 1976) or visiting parent (Wallerstein & Kelly, 1980a). In cases in which both parents desire to continue their parenting roles, two interrelated households can form one family system, the binuclear family system (Ahrons, 1979). This pattern can occur whether joint custody has been awarded or not, as long as the co-parenting relationship is maintained. Ahrons (1980b) and other observers of custody arrangements (Abarbanel, 1979; Galper, 1978; Greif, 1986; McKee & O'Brien, 1982; Roman & Haddad, 1978) estimated that this co-parenting pattern may soon be the rule rather than the exception.

However, with few institutional supports for the noncustodial role, the father–child subsystems that emerge vary considerably, usually falling between the extremes of an "empty shell" relationship involving erratic and infrequent interaction and a "vital" relationship involving frequent interaction and cohesiveness. Tentative findings suggest that the quality of the father–child relationship initially improves, at least for a while (Earl & Lohmann, 1978; Earls & Siegel, 1980; Grief, 1985). Over time, however, this relationship is often reduced to infrequent interaction and to a less involving relationship. The father's involvement is often diminished when custody is not shared (Abarbanel, 1979; Ahrons, 1980b), when loss of everyday life with family rituals and routine is either blocked by visitation restrictions or a strained relationship with the custodial mother (Benedek & Benedek, 1979; Cline & Westman, 1971, Fulton, 1979; Weiss, 1979), or when the father was marginally involved with the children in the first place (Keshet, 1980; Minuchin, 1974).

Even when strained interaction characterizes the parents' relationship "most single-parents do what they can to foster their children's relationship with their noncustodial parents. They do so despite their own feelings, because they believe it important for the children" (Weiss, 1979, p. 159). Goldsmith (1980) and Wallerstein and Kelly (1980b) corroborated this finding, reporting that the majority of parents (both fathers and mothers) felt it important for the noncustodial parent to stay involved with the children. Thus, the noncustodial father may be psychologically inside the single-parent family boundary for some time, even in families where he is physically absent (Boss, 1980; Lopata, 1979). It would also be misguided to assume that the absent father diminishes in saliency in the eyes of the child even if the interaction is reduced. Children frequently continue to think of themselves as children of two parents, despite the low level of interaction with the absent father. Based on their study of children of divorce, Wallerstein and Kelly (1980b) commented: "Although the mother's care-taking and psychological role become increasingly central in these families, the father's psychological significance did not correspondingly decline" (p. 307).

Evidently there is good reason to question the stereotype of parent "absence." Yet a perspective commonly found in the literature appears to be that when a marriage dissolves, the family dissolves; and if a marriage was never present, a family never existed. But as Sprey (1979) wrote: "Divorce ends a marriage but not a family. It removes one parent from the household. It changes the relationship between the parents, it does not end the relationship; psychological and interactive ties continue to connect all family members, but under widely different circumstances" (p. 155).

There are apparent risks, however, with the father's active involvement in the family's life. Inability to manage and contain the conflicts between the parents can add subjective stresses to the lives of all family members (Atkin & Rubin, 1976; Fischer & Cardea, 1981; Fulton, 1979; Wallerstein & Kelly, 1980b), and an interactively absent but psychologically present father can increase boundary ambiguity and jeopardize the mother's ability to reorganize the family (Boss, 1980; Keshet, 1980). As Boss suggested, "stress continues in any family until membership can be clarified and the system reorganized regarding (a) who performs what roles and tasks, and (b) how family members perceive the absent parent" (p. 549).

Mother–Child Relationships in Single-Parent Families

Until recently there was no systematic research on custodial-mother single-parent family as a system with its own authority structure, norms, processes of conflict management and boundary maintenance, patterns of exchange and reciprocity, and decision-making rules. The second, albeit corollary, sphere of family life that remains virtually uncharted thus has to do with the concept of "boundary redefinition" and life inside mother-headed single-parent families over the course of the family career.

When the father leaves the family household two dramatic changes follow. First, as Weiss (1979) noted, the loss of a parent tends to decrease the social distance, and opens normal boundaries between the mother and the children. More specifically, the authority structure in a two-parent family is grounded on the implicit coalition of two adults aligned against the children. In single-parent families, superordinate/subordinate "echelon structure" collapses. Weiss (1980) suggested that the children are promoted: The custodial mother relinquishes some decision-making control and then begins to engage the children "as if" they were junior partners. The parent wants to be able to rely on the children as full participants in the functioning of the family. Then, when the children do accept the increased responsibility, it becomes natural for the single-parent to consult the children regarding household decisions.

Second, decomposition of the authority structure and group size, to paraphrase Simmel (Wolff, 1950), increases communication and disclosure. Given this and the fact that single-parent families are often more isolated from friends and community groups (Burgess, 1970; Kitson, Lopata, Holmes, & Meyering, 1980; Smith, 1980; Weiss, 1975, 1979), a type of parent–child relationship "dyad" forms, which is markedly different from the traditional parent–child relationship. Characterized by greater equality, more frequent interaction, more discussions, and heightened cohesiveness (i.e., greater intimacy and companionship), the relationship fosters a wholly different affective structure (see Blechman & Manning, 1976; Hess & Camara, 1979; Keshet, 1980). "The condition of intimacy consists in the fact that the participants in a given relationship see only one another, and do not see, at the same time, an objective, super individual structure which they feel exists and operates on its own" (Simmel, cited in Wolff, 1950, pp. 127–128).

There has been as yet little in-depth study of this single mother–child relationship. Assuming that the dyad shares household tasks, problems, feelings, and often recreational activities (Keshet & Rosenthal, 1978; Klein, 1981; Wallerstein & Kelly, 1980b; Weiss, 1979), one could predict a higher level of mother–children intimacy than exists in most two-parent families.

But one is left at the present with more questions than data. Do signs of affection increase and signs of hostility decrease (see Blechman & Manning, 1976)? Does mother–children communication improve in terms of openness, depth, and breadth of topics discussed and issues shared (Kieffer, 1977)? Is the situation a type of "fox-hole" intimacy, eroding once the crisis situation passes, or does the relationship gradually increase in closeness? Does the "intimacy drain" on the parent translate into further emotional and social isolation from other adults, thus helping to explain the fact that many single mothers never remarry (Greenberg, 1979; Weiss, 1979)? Or does the closeness of the family make singlehood less painful and thus contribute to the tenure of single parenting (Libby & Whitehurs, 1977)? Do these children, who Weiss (1979) suggested grow up a little faster, fare better in their own ability to develop intimate relationships?

Although parent–child relationships in single-parent families are often strained, both Wallerstein and Kelly (1980b) and Weiss (1979) reported that the problems will differ depending on the ages of the children. In families with preschool children, Weiss contended that one major problem is the amount of attention small children seem to demand from their mothers. He stated that this demand can be extremely wearing on the single mother, especially because there is no second parent to provide relief. Weiss also noted that during the preschool toddler age, children are old enough to be negative, irritating, and extremely demanding, but not old enough to recognize the wearing effects this has on their parents. Furthermore, Havighurst (1961) suggested that parents must struggle a great deal with these children in order to manage their initiative. According to Weiss (1979), the single parent must often suppress an enormous amount of anger and rage toward the preschool child who insists on exerting a certain amount of will.

School-age children seem to be more in touch with a parent's emotional state, however, they also make many demands on the single parent. Weiss (1979) reported that single mothers of school-age children want to give their children the same experiences and opportunities that two-parent families have, however, in trying to do so, they overburden themselves with their children's extracurricular activities. He further contended that mothers who have sons are particularly concerned that their boys are provided with male role models. These women tend to feel guilty if they are not helping their sons become involved in sports, cub scouts, and other activities where these models exist.

The literature contains much material describing the many conflicts between adolescents and their parents. David Ausubel's theory (Ausubel, Montemayor, & Svajian, 1977) and Montemayor's studies (e.g., 1982) point out that the major source of this conflict lies in the fact that parents often encourage their adolescents' autonomy while at the same time trying to control them. Weiss (1979) found that single mothers in particular have a difficult time controlling adolescents and their many adolescent activities such as drinking, drugs, and sex. Ambert (1982) reported that many adolescents blatantly disregard their mothers' wishes because they realize that without spousal support, their mothers have much less control over them. Furthermore, Ambert found that custodial fathers have less trouble handling their children than do custodial mothers. In support of Ambert (1982), Hetherington, Cox, and Cox (1976) found that 2 years after divorce, single mothers have much more difficulty controlling their children (i.e., children complied with 40% of their mother's commands), as compared with single fathers (i.e., 50% compliance to father's commands). These women had more difficulty controlling their sons (i.e., 32% compliance to commands) as compared to their daughters (i.e., 40% compliance to commands).

The relationship between a single mother and an only son may resemble a marriage (Weiss, 1979). The mother may look to the son for emotional security, feeling that he is all she has in the world. In this type of situation, the parent may invest everything she has in the child, creating an overprotected individual who is not prepared to function autonomously and face the rigors of the modern world (Allison & Furstenberg, 1989). Many of these children tend to stay at home with their mothers for too long a time, resulting in their lack of maturation (Bowen, 1978).

One may expect that only sons would be particularly vulnerable to becoming "parentified" (Boszormenyi-Nagy & Spark, 1973) by a dependent mother. That is, the son may take over many of his mother's burdens, and she may turn to the son with expectations of devotion and caretaking. Wallerstein and Kelly (1980b) termed this *role reversal* (p. 117). They feel that children are not prepared to take on these tasks and that many children are depleted by the responsibilities, and by their own needs for parenting that were not met.

The mother–only daughter family system can also result in parentification of the daughter, however, Weiss (1979) found that competition is the main problem in this situation. Weiss reported that the daughter may want to emulate her mother (e.g., stay up late), whereas the mother may be jealous of her daughter's youthfulness and attractiveness. This might be accented if the daughter is particularly outgoing and has a number of male suitors.

The mother who has more than one child might receive more help with the household chores, however, she must be careful to share herself equitably. Weiss (1979) reported that sibling rivalry is often a major problem in this family system. He stated that each child tends to vie for the parent's attention, thus creating great competition. Increasing the tension is the fact that the eldest child often becomes a second parent, and is given power over the younger siblings who often resent this.

Many of these dynamics may change over time and situations. Simmel noted that when the mother–child dyad is expended, as when the mother begins to date, the parent–child relationship completely changes its character. A new oligarchical, adult clique emerges, competitive conditions follow, and coalitions replace solidarity. In effect, when the mother begins dating, the parent–child dyad once again becomes a subsystem within the total family structure. Both the parent and the children must relinquish some of the closeness and time shared (Rosenthal & Keshet, 1981; Staples, 1985; Walker & Messinger, 1979), leading some children to report jealousy (Staples, 1985; Weiss, 1979). Much more systematic research is needed to understand the nature, extent, and effects of this boundary reorganization. When there are two or more children in the family, does the presence of an "outsider" prompt the children to form a coalition, a competitive power, or does the fact that there are two reduce the likelihood of enmeshment with the mother, and hence the possessiveness? Does the addition of another adult inside the family boundary cause a redistribution of power, reestablishing an echelon authority? Do changes in the dyad alter the affective bonds between the mother and her children, and do the changes provide members more or less autonomy?

It is clear that there are both theoretical and empirical reasons to begin to conceptualize single-parent families as family systems with their own structure, norms, and internal processes of boundary reorganization. Recent research has offered some suggestion of what life is like inside these families. Mothers are often overloaded (Weiss, 1979), and children are precariously occupying a junior partner status (Wallerstein & Kelly, 1980b; Weiss, 1979). Although the amount of research is still small, there is a growing awareness among researchers that we must concentrate on the mother-headed family as a family unit, examining its own unique internal organization and its reorganization over time.

Quality of Single-Parent Family Life

Although "pathology is prominent element of the public view of single parenthood" (Schorr & Moen, 1979, p. 15), research suggests that single-parent families of divorced women are not inherently disorganized nor necessarily detrimental to the children. Rather, they simply differ in structure and internal organization (Blechman & Manning, 1976; Burgess, 1970; Mendes, 1979). Just as there are variations within the two-parent family systems, some single-parent families meet the needs of the family members and society and some do not.

Until very recently, only those single-parent families seeking help for problems in living were studied. Because single mothers are more open to seeking help (Blechman & Manning, 1976; Guttentag et al., 1980) and clinicians tend to anticipate pathology, many studies reported that single-parent family life was producing troubled and anxious children, and neurotic parents. Kalter's (1977) review of the clinical "research" found only five studies that systematically attempted to compare two-parent and single-parent family systems. However these five also fall into the long tradition of research on the "single-parent condition" with the standard conceptual biases and methodological limitations (for review and critiques, see Adams, Milner, & Scherpf, 1986; Biller, 1970; Herzog & Sudia, 1968; Lamb, 1976; Sprey, 1967).

Much of the research purportedly examining the single-parent family system has instead focused on the individual family members (e.g., Stolberg & Garrison, 1985). It assumed living in a single-parent household was at best problematic and at worst the source of major social problems, and thus sought to identify what negative effects the single-parent condition had on which family members. The single-parent home was assumed to be the cause of a family member's inappropriate gender role behavior, achievement problems, low self-esteem, depression, immaturity, and sexual precocity (see Blechman, 1982; Goetting, 1979, for reviews). Few studies controlled for other casual explanations, such as the family's socioeconomic status and degree of access to social supports, the custodial parent's gender and employment opportunity, the child's age, gender, and involvement with the father, or the relationship between the parents before and after the separation and/or divorce.

Billingsley and Giovannoni (1971) noted that "The unfortunate assumption that there is a one-to-one relationship between this type of family structure and all kinds of social and psychological pathology has resulted in almost total ignorance about [those single-parent] families — the majority — who somehow circumvented this 'inevitable' pathology" (p. 368). Since the 1970s, however, investigators have begun the necessary systematic comparison of families, assessing whether interaction within single-parent and two-parent family systems differentially affect individual members. Some have examined the mother–child relationship (e.g., Hetherington, 1972; Hoffman, 1971; Sanik & Mauldin, 1986), whereas others have focused on the psychosocial climate within the families (e.g., Berg & Kelly, 1979; Bisnaire, Firestone, & Rynard, 1990). Although most of this research still focuses on the individual and does not directly assess the family system, it is nonetheless important because it substantiates the idea that family processes supersede family structure. Studies have examined the interaction patterns and coorientation between mothers and children (Aldous, 1977; Longabaugh, 1973; Stolberg, Camplair, Currier, & Wells, 1987); the degree of inaccessibility of both parents in two-parent systems (Blanchard & Biller, 1971; McLanahan, 1983; Minuchin, 1974; Reuter & Biller, 1973); the quality of the parent–child relationship before and after marital separation (Block, Block, & Gjerde, 1989; Hess & Camara, 1979; Wallerstein & Kelly, 1980b); the quality of the marital relationship across families (MacKinnon, Brody, & Stoneman, 1986; Raschke & Raschke, 1979); and the emotional quality of the home environment (Bisnaire et al., 1990; Block et al., 1988; Herzog & Sudia, 1973; Raschke & Raschke, 1979). The family systems approach in studying divorced families was adapted in a recent study by Ellwood and Stolberg (1991). They reported that although the levels of family cohesion and democratic style were positively related to family functioning, levels of conflicts and a laissez-faire parental style were negatively related to both the children's and the parents' functioning. Thus, overall, results suggest that it is the psychosocial characteristics of the family unit, independent of the number of parents, that affect the individuals in the family. Living in a single-parent family need be no more harmful than living in a two-parent family.

However, there is as yet little evidence indicating the comparative effects of living in a single-parent family. Living in a single-parent family is probably less detrimental for children than living in an unhappy, conflict-ridden two-parent system (Nye, 1957; Staples, 1985), and less permanently troubling than previously anticipated (Kulka & Weingarten, 1979; Luepnitz, 1979). But at present there is little information grounded in methodologically sophisticated work. For the time being, conclusions must remain tentative.

Research needs to move ahead in new directions. First, more extensive comparison of a broad range of families (both mother-headed single-parent and two-parent systems) would test the validity of the notion that the single-parent family system is inevitably pathological and its family members disadvantaged. Second, it is important for researchers to untangle the effects of the crisis period that triggers the single-parent family situation from the family system's pattern of interaction following the separation. Are the problems so often experienced by single parents and their children a result of life in a single-parent family per se or of the trauma of the separation (Boss, 1980; Hansen & Johnson, 1979; Levitan, 1979; Luepnitz, 1979)? Research is needed on both the short- and long-term impact of the separation (Berkman, 1969; Bloom et al., 1978; Luepnitz, 1982) and on life at various stages in the single-parent family career. Third, a typology of the different stages in the single-parent family career is needed, one that captures the changing patterns of interaction and conflict management. Fourth, the effects of family formation and reorganization need to be separated from the effects of the family's place in the larger society. To what extent are the problems commonly attributed to single-parent families a consequence of the dynamics of living in that family or of the discrimination these families often encounter in a two-parent society ("stress pile-up"; Dill, Feld, Martin, Beukma, & Belle, 1980; McCubbin et al., 1980)?

Support Networks and Social Life

The relationships that single-parent families maintain with friends and kin can only be obtained by piecing together studies that have focused on the mother's social ties or the child's kin relationship. Because we must borrow bits and pieces from the available information, the linkage between single-parent families and their social networks cannot be clearly defined.

Some literature suggests that custodial mothers maintain or increase their exchange and affectional ties with their own relatives after the divorce (Anspach, 1976; Gongla, 1982; Spicer & Hampe, 1975). Relatives basically feel a commitment to help, and that commitment provides the family a sense of continuity and security whether or not help is actually given (Leslie & Grady, 1988; Weiss, 1979). This is particularly true during the first year following the divorce (Anspach, 1976; Leslie & Grady, 1988). Nonetheless, turning to the children's grandparents for help can create a "catch 22." Returning home for services and support often results in tension and dependent feelings (Colletta, 1979a; Dell & Applebaum, 1977; Weiss, 1975, 1979). Particularly acute are the problems of boundary ambiguity when relatives offer unsolicited advice about childrearing (Leslie & Grady, 1988) or in cases of custody disputes (Johnston & Campbell, 1986).

Interaction with in-laws usually diminishes with divorce, unless the noncustodial parent continues to maintain contact with the family and thus provides a pathway to the in-laws (Anspach, 1976; Gongla, 1982). In effect, relationships with in-laws remain contingent upon the interactive presence of the noncustodial parent and generally worsen as the noncustodial parent withdraws from the single-parent family.

Ties to friends seem to follow a different pattern. As the single-parent family emerges, defines, and organizes itself, so too does the family's community of friends. For the custodial mother, the first reaction is a sense of being marginal to the family's former community and a sense of social, if not emotional, isolation (Hetherington et al., 1979a; Kitson et al., 1980; Smith, 1980; Weiss, 1979). Unlike single fathers, many single mothers are able to maintain or increase their intimacy pattern with their old friends (Gongla, 1982). As time goes on and the family is able to more clearly define itself, a new community of friends is often formed (McLanahan et al., 1981; Rosenthal & Keshet, 1981). Such friends may be more effective than kin, providing more support for the single mother and respecting the family's external boundaries (see Greenberg, 1979). However this finding may only be valid for those custodial mothers who strongly identify with the role of a single parent and who are attempting to reorganize their lives in a way that increases their independence (McLanahan et al., 1981).

Single mothers often have problems establishing new friendships as well as maintaining old ones. Many single mothers have been out of the single social life for so long they do not know where to meet people (Goode, 1956b). According to Goode and to Weiss (1979), many of these women do not have the time nor the energy needed for frequent social activities. Single mothers who work have a hard enough time balancing their job's demands and family life. They are often too occupied and exhausted to socialize or to contribute the time needed to maintain a solid friendship.

Although few friends may remain close to the single mother throughout the divorce process, most of her friendships with married friends may fade away. According to Weiss (1979), many married friends tend to lose interest in the relationship because they feel that they have nothing in common with the unmarried woman.

Many of the people who formally made up the community of friends are confronted with a conflict of allegiances; therefore, they may withdraw all together from both divorcing parties. Some may sever their relationship with the single mother because they disapprove of separation/divorce and/or because they feel "superior" (Miller, 1970, p. 74) to a divorced person. Most often however, the friends closest to each spouse either before or during the marriage will side with that person after the separation/divorce (Kohen et al., 1979; Miller, 1970).

Finally, many married people may feel that their friends' separation might negatively effect their own marriage. According to Bohannan (1968), divorce in particular can become contagious within cliques of friends. Burgess (1970) and Weiss (1973, 1975) reported that the female of the married couple may feel sexually threatened by the single woman, and insist that her husband follow her in severing their former friendship with the woman. This is in accordance with the fact that single mothers, particularly divorcees, are stigmatized as being sexually needy (Marsden, 1969), and thus may be susceptible to propositions by their friends' husbands (Miller, 1970).

Even though friends tend to abandon the single mother, it is important to realize that the single mother may also abandon them. Although she may be too busy to invest time she may also feel uncomfortable among her married friends (Bohannan, 1968). The single mother may also, because of financial problems, not be able to keep up with her friends' style of living and entertainment.

But almost regardless of the particular situation, the single mother will no doubt lose some friends. However, most will eventually make up for the lost friends by making new ones, most likely also single mothers. According to

Goode (1956b) and Weiss (1973), these new friends can better share with the single mother dilemmas and experiences and at the same time help to reestablish her socially.

Neighbors can often be supportive of the single-parent family, especially if they perceive the mother to be a "victim." Many may offer food, shelter, and in some cases, a financial loan in order to help in times of distress (Weiss, 1973). Other neighbors, however, may become hostile toward the single mother and her family, particularly if the woman is a divorcee and the neighbors disapprove of the single-parent family system. In a study of social networks and social support in Sweden, Tietjen (1985) found that neighbors provided less instrumental, personal, and social support to single mothers than did friends, relatives, and workmates. Many of the divorced mothers in the Swedish sample reported that they felt gossiped about by their neighbors following the divorce.

Neighbors were also known to totally ignore the single-parent family and to even disallow their children to associate with the family's children (Marsden, 1969). Many children of single-parent families are made to feel ashamed about their family background and often lie about the absent parent's whereabouts (Gibson, Range, & Anderson, 1986; Landis, 1960).

Relatives, particularly siblings and parents, can be quite supportive to the single-parent family. They may help in some everyday chores and financially (McLanahan et al., 1981; Weiss, 1975). Tietjen (1985) reported that parents of single mothers provide frequent child-care services for which single mothers are greatly indebted.

Although there may be some drawbacks to family support in that it may bring about new and renewed conflicts, decrease the chances for the single mother's independence, and so on, the importance of different kinds of networking cannot be overstated: Serving as a buffer to external stresses and providing emotional and instrumental assistance as needed, social supports do seem to have an effect on the fact and the feeling of doing it alone (Bloom et al., 1978; Chiriboga, Roberts, & Stein, 1978; McLanahan et al., 1981; Spanier & Casto, 1979; Wilcox, 1981).

Psychological Consequences of Divorce

In 1956, Goode noted that 63% of the divorced mothers in his study suffered from high or medium trauma during the divorce process. More specifically, approximately 66% of these mothers had a greater feeling of loneliness, poorer health, and greater difficulty sleeping during the divorces. Gardner (1974) found that women suffer intense guilt during the divorce process, particularly after they inform their children that there will be a divorce. Bohannan (1968), Brown (1976), and Kaslow (1981), among others, also found that women who are involved in the divorce process exhibit a variety of emotional symptoms. They are as follows: alienation, anger, anguish, despair, disillusionment, emptiness, grief, guilt, helplessness, hurt, inadequacy, loneliness, low self-esteem, and rejection.

The aftereffect of divorce may also cause women psychological problems. Gurin, Veroff, and Feld (1960) found that divorce affects the adjustment of women more than it does men. According to these authors, divorced and separated custodial mothers reported immobilization, feelings of an impending nervous breakdown, and consistent worrying.

Malzberg (1964), also reported that unmarried people in general had higher rates of mental disease than married people. And Briscoe and Smith (1974, 1975) reported that in 92% of their divorced units, one or both ex-partners experienced psychiatric problems, compared to 43% of the married control units. In contradiction to Gove and Geerken's (1977) assertion that the high rates of emotional difficulties in women can be attributed to their being married, Warheit et al. (1976) found that the highest rates of psychiatric disturbance existed in women who were separated for 1 year or less, compared with those who had been separated for more than 1 year.

Early reports (e.g., Gibbs, 1969; Gove, 1972) indicated a high correlation of suicide rate with marital status. U.S. government data revealed similar information years later. It showed that the suicide rate was higher among the divorced women than among the married and the widowed; the risk of death by homicide for women was more than four times higher among the divorced than the married, and more than twice as high as the widowed; and that automobile fatality rates were higher among the divorced than among the widowed, and about three times as high as automobile fatality rates among the married (National Center for Health Statistics, 1984; U.S. Bureau of the Census, 1984).

In conducting a study of 2,300 people in the Chicago area, Pearlin and Johnson (1977) found the following: (a) separated and divorced women were more depressed and experienced more hardships than the married, widowed, and never married women; (b) the number of children for which the divorced woman is responsible reflects the most direct indication of parental burdens — the more children the more depression; (c) separated and divorced women with children were disposed to more depression than separated and divorced men; (d) those who were simultaneously single parent, isolated, exposed to burdensome parental obligations, and, most importantly, poor, were most susceptible to psychological difficulties. The authors felt that many of these women's depression could be attributed to economic hardships, social isolation, and parental role overload.

According to MaLanahan and his colleagues (1981), divorced custodial mothers experience a considerable amount of psychological distress. In fact, Guttentag et al. (1980) reported that divorced mothers were the major consumers of mental health services. Weiss (1976) reported that newly divorced/separated women exhibited continued attachment to the ex-spouse, anger, guilt, restlessness, hyperalertness, and feelings of panic and fear. To summarize, Weiss' words seem to capture it all. He said: "The symptoms of separation distress in adults are very similar to those exhibited by young children who have lost an attachment figure" (Weiss, 1976, p. 140).

Economic Consequences of Divorce

One obvious exception to the lack of a thorough study is the research on the economic consequences of divorce. Goode (1956) presented his sociological study of "Women in Divorce," which subsequently became a classic study. His findings demonstrated that there is a rough inverse correlation between class position and the rate of divorce. Prior to Goode's study, higher income classes were thought to be more prone to divorce. He also noted that child support payments to the divorced mother are small and irregular. He further indicated that over time the economic position of the divorced mother improves and that this improvement was almost entirely a function of remarriage.

Since then, evidence has accumulated to conclusively document the low economic status of single-parent families—their low income, high rates of poverty, and fewer employment opportunities than two-parent families (Bane & Weiss, 1980; Bianchi, & Farley, 1979; Bradbury et al., 1979; Dinerman, 1977; Epenshade, 1979; Stirling, 1987; Weitzman, 1981, 1985). As Cherlin (1981) and Colletta (1979b) summarized, the major problem faced by single-parent families is not the lack of a male presence, but a lack of a male income.

Nowhere is the linkage between major social institutions and single-parent families as pointed as it is in the areas of economics and employment. Throughout most of the 1970s, the income of single-mother families remained less than one third the income of two-parent families, and the income differential appears to be increasing. By the end of the decade, single custodial mothers commanded half the income of single fathers, and half again the average income of the two-parent family.

More recent research (Corcoran, 1976; Epenshade, 1979; Weiss, 1984; U.S. Bureau of the Census, 1988; Weitzman, 1981, 1985) compared the economic status of married couples to divorced men and women. There is a consensus among these studies that married couples and divorced men fare much better than divorced women, even when they adjust for the smaller family size of the divorced families (Mnookin & Kornhauser, 1979; Seltzer & Garfinkel, 1990). Hampton (1975), for example, concluded that the economics status of the former husbands improves, whereas that of former wives deteriorates. He found twice as many ex-husbands as ex-wives in the top three income-to-needs ratio (i.e., the total family income adjusted for the needs of different-sized families) decile position, whereas only 15% of ex-husbands are in the lowest three deciles compared to 37% for ex-wives. His explanation is that children hinder the mother's labor force participation and thus her economic status deteriorates.

Data from research also indicate that divorced women run a disproportionately high risk of falling into and remaining in poverty (Duncan & Hoffman, 1985). For example, Duncan and Morgan (1975, 1981) examined the impact of divorce on a family's chances of being in poverty. They observed a cohort of married couples in 1967 and then reexamined them in 1973. Only 6% of those couples who remained married and 13% of the men who divorced became poor during the time period, but 33% of the women who divorced fell into poverty. Conversely, of the married couples who were poor in 1967, 45% were not poor in 1973, 67% of the poor men who divorced escaped poverty, and only 26% of the poor women who divorced during this period managed to escape poverty.

With such an income differential, it is not surprising that families maintained by a single mother are over three times more likely than those headed by single fathers, and six times more likely than two-parent families, to have an income below the poverty threshold (U.S. Bureau of the Census, 1985). A major reason for the single parent's poor economic status, especially the single custodial mother's status, is the sizable reduction in family income most families experience following separation. In recent years, the magnitude of this reduction becomes even more severe; it is the single most important factor explaining the economic gap between single-parent and two-parent families (Bane & Weiss, 1980; Bianchi & Farley, 1979; Epenshade, 1979; Weitzman, 1985).

But a number of other factors contribute to the poor economic conditions of a single-parent family: the father's inability or unwillingness to contribute to the family income (U.S. Bureau of Census, 1990; Weitzman, 1985); the cost of child care (Sawhill, 1976; Schorr & Moen, 1979); the catch 22 governing policies of public assistance and "workfare" (Dinerman, 1977); the labor market "squeeze," which results in younger single mothers receiving the lowest income, experiencing the highest rate of unemployment, and obtaining the fewest benefits (Schorr & Moen, 1979; Weitzman, 1985); and the recurring problem of discrimination against women in the workplace (Sawhill, 1976; Schorr & Moen, 1979).

The form of welfare encountered by most single-mothers is Aid to Families with Dependent Children (AFDC). AFDC is largely federally funded, but each state dictates its own payment schedule. To be eligible for AFDC, the single mother usually must provide evidence of her expenses, and sometimes a birth certificate to prove that she indeed has children. A home visit by a welfare worker to corroborate this information usually follows. Also, the single mother must aid the welfare bureau in securing support from her ex-husband. In fact, many offices require the separated/ divorced mother to bring legal action against her ex-spouse for nonsupport (Weiss, 1979).

Burden (1980) referred to AFDC as a punitive program that reflects the general stigmatization and negative social attitudes toward women and children who are not supported by men. Weiss (1975) reported a former applicant as saying:

> I had to bring my rent, heat, light, doctor's bills, dentist's bills, my last five paychecks, and explain what happened to my support check. My ex had a very bad winter and he wasn't sending anything. And I had to bring my bank account and say if the children had a bank account. They destroy any pride, any dignity that an individual would have. You have to plead poverty, say you are starving to death, before they'll give you anything. (p. 31)

Implication

Demographically, it is clear that single-parent families are now within the mainstream of U.S. society. Moreover, after at least four decades of work that emphasizes their deviation from the two-parent family and the pathological effect on the individual member (Shaw & McKay, 1932), single-parent families are now gradually coming to be recognized and studied as whole, often healthy, families.

Some manage to adapt and reorganize easily, even to thrive, coping effectively with stresses both from within and outside the family unit. Others do not. Research findings suggest that the factors directly associated with successful families are the age of the custodial mother and her children (Wallerstein & Kelly, 1980b), family income (Colletta, 1979b; Ross & Sawhill, 1975), residential stability (Bane & Weiss, 1980), development of an adaptive informal support system (McLanahan et al., Adelberg, 1981), systematic separation of marital and parenting roles (Keshet, 1980; Weiss, 1975), the interactive and psychological presence of the father (Boss, 1977), ability to manage conflict (Goldsmith, 1980; Raschke & Raschke, 1979; Weiss, 1979), abandoning old rules and rituals and establishing new family norms (Ahrons, 1980; Weiss, 1975), and access to child-care alternatives (Sawhill, 1976; Schorr & Moen, 1979).

Yet, even the studies cited here must be interpreted cautiously. Few studies have been designed to compare families, and our knowledge is too limited to suggest what resources have an ameliorative effect on the life of a single-mother family in a two-parent society. Most, if not all, of the factors mentioned here also probably apply to the maintenance of well-functioning two-parent families. Data suggest that there are more variations within single-parent and two-parent families than between them. Hence, continued concern with the structural variable of number of parents within the household may be less helpful than a search for those characteristics that all well-functioning families share.

Custodial single-mother families desperately need to be studied as family systems that involve internal and external boundaries and some degree of embeddedness in the social environment. There must be a continued focus on single-mother *families,* with attention to the diversity of their internal organization and boundary reorganization over time, the degree of involvement with kin and friends outside the household, and their interaction with the large social environment. Recent research strongly suggest that new investigations of custodial mothers' families recognize the possible existence of a second parent who continues to be present within the family system. Although findings are at present tentative, the second parent continues to play an important role in the family after separation/divorce. The interactive and/or psychological presence of the second parent must certainly have its attendant benefits and costs, but it is difficult to specify when benefits will outweigh costs.

Although most single-parent families will continue to experience the effect of their low economic status, and although the full impact of the change in economic lifestyle is far from fully explored, families appear to differ in their degree of vulnerability and with regard to the stage in their family career at which they are most vulnerable.

NONCUSTODIAL MOTHER

As was previously noted, the divorce rate has increased dramatically, creating millions of divided families. Most often the mother is awarded custody of the children, although increasingly joint custody is considered. However, in more than 13% of the cases, the mother is either forced, or chooses, to relinquish custody of her children to the father (Orthner, Brown, & Ferguson, 1976). Of the noncustodial mothers Gersick (1979) studied, 90% had given their pretrial consent to have the children raised by their fathers. But whether voluntarily or not, mothers who relinquish custody appear to challenge the fundamental belief of our society that motherhood is a woman's highest calling (Doudna, 1982). These noncustodial mothers are then viewed as deviants in a culture that idealizes motherhood and believes that a mother should live with her children (Paskowicz, 1984). Mothers who do not live with their children frequently face ostracism, condemnation, and derogatory labels (e.g., selfish, irresponsible, promiscuous, crazy, or unfit; Paskowicz, 1984).

Society and the Noncustodial Mother

Fischer (1983) reported the results of a study undertaken to document societal attitudes toward various child-free lifestyles. Subjects were asked to compare each child-free lifestyle with the married couple with children, the lifestyle that appeared to be the most common and approved of by the general population. The results indicated that homosexual couples and noncustodial mothers were judged the harshest.

It is not surprising, then, that the stigma and guilt of being a noncustodial parent are much greater for a mother than for a father (Koehler, 1982). It appears that if the single parent with custody is a mother, she is only doing the expected. If she relinquishes custody of her children, she is negatively evaluated and ostracized. In contrast, a father who relinquishes custody is only doing the expected. If he should retain custody of his children, he is practically deified. Consequently, the possible evaluation of a noncustodial father range from neutral to very positive, whereas the best rating achievable by a noncustodial mother seems to be in a neutral range.

Paskowicz (1984) pointed out the negative stereotypes of the noncustodial mother that have been perpetuated by novels and movies. The mother without custody is viewed as a "self-centered bitch," as "sexually promiscuous," or as a "cold-hearted career woman."

For many years the belief that a noncustodial mother must be unfit was coded in law (Doudna, 1982). During most of this century, the legal standard for custody decisions was the "doctrine of tender years," which assumed that children benefitted most by living with their mother during their tender years. The only exception to the doctrine was if the mother was judged unfit, which included a wide variety of behaviors and attitudes, such as adultery, other sexual misconduct, substance abuse, and unpopular religious, political, or social beliefs (Saposnek, 1983). Because of sex discrimination inherent in the tender years doctrine, most courts have replaced it with the "best interest of the child" standard. Theoretically, the best interest guideline counteracts the tendency to award custody by finding one parent at fault or unfit. Nevertheless, in practice, custody may still be denied to a parent who is perceived as unfit in some way under the pretense that it is in the best interest of the child (Saposnek, 1983).

Furthermore, the best interest doctrine often favors the father (Fischer & Cardea, 1981; Shulman & Pitt, 1982). An important issue in any custody decision is money. Women still earn only 59¢ for every $1 that men earn in similar positions. Therefore, the divorced mother typically finds herself with less money to support herself and her children than her ex-husband has to support himself alone (Weitzman, 1985). This discrepancy in financial resources leads to a situation in which judges, fathers, mothers, and even the children themselves may decide that the children's best interest will be served by awarding custody to the father.

In her survey of 100 mothers who had relinquished custody of their children, Paskowicz (1984) found that 75% of the women voluntarily gave up custody, whereas the other 25% did so involuntarily. Of the 25 women who had separation from their children imposed on them, 12 of the mothers lost custody of their children through legal judgment; 13 lost custody because their children chose to live with their fathers. Voluntary noncustodial mothers are women who chose to relinquish custody of their children. These mothers cited the following reasons for their decision to relinquish custody: emotional problems, need for self-realization, intimidation by the children's father, problems in a second marriage, and/or the father was the more nurturing or established parent.

Noncustodial mothers report an awareness of society's negative attitude toward them. Fischer and Cardea (1981) found that 86% of the custodial mothers and 83% of the noncustodial mothers were of the strong opinion that society's attitudes toward the noncustodial mother are negative.

Searching for an answer as to why noncustodial status is so stressful for divorced women leads to an examination of the motherhood literature. As one views the history of motherhood, it appears that mothers have always been with us; however, the exaltation of motherhood and the invention of maternal instinct are relatively recent phenomena (Howell, 1973; MacBride, 1973).

Badinter (1981) reviewed the history of different forms of maternal behavior in France across four centuries and has clearly demonstrated that the maternal instinct is a myth. She drew on a wide variety of sources to show that mother love is not innate or biologically determined, but rather is a culturally conditioned response that is relative to time and place. She cited periods in history when French mothers freely abandoned their children and did so with an apparent indifference. Badinter is not at all opposed to mother love; however, she viewed it as more of a gift than a given.

Dally (1982) discussed the changes that have occurred in the theory and practice of mothering throughout the years. Love for individual children was largely absent among our ancestors, partially due to the number of children who did not survive infancy. Abandonment of children was fairly common in Europe up to the 18th century. Dally explained how the social and economic developments that have occurred in the last 200 years have separated the place of work from the home, eliminated the domestic servant, and have largely isolated the mother and her children in the home. She noted how the theories of childrearing that have evolved since the 1940s match the social situation, thereby justifying and idealizing the segregation of mothers. She cited Bowlby's theory regarding the deleterious effects of maternal deprivation as central in segregating mothers and children into the home. Dally pointed out that Bowlby's studies were conducted on children in institutions who were totally deprived, lacking much more than just mothers.

Dally further suggested that the 20th century could be termed the age of the idealization of motherhood. For the first time in human history, mothers have been closed up alone with small children for long hours, with the appearance that "this was the ideal, the norm, essential for the healthy psychological development of the child and a demonstration of feminine normality in the mother" (p. 10). However, Dally argued that by insisting that the only psychological essential is to keep mothers and children together is to conveniently ignore the individual needs of both the mother and the children.

Finally, Dally examined the consequences of the mother ideal for women. She pointed out how women have been affected socially and psychologically. Some of these consequences include the sacrifice of social life to maternal duty, making the "working mother a bad mother," and the worsening of any of the mother's emotional problems.

Bernard (1975) pointed out how motherhood has varied greatly depending on time and place. She explained how motherhood in our modern industrial society is much different from motherhood in preliterate and preindustrialized societies. She referred to motherhood as we know it today as new and unique and suggested that the way we institutionalize motherhood in our society is not a particularly positive way for mothers or their children. Assigning mothers the sole responsibility for child care without help from others, segregating mothers and children in the home, and requiring constant, loving care by the mother, she argued, may be the worst way to structure motherhood. "It is as though we have selected the worst features of all the ways motherhood is structured around the world and combined them to produce our current design" (p. 9).

Schaffer (1977) questioned the instinctual nature of mother love and has concluded that mother love is not inevitable. He cited the lifestyle of the IK tribe of Uganda and the Mundugumor people of New Guinea as evidence that lovelessness toward children can become institutionalized. In the IK tribe, children are turned out on their own at the age of 3, and among the Mundugumor, it is not unusual for babies to be thrown in the river. In addition, Schaffer (1977) pointed out that even in Western society, many children are taken into public care because of parental cruelty, neglect, or desertion. Having children, Schaffer stated, should be only for those who want children. He concluded that the best way to improve the quality of motherhood is to make it genuinely a matter of choice.

Russo (1979) discussed the mandate for motherhood in our society that requires that a women have at least two children and raise them well. She argued that motherhood is chief among the prescriptions of gender typing, and that most people in our society believed that the major goal of a woman's life is to raise well-adjusted children. She pointed out how fulfilling the motherhood mandate limits a women's access to educational and occupational options. Russo concluded that the motherhood mandate has been very resistant to change because it is so deeply rooted in our societal institutions.

Noncustodial mothers stand in stark contrast to the mother mandate, the idealization of motherhood, and the notion of maternal instinct. The literature cited here sheds some light on the reasons behind the stressful nature of noncustodial status. Not only is the noncustodial mother at conflict with society, but she also experiences dissonance within herself to the extent that she has internalized society's expectations of her as a woman. Nevertheless, some evidence has been reported to suggest that societal attitudes toward motherhood may be beginning to change.

In their investigation of attitude toward motherhood, Hare-Mustin, Bennett, and Broderick (1983) found that older women who have lived the mother mandate embrace more conventional attitudes toward motherhood than do younger women. For the younger women, a theme of reproductive freedom emerged that includes autonomy in the choice of motherhood as well as personal fulfillment.

Characteristics of the Noncustodial Mother

Very few studies have focused on the characteristics or personality patterns of noncustodial mothers. The typical noncustodial mother in Greif's (1987) study was not remarried, White, 39 years old, and had completed 2 years of college. Fischer and Cardea (1981) administered the Ben Sex Role Inventory and the 16 PF Neuroticism Scale to the 16 custodial and 17 noncustodial mothers participating in their study as a check on the personality characteristics of the two groups. The researchers reported finding no differences in mean scores on masculinity, femininity, or neuroticism for the two groups. One third of the mothers in Greif's (1987) study felt "comfortable" with their role and relationship with their children. One third felt "uncomfortable" and one third had "mixed feelings" about their life without their children. The mothers (according to the custodial fathers' report in Greif's 1985 study) tended to remain involved and about half visited at least once in 2 weeks. This pattern of involvement was more apparent when only girls were involved, but even then the mothers' involvement decreased as the children got older.

As reported in Greif's (1987) study, more than 90% of the mothers had given up custody without a court battle. The dominant reason, as reported by the mothers, was the lack of money. They thought that for financial reasons they could not raise the children or that the children preferred the father. By custodial fathers' account, 20% have the children after winning custody suits; 37% through mutual agreement; and 26% by the children's choice (Greif, 1985). This latter information is drawn from custodial fathers, thus it must be taken with some skepticism.

Psychological Consequences

Noncustodial mothers, whether voluntary or involuntary, have reported facing similar difficulties in the years following separation from their children, such as isolation, loneliness, guilt, depression, and rejection (Paskowicz, 1984). Even voluntary noncustodial mothers are likely to feel rejected by their children and to worry about the long-term effects of their decision on the development of the children (Todres, 1978). It appears that noncustodial mothers suffer from self-imposed, as well as societally inflicted, punishment.

Although the dramatic increase in divorce has engendered a proliferation of research and articles regarding divorce, single-parent families, remarriage, and stepparenting, the noncustodial mothers remain an enigma, having been largely ignored. Although the popular press has exhibited interest in the subject in the last few years, there have been very few empirical studies comparing the characteristics and lives of noncustodial and custodial mothers.

Nevertheless, it has been estimated that at least 565,000 mothers nationwide have relinquished custody of their children, either voluntarily or involuntarily (Doudna, 1982). The number may be even greater because this figure does not reflect the fathers with custody who have remarried or those mothers who relinquished custody to someone other than the fathers.

The available literature on mothers without custody indicate that noncustodial status is stressful. Fischer and Cardea (1981) examined stress and coping in four areas through interviews of 17 noncustodial and 14 custodial mothers. They found that the stressfulness of the noncustodial situation was reelected in negative evaluations of women who do not have custody, in the difficulties in dealing with ex-husbands over custody, in a lack of support from their families, and in the fewer hopes for the future reported by these women. The study also indicated that custody arrangements are transitory. Fifty-nine percent of the noncustodial mothers reported that they originally had custody of all their children. However, at the time of the interviews, one or more of their children had left to live with the father. Thirty-five percent of the noncustodial mothers reported feeling helpless in the face of the father's efforts to win custody. No evidence was found to indicate that noncustodial mothers were more "unfit" than custodial mothers, in terms of feelings for the children, type of living arrangements, abuse, alcoholism, or other problem areas (Fischer & Cardea, 1981).

Mother-Child(ren) Relationships

Research results also suggest that the mother–child relationship is stressful for noncustodial mothers. Fischer and Cardea (1981) examined divorced mothers' perception of the mother–child relationship when mothers lived with or apart from their children. The noncustodial mothers in their study reported more negative, hostile, and nonexistent relationships with their children than did custodial mothers. In addition, the noncustodial mothers perceived more of a negative shift in the relationships with their children following the separation than did custodial mothers. Fischer and Cardea suggested that the negative shift may be related to the sense of loss of the parental role reported by 35% of the noncustodial mothers, and that the stresses of separation from the children may have created barriers in the mothers that inhibited their overtures to the children.

Fischer and Cardea posited that the more negative mother–child relationships with noncustodial children represent a complex set of circumstances, involving the mothers, the fathers, and the children. They speculated that when the father has gained custody through material means, he may be apprehensive that the mother could get them back in the same manner. This insecurity may promote interference in the mother–child relationship by the father. Fischer and Cardea further reported that many of the negative mother–child relationships result from nonexistent mother–child contacts where the father has successfully interfered in the relationship. In other situations, where the father's attempts to interfere in the mother–child relationship have failed, the mother is frequently angry with the children for leaving and may set up obstacles of her own. The children, the authors suggested, may react to the whole situation by withdrawing. Moreover, the children may disparage the mother and enhance the father in an attempt to justify their nonnormative situation. Fischer and Cardea concluded that professional intervention may be necessary to resolve the tensions inherent in these situations.

The stressfulness of the mother–child relationship for noncustodial mothers is also reflected in the results of other studies (Davenport, 1981; Greif, 1987; Todres, 1978). Davenport's investigation sought to determine if attitudes toward children and childrearing are different between divorced fathers and mothers, between divorced custodial parents and divorced noncustodial parents, and whether an interaction exists between custody and sex. The results indicate that the divorced noncustodial mothers had the lowest score on the Protective scale of the Maryland Parent Attitude Scale, indicating a nonprotective attitude toward children. Moreover, the noncustodial mothers had the highest Rejecting score, which Davenport interpreted as suggesting that they feel burdened by their children. These results are congruent with Fischer and Cardea's (1981) analysis of the mother–child relationship. Perhaps a nonprotective, rejecting parental attitude on the part of noncustodial mothers is one of the obstacles set up by the mothers who are angry at their children for leaving. Somewhat more positive results are reported in Greif's (1987) study. Twenty-five percent of the noncustodial mothers reported being satisfied with the relationship with their children. Together with those mothers who reported "mixed reaction," more than 50% of the noncustodial mothers felt somewhat positive about their relationship with their children.

It seems that the aforementioned studies have only begun to explore the unique situation of noncustodial mothers. In view of the number of noncustodial mothers, the psychological stress reported by this population of women, and the paucity of relevant studies in the literature, it is clear that there is a need for research pertaining to noncustodial mothers. Such research may provide meaningful data that can be used by mental health professionals for the development of effective interventions with these women.

5 Divorced Fathers

For the majority of fathers, divorce means losing custody of their children. In 90% of divorce cases the mother is awarded custody (National Center for Health Statistics, 1985). However, as a result of the frequency with which couples seek divorce, of the pressures from the feminist movement, and of a gradual change in the attitudes and perceptions of the courts, the number of children living with single fathers is slowly rising (U.S. Bureau of the Census, 1985). Only a few studies investigating children under their fathers' custody have been reported to date, but those studies indicate that this arrangement is no worse than maternal custody (Gasser & Taylor, 1976; George & Wilding, 1972; Greif, 1985; Jacobs, 1986; Levine, 1976; Mendes, 1976; Schlesinger, 1978). Researchers have reported that the problems facing fathers and children in motherless families do not impair the children's normal development. The negative result reported by Katz (1979) in his study of Australian fathers was a noted exception.

Yet, despite these findings and the new recognition of the importance and ability of the father to be a functional parent, fathers are still very much the "forgotten parent." This fact not only is evident in the way courts are dealing with issues of divorce in general and custody in particular but is also apparent in the way the available professional literature deals with the topic. However, this disregard of the divorced father is, as we see here, only a logical extension of the commonplace and professional references to the father's functions in a two-parent family and to his influence on his children's development.

A bold sign as to the pressing need for a penetrating discussion of the

111

subject of fatherhood is found in a guide to advocates published by the Family Law Committee of the Minnesota Bar Association (Rorris, 1971):

> Except in very rare cases, the father should not have the custody of the minor children of the parties. He is usually unqualified psychologically and emotionally; nor does he have the time and care to supervise the children. A lawyer not only does an injustice to himself, but he is unfair to his client, to the state, and to society if he gives any encouragement to the father that he should have custody of his children. (p. 75)

These words represent not only the perceptions and attitudes of lawyers and of the general public, but also an issue expressed in much of the professional literature and family policy (Girdner, 1985; Woody, 1977). The blunt words just cited stem from stereotypical attitudes toward fathers and their roles in raising children, from unproven theories, and from misinterpretations of studies that seem to give scientific legitimacy to this stereotype. Although rapid changes are occurring in the legal arena, the tender years doctrine is fading all too slowly.

Therefore, this chapter deals first with the myth and reality of fatherhood. It reviews the relevant literature and relates to the current renaissance of interest in and research on and with fathers. This interest leads to a reappraisal of a father's roles and of his significance in his family's and children's lives. We examine the problems faced by the divorced father, both as a man and as a parent, when he is granted the children's custody and when he is not.

FATHERHOOD: MYTH AND REALITY

Historical Perspective

Haim Ginott (1975), a psychologist, remarked that the "natural order" of things forces fathers to take a distant and a secondary role in the caring and raising of children. Margaret Mead (1964) said that although fathers are a biological necessity, they are a social nuisance. Benson (1968), in a sociological and historical analysis of the father's role in the postindustrial era, concluded that fathers indeed were not important figures in their children's lives.

Without attempting a comprehensive historical analysis of the development of the natural order myth, yet to gain some perspective on the issue, it would be helpful to recap the drastic changes in the father's role following the industrial revolution.

The creation of workplaces outside the home and of men becoming hired labor forced a division of roles between men and women in the household. Fathers had to give up their traditional roles in the household and their part in raising the children; women had to stay behind and care for the house and children. The patriarchal structure of the traditional family fell apart. The role of the father became more instrumental, whereas that of the mother became more expressive. She had almost sole responsibility for raising the children; he had almost sole responsibility for providing for the family. Both parents had to learn to be content with their roles.

Because of these changed roles, the fathers were considered to be a distant model for their sons (for their daughters they were not even that), and they were supposed to be a moral and materialistic support to their wives. The social emphasis and push toward materialistic success, the developing new economic order, and the need for the family to be mobile gave further prominence to the nuclear family and brought about an increased rigidity in the division of roles in the family. This division caused, among other problems, the critical confusion about and lack of differentiation between the existing gender roles and the "natural" gender roles. Because women more than men are involved in housework and child care, they are viewed as being more naturally oriented toward (hence better at) an expressive role. The "proof" of nature's intentions was thus found in practice. And yet, despite endless reinforcements to the belief that parenthood is biologically based and not learned, there is no scientifically conclusive evidence to sustain the claim that fathers cannot or should not fully participate in caring for and raising children.

FATHERHOOD: A SCIENTIFIC PERSPECTIVE

Although motherhood has been extensively theorized, researched, and investigated, little scientific attention has been given, until recently, to fatherhood. In 1974, LeMasters published a comprehensive review of the relevant literature; it revealed an almost total disregard of the father, his role in the family, and his influence on children. LeMasters cited studies that support terming the whole of social science's approach to the investigation of the family as women/mothers/wives sociology.

Sears' (1957) classic study, titled "Methods of Child Raising" was based on interviews with 379 mothers—no fathers. Another classic study, conducted by Miller and Swanson (1958), examined the changes of parental roles in U.S. society. It was based on interviews with 582 mothers—again ignoring fathers. The clearest example of the trend of minimizing the importance of the father's role in childrearing is found in the *Handbook of Socialization* (Goslin, 1969) where there are only 5 specific references to fathers (Levine, 1976).

Such total lack of regard of a father's parental role reached absurdity in a study by Pedersen and Robson (1969) entitled "Father Participation in Infancy." The authors wrote: "It causes [us] great embarrassment to report that the actual data on father participation were secured by interviewing the mothers" (p. 467). Other than the writers' unusual candidness, nothing in the study's rationale and execution was, for that time, uncharacteristic.

One of the main reasons for such biased treatment of fathers relates to psychological theories concerning child development. It is not within this book's scope to present a thorough discussion of different theories and the significance they attribute to the father. Suffice to point out the minor role that the father has in caring for and raising his children in Freud's psychoanalytic theory, and the clear role differentiation that Franscois and Balas indicate in their role theory. However, when this chapter mentions theories, it is important to remember that they represent merely an attempt to explain, on the basis of intuition, clues, or "the best explanation," the way in which the world around us behaves. From these theories researchers extracted their assumptions and working hypotheses. Given this process, theoreticians and researchers not only suggest explanations, but also choose the issues and problems that are studied and discussed. Thus, theories not only may offer new insights into the nature of nature but also may limit and divert us from considering and investigating other issues or aspects not represented in a theory.

And so, we did not simply forget the existence of fathers. We ignored them because we were led to believe, on the basis of theories, that fathers are of lesser importance than mothers in their influence of children's development. Because theories are the basis and the rational justification for research questions, studies investigating the relationship between the development of children and the family setting reflect the same relative importance of the father as is represented in the theory. Suffice it to say that until recently, very few questions were asked with regard to the father and his role as a parent; hence, there are few answers. It is possible, therefore, that the relative importance of the father and mother in their children's lives as it is much perceived today, is not a reflection of some natural order but merely a result of particular questions asked. Most research investigating the influence of the father on his children has been conducted by studying families where the father was absent. Following this logic, where researchers found deficiencies in the children's cognitive, social, and emotional development, these problems were attributed to fatherlessness, hence to the lack of his influences (see Adams et al., 1984). Much research has been based and focused on the assumption that father deprivation or his prolonged absence during critical developmental stages will cause the children serious psychological problems. Like Freud, other theoreticians viewed the father as a critical factor (not before the first 3 years, however) in the adequate development of the son. But like Freud, many others had an almost total disregard of the father's significance on his daughter's development. Thus, it was the boy who was "awarded" the center stage of research conducted to appreciate the effect that a father's absence has on children. Still, this type of research did not alter the view as to the importance of the father's role in the family in general and in his children's lives in particular. As before, his role was perceived as being minor.

THE FATHERS' ROLE

In a comprehensive review and analysis of fathers' roles in today's Western society, LeMasters (1974) indicated three characteristics of a father's role:

1. The role of the father is perceived as minor and peripheral to most men, their wives, and their children. His central role is considered to be that of a breadwinner. The father's relationship with his children is often maintained through his wife, who bears the major responsibility for childrearing. When a father does take an active role in the children's day-to-day life and care, it is the mother who usually assigns him that role.
2. LeMasters (1974) characterized the father–child bond as weaker and less natural than the mother–child bond.
3. The father's role is contingent upon the success of his marital life because being a good father and a good husband have much to do with being a good provider: A good father is also a good husband.

To these three role characteristics, there should be added that just as the wife is defined and judged by her success in her role of raising and educating the children in the home, the father is judged by the performance of his duties outside the home (Bernard, 1986). A "real man" or "manliness" is seldom associated with such an expressive role as functional fatherhood (as distinguished from functional husbandhood). Although the quality of the mother–children relationship is a critical factor in determining the quality of a mother's functioning, the quality of fatherhood is determined more by the man's ability to satisfy his family's needs than by the quality of his relationship with his children. Rosenthal and Keshet's (1981) study underscores this point. They found that all participating fathers (N = 98) evaluated themselves as good parents without any real consideration of the time they spent with their children or of their day-to-day involvement in their children's lives.

The modern family's working structure has created a situation where the father's relationship with his children is based on social values and expectations rather than on personal involvement. His relationship has had a practical-instrumental quality and not an emotional-expressive one (Green, 1977). Thus, fathers have been assigned and have adopted the educational role of being some kind of bridge between the child and society. It is, therefore, understandable that many fathers feel more comfortable with their children as the children grow up (Green, 1977). That is because, over time, the link to society becomes not only more important to the child but also something the father knows more about. This crossroad of interests allows the father to partake, for a time, more fully in his child's life. But this involvement, too, diminishes as the child becomes more capable of independently relating to society.

Although some people consider this to be a reliable description of Western societies' perceptions of fatherhood, others judge this description to be not only the right state of affairs but an inevitable one. In an article published by *Parents' Magazine* entitled "Fathers Shouldn't Try to be Mothers," Dr. Bruno Bettelheim (1956) wrote:

> Today's father is often advised to participate in infant care as much as the mother does, so that he, too, will be as emotionally enriched as she. Unfortunately, this is somewhat an empty advice because the male physiology and that part of his psychology based on it are not geared to infant care . . . infant care and child-rearing, unlike choice of work, are not activities in which who should do what can be decided independently of physiology. . . . The relationship between father and child never was and cannot now be built principally around child-caring experiences. It is built around a man's function in society: moral, economic, political. (pp. 124–125)

Almost 20 years later, in his best-selling book, *Between Parents and Children,* Ginott (1975) warned us in much the same way:

> In the modern family . . . many men find themselves involved diapering, and bathing a baby. Though some men welcome these new opportunities for closer contact with their infants, there is a danger that the baby may end up with two mothers, rather than with a mother and a father. (pp. 168–169)

It is hard to evaluate the impact of such statements on our perceptions and beliefs regarding fatherhood. But such declarations made by well-known social scientists help to maintain, indeed provide, scientific justification for the fatherhood stereotype and popular myth. They contribute to the belief that today's dominant structure and division of roles in raising children reflect a natural order of sorts. But does such a natural order exist? Are there biological differences in the capacity of men and women to raise children? Are there inherent differences in the "naturalness" and "strength" in the relationship mothers and fathers can have with their children? Or perhaps the division of labor between the parents represents a social order that is rooted in social conditions and a social heritage?

The "Natural" Gender Role Division

The work of Bowlby, the British psychoanalyst, during the 1940s and 1950s probably had the strongest influence during our time on our perceptions and understanding of the significance of role division between the mother and father in raising children. Bowlby's assertion was that the mother has a natural tendency, which the father does not possess, to care for her offspring. Although Bowlby did not totally disregard the importance of the father's role, he perceived it to be limited and having only indirect influence on the children. The man's main role in raising the children, he judged, is to maintain and support the mother–child relationship (Bowlby, 1958, 1969).

The most popular argument for the difference in men's and women's abilities to care for children is the one that assumes this difference is a result of a biologically determined predisposition. To prove the point, researchers advanced examples of animals' parenting behavior. From their studies in the animal world, researchers (most notably Harlow in the 1960s) learned of the seemingly "natural role division" in parenting behavior between males and females. The results found in animal research (e.g., Moltz, Lubin, Leon, & Numan, 1970; Redican, 1976; Rosenblatt, 1969) were generalized to humans. Such reasoning falls down in two important respects. First, not all findings from the animal world show the same pattern of parenting behavior (Mitchell, 1969; Mitchell, Redican, & Gomber, 1974; Redican, 1976; Rosenblatt, 1969). Second, the validity of the generalization from animals' behavior to that of humans' is highly questionable (Lamb, 1976; Maccoby & Jacklin, 1975). There is, of course, great variance among different species of animals in the amount of male involvement in caring for the young. Some of these differences may, in fact, be explained, as implied by Rosenblatt's (1969) study, by the amount of involvement allowed by the female. The important point is that animal research does not exclusively support the thesis that animals' "fatherly" behavior is biologically impossible.

The second point of difficulty in the predisposition argument results from an attempt to generalize the results of animal research to humans. The problem arises from attributing the same significance to biological factors in human parenting behavior as to those in animal behavior. Maccoby and Jacklin (1975), authors of *The Psychology of Sex Differences,* reviewed hundreds of studies dealing with gender differences among humans. They concluded that "little is known concerning the possible (biological) basis of maternal behavior in species higher than rodents" (p. 216). Lamb (1976) pointed out that the importance of biological predispositions decreases the higher one goes up the phylogenetic scale.

Some anthropologists contest the biological predisposition argument from a different angle. Mead (1964), for instance, found cultural reasons and male chauvinistic motivation to be the forces behind the assumption of a close relationship between biological order and human behavior. In an article published in the mid-1960s, she maintained that claiming that women have an inborn ability to care for children and that children have a biologically rooted dependency on their mothers is "a new and subtle form of anti-feminism in which men, under the guise of exalting the importance of maternity, are tying women more tightly to their children" (p. 480). On the basis of her many studies of different societies where men take an equal role and share the responsibility of raising the children, Mead firmly believed that cultural and not biological factors determine the division of roles in the family and in child care. Similarly, LaBarre's (1954) and Parsons and Bales' (1955) anthropological studies support the notion that the role of fatherhood is not of universal content and construct and, therefore, cannot be biologically determined.

In light of this information, Howell's (1973) conclusion seems appropriate: "The near-exclusive assignment of functional parenting to women is a condition of our society that is not universally shared by all human societies, not even by all primate groups. We should, therefore, remember that the child care usually performed by mothers might be just as well carried on by fathers" (p. 7). Thus, stating that men are biologically unfit for parenthood does little to justify the traditionally limited role of the father.

The Father's Changing Role

Whether the father stereotype ever existed in large numbers is debatable. Today, however, it is evident (e.g., Bernard, 1986; Hanson & Bozett, 1985; Robinson & Barrett, 1986) that any rigid generalization of how fathers function as parents is increasingly missing the point. Although some fathers' involvement in their children's lives is still minimal, others fully share with their wives the responsibility, work, and pleasure of caring for and raising the children. And yet others, in growing numbers, do all that alone.

Today, "there is no accepted theory of fatherhood that necessarily consigns fathers to a secondary role in child care" (Parke, 1981, p. 5). And no respected theory of fatherhood prescribes the father and suggests that his significance and influence on his children's course of development is necessarily minor. Similarly, judging and comparing quantitatively the influences mother and father have on their children (i.e., who has more influence) seem to be a simplistic approach. Such an approach overlooks the qualitatively different, yet still complementary (even compensatory), influences each has on the children.

Many reasons account for this change. New definitions and perceptions of the role that mothers and wives have affect our perceptions of the father's role as well. Because materialistic success is not the only criterion for marital satisfaction (Blumstein & Schwartz, 1983), redefinition of the roles between husband and wife or father and mother has been necessary. Until recently, one might have characterized the division of roles in the family, along with much of the theory and research dealing with the issue, as stemming from two basic myths. First, it is the natural role of the father to be the financial supporter of the family. Second, it is the natural role of the mother to care for the children. The doubt that is placed on the validity of the second myth allows, and in fact encourages, contemporary changes in the woman–mother role both in and out of the home. Although the first myth regarding the father's role is changing, it is still considered by many to be valid. These changes are especially relevant to a divorced father because they greatly affect his adjustment to his new role as a parent and as a single-again man.

As in other areas of the family's life and dynamics, until quite recently little work was done concerning the subject of fatherhood in general and of divorced fathers in particular. But the emergence of interest in fatherhood issues has brought forth a concomitant interest in the divorced father. To date, the subject of divorced fathers has been investigated mainly in regard to their parental functions and postdivorce relationships with their children and former spouses. But the divorced father's difficulties as a person and as a parent, with or without custody of his children, has only very recently been touched upon.

DIVORCED FATHERS

The Impact of Divorce

The findings of many studies support the idea that marriage is psychologically more important for men than for women and that the experience of divorce represents a psychological crisis of greater magnitude for men than for women (Carter & Click, 1976; Goldberg, 1976; Zeiss, Zeiss, & Johnson, 1980). Studies have shown that men are less prone than women to initiate divorce (Hill et al., 1976; Zeiss et al., 1980); that more men than women remarry (Albrecht et al., 1983; Glick, 1984); and that men are more inclined than women to express a desire to resume their relationships with their former spouse (Zeiss et al., 1980).

The most substantial support, however, for the view that men more than women need marriage for their psychological well-being is furnished by research investigating the relationships between sex, marriage, and mental health (Briscoe & Smith, 1973, 1975; Briscoe, Smith, Robins, Marten, & Gaskin 1973). Family status is the most significant social variable accounting for a disparity between the genders in adult psychopathology — namely, that a higher percentage of married women than married men have mental health problems, whereas a greater percentage of divorced men than divorced women have mental health problems. Bloom and Hodges (1981) reported that divorced men were nine times more likely to be admitted to psychiatric hospitals for the first time than men from intact families (for divorced women there is a threefold increase). His data further indicate that admission rates were higher for separated men than for legally divorced men, suggesting that the separation stage is particularly critical and that the crisis ebbs as the divorce process unfolds and ultimately becomes legally final.

Other studies on the effect of divorce on men cited by Atkins and Cath (1989) found that divorced fathers are nine times more likely to be hospitalized for psychiatric reasons than married fathers. Separated and divorced men are also overrepresented in surveys of successful suicide, homicides, and deaths caused by a variety of medical illnesses. The greatest risk for stress-related morbidity seems to exist around the time of separation.

In his attempt to explain these figures, Bachrach (1975) invoked stress theory, selectivity theory, and role theory. Stress theory assumes that personal crises may cause an individual's latent tendencies and problems to become manifest. According to the selectivity theory, persons with different psychological structures tend to have different family statuses. That is, the conditions of being single or married have to do with "states of mind" that are associated with varying chances of a person becoming subject to mental problems. This would account for the high frequency of mental problems among people who have never married, as well as the tendency among some persons who do marry to divorce.

Finally, role theory proposes that the different roles assumed by people with respect to different marital statuses are connected with the degrees of exposure to situations of high psychological risk entailed by each marital status. Accordingly, the condition of being divorced is inherently more risky than that of being married. And it might also be argued that the condition of being a divorced parent without custody of children (the situation of most men in this category) is psychologically more risky than being a divorced parent with custody (as are most women in this category).

From the foregoing, two main hypotheses may be extracted. First, marital discord may be a result of psychological problems, which then serve as mediating variables in the change of marital status. Second, the change in marital status may create different stressful situations, which account for the differences in psychopathological response. Thus, although there is an evident relationship between family crisis and an individual's physical or mental health problems, it is difficult to pinpoint the reasons why this relationship should be so (Bachrach, 1975).

Some research indicates that single fathers have basically similar emotional reactions and feelings as single mothers (LeMasters & DeFrain, 1983; Orthner et al., 1976). In the work of LeMasters and DeFrain, both fathers and mothers viewed the divorce process as stressful and described the reactions of friends and family in a similar way. Single fathers, however, more than single mothers encouraged their children to take sides in disagreements with the ex-spouse. Contrary to the image of the swinging playboy after the divorce, custodial and noncustodial single fathers suffer serious emotional and physical effects (Roman, 1977; Roman & Haddad, 1978; Silver & Silver, 1981). Typically, single fathers undergo a great deal of stress and describe an array of feelings such as anger, sadness, resentment, and depression (Grief, 1985; Keshet & Rosenthal, 1978; Miller, 1982). Feelings of inadequacy and uncertainty about future relationships with children are also reported in these studies. Loneliness and social isolation are, however, the major problems reported by most men following divorce (Smith & Smith, 1981; White & Bloom, 1981). Loneliness and a sense of loss of spouse and children are especially hard for noncustodial fathers.

Variables Associated With Adjustment

A person's ability to reestablish psychological balance following a crisis derives from the combined influence of a great many variables. The most important of these are age, gender, prior psychological stability, education, socioeconomic status, number of crises occurring simultaneously, past experience in dealing with stress, and availability of support systems at the time of crisis (Falek & Britton, 1974). In divorce, other variables are significant as well. These include the number of years that the marriage has lasted; the extent of commitment invested in the relationship; the attitudes toward gender roles; the degree of self-esteem; the quality of the current relationship with the former spouse and with other family members; and who it was that initiated the divorce (Blair, 1970; Brown & Manela, 1978; Chiriboga & Cutler, 1977; Chiriboga et al., 1978; Gray, 1978; Hetherington et al., 1978; Norton & Click 1976; Spanier & Casto, 1979; Weiss, 1975).

The presence of such a diversity of independent variables complicates efforts to assess the influence of each variable. Few studies have managed to control all these variables, and whatever generalizations may be made must be treated with circumspection. When the time that elapsed since separation of the partners was singled out as a variable, it was found that the period immediately following separation was probably more difficult for the man than for the woman (Chester, 1971; Chiriboga & Cutler, 1977; Weiss, 1975). Separation in divorce means confronting the social and practical manifestations of being single again. A deepening of the crisis reaction takes place (Krantzler, 1975; Toomin, 1974), and the resultant "impact of stress" arouses feelings of confusion and loss of direction (Jacobs, 1982).

Hetherington et al. (1976) studied 48 divorced fathers and found that 2 months after the divorce, the fathers were spending more time at work, in household and solitary activities, or with friends. They had a great need to avoid solitude and inactivity. Many men began to lose contact with old friends, and dating and casual sexual encounters were more frequent throughout the first year. Two years after the divorce, these men were still complaining of feeling shut out, rootless, and at loose ends. Most fathers yearned for intimate love and stable relationships, which they considered paramount for their own happiness and self-esteem.

Initially, most of these men did not get along well with their ex-wives. Their relationship with former partners was characterized by acrimony, anger, feeling of desertion, resentment, and memories of painful conflicts. By the end of 2 years, however, both conflict and attachment between the ex-spouses had substantially decreased. Although about one third of the fathers reported an excited sense of freedom immediately following the divorce, this feeling changed with—and by 1 year had been replaced by—depression, anxiety, or apathy. By the end of the 2-year follow-up all these effects had markedly decreased. This development in men's reaction to divorce was generally found also in Greif's (1979) and in Keshet and Rosenthal's (1978) studies.

The variables found to have had the most significant effect on the magnitude of the impact of stress experienced by divorced men are separation from the children (Asher & Bloom, 1983), loss of familiar and institutionalized activities (Kessler, 1975; Weiss, 1975), and the need to learn new roles and behaviors (Hunt, 1966; Krantzler, 1975). Even the issue of deciding what to do in one's spare time—which had formerly been devoted to activities centered around the house—is problematic because it accentuates the feelings of emptiness and being alone. White and Asher (1976) interviewed 30 men who had been divorced 6–12 months earlier. Apart from the difficulties that they reported regarding their work, finances, and management of their household, most of these men felt that the biggest problem they faced was loneliness. The level of adjustment to separation among divorced men was inversely correlated with their dependence on their wives during marriage; it was positively correlated with their establishment of an independent social network.

Theoreticians and researchers stressed the important part that is played by social support networks and social reactions in the divorce experience. Although society furnishes models of conduct and defines the roles of married men, it does not do so for divorced men (Johnson, 1977). In the absence of a socially sanctioned role model, divorced men are unsure about how they should behave and relate to their children, their ex-wives, their families and friends, and society at large. Similarly, although there are norms, rituals, and traditions to guide and assist us in coping with bereavement, there are none that perform the same service in regard to divorce (Freund, 1974). This sense of a "social void" accounts for the findings of Hetherington et al. (1976), who reported that divorced fathers claim that they have lost their identity and roots. Divorced fathers view their lives as lacking in structure, and they are troubled by feelings of loss, guilt, anxiety, and depression.

Some of these feelings are closely associated with having left familiar surroundings. Because men do not ordinarily obtain custody of their children following a divorce, they are almost always the ones to leave home; in about half the cases, they also leave the neighborhood (Asher & Bloom, 1983). Indeed, men's mobility following divorce has been found to be inversely related to their adjustment and mental health (Bachrach, 1973; Bloom et al., 1978; Levinger & Moles, 1979; Pihl & Caron, 1980). Although the very fact of moving away may itself contribute to the adjustment difficulties of divorced fathers, it may also be plausibly argued that those among them who are better able to adjust tend to remain near their former home rather than "run away." When divorced men were questioned about their main cause of moving away, 55% cited work as the principal reason. The second most important reason was their need to distance themselves from their former spouses. However, when researchers compared the level of adjustment to divorce between men who had left the vicinity of their former home and those who had remained, the latter adjusted more successfully (Asher & Bloom, 1983).

Many single fathers are able to cope with their initial feeling of loss, depression, and anxiety and usually do not feel the need for counseling (Chang & Deinard, 1982). The ability to adjust well to divorce was associated with personal characteristics such as high intelligence, assertiveness, a creative and imaginative approach to resolving problems, self-confidence, openness to personal and social experiences, and independence (Thomas, 1982). As much as these attributes are undeniably important for adjustment, their becoming manifest depends on the particular life circumstances of the individual. One of the paramount aspects of the life situations of most divorced fathers is that they do not have custody of their children.

VISITATION FATHERS

A Historical Perspective

Prior to the 20th century, fathers were automatically granted custody of their children. Both the law and practice in those days were based on the premise that a father had a sacred and virtually inviolable right to bring up his own legitimate children (McKee & O'Brien, 1982). Just how much attitudes have changed in this regard may be gauged from the following remark of Judge L. J. Bowen, who stated in "Re Agar-Ellis," 1883: "To neglect the natural jurisdiction of the father over the child until the age of twenty-one would be really to set aside the whole course and order of nature and it seems to me it would disturb the very foundation of family life" (as quoted in Lowe, 1982, pp. 27–28).

However, the reasoning that was reflected in Judge Bowen's statement was merely one upshot of philosophy that granted social status and rights to men, but on the whole denied them to women and children. Given women's lowly legal and social standing at the time, and their inability to adequately support themselves and their children on their own, they were very unlikely to obtain custody of their children (Derdeyn, 1976).

The status of women and children began to alter in the late 19th and early 20th centuries, along with the dramatic changes brought on by the industrial revolution. These changes were also a result of the general climate of progress that attended a transformation of the means of production. The idea that a child was the father's property was gradually supplanted by the view that children had rights of their own. The role of mothers altered as well under the impact of the industrial revolution because they were constrained to remain at home and to care for their children. This circumstance helped to bring about a change of view concerning the importance of mothers in the life of their children. Finally, the activities of the women's suffrage movement, and later the work of notable thinkers such as Freud and Bowlby, augmented consciousness of the vital role of mothers—especially in the early years of childhood. These changes of attitude affected the way in which courts ruled in child custody disputes.

The bias favoring mothers since the middle of this century (although there has been some degree of change in this regard during the last few years) has been such that about the only way in which a father could obtain custody was to prove that the mother was unfit to raise the child (Orthner et al., 1976). Most courts adhere to the tender years doctrine, which has dominated divorce and custody proceedings. Therefore, typically, fathers have had nothing close to equal rights in child custody disputes (Bernstein, 1977). Only in 1973 did the case of *Watts v. Watts* (1973) in the New York court system recommend that the tender years principle be discarded because "it is based on outdated social stereotypes rather than a rational up-to-date consideration of the welfare of the children involved" (p. 288).

In roughly 90% of custody dispute cases that are adjudicated in U.S. courts today, the mother is awarded custody of the children (Seltzer & Bianchi, 1988). This imbalance is not merely a result of arbitrary judicial decisions and practice. Of divorced couples, 80% enter the courtroom after having already decided that the mother should receive custody (Kohen et al., 1979). Thus, the high proportion of cases in which mothers are awarded custody is the result of a combination of factors that include the will of the parents, the orientation of the court, and the force of circumstances that both parents have to take into account in planning for their lives after the divorce. Because the income of most men is higher than their wives' current or potential earnings, it is easier for men to continue working after the divorce than for the woman either to continue to work or to begin a career. However, more important is the fact that no matter how much a father may have been involved with his children prior to the divorce, it was probably the mother who carried the greater burden in bringing up the children. It was this fact that enabled her to develop her skills as a parent, educator, and homemaker. As a result, the children became more dependent on her than on the father; once that relationship is formed it is not easily modified or changed. Moreover, the children and the mother (and in some cases the father as well) may actually fear altering the relationship. The recognition both by the courts and by the parents that awarding custody to the father would require a greater change in the parent–child relationship than if the mother were awarded custody has been translated into custody agreements that effectively separate the father from his children.

Away From the Children

Being apart from their children is the most painful experience for divorced fathers and it significantly affects their adjustment. Some researchers see divorce as the father's "child-centered crisis" (Jacobs, 1983). Hetherington et al. (1976) reported that of the 48 fathers who had been affectionate parents and highly involved with their children while married, 8 could not tolerate the pain and frustration of intermittent contact with their children. Two years after the divorce, these fathers had decreased their visits with the children in order to lessen their own unhappiness. They still, however, continued to experience a great sense of loss and depression. This was true even for those fathers who remarried.

Greif (1979) studied 40 divorced fathers who differed widely in the amount of contact they were allowed to have with their children. Of these men, 60% developed physical symptoms such as weight loss, dental problems, headaches, rheumatoid arthritis, and hypertension. The fathers who experienced "child absence" have shown signs of depression and difficulty in sleeping, eating, working, and socializing. Many of these fathers felt overwhelmed by feelings of loss of their children and devaluation of themselves as parents. Given such feelings of exclusion, it is not surprising that one third of the fathers in Fulton's (1979) study took issue with the custody decisions of the court and that many more regretted not having fought to obtain custody of their children at the time.

In *Part-Time Father,* Atkin and Rubin (1976) pointed out that many men are fearful of losing significance in their children's lives. In a recent study, Maccoby, Depner, and Mnookin (1990) reported that only about 17% of divorced parents were able to functionally "co-parent" and have the fathers play significant roles in their children's life. And Dominic and Schlesinger (1980) found that "a great many fathers . . . were afraid that the children would experience the separation as a desertion on their part [and] that their ex-spouses might attempt to antagonize the children against them" (p. 246). The father's wish to remain significant in his children's life, on the one hand, and the painful experience associated with being a part-time parent, on the other, is probably the most difficult approach–avoidance conflict facing the divorced noncustodial father.

Visiting Fatherhood

It has been reported that many divorced fathers forego their rights of regular visits with their children (Greif, 1985; Maidment, 1984; Mott, 1990; Seltzer & Bianchi, 1988; Wallerstein & Kelly, 1980b). These parental visits reach a peak about 2 months after the divorce and dramatically decline shortly afterward (Hetherington, 1979); they are most frequent when the children are ages 2 to 8 and least frequent when the children are 9 to 15 years old (Wallerstein & Kelly, 1980b). The typical pattern is that visitation is maintained on a fairly stable level for the first 2 years, then declines. Furstenberg (1982, 1983) found that fewer than one half of the national sample of approximately 500 children had seen their father even once during the preceding year, and fewer than one sixth of the children saw their fathers as often as once a week. And when the frequency of the visits declined, so did the phone calls and the letters. Money for child support was maintained for a longer time than visitation, but it too declined over time (Francke, 1983; Furstenberg & Spanier, 1984).

Other researchers (e.g., Greif, 1984; Luepnitz, 1982) found that only between 20% and 40% of single fathers maintained regular visits with their children. Following a review of the relevant research, Maidment (1984) commented, "For many noncustodial parents, divorce not only ends their marriage but also their participation as parents" (p. 238).

Yet many divorced fathers appear to be dissatisfied with the extent of their influence on their children and with the cooperation they receive from the mother regarding the children's education and upbringing (Fulton, 1979; Maidment, 1984). Many divorced fathers have claimed that their former wives prevented their real involvement in their children's lives; by not sharing relevant information with these men, their ex-wives diminished the fathers' significance in the eyes of the children (Goldsmith, 1980).

There seemed to be a contradiction between the statistics revealing the low frequency of visits of divorced fathers with their children and the findings that show fathers to be fearful of the attenuation of their ties with their children. Studies of divorced fathers indicated five possible explanations for this contradiction.

Cultural Biases.   As we noted before, our culture implies that fatherhood is not very important. The visitation father who rarely visits with his children is merely following this implication to its conclusion. Some self-help books dealing with divorced families actually counsel fathers to give up visitation when children do not want to visit him or when the relationship between the parents is conflictual (Atkin & Rubin, 1976; Gardner, 1978). Goldstein et al., (1973) even suggested that "once it is determined who will be the custodial parent, it is that parent, not the court, who must decide under what conditions he or she wishes to raise the child. Thus, the noncustodial parent should have no legally enforceable right to visit the child" (pp. 37–38). Although these types of statements are not common any more, their impact or the attitudes they reflect still affect noncustodial fathers.

Visitation That is Emotionally Difficult.   Many fathers claim that distancing themselves from their children is their way of combating the pain entailed in the visits (Furstenberg, 1982, 1983). Some fathers seem to go as far as to cultivate "a certain numbness" about their children, not wanting to even think about them because these thoughts are too painful (Loewen, 1988). Feelings of anger and unfairness are almost always built into visitation. Having to ask to see one's children can be a demeaning experience (Sturner, 1983). Fear of being rejected by the children also threatens fathers.

Another painful aspect of visitation is the fathers' sense of diminishing significance in their children's lives (Anderson-Khleif, 1982; Wedermeyer, 1984). Only one fifth of the fathers in Furstenberg's (1983) sample felt that they had much influence over their children. So rather than experiencing the pain of watching their children turn into strangers, some fathers withdrew from the relationship altogether. This action created a vicious cycle in which the father's perception of his waning significance to his children was only reinforced by the pain-avoidance strategy he had adopted, which had the effect of augmenting his estrangement.

The Artificiality in Visiting Parenthood. Maintaining a close and meaningful bond by adhering to a rigid visitation schedule tends to obstruct the natural ebb and flow of a normal relationship. As Wedermeyer (1984) said, "Parents and children who see each other infrequently and only under visiting circumstances tend to lose the sense of intimacy they used to have" (pp. 109–110). Conjoined to discourage the father from visiting are the facts that the father often lacks experience in dealing with his children, he often lacks suitable living accommodations, and he has problems of where and what to do with the children.

Fathers' Other Commitments. As important as their parental role is, divorced fathers have many other roles and commitments. While married, fathers have the flexibility to interact with their children whenever they can and want. When fathers are divorced, the rigid visitation schedule may often create a conflict in their commitments, a conflict that may cause fathers to cancel a planned meeting with the children without having the ability to compensate themselves and the children for the lost time. Also, as Wedermeyer (1984) observed, "Seeing their children infrequently simply makes the children seem less important and less central to their lives. . . . Four days a month of seeing your children may not seem sufficiently important to refuse a job promotion which requires a move to another city or state" (pp. 109–110).

The effects of remarriage on visitation seem to be mixed. Hetherington (1982) found that father's remarriage usually brings a decrease in visitations. Kerpelman (1983) noted that a father's remarriage frequently caused renewed conflicts between the former spouses over the issue of visitation. Furstenberg (1983), however, observed that although in some cases, remarriage aggravated tensions between ex-spouses, in many other cases it actually helped to put aside some old, unresolved conflicts.

Conflict With Custodial Parent. Although the previous four reasons are undoubtedly important, the relationship between the ex-spouses accounts for the most variance in the postseparation involvement of fathers with their children (Koch & Lowery, 1984). Researchers have found that as many as half of all custodial mothers resist the father's visitations (Ambrose, Harper, & Pemberton, 1983; Anderson-Khleif, 1982; Furstenberg, 1983; Goldsmith, 1980) even if, when asked, these women claim to be supportive of the father's visits (Wallerstein & Kelly, 1980b). Thus, a father who does not visit with his children may, in fact, be responding to his ex-spouse's pressure and/or expectations (Bohannan, 1985; Maidment, 1984). A father's visitation is often affected by his ex-wife's perception of his ability to be an effective parent, her still-unresolved feeling about the divorce, and the children's needs. Because her available time with the children also decreases due to her increased workload and the father's visitation, she too may become jealous of every opportunity to be with the children (Francke, 1983).

Ex-spouses often do not perceive visitation in the same way. Custodial mothers may see a father's visits as "regular and reliable," whereas the ex-spouse may see it very differently (Anderson-Khleif, 1982). Very different also is the power and control each parent has over the children and over allowing the visitation to take place. Custodial mothers have far more power than noncustodial fathers in determining "guidelines for routine visits . . . setting down rules and limits, and in making final decisions on the extent of visitation allowed" (Anderson-Khleif, 1982, p. 94).

When the ex-spouse's relationship is hostile, as is often the case (Anderson-Khleif, 1982; Hetherington, 1982; Wallerstein & Kelly, 1980b), the details of the visiting could become a weapon against the visitation parent (Wallerstein & Kelly, 1980b). The custodial parent can make scheduling the visit difficult "in a thousand mischievous, mostly petty devices designed to humiliate the visiting parent and to deprecate him in the eyes of his children" (Wallerstein & Kelly, 1980b, p. 125). Under these circumstances, the noncustodial parent may be inclined to avoid visits in order to escape the humiliation in this unequal power relationship. With this in mind, Anderson-Khleif (1982) concluded that "Just as women who try to collect child support often give up, fathers who cannot 'collect' their visitation rights give up. They just get worn down" (p. 109).

Visitation and Fathers' Adjustment to Divorce

Greif's (1979, 1982, 1985) studies and others (e.g., Hetherington et al., 1976; Wallerstein & Kelly, 1980b) suggest that just as a child's postdivorce adjustment is enhanced by regular and frequent contact with his or her father, fathers who spend the most time with their children tend to be less depressed and better adjusted following a divorce. Frequent and regular visits with children help fathers feel they are important to the children, are still part of a family, and have reasons to live and work for (Little, 1982). Fathers who kept up visitation said that they "felt closer to their children than they did before the separation" (Rosenthal & Keshet, 1981, p. xii). They found that the time they spent alone with the children added to the intensity and meaningfulness of their relationship. They enjoyed doing things for and with the children.

Hetherington (1979) noted that "there is little continuity between the quality of pre- and post-separation parent–child interaction, particularly for fathers" (p. 855). Some fathers rediscover their children and their fatherhood after the divorce. This may be so because, although divorced, presence can no longer serve as a cover for inaction. In a two-parent home, the father is assured of the availability of his children. But once he leaves, his fatherhood must be "earned." When his children are not permanently available to him and he is afraid of losing them, then he becomes aware of the greater need and his will and ability to invest time and effort in his relationship with them.

Maintaining visitations helps fathers stay in touch with their own feelings and even challenges their old values and hierarchy of needs and importances. Some fathers reported that visitation not only increased their sense of purpose but also gave them a sense of heroism and exhilaration that they had persevered in face of legal and cultural odds (Brandt, 1982).

A noncustodial father who maintains an extensive visitation schedule is awarded with more support from family and friends than otherwise (Loewen, 1988). Family and friends help these fathers struggle with their sometimes conflicting commitments, with learning their new roles of fatherhood, and with day-to-day management of the children.

A significantly growing number of fathers, both married and divorced, are intent on actualizing their potential for positive psychological presence in the lives of their children. This is a consequence of the increasing awareness among men of their need to realize their expressive selves. Doubtless the enhanced awareness among married and divorced women that they must share the duties and pleasures of raising children with men in order to actualize their instrumental selves must also have a significant effect on the situation.

SINGLE-FATHER FAMILIES

Background and Statistics

The category of a single father having a family includes families that are different in a very fundamental way. Some men may have adopted children, others may have the children because of a spouse's death, and still others may have the children following separation or divorce. Even fathers in one-parent families as a result of separation or divorce are not a homogeneous group. Fathers who have insisted on or fought for the custody of their children must be distinguished from those who have the children by mutual agreement, because of the children's choice, or because they had no choice because the mother neglected, abandoned, or did not want the children. As this distinction has rarely been investigated, a discussion of the issues must be limited to a broad general account.

Single-father families have appeared in the literature only since the mid-1970s. Some researchers have written about the subject from a personal perspective (e.g., Krantzler, 1975), others have offered practical advice (e.g., Bowskill, 1980; Brown, 1985), and still others have described the involvement of professionals in attempting to assist such families (Brown & Stones, 1979). And quite a number of empirical studies have been carried out that investigate families in which the father is the only parent.

It is estimated that of single-parent families, 89% are headed by mothers and 11% headed by fathers (U.S. Bureau of the Census, 1985). Due to the changing ideology about gender role stereotypes and the changes in the social and the courts' attitudes toward custodial fathers, there has recently been an increase in the number of fathers who ask for and are awarded custody of their children. Following separation or divorce, the number of father-custodial families increased from 241,000 in 1970 to 683,000 in 1984 (U.S. Bureau of the Census, 1985). Lewis (1978) estimated that the number of children living with their father was more than twice the reported 1.5 million because of informal custody arrangements made between parents. With the same reasoning, one may argue that the number of father-custodial families today exceeds 1 million.

Although most custodial fathers have sole custody of their children, some arrangements are part of a split-custody agreement (one parent receives sole custody of one or more children); others are part of a joint-custody agreement (both parents have equal responsibilities for the welfare of all children). Based on very small samples, statistics show (Weitzman, 1985) that fathers are now winning custody in as many as 38% of contested cases in Alameda, California ($n = 13$) and 33% in Los Angeles County ($n = 15$). Of the fathers in a much larger sample ($n = 1,136$), 19% reported winning custody when it was contested (Greif, 1985). These numbers are significantly higher than the latest national statistics indicate (U.S. Bureau of the Census, 1985). Because most of these investigations cover small samples, we need to await further study to learn the current national statistics.

The Research and its Limitation

Much of the results of the studies dealing with single-father families have limited generalizability, especially because of the lack of representativeness of the samples. Most samples in these studies are too small to be representative of any but a very limited part of the population of divorced fathers. Fathers in the lower income brackets and even some with middle-class incomes are prevented either financially or by the nature of their work from adopting the sort of flexible lifestyle that is required to look after children. For this reason such men are highly unlikely either to demand or be granted custody. Although this discussion points up an important social factor that differentiates between fathers who obtain custody of their children and those who do not, it also militates against our ability to generalize about divorced fathers who live with their children and, even more importantly, about the effect of such an arrangement on their children.

Another problem concerning the representativeness of samples in this field derives from the social and individual differences among fathers with regard to their willingness to participate in research studies. It could be argued that fathers who do not fare well will be more reluctant to participate in an investigation. And fathers who need to work hard and for long hours will also tend not to be represented in these studies. Even in a large, heterogeneous sample such as the one used by Katz (1979), the researcher was unable to make up a suitable control group of single-parent families headed by mothers. As a result, it was impossible to assess the particular difficulties that fathers encountered in raising their children alone.

Moreover, the data-collecting methods used in the studies of single-father families varied greatly and, therefore, their comparison was much restricted. In some studies, the subjects were interviewed (McKee & O'Brien, 1982; Mendes, 1976); in others, they were given questionnaires (e.g., Chang & Deinard, 1982; Greif, 1985); and in other instances, information was gathered by asking former wives and the children about the father (e.g., Ambert, 1982; Hanson, 1985).

Most studies were descriptive. Some, however, went beyond description and compared custodial to noncustodial fathers (Gersick, 1979); intact to single-father families (Santrock & Warshak, 1979); widowed to divorced custodial fathers (Greif, 1985; Katz, 1979); and father with different kinds of custody (Hanson, 1986a; Hanson & Trilling, 1983).

With this comparison in mind, the following discussion examines the reasons for fathers' custody, the unique characteristics of these men, how their children fare, and how they live and cope.

Reasons for Custody

Single fathers give various reasons why they have the custody of their children. In Greif's (1985) study, for instance, 37% of 1,136 fathers cited "mutual agreement" as one of two reasons for having custody; 26% said that "the children picked" them; 22% said that they "offered a more financially and emotionally secure home"; 20% claimed that their wives "could not handle the children"; and 19% said they "won a custody suit." Some other researchers made a more global distinction and differentiated only between two types of reasons: (a) actively seeking custody, and (b) resigning to it or having it by default (Gasser & Taylor, 1976; Green, 1977; Hanson, 1981; Mendes, 1976, 1979; Risman, 1986). Most often, however, fathers had custody because of an uncontested arrangement (e.g., Chang & Deinard, 1982; Greif, 1984, 1985; Risman, 1986).

Fathers who had been extensively involved with their children prior to divorce were more likely to seek and fight for custody and were better equipped both physically and emotionally to assume the single-parent role (Hanson, 1986a, 1986b; Mendes, 1976, 1979; Risman, 1986). In the studies reported, these fathers were found to adjust better and faster to their single-parent role than those who assented to custody, although the latter fathers also learned and adjusted to their role.

Men tended to seek custody, generally, for positive reasons. Chang and Deinard (1982), for example, found that most single fathers wanted custody because they considered themselves to be better parents. Very few men sought custody to spite their former wives or thought that their former spouses were unfit mothers (Greif, 1985; Risman, 1986). In fact, many single fathers thought that their children's mother could care for the children as well as they could but these fathers "just happened to have the custody at this time" (Hanson, 1988, p. 180). But regardless of the reasons for having custody, these men, as a group, were not the average group of men one would randomly find, not even among divorced men.

Fathers' Characteristics

The majority of studies investigating male single parents yielded very similar results. Virtually all U.S. demographic reports indicated that divorced fathers who had custody were at the higher socioeconomic levels. They had higher than average income. For instance, almost half of the 80 fathers in Chang and Deinard's (1982) study earned over $20,000 a year, and the median income of 1,136 fathers investigated by Greif (1985) was $30,000. Custodial fathers also had a higher than average educational level. Of the 20 fathers in the study by Orthner et al. (1976), 80% had post-high school education; 50% of the 141 fathers investigated by Risman (1986) had BA degrees or higher; and the mean number of years of formal education in Greif's (1985) study was 14.6. Studies showed these fathers were mostly white-collar professionals and about 90% of them were Caucasian (Chang & Deinard, 1982; Greif, 1984; Risman, 1986). Higher socioeconomic status, however, was not the characteristic of most fathers in studies in Canada, England, and Australia, where single fathers were men from all social and socioeconomic levels (Bain, 1973; George & Wilding, 1972; Katz, 1979; Schlesinger, 1980, 1982b).

Another exception is the U.S. military where many custodial fathers are non-White (Orthner & Bowen, 1983). Although not much is known about the religious affiliation of single fathers, its distribution seems to approximate that of the general U.S. population (Hanson, 1981; Risman, 1986).

Single fathers in the research literature were found to range in age from 30 to 54, with a mean of 40 and below (Chang & Deinard, 1982; Greif, 1984, 1985; McKee & O'Brien, 1982), which are the childrearing years for most fathers. The ages of these custodial fathers also indicated that their children were more often than not, adolescents.

Notwithstanding the lack of independent outside evidence, many studies have suggested that divorced fathers with custody excel in nurturing skills, and that they are not only warm, assertive, and self-confident but are well able to organize and manage the tasks of everyday living (Bartz & Witcher, 1978; Gersick, 1979; Hanson, 1985; 1986a, 1986c; Orthner et al., 1976; Risman, 1986; Rosenthal & Keshet, 1981). Analyzing custodial fathers' reports, Smith (1976) found four major characteristics among fathers who managed to overcome the difficulties entailed in childrearing with relative ease. These characteristics account for the high level of adjustment attained by these men. Prior to their divorces, these fathers were greatly involved in bringing up their children; they shared the responsibilities of housekeeping, had some theoretical knowledge of children and their development, and maintained a warm and loving two-way relationship with their offspring. Thus, becoming a sole parent appeared to be easier for men who possess a high level of self-confidence and self-motivation, who required no social approval of their success as parents, and who had the knowledge and resources to meet the emotional and general needs of their children. It is unclear why some men would seek the role of primary caretakers when men are generally not supposed to be prepared or socialized for such a role. Custodial fathers were not more likely to come from divorced homes. Interestingly, the men who had custody of their children had had a more intense relationship with their own mothers and had been more distant from their fathers than the men who did not have custody who were closer to both parents. The mothers of these custodial fathers generally had assumed more complete responsibility for child care and had worked more outside the home (Gersick, 1979). These men may have patterned themselves after their mothers, who provided a child-oriented model of parenting. The intriguing aspect of this pattern, in Gersick's (1979) words, is that "men from traditional families are more likely to make the extremely nontraditional decision to seek custody of their children" (p. 320).

Children in the Custody of Fathers

Although fathers have custody of both boys and girls of all ages, some studies reported that the number of boys exceeded that of girls (Chang &

Deinard, 1982; Greif, 1985; Hanson, 1986b). Although the numbers of boys and girls were equal in single-mother families (U.S. Bureau of the Census, 1980), studies showed that, on the average, 57% of single fathers had custody of boys, and 43% had custody of girls (Ambert, 1982; Hanson, 1981). In some cases, the father had custody of the boys, whereas the mother had custody of the girls. It would appear that men sought custody of their sons and that the courts assumed that fathers were better parents to boys than to girls.

Few researchers have investigated the influence of the mother's absence on children who live only with their father. Early research on the subject of the mother's absence was concerned with parental rather than maternal deprivation, so it offered little of relevance to the present discussion.

The data contained in some earlier research studies (e.g., DeFrain & Eirick, 1981; Lowenstein & Koopman, 1978; Schlesinger, 1978) suggested that children in custody of one parent revealed lower levels of self-confidence and that they experienced some behavioral problems immediately following their parents' divorce. However, after a few months, they showed signs of adjustment to their new situation, and their conduct greatly improved over time.

Guttmann (1982) compared 15 mother-custody children (7 boys and 8 girls) with 15 father-custody children (8 boys and 7 girls) with regard to their school performance as assessed by teachers, their popularity in class as assessed by a sociometry tests, and the extent of their dependency. No significant differences were found either in the main effects of the parent's or child's gender or in the interactions. Lowenstein and Koopman (1978), too, have reported no significant effects in comparing the self-concept of boys living only with their fathers with that of boys living only with their mothers.

Santrock and Warshak (1979; Warshak & Santrock, 1983) found significant effects in what is to date the most intensive series of studies of single-father families. The results of their studies are based on a sample of 60 White, middle-class families with children from 6 to 11 years old; 33 of the children were boys and 27 were girls. One third of the children came from single-father families, one third from single-mother families, and one third from intact families. The three types of families were matched for socioeconomic status, family size, and age of children. The two groups of children from single-parent families were also matched for the child's age when parents separated and for sibling status. The parents had been separated for an average of 2.9 years.

The studies' results were based on a careful evaluation of how a custodial father, a custodial mother, and a matched-for-gender parent from an intact family related to their children in a problem-solving task in the laboratory. These results also included interviews with the parents and children. The overall findings suggested that children who lived with the same-gender parent were better adjusted than those who lived with opposite-gender parent. For boys, paternal custody appeared to be beneficial: The boys were less demanding, more mature, socially competent, and independent than boys in maternal custody. For girls, maternal custody appeared best: They were less demanding and more independent, mature, and sociable.

When children from single-parent families were compared with children from intact families, an interesting and puzzling picture emerged. Boys in their mothers' custody showed higher self-esteem and less anxiety than boys from intact families; for girls, the opposite was true. They showed lower self-esteem and more anxiety than girls from intact families. Boys from single-father families were "much more" socially competent; had higher self-esteem; were more sociable, mature, and independent; were less demanding; and were observed to be warmer in their interactions with their fathers than boys from intact families were with their fathers. Girls from single-father families fared worse. They showed lower self-esteem and were less mature, warm, sociable, conforming, and independent with their fathers than girls from intact families.

Santrock and Warshak (1979) correlated three parenting styles—authoritative, authoritarian, and laissez faire—with the ratings of the children's behavior in their interactions with their parents. Regardless of the custodial arrangement, authoritative parenting that was associated with warmth and with setting clear rules and regulations yielded significant results: These children showed higher self-esteem and more warmth, social conformity, sociability, and maturity.

Although there may be no inherent reasons that boys living with their fathers should fare better than those living with their mothers, the data indicate this to be the case. These findings, however, can be partially accounted for by variables that do not bear directly on the quality of parenting.

First, studies that have based their conclusions on the self-reports of fathers (even Warshak & Santrock, 1983, based some results on interviews with fathers) may reflect the strong wish of the respondents to represent themselves as succeeding in their parental roles, whereas the actual situation of their children may be different. Second, the close scrutiny to which fathers are submitted before being granted custody of their children may ensure that those who actually obtain custody are the most suitable for the job. Third, some evidence suggests that fathers who are sole parents are more likely than their female counterparts to receive practical assistance in their child-care activities (Ferri, 1976; Santrock & Warshak, 1979). Interview studies have indicated that there is no shortage of sympathy from the community for such fathers (McKee & O'Brien, 1982). Teachers, for example, were found to be very supportive of single fathers, often providing them with the needed information on child development matters (Briggs & Walters, 1985). Finally, the secure financial circumstances of these fathers may place them in a position of being able to prevent their children from appearing to have problems, although their children might actually be problematic.

Managing Life and Parenthood

Because the role of the father in a single-parent family has yet to be institutionalized and because both the social system and the workplace have so far failed to recognize the special demands of such a lifestyle, men in this position are constrained to alter the patterns of their lives in radical ways (Mendes, 1976). To meet the demands of single parenthood, men reported that they had to make substantial adjustments in their personal and professional priorities. They had to alter their attitudes toward success in their careers, the number of hours they dedicated to work, and the necessity of realizing professional opportunities (Chang & Deinard, 1982; Mendes, 1976). These adjustments can be greatly complicated by the absence of appropriate models, by the widespread prejudices concerning parenthood, and by the inexperience of men in running a household. Not only do such factors complicate and make difficult the task of adjustment, but they may also discourage a great many men from even trying.

During the first year following divorce, fathers with sole custody tend to keep to themselves and their homes. Most have reported experiencing feelings of loneliness and depression, and a few complain of physical problems that, by their own assessment, are related to their psychological state (e.g., Chang & Deinard, 1982; Hanson, 1986b). Yet when asked about their general well-being, many men characterized it as being good, even during the difficult first year of their single parentage (Risman, 1986; Rosenthal & Keshet, 1981). It is possible that in their response to a direct question of this kind, they merely wished to present their situations — and therefore themselves — in a favorable light (some fathers were still afraid that the court might reverse its decision to grant them custody).

Still, fathers did admit to experiencing some difficulties. The financial burden was mentioned as a major problem in several studies (Bartz & Witcher, 1978; Gersick, 1979; Katz, 1979; McKee & O'Brien, 1982; Risman, 1986). Juggling home and work demands were also difficult for some men (Chang & Deinard, 1982; Greif, 1985). But the most disturbing problems were related to the fathers' ability to meet their children's emotional needs (Bartz & Witcher, 1978; Katz, 1979; Rosenthal & Keshet, 1981), especially the needs of adolescent girls (Chang & Deinard, 1982; Greif, 1985; Mendes, 1976; Orthner et al., 1976). Katz (1979), however, believed that the reported difficulties represented only "the tip of the iceberg" (p. 527), and that fathers are worse off as single parents than are women in a similar situation. Katz's evaluation, however, was based on a sample of Australian men who were members of a social organization called "Parents without Spouses" whose purpose is to help its members find new marriage partners. Thus, his sample probably consisted of men who were more dissatisfied with their circumstances and were not as good at handling their sole parent role as other men.

After interviewing U.S. men who sought custody of their children, Levine (1976) concluded that fathers in this category "are brave explorers of the new sex role frontier" (p. 48). Indeed, 80% to 90% of fathers with sole custody did all of the housework and household chores, often with the assistance of their children (Mendes, 1976; Risman, 1986). Most fathers reported very few difficulties adjusting to their homemaker role. One study even reported that many of these fathers perceived themselves as better homemakers and parents than the "average" father in an intact family (Chang & Deinard, 1982).

Strong support of social and family networks help fathers adjust and function well as single parents (Greif, 1985; Hanson, 1986c). They tend to make use of their friends (mostly single mothers), extended family, and community resources to help manage their day-to-day obligations. Because single fathers elicit much sympathy, others' help is often willingly extended.

Fathers appraised the time that they spent with their children as highly positive (Greif, 1985; Hanson, 1981; Katz, 1979; Risman, 1986; Rosenthal & Keshet, 1981). Soon after the divorce, they made their children and their relationship with them top priority. Many of the fathers reported feeling closer, more affectionate, and more comfortable with their children. The film *Kramer v. Kramer* seemed to validly describe the father–child relationship in this regard. Fathers, who for a long time were excluded (or exempted themselves) from assuming a full share in the responsibility of caring for their children, are now increasingly devoting themselves to the task. Not only is the type of father who assumes an active and significant role in his children's lives becoming socially acceptable, but increasingly this role is preferred by many fathers, both married and divorced.

More and more men (and women) are coming over to the view that actualizing fatherhood does not contradict manhood but rather enhances it. More men than before are aware that functioning "expressively" assists instrumental functioning just as many women now realize that the reverse is true.

THE STUDY OF FATHERS: CONCLUDING REMARKS

Until the 1970s, little research was undertaken on the subject of the father's role in the family. And although even now the field remains a minority interest among researchers, there has been a considerable increase in the amount of work being done. Nevertheless, the bulk of this growing body of research is in effect merely an extension of the work that has been carried out with mothers. It largely represents an attempt to redress the balance of the nearly exclusive concentration on mothers that had characterized earlier research, rather than being devoted to discovering factors that are unique to fatherhood (as opposed to either motherhood or parenthood in general). Men as parents are treated as merely surrogate mothers, and much of what has been written is concerned with demonstrating men's adequacy as parents. Little of this research explicitly or implicitly goes beyond the comparison of the behaviors of men and women in dealing with their children (McKee & O'Brien, 1982).

The expansion of the work being done on fathers is essentially a response to external pressures, not the result of developments in theory and research per se (Richards & Dyson, 1982). These outside pressures have taken many forms and are complex in origin. In part they derive from feminist attacks on psychology for its overwhelming preoccupation with the role of mothers and its adherence to the idea that child care is exclusively the business of women. The increasing involvement of fathers in child care has had an effect as well. And the academic world has responded to these pressures, not least of all because investigating the subject seems to satisfy the growing call for social relevance in research. The result is that research is all too easily justified by its object rather than by theoretical or methodological arguments. The upshot of all this has been that the various mechanisms that are needed to weed out poorly thought out or badly conducted research have been desensitized. Therefore, old issues, approaches, and theories have often been simply carried over into new areas of investigation (Richards & Dyson, 1982). On·the other hand, there has been very little pressure for creating new orientations, theories, and research methods.

For a time, because of the particular stage in developing of research on fathering, it seems proper that the most ambitious studies in this area should use descriptive methods whose primary aim was to adumbrate and make familiar the scope of the subject. However, if the study of fathers is to become more than a mere elaboration and expansion of the study of mothers, then quantifying and experimental methodologies will have to be applied. We must concern ourselves with the issues of how an individual grows up to become a father and with the manner in which the expectations, needs, desires, and attitudes of fatherhood are passed on and learned. Notwithstanding the considerable psychological work that has been done in the areas of gender differences and of gender role and identity, relatively little attention has been given to how parental roles of fathers are transmitted from one generation to the next (Richards & Dyson, 1982). Although quasi-experimental and experimental approaches have recently become more common in studying the effects that fathers have on their children, these studies have not spilled over to research about divorced fathers. A more penetrating and relevant look at the unique situation of divorced fathers would encourage researchers to develop more creative research questions and data collection methods. For example, to deal with the process of fathering and the changes manifested in it over time, research will have to be pursued longitudinally.

Most research studies devoted to fathering have been one-shot affairs. Longitudinal investigations, on the other hand, would offer a better insight into the personal changes experienced by the father in his capacities both as an individual and as a parent, as well as to deepen our understanding of the father's relationship with his child. Moreover, it is no longer sufficient to study the father, or even the father and child, in isolation. To obtain a broader perspective, we must consider the influence of others — especially the mother and other family members — who are involved in childrearing. The challenge that researchers will face in the future will be to continue to develop the theoretical framework and the research methods and designs that will fully incorporate already existing knowledge and will help move their investigations in a direction that will connect the lives that men lead inside and outside the home.

6

Children of Divorced Parents: Theoretical and Research Considerations

Since the late 1950s, the subject of divorce has aroused considerable academic interest, beginning with Nye's (1957) seminal and revolutionary study of children from "broken" and "unhappy unbroken" homes. Nye reported that children from broken homes showed similar or better social adjustment than their counterparts in unhappy intact families. Nye had thereby thrown down the gauntlet, challenging theorists and researchers in a broad spectrum of disciplines who had assumed that the nuclear family, with its fixed roles and prescribed functions, was the only setting in which normal growth and development could occur. The initial and most serious challenge was to the notions about the father's role in the subsequent development of his children. Following the publication of Nye's work, there followed more than a decade of research on the varying effects of the father's absence, chiefly regarding the development of male children.

In the early 1970s, researchers concluded that a paternal absence could not be considered in isolation from other factors (Biller, 1970; Herzog & Sudia, 1973), and the search for such "other factors" began in earnest. Thus, since the early 1970s, researchers have recognized the complexity of divorce, seeking to define the shifting constellation of events that surround it, and to identify mediating factors and short- and long-term effects of these on the various aspects of the development of children. Nevertheless, the focus of much of this research was determined in 1957, following the overwhelming response to Nye's challenge to the established view of the principles of child development. Many of the more recent studies sought to identify which aspect of divorce—if not the absence of the father—does indeed affect children's development. The fact that the process of divorce takes place in relation to a complex network of social, cultural, legal, economic, and psychological variables makes it difficult to determine a real net effect of divorce on children. The interactions among numerous variables has tended to complicate research designs and the interpretations of their results.

An attempt is therefore made in this chapter to furnish the reader with a theoretical framework within which much of the research on the "children of divorce" that is reviewed in chapter 7 can be considered and interpreted. It is my goal here, as well, to highlight some of the research considerations that bear on the generalizability of results in investigations of this kind. Such a focus requires a knowledge of the relevant statistics, as well as an understanding of how divorce and child development have been conceptualized in the literature, and of the experience of divorce from the child's perspective.

Children of Divorced Parents: Statistics. The importance that is attached to issues of the effects of divorce on children increases in proportion to the number of children whose parents are divorced. Statistical data show that the number of families in which parents divorce has risen dramatically in the last three decades. From 1950 to 1980, for example, the rate of divorce doubled (see National Center for Health Statistics, 1984; Fig. 1, p. 2). In 1982, 5 million children in the United States under the age of 18 (8%) lived in single-parent homes (U.S. Bureau of Census, 1983). But because these data include neither divorced parents who remarried nor parents who were separated at the time of the study, the number of children who experienced parental divorce and separation must be assumed to have been even higher. Glick's (1979) study indicated that in 1978 as many as 18.6% of all children in the United States were living in one-parent families. Furstenberg, Nord, Peterson, and Zill (1983), whose data was obtained from a large-scale national sample, estimated that about 39% of all children will experience parental divorce by their 15th birthday. Although 1 year later, Bumpass (1984) projected that 38% of White children and 75% of Black children, born to married parents will experience parental divorce before reaching the age of 16. Recent national statistics (U.S. Bureau of the Census, 1989) indicate that currently 1 million children, every year, experience divorce of their parents.

Only in 1980 did the number of divorces in the United States decline, for the first time in 20 years. There were 3.5% fewer divorces in 1980 than in 1979 (National Center for Health Statistics, 1980). Actually, the trend in the divorce rate started to turn around after 1979, falling by about 5% between 1979 and 1985 (Hernandez, 1988). But if this decline may suggest a leveling off, or even a slight decrease in the rate of divorce, the large number of children experiencing parental divorce makes the impact of divorce on children a continuing concern of researchers and clinicians, and of the public at large.

DIVORCE: FAMILY DYNAMICS

A dynamic view of divorce – as opposed to a structural view – is strongly suggested by the data, if we are to deduce from the data different ways in which children respond to a useful conceptualization of divorce that approximates what matters most to children. Without exception, relationship measures have accounted for more of the differences in children's behavior than has family type.

If we can conclude that process is what matters most to children, then researchers may have pointed the way for pragmatists who wish to develop focused intervention, prevention, and education. Relationships, it is believed, can be reshaped and redirected by these processes. A structural view, on the other hand, can only suggest that we advocate or explicitly legislate a ban on divorce, separation, or desertion in families. In addition, a process view extends our concerns as researchers and practitioners beyond a biased sensitivity toward the needs of children from "broken homes," and the needs of children experiencing conflict and tension in all family types.

Although the father-absence approach to divorce focuses on structural changes in the nuclear family, there are researchers who have conceptualized divorce as a change in family dynamics. From the latter perspective, if interparental conflict is reduced and parent–child relationships are unchanged or improved, divorce can be expected to produce positive effects on children. Negative outcomes, on the other hand, are attributed to the cumulative effect of past and/or continuing interparental hostility and/or deterioration in parent–child relationships.

In his study, Nye (1957) compared 780 high school male and female students from broken homes; unhappy, unbroken homes; and happy, unbroken homes. These determinations were made by the subjects and required a rating indicating that both parents were happy or unhappy in their marriage. No significant differences were reported regarding variables such as socioeconomic status (SES), educational levels of the parents, and type of employment that were measured across groups. Adolescents from broken homes showed less psychosomatic illness and delinquent behavior than did adolescents from unhappy, intact homes. On dependent measures, Nye found no significant differences in school adjustment, church attendance, or delinquent companionship. And, as opposed to unhappy, intact homes, Nye reported superior mother–child relationships in broken homes.

Progressing beyond issues of structure to the "sociopsychological success or failure of the family," Nye's study contributed significantly to a more sensitive analysis of the "intact" family. Unfortunately, the same depth of analysis was not extended by Nye to the sociopsychological well-being of the broken home, in that he compared adolescents from divorced homes on the basis of structure, and applied dynamic analysis only to the intact families. As a result, he was forced to conclude that positive adjustment in adolescents from broken homes is the result of a new equilibrium that is achieved in the divorced family after a period of adjustment. The basis for his hypothesis cannot be verified because Nye provided no information concerning the length of time since separation for the broken homes.

In this view, therefore, it must be assumed that (a) the variables accounting for disruptions in children's growth and development are interparent hostility and poor mother–child relationships, and (b) divorce results in a cessation of interparent hostility and an improved mother–child relationship resulting in positive adjustment in children.

Westman, Cline, Swift, and Kramer (1970), in their study of the role of child psychiatry in divorce litigation, concurred with Nye's view that divorce represents a change in family relationships. However, these researchers found that in one third of their sample, divorce did not terminate conflictual interaction between parents. Furthermore, in 23 clinical psychiatric cases in which the child had experienced separation or divorce, the marital disruption had occurred more than 2 years before referral, and was followed by interparental conflict or complete loss of contact with one parent, usually the father. Cessation of interparent hostility, or a readily achieved new equilibrium, is therefore not experienced by all divorced families. Clearly, then, assumptions about family process cannot be made on the basis of family structure in divorced families, any more than such assumptions can be accurately made about intact families.

The relative contribution of process versus structural variables was assessed in a study by Hess and Camara (1979) of postdivorce family relationships with 16 fourth- and fifth-grade boys and girls who had experienced parental separation or divorce within the preceding 2 to 3 years. In their initial study, these researchers compared children by family type (intact vs. divorced) on measures of stress, work style in school, aggression, and social behavior. They reported (a) significantly higher levels of stress and aggression in children from divorced families, and (b) less work effectiveness in school for both boys and girls from divorced families. No differences in social behavior were reported. The researchers noted that some children from intact families showed more stress and aggression than those from divorced families, although the mean group differences were statistically significant. This finding was similar to Nye's (1957) report.

Hess and Camara (1979) completed a second study, in which they compared all children on the basis of interparental interaction measures and parent–child interaction measures irrespective of family type, avoiding the structure versus process comparison used in Nye's work. In a comparative analysis of relative contribution in order to explain variance in child outcomes, the process variables had a larger unique contribution to child outcomes than did the structural variables. The parent–child relationship, and not the interparental relationship, was found to be the most powerful predictor of the child measures. The quality of contact was a significant predictor of stress and aggression, as reported in the study; whereas the amount of contact with the father was not significant for children from divorced families.

In a study by Raschke and Raschke (1979), significant differences in the self-concept scores of children ages 8, 10, and 12 were attributed to levels of interparental conflict and parental unhappiness regardless of family type. However, the quality of the parent–child relationship was not measured by Raschke and Raschke's study.

Whitehead (1979), examining 2,775 British children, found that divorce and separation were significantly associated with antisocial behavior in 7-year-old boys and with withdrawal behavior in 7-year-old girls, but to a lesser degree than in cases of marital discord of other types, as in the case of Raschke and Raschke's work. The dynamics of the parent–child relationship were not, however, evaluated in this study.

Suggesting that the quality of the parent relationship affects the quality of parenting and consequently children's adjustment, Rickard, Forehand, Atkeson, and Lopez (1982) found that both divorced and unhappily married mothers gave their children significantly less positive attention than did happily married women. Social behavior, social withdrawal, and cognitive functioning of young adolescents were found not to be related to family structure. Interparental conflict, on the other hand, was revealed to exert a significant main effect on these dependent variables (Forehand, McCombs, Long, Brody, & Fauber, 1988).

The relative strengths of two models were compared in a recent study by Partridge and Kotler (1987), who investigated the long-term effect of the father's absence as a result of divorce or bereavement on the self-esteem and adjustment of adolescents. The family deficit (FD) model predicted poorer outcomes for adolescents from single-parent families than for those from intact families. The family environment (FE) model predicted that the quality of family interaction, rather than family type, would influence the outcomes for adolescents. Subjects were interviewed from three closely matched groups, consisting of adolescents from bereaved, divorced, and intact families, respectively. The results supported the FE model. The FE model accounted for between 12% and 29% of the variance in the dependent measures, whereas the family type accounted for less than 1% of the variance.

Notwithstanding the value of an interpersonal process view of divorce, it is important to keep in mind that, although process variables have accounted for more variance in children's well-being across family types, children from divorced families nevertheless have systematically done more poorly in mean comparisons than have children who did not experience parental divorce. Several explanations may account for this failure:

1. No study has evaluated the effect of negative change in a relationship as opposed to the effect of a negative but stable relationship on outcomes for children. It may be that change in family relationships, which is more inherent in situations of divorce than in intact but unhappy family situations, produces alterations in children's behavior.

2. No study has assessed the interaction effect of family tension and family type on measures of children's adjustment. It may be that such an interaction exists and is further complicated by the children's gender and developmental stage. Possibly, the experience of divorce and separation, as events in and of themselves, will render children more vulnerable to tension in family relationships.

3. It is possible as well that in divorce the more powerful variables are masked by, or interact with, discord in family relationships. And these variables and/or their interaction may ultimately shape the divorce experiences of children. The data clearly indicate that in all children the process variables are associated with stress, learning disabilities, problems of overcontrol and undercontrol, and low self-esteem.

Father's Absence

In the literature on paternal absence, divorce has been conceived of as one of a number of events—such as military service, long-distance employment, and death—that results in the loss of the male parent (Herzog & Sudia, 1973; Longfellow, 1979). In this view of divorce, the loss of the male parent is considered to be the critical independent variable; although types of father absence are typically compared to determine whether the cause of the loss is significant. In the areas in which fathers are presumed to be of primary importance, the dependent variables are the measures of the child's growth and development.

An area considered to be critically at risk in the case of the father's absence is that of the child's psychosexual development. Students of paternal absence have hypothesized that gender role development will be disrupted (Biller, 1970; Santrock, 1970, 1977), resulting in poor social knowledge and adjustment (Hetherington, 1972; Koziey & Davies, 1982; Young & Parish, 1977), and in subsequent marital disruption (McLanahan & Bumpass, 1988; Pope & Mueller, 1976). The father is viewed as the familial model of logical, qualitative thought and of achievement-oriented behavior (Biller, 1970; Blanchard & Biller, 1971; Gershansky, Hainline, & Goldstein, 1978; Shinn, 1978). The father is also considered to have a critical role in the development of his children's moral thinking and behavior (Parish, 1980; Santrock, 1975).

All types of paternal absence should result in similar levels and types of disturbance, if it is in fact useful to conceptualize divorce as one type of paternal absence, and to understand its effects as resulting from the loss of the male parent. However, if this is not the case, we must assume that children experience divorce as a qualitatively different event from other types of paternal absence, and that children are therefore affected by it in very different ways.

Children from homes that were disrupted by either divorce or the death of a parent were found to score lower on measures of self-acceptance, self-control, and sociability when compared with children from intact families (Koziey & Davies, 1982). Santrock (1977) found more aggression, disobedience, and independence among father-absent boys in general, and boys from divorced homes in particular, in a comparative study of gender-typed behaviors among father-absent and father-present boys.

The findings are contradictory in three studies of the responses of adolescent females to the father's absence. Hainline and Feig (1978) found no differences at all in measures of heterosexual behavior between all father-absent and father-present girls. Significantly different heterosexual behavior and lower self-esteem was found by Hetherington (1972) among daughters from divorced homes than among those from widowed homes; whereas Young and Parish (1977) found significantly lower self-esteem among both types of father-absent girls, with no differences between daughters from divorced or widowed homes on either this measure or measures of heterosexual attitudes.

In a study of intergenerational transmission of marital instability, Pope and Mueller (1976) found higher rates of marital instability in children from both widowed and divorced homes, with significantly higher rates in homes disrupted by divorce. Parish (1980) found lower levels of moral judgment only in young adults who had experienced paternal absence as a result of divorce, but no differences between young adults from widowed and intact homes. In earlier studies of the effects of the father's absence on moral development, Santrock (1975) found few differences between all types of father-absent and father-present boys when he controlled for IQ, SES, age, and sibling status; although he did find significant differences between the discipline styles of divorced and widowed mothers.

After reviewing 54 studies of the effects of the father's absence on cognitive development, Shinn (1978) concluded that cognitive deficits in father-absent children were due to financial hardship, high levels of anxiety, and low levels of parent–child interaction, rather than to paternal absence per se. Similarly, Biller (1970), in his review of the father-absence literature, concluded that the values of the mother and of the peer group, as well as the presence of female authority figures at school, are significant factors contributing to reported differential dysfunction. Blanchard and Biller (1971) found significant differences in academic achievement and grades between father-present and father-absent boys, with no differences that related to the cause of absence. However, they found low father-contact boys performed no differently from father-absent boys when, as Shinn and Biller suggested, a comparison was made between boys who had less than 6 hours a week of contact with their fathers and boys who had 2 hours per day of contact with their fathers.

Kurdek and Sinclair (1988) compared children from families that were divorced, families with a stepfather, and intact families on measures of psychopathology, goal directedness, and school-related problems. They found that measures of psychological adjustment were unrelated to family structure. The authors concluded that adjustment was negatively related to the level of family conflict, and positively related to family cohesiveness. However, adolescent boys from divorced families were found to score lower in self-esteem; and they perceived their parents, and especially their mothers, as being less caring than did their peers from intact families or whose fathers were deceased (Harper & Ryder, 1986).

Regarding the assessment of the value of conceptualizing divorce as one instance of father absence, a preponderance of the studies reviewed do indeed suggest that father-absent and father-present children reveal differences in patterns of growth and development. The findings suggest that loss or prolonged absence of a father has a telling impact on his children's subsequent development. Specifically, father-absent children show lower levels of self-esteem, marital stability, and academic achievement, and higher levels of aggression and disobedience; and, equivocally, disruptions in moral development and heterosexual functioning. (For a more detailed review, see Adams et al., 1984.)

A definition by which divorce is conceptualized as one instance of paternal absence appears simplistic in the face of the different effects deriving from each type of absence. It precludes more refined analysis of such variables as the amount of time lost with the father, the changes in the quality of the mother–child relationship, the family's SES, and the child's own perceptions and understanding. According to these father-absence studies, the variables just cited can be expected to be significantly different from, possibly even unique to, the child's experience of divorce as opposed to paternal death or prolonged absence. However, the simple fact that the loss of significant contact with a male parent (in addition to other aspects of the child's experience of divorce) may be detrimental should not be overlooked in the search for a more useful conceptualization.

CHILD DEVELOPMENT

The child's own level of psychosocial, psychosexual, emotional, and cognitive development has a decisive role in the way in which he or she responds, at different stages in the process of parental divorce, to such external factors as the absence of one parent, changes in socioeconomic status, altered parent–child relationships, and family conflict. There is a conceptually and methodologically diverse body of literature in which hypotheses are generated and conclusions explained from a wide range of developmental perspectives. Typically, in dealing with the effects of divorce on children, these studies have assessed the effect of a single external factor on one aspect of the child's development. This external factor is conceptualized as "divorce." Presented here are the three predominant paradigms of child development that are featured in the literature.

Social Cognitive Developmental Theory

Social cognitive developmental theorists and researchers have argued that children's responses to divorce can be explained in terms of the child's level of interpersonal reasoning (Kurdek & Berg, 1983; Kurdek, Blisk, & Siesky, 1981; Longfellow, 1979; Neal, 1983). Social cognitive developmental theory is hierarchical in nature. The child's interpersonal reasoning skills are enhanced at each stage, as is his or her capacity for understanding and interpreting the self in relation to the external world. According to Selman (1980), social cognitive development and interpersonal reasoning skills develop in four stages.

Level 0 (Egocentric Pre-Oedipal).   At this level, the child fails to distinguish his or her own viewpoint from that of others. Therefore, in interpersonal reasoning, the child confuses the subjectivity of the self and of others, but can identify subjective feelings. The child can understand only one subjective state at a time, and will conceptualize interpersonal relationships in terms of their physical aspects. Any situation is defined by the child as being synonymous with his or her personal reactions to it.

Level 1 (Subjective Early Latency).   At Level 1, the child is capable of understanding that, distinct from his or her own perspective, all other people have their own subjective perspectives. In interpersonal reasoning, the child does not understand that it is possible to hold two opposing feelings toward one person simultaneously, but is more aware of his or her own feelings. No account is taken of the different quality of each relationship; the consequences of behavior in interpersonal relationships are understood in absolute terms.

Level 2 (Self-Reflective Late Latency).   The child, at Level 2, can reflect on his or her own thoughts and behavior from another's point of view. In interpersonal reasoning, the child is still not capable of understanding how it is possible to integrate or express two opposing feelings toward the same person, but does understand that such feelings are possible.

Level 3 (Third-Person Reasoning Adolescence).   At the final level, the adolescent can adopt a viewpoint that simultaneously considers the perspectives of the self and of another as these relate to each other. In interpersonal reasoning, the adolescent has the ability to conceptualize interpersonal relationships as the product of mutual motivations, feelings, and behavior.

Longfellow (1979), in a review of the effects of personal divorce on children, proposed the social cognitive developmental perspective as a basis for explaining the clinical reports of Wallerstein and Kelly (1974, 1975, 1980b). For example, Longfellow attributed young children's fear regression and self-blame to the subjective and egocentric quality of their reasoning. Because children at the early latency level do not perceive divorce as mutual or distinguish between the marital and the parent–child relationship, the perception of relationships as absolute would be expected to result in inhibition and fears of abandonment. Divorce is consequently perceived by these children as the abandonment by one parent of another, a crisis that may also befall themselves. Longfellow proposed that the self-reflective interpersonal reasoning of older latency-aged children resulted in defensive posturing and social self-consciousness about the divorce. A type of protective "distancing" and objectivity about the divorce in their families might result from the ability of adolescents to understand others, independent of the specific contexts of relationships.

No single development theory can encompass children's responses to the highly complex phenomenon of parental divorce, although some support for each of these perspectives is to be found in the literature. Arguing in favor of such theoretical diversity, Levitin (1979) observed that "it is yet premature to search for a framework or schema that will integrate the various perspectives and findings" (p. 23).

Psychosocial and Psychosexual Developmental Theories

The developing child advances through discrete stages from infancy to adolescence with regard to both psychosocial and psychosexual perspectives. At each stage, the child's physical and psychological energy is focused on the achievement of distinct developmental tasks.

According to Erikson (1963), psychosocial development progresses in five lateral stages from infancy to adolescence, and occurs simultaneously with the consolidation of sexual identifications. Healthy adjustment depends on the achievement of a positive balance between a polarity of developmentally enhancing and developmentally disruptive outcomes.

Trust versus mistrust and autonomy versus shame and doubt are the polarities during infancy. In psychosexual theory, these stages encompass pre-Oedipal development, during which the child recognizes that he or she is male or female (Lamb, 1977). Erikson described the tasks of the subsequent Oedipal period as marking the achievement of a comfortable sense of initiative versus guilt. In part, this polarity is determined by the psychosexual task of gender identification. During the Oedipal stage, the child views the parent of the same gender as a rival for the affectional resources of the opposite-gender parent; fear of the consequences accompany these rivalrous fantasies. Gender identification will, theoretically, be successful if fear overcomes desire, producing identification with the same-gender parent and a self-protective alignment. The superego develops as the fear is internalized (Anthony, 1974; Toomin, 1974). These tasks, according to Erikson, must be accomplished without an overincorporation of guilt or destroying the child's sense of initiative (conceived in psychosexual terms as a libidinal drive toward the opposite-gender parent). Latency was characterized by Erikson as a struggle for a sense of industry versus inferiority. In psychosexual theory, the child is understood to be actively mimicking and identifying with significant adults of both genders. Nonsexual aspects of masculinity and femininity are integrated into the child's behavior (Westman, 1972).

Psychosocial and psychosexual tasks converge during adolescence. Identity involves an integration of one's sexual, intellectual, and moral self in all aspects of social functioning. It is during this period of adolescence that Erikson conceptualized a polarity between identity achievement and role confusion.

Clinicians have characteristically explained their observations in psychosocial and psychosexual terms (Anthony, 1974; Gardner, 1977; Schlesinger, 1982a; Sorosky, 1977; Toomin, 1974; Westman, 1972). Summarizing the psychosocial and psychosexual perspectives of the effects of divorce on children in a brief review, Westman (1972) proposed, for example, that disruptions in parenting precipitated by the divorce would impede the development of trust and autonomy in the pre-Oedipal child; whereas father absence during the Oedipal stage would disrupt gender identification. Westman hypothesized that when divorce occurs during latency, children's integration of gender identity and self-esteem would be impaired by parental involvement in their own crisis at the point when the child is actively involved in identifying with both parents. From a psychosocial and psychosexual perspective, the divorce experience is expected to have the least impact on the period of adolescence.

Divorce as a Developmental Process

Divorce is a long process within the family's history that is parallel to the child's personal development. It is not a specific entity or event. Divorce is attended by a sense of failure, a sense of loss, and marks the beginning of an often difficult transition to a new family lifestyle (Magrab, 1978). For the necessary equilibrium to be reestablished, the family system as a whole needs time, as does the child who is taking part and involved in the process. The process requires dealing with a different family environment that involves a new network of communication, visitation, and support, and the potential entry of additional people into the family schema, such as lawyers, judges, therapists, and stepparents.

The delicate balance between a child's family environment and the specific state of the child's physical and psychological development have intrigued developmental theorists, clinicians, and research investigators. Divorce gives rise to issues such as the new roles of the parents in raising the child, the effect of single-parent households, the type and implementation of appropriate visitation rights, the psychological meaning of divorce for the parents, the parents' adjustment to divorce, and their adjustment to their new parental roles. Most of the factors in which divorce specifically alters the child's environmental structure have yet to be sufficiently analyzed.

The basic life support that ensures the physical survival of the child must be provided for by an adequate family environment. The family environment should, as well, stimulate the child's emotional, social, and cognitive achievements; promote stability of intrapsychic development to ensure adequate control over impulses; provide for regulation and moral stability; and give the child the ability to disengage from the family constellation as part of a process of lifelong individualization (Klebanow, 1976).

Wallerstein and Kelly (1980b) noted that during the divorcing periods, parent–child relationships are fluid and subject to radical changes in character. The role of the child in providing support for the distressed parent, sometimes becomes magnified. Citing Anna Freud's observation that "the reason why broken homes are destructive for a child's development is less in the absence of a parental figure for identification than in the fact that the remaining parent will tend to cast the child into the absent parent's place," McDermott (1970) noted that identification with the absent parent was a frequent reaction of the children of divorce parents.

The significance of the interval between the time of parental separation and the point at which the child is studied has been recognized by many researchers. They have studied the effect of divorce and separation on children and have controlled for the length of time since separation by means of sampling (e.g., Fulton, 1979; Nelson, 1982), statistical procedures (e.g., Farber, Primavera, & Felner, 1983; Kurdek, 1986; Nelson, 1981), and longitudinal studies (Cherlin, Furstenberg, Chase-Lansdale, & Kiernan, 1991; Hetherington, 1979; Wallerstein, 1984).

Only a few scholars, however, have described the unfolding sequence of stages that define divorce as a developmental process. Kressel and Deutsch (1977), in a survey of experienced clinicians, attempted to define the process that is set in motion when a marriage is being terminated. Defining this process as *psychic divorce,* they focused on the experience of the parents. According to Kressel and Deutsch, psychic divorce brings with it unavoidable but predictable feelings that impair decision making and rational planning. Occurring in discriminable stages, it is also an inevitable process that may or may not be successfully completed. The specific stages identified by them were the predecision period, the decision period proper, the period of mourning, and the period of re-equilibration.

The predecision period, according to the clinicians surveyed by Kressel and Deutsch, involves increasing marital dissatisfaction and fluctuating attempts at reconciliation that are followed by a break in the facade of marital solidarity, a stage that may last for months or years. The effect on children's development and its duration are as yet unclear. Kelly (1980) proposed that the predivorce state in families ranges along a continuum from minimal conflict to continuous fighting and violence. Family-process literature strongly substantiates that family conflict is associated with stress, learning disabilities, low self-esteem, and problems of over- and undercontrol. However, the effect of changing, or possibly ending, the conflict by divorce cannot be predicted from the literature.

Clearly related to the quality of the predivorce family is the global adjustment of children. This was reported by Kurdek et al. (1981) and Kurdek and Berg (1983) as highly correlated with children's divorce adjustment. Similarly, from a clinical perspective, Anthony (1974) reported that if the predivorce marital relationship was within the normal range, children did not exhibit long-term divorce adjustment problems. He speculated that what is a good divorce from the point of view of the parents may lead to an internalization of disorders in children who cannot make sense out of the juxtaposition of an amicable relationship that is being voluntarily terminated. Anthony accounted for the possibility that unexpressed conflict and emotional withdrawal may be as damaging for children as high levels of overt hostility.

Internalization of disorders is not, however, limited to unexpressed conflict. Jacobson (1978) reported that children ages 3–17 who had been exposed to high levels of interparental conflict prior to divorce showed higher levels of behavioral inhibition following divorce than did children who had not been so exposed. In addition, the longer the children had known about the marital difficulties before the divorce, the better adjusted they were on measures of aggression, irritability, and cognitive and learning disabilities.

Evidence suggests that the time preceding separation may be as powerful a determinant of the children's divorce experience as the quality of their postdivorce life (Beal, 1979; Luepnitz, 1979). The view of divorce as a sequential developmental process can be useful in extending the scope of the consideration of clinicians and researchers as regards this stage. The meaning of children's short- and long-term responses are, however, difficult to measure and interpret. Clinical insight puts sensitizing, if annoying, restraint on our current ability to predict divorce adjustment on the basis of children's experience of the predivorce stage. Before this issue can be well understood, dependent measures that capture the subjective meaning of children's short- and long-term responses must be carefully developed and applied.

In the stage sequence outlined by Kressel and Deutsch (1977), the stage following the decision period proper is designated as the period of mourning. In parents, this stage is marked by intense feelings of guilt, a sense of failure, diminished self-esteem, loneliness, and depression. Hetherington et al. (1978), in a longitudinal study covering the 2 years subsequent to separation, also noted that parents were subject to feelings of depression, incompetence, and loss of self-esteem in the immediate postdecision or mourning period. The researchers found that these feelings were most intense in the first year after separation. In children, feelings of distress and anxiety peaked during the first year following divorce; and particularly in boys there was an increase over the first year in dependency and play disruptions, as well as in aggression toward the mother. Hetherington et al. (1979a) concluded that, for both parents and children, the first year after divorce was the period of maximum negative behavior.

Wallerstein and Kelly (1980b), in their 5-year longitudinal study, also found that the acute crisis reactions at all developmental stages subsided for most children at 18 months following separation. Parents, on whom children normally rely for support, may be as decompensated as their offspring during this period. Regarding intervention, this is clearly a high-risk period for children. Because access to such outside support as the public schools appears to be critical, the attention of policymakers and mental health professionals is necessary. It is possible that the children who are most seriously threatened are those who continue manifesting increasingly chronic and/or new and specific developmental disturbances beyond the mourning period. For people concerned with identifying children who are at risk in regard to long-term adjustment disorders, the perspective of time has additional value because it defines a period of between 1½ and 2 years in which some behavioral deficits and emotional difficulties may be normal. The perspective of time and predivorce level of children's functioning was also found significant in the Cherlin et al. (1991) longitudinal study.

Parents enter the final stage of re-equilibrium, according to Kressel and Deutsch (1977), if the mourning stage is successfully completed. For most families, this stage is reached 18 months after separation (Wallerstein & Kelly, 1980b). In the case of the sample of Hetherington et al. (1979a) re-equilibration was reached after 2 years. These researchers and others (Emery, 1982; Jacobson, 1978; Westman, 1972; Westman & Cline, 1971) reported, however, that not all families nor all children reach this stage. Unresolved postdivorce parental conflict can continue for years. In these circumstances, children are frequently among those referred for clinical treatment (Luepnitz, 1979; Westman et al., 1970).

For children who will show short-term crisis responses followed by recovery and for those whose responses become a chronic disturbance, failure to complete the mourning process and resulting ongoing postdivorce conflict is only one factor in their differentiation. The functioning of the custodial parent is another primary determinant. Specifically, children with less mature and able mothers, or with mothers who are unable to cope with their situation following divorce, were revealed to have more lasting problems than did children with well-adjusted, competent, and responsive mothers. Two years following parental divorce, these children were adapting well both at home and in school (Hetherington, 1979; Hodges, 1986).

Severe and chronic disturbances were attributed by Anthony (1974) to the gathering stress accumulations from the predivorce and decision stages. The most salient of these cumulative stresses include changes in family dynamics and in social and economic conditions that are most powerfully expressed within, and mediated by, the custodial parent–child relationship. An integration of the perspectives of divorce presented here suggests that children who fail to reach equilibrium within the span of 1½ to 2 years are indeed responding to cumulative stresses from the predivorce and decision stages.

Children's Adjustment to Divorce

A central and still unresolved issue is how to define and assess the adjustment of children to the divorce of their parents. The issue has both theoretical and research implications. Methodologically, the question concerns how children's adjustment is to be assessed and what are the various degrees of adjustment. Conceptually, the question concerns whether divorce adjustment is independent of general adaptive behavior (Kurdek, 1981).

Two not mutually exclusive, yet distinguished approaches to the problem have been used by researchers. In one of these, children's reaction to divorce is evaluated by tapping on the children's specific characteristics (e.g., self-esteem, anxiety level, gender role). In a second approach, adjustment is assessed by the children's general adaptive behavior (e.g., school achievement, home and social behavior).

Some overlap is shown in the scores of children's specific measures and general adaptive behavior (Kurdek, 1986), but these behaviors are not interchangeable. Kurdek et al. (1981) reported that parental ratings of children's adjustment were inconsistently correlated with the children's own ratings. They also found that children's responses to a structured, open-ended questionnaire and an objective rating scale were nonsignificantly correlated. Part of the problem may be the lack of a theoretical framework within which children's adjustment to divorce is conceptualized (Kurdek et al., 1981).

Several theoretical approaches depicting the process of children's adjustment have been proposed. None, however, included an operational definition.

Hozman and Froiland (1976) delineated a series of five stages in the process of children's adjustment to their parents' divorce based on the Kubler-Ross (1969) model. Although there are points that overlap with those mentioned by Wallerstein (1983), the process as a whole is different and therefore noteworthy. There are five stages, during each of which the child needs to "work through" a dominant emotional reaction.

Denial is the first stage. In it, the child needs to resolve the tendency to perceive the world as he or she would like it to be, and to accept the painful reality of the parents' separation.

The second stage is anger, which is when the child attempts frequently to strike out at anyone who is perceived to be in the way of reconciliation. The target may be both or only one parent, or anyone who attempts to replace one of the parents.

Children will enter the third, or bargaining stage, when denial and anger prove to be nonproductive. Imagining that improvement in their behavior (or any other kind of manipulation) will result in a reconciliation, children attempt to overcome their loss by "making a deal" with themselves.

Stage 4 is that of depression, which is reached when children realize that they cannot control the situation.

Finally, Stage 5 is acceptance, which comes when children learn to accept reality whether they like it or not. Only after having come to terms with things as they are can children discover the possibility of reestablishing a satisfactory relationship with both parents.

Wallerstein (1983) outlined six developmental tasks that children from divorced families need to master. The first two tasks require being resolved within the initial year, whereas the others may need to be reworked several times. The tasks are:

1. Acknowledging the reality of the parents' separation. This may involve dealing with fears of being overwhelmed by intense feelings of anger, rejection, sorrow, and abandonment. In emotional and behavioral terms, the child needs to overcome a powerful tendency to deny the reality of the parents' separation in order to accomplish this task.
2. Disengaging from parental conflicts so that daily activities can be pursued. To do this, children must establish and maintain some degree of psychological distance from the parents; and thereby remove the family crisis from a dominant position in his or her life.
3. Resolution of loss. Here the child needs to come to terms with the loss of the family's old routines and customary patterns, as well as with the partial loss of a parent. There may even be a need to deal with the loss of familiar and supportive environment and friends.
4. Resolution of anger and self-blame. According to Wallerstein, self-blame stems from hidden wishes for divorce or for failure of the family's restoration. The anger stems from the fact that divorce is not inevitable.
5. Accepting the finality of the divorce. The older a child is at the time of divorce, the less difficult this task tends to be.
6. Achieving realistic and independent expectations regarding one's own ability to establish and maintain future relationships.

In both the preceding theoretical descriptions, acceptance of divorce is just about the final stage in the process of children's adjustment. Both models also share the "stage-developmental" approach, and highlight the psychological aspects of the adjustment process. Neither model, however, attempts operationally to define the process or criterion for a successful adjustment. Neither was set out to propose a model that encompasses the whole complex of factors, social as well as psychological, which affect children's reactions to parental divorce. There is an evident need for such a model. A comprehensive adjustment model could serve not only as a framework within which to consider the numerous studies published every year on children's adjustment to parental divorce, but also as a basis for an orderly formulation of research questions.

CHILDREN'S EXPERIENCE OF THEIR PARENTS' DIVORCE

For children, as for adults, divorce is a long process of negotiating one's way through disruption and reorganization. For adults, divorce can be viewed as a crisis that starts with marital disharmony and, over the course of time, approaches a potential resolution. For children, divorce represents a traumatic transition from life with both parents to the condition of living with only one, attended by the intermediate stages of personal imbalance, confusion, and disorganization.

The Divorce Crisis

For children, one of the outcomes of the divorce is permanent, or total, or partial separation from a parent. The result is often a reaction described as grief. Leaving aside the question of whether the response is appropriately named, it differs from the grief that attends the death of a parent. First, because divorce is a voluntary action on the part of parents, it can be discussed, planned, and prepared for. Second, each parent has the option of continuing to play a real and meaningful part in the child's life, so the child may continue to express feelings of anger, anxiety, and sadness to the separated parent, as well as to ask questions and solicit opinions. This circumstance potentially allows for working through the loss, and a possibility of reestablishing a new kind of relationship with this parent. Finally, divorce may even have positive effects on the child by defusing a previously highly conflicted family situation. Subsequent to a divorce, the parents can serve more competently as role models and ego supports, and are in a position of positively promoting both the adjustment of the child to the new family situation and the further growth and development of the child's personality (Wallerstein & Kelly, 1974).

Relief often typifies the feelings of partners in the period immediately after the decision has been taken to end the marriage (Kressel & Deutsch, 1977). These same feelings cannot, however, be expected of children. Studies have reported that an announced decision to divorce is a significant independent stressor that is by no means necessarily anticipated by children, even when the predivorce conflict is readily apparent (Jacobson, 1978; Kelly, 1980; Kurdek & Siesky, 1980). Regardless of the level of predivorce conflict, children remain intensely loyal to the two-parent family, as is revealed by Wallerstein and Kelly (1980b) in their longitudinal clinical study of divorced families. According to their study, children were profoundly upset by the news of the family disruption.

Although for most children the news of their parents' divorce is distressing and shocking, to some extent the degree of distress they experience depends on how parents convey the news. Jacobson (1978) attempted to study the degree to which cognitive preparation by the parents for the impending decision to divorce affected children's ability to adjust. In Jacobson's sample of 30 families, the number of parents who had prepared their children for the separation was insufficient for a statistical analysis to be carried out. Adjustment was improved for the few children who had experienced preparation. The ability of parents to comfort their children and to provide a clear, rational explanation has been found to be strongly related to the lower intensity of children's reaction and fearfulness (Wallerstein & Kelly, 1980b).

Wallerstein and Kelly reported that children's perceptions of the decision of the parents as being carefully considered, rational, and bringing some measure of happiness to at least one parent appears to have a direct effect on their ability to cope. Several authors (e.g., Anthony, 1974; Whiteside, 1983) emphasized that without a clear understanding of the divorce, children are less able to move toward acceptance of their new family structure. But, regardless of how parents inform their children of the impending divorce, children are rarely prepared and seldom able to immediately accept the separation. Because children often respond to the announced decision with denial and detachment, parents are misled into believing that the divorce decision was anticipated and readily accepted by their children (Anthony, 1974; Toomin, 1974).

Family Economics

Following a divorce, many mothers and children experience unprecedented economic deprivation and downward socioeconomic mobility. In a detailed analysis of the economic situation of divorced mothers and their families, Weitzman (1985) noted that divorce and poverty are intimately related. Weitzman found that about one third of mother-headed White families were poor, compared to less than 8% of father-headed families. Among non-Whites, 20% of father-headed families were poor, compared to over half of mother-headed families. Bane (1976) reported that 51% of children under 18 in female-headed families fell below the poverty level in 1975.

In the sociopolitical view, the salient features of the divorce are conceptualized as second-order effects on the quality of the parenting of a mother who is economically, professionally, and socially discriminated against on the basis of her gender and marital status.

DeSimone-Luis, O'Mahoney, and Hunt (1979) examined a wide range of environmental change factors and their correlation with the children's behavioral profiles in a study of the factors influencing the adjustment of 25 children ages 7–13 of divorced and separated families. Among some 30 factors that were studied, loss of income was the only one that proved significant. Of the five subjects who showed deviant profiles, all had custodial parents who suffered a 50% drop in income immediately following separation.

Hetherington et al. (1978) applied a broader systems view in their study of stress and coping in mother-headed households during the 2 years following divorce. In their sample, mother's ratings of economic stress were significantly correlated with ratings of depression, incompetence, and external locus of control; these, in turn, showed significant correlations with observer ratings of children's aggressions and frequency of noxious behaviors. Children showed a higher incidence of conduct disorders and emotional problems as the divorced parents in the researchers' sample were more likely than married parents to increase their workload (Hetherington et al., 1979a).

The effects of divorce and maternal employment were specifically studied by MacKinnon, Brody, and Stoneman (1982). According to this study, maternal employment per se did not negatively affect the degree of cognitive and social stimulation that preschool children experience. A significant interaction effect of maternal employment and marital status on the home stimulation inventory was found by these researchers. The children of the divorced working mothers experienced significantly lower home stimulation than did the children of married working or nonworking mothers. However, in additional analyses of the effect of income on the dependent measure, MacKinnon et al. concluded that on the subscales of physical environment, encouragement of social maturity, and a variety of stimulation and physical punishment, the level of income could have accounted for the differences reported. Accordingly, these researchers described an "ecological reality namely, that children within divorced (mother-headed) households often spend several years in milieus that contain the stresses of a low-income environment" (p. 1397). They hypothesized that the multiple roles and responsibilities of divorced mothers were indirectly related to the decreased home stimulation. This hypothesis is consistent with the descriptions by Hetherington et al. (1978) and by Wallerstein and Kelly (1980b), who observed that from the children's point of view, everything seemed to have fallen apart. These researchers described a group of divorced mothers who were overwhelmed by the sheer number of tasks confronting them, and felt they had neither the time nor the energy to deal competently with routine financial tasks, household maintenance, child care, and occupational and social demands.

Ambert (1982) suggested that (a) children in postdivorce families are also the recipients and transmitters of society's view of women, and (b) the parent–child relationship is reciprocal, so that the attitudes of children shape parental behavior and vice versa. With these premises in mind, Ambert studied the differences in children's behavior and attitudes toward low and high SES custodial mothers and fathers. She found an intimate interaction between SES, child behavior, parental adjustment, and gender. Ambert further hypothesized that, in response to their disadvantaged position, children were led to acts of rejection toward the mother, who becomes the scapegoat for their frustration. On the other hand, in observing both high and low SES custodial fathers and children, Ambert reported that fathers commanded almost automatic authority and respect from their children.

In the sample they studied, Hetherington et al. (1978) reported that divorced mothers described their relationship with their children as "a declared war" and "like being bitten to death by ducks." Children (particularly boys) exhibited greater negative behavior in the presence of their mothers than of their fathers. This pattern was characterized by the researchers as a cycle of coercion, in which the mother's lack of management skills leads to noxious behavior in her children that, in turn contributes to the mother's feelings of low self-esteem, depression, and incompetence. Ambert's hypothesis thus adds a missing perspective to the supposedly reciprocal view of Hetherington et al. Although these researchers attempted to analyze reciprocal dynamics, they identified the origin of the cycle as being the mother.

Clearly, a broad-based systems view of divorce provides some understanding of the factors that cause change in both the custodial parent–child relationship, and in the interactions among factors. However, a detailed analysis of the meaning and differential effects of the myriad factors involved should not be precluded by the breadth of conceptual focus. For example, Hetherington et al. (1978) and Wallerstein and Kelly (1980b) noted that income loss following divorce is typically combatted by the sudden introduction of maternal employment or an increase in the mother's working hours outside the home.

The effects of income loss, however, should not be equated with the effects of maternal employment. In the studies reviewed, the efforts of mothers to recoup economic status brought them into confrontation with discrimination in employment and financial institutions. Moreover, income loss was repeatedly associated with the mothers' experience of an overwhelming multiplicity of roles associated with inadequate parental attention and control, depression, loss of self-esteem, and parental incompetence. On the other hand, divorced mothers who were able to work, generally reported having positive feelings of self-esteem that derived from companionship with colleagues, and reported a sense of enhanced personal competence in parenting as well (Hetherington et al., 1978; MacKinnon et al., 1982). Thus, maternal employment and income loss do not produce the same effects. It may be that for custodial mothers the negative effects of income loss on their relationship with their children is offset by employment.

Nevertheless, from the child's perspective, income loss and mother's employment may confound negative effects because both these factors are associated with loss of nurture and attention, and with reduced social and cognitive stimulation (Hetherington et al., 1978; MacKinnon et al., 1982; Wallerstein & Kelly, 1980b).

We cannot assume that all factors affecting the custodial parent will similarly affect the child and vice versa, if we are accurately to conceptualize divorce from the perspective of the child. The process view would suggest that the critical issues are the manner in which the parent and child respond to sociopolitical changes in their postdivorce lives, and the degree to which these responses are introduced into the parent–child relationship. Bane (1976) placed responsibility for economic hardships of mother-headed families squarely on the policymakers whose supposed domain of concern is the welfare of the children of maritally disrupted homes. Indeed, the nature of children's experience of divorce may ultimately prove to be more a matter of policy than pathology and ignorance.

Family Relationships

When divorced parents are asked about their children's life following separation, they most often mention the changes that occur in the course of reorganizing family life, and the part children play in the process (Weiss, 1979, 1980). One change that is made dramatically apparent in analyzing divorce from the viewpoint of children's adaptation to such reorganization has to do with their status in the family hierarchy. In one-parent families, the child's position is that of a junior partner, whereas in dual-parent families it is mainly that of a subordinate (Farson, 1978).

This transition in status occurs when the custodial parent faces the problem of filling the void created by the departure of the partner. The custodial parent then discovers a need to rely on the children in practical matters as well as for emotional support (McDermott, 1970). In their reports, parents describe the change in the children's status as one of accelerated development and growing up (Kurdek & Siesky, 1979).

In their new position, children assume a growing share in the chores, and concerns of the household, as well as becoming more involved in making decisions concerning the family and carrying them out. Older children often take care of their younger siblings, and sometimes even partially of the parent (Kurdek & Siesky, 1980). In obtaining a larger scope in making decisions and greater independence of action, children in one-parent families also acquire the sort of privileges and a degree of authority that children in two-parent families are rarely awarded. Such single parents are more inclined to take their children's wishes into consideration and to act more through the medium of cooperation and understanding than by imposing their authority (Atlas, 1984; Hanson & Trilling, 1983). These changes result in a more democratic family identity in the matter of making and carrying out decisions; although some of the changes came about not because they were planned, but come with time and are essential to the continuance of normal family functioning.

After divorce, parents appear to be less consistent, less affectionate, and weaker in their disciplinary control (Hetherington, 1979, 1989). Kelly and Wallerstein (1977) noted that parent–child relationships are then fluid and subject to radical changes in character. Other researchers concur, and conclude that the quality of the custodial parent–child relationship is the most powerful determinant of the child's divorce experience (Lowenstein & Koopman, 1978; Hetherington, 1979; Hetherington et al., 1978; Pett, 1982; Wallerstein & Kelly, 1980b). Parental responsibilities include meeting the emotional and nurturing needs of children, providing for their financial security, and furnishing them with a model of adjustment. But the preoccupation of both parents with their own sense of loss and with their struggle to survive the crisis becomes one of the difficulties in providing the child with these needs.

In studying postdivorce family dynamics, Jacobson (1978) and Hess and Camara (1979) concluded that attention from parents accounted for more variance in the overall adjustment of children ages 3–17 than did interparent hostility. As the custodial parent is typically the mother, perhaps the most appropriate comparisons in divorce research should be made along the dimensions of maternal deprivation (Brandwein et al., 1974). Such studies should assess variables that would interfere with or enhance the mother's ability to provide adequate mothering.

The availability of support sources for the child is a key related factor. For adults, support has been found to correlate with good postdivorce adjustment (Bloom et al., 1978; Chiroboga et al., 1979). Indeed, such support for parents has been shown to be connected both with the children's postdivorce adjustment (Kurdek & Berg, 1983) and the quality of parent–child relationship (Hetherington et al., 1978).

A highly important related intervening factor in the adjustment of the children is the quality of relationships between the ex-spouses. The more amicable the settlement between the parents, the happier the mother and father upon separation; the shorter the separation, and the longer the passage of time since separation, the better the positive emotional adjustment of the children (Nelson, 1981). Conversely, prolonged and continued tension between the divorced parents has been found to hinder the well-being of the children (Hess & Camara, 1979; Jacobson, 1978; Kurdek, 1981; Wallerstein, 1983).

In recent years, the emphasis on family dynamics has led a number of researchers to consider the question of what factors shape family process, as well as to seek to determine how family dynamics interact in and of themselves. The parental relationship was identified as one determinant of the custodial parent–child relationship in one of the few extensive systems analysis studies of postdivorce mother-headed families (Hetherington et al., 1978). In essence, parental interaction is viewed as a second-order effect on children's experience. Wallerstein and Kelly (1980b) concluded that the custodial parent–child relationship is the most salient feature of the child's experience; they identified the parental relationship as one of several second-order effects on children. This conclusion is similar to the hypothesis by Rickard et al. (1982) that marital satisfaction affects parenting across family types.

The effect of divorce on children may be as much due to the marital discord that preceded the divorce as it is to the trauma associated with the loss of family structure (Felner & Farber, 1980; Guidubaldi, Cleminshaw, Perry, & Mcloughlin, 1983; Kurdek, 1981; Wallerstein, 1983). Indeed, current thinking on children's reaction to divorce indicates that marital tension and family discord before separation and divorce may be more strongly related to children's adjustment than was previously thought.

For children, divorce is more than just a change in their relationship with their parents; it is often the impetus for a long chain of changes that individually and collectively influence them. So, for example, a common outcome of divorce for children is the loss of the familiar surroundings of their home, school, and friends as a result of moving away (Fulton, 1979), which has the effect of increasing their social isolation (Marsden, 1969; Pearlin & Johnson, 1977). For many children, divorce also means a significant drop in standard of living. Following the divorce, many mothers are compelled to go to work or to work longer hours, a circumstance that only doubles the child's loss. That is, the child has an absent full-time father and a less-available mother (Wallerstein & Kelly, 1975).

RESEARCH WITH CHILDREN OF DIVORCE

Some Critical Comments

Much of our understanding of the effect of parental divorce on children derives from the research of Hetherington and her colleagues and Wallerstein and Kelly. These studies are benchmarks in the field. However, they have some design limitations that raise questions regarding the extent to which they can be generalized and applied to other populations. Thus, among the design limitations of Wallerstein and Kelly, is the study's failure to include a comparison group of nonseparated families, and their reliance on subjects from the clinical population (families that sought help from a counseling service and were subsequently asked to participate in the research). The study by Hetherington and her colleagues can be criticized on the grounds that their sample was predominantly made up of middle-class families.

A number of authors have integrated and critically reviewed the available research on the effect of divorce on children (e.g., Atkeson, Forehand, & Rickard, 1982; Blechman, 1982; Derdeyn & Scott, 1984; Kurdek, 1986; Voelker & McMillan, 1983). The reviewers are unanimous in concluding that the literature concerning the effect of divorce on children is "fraught with methodological difficulties," as was observed by Kurdek (1986). The specific problems identified by Kurdek in this regard are as follows:

1. The use of small nonrepresentative samples of voluntary White middle-class subjects.
2. The classification of subjects according to time elapsed since divorce rather than time since separation, thereby ignoring the major psychological changes occurring before the marriage has legally ended.
3. The use of retrospective data that has been submitted to subjective distortion.
4. The lack of appropriate comparison groups.
5. The failure to control for developmental effects.
6. The failure to examine changes in the family's functioning and relationship from a process rather than a structural perspective.
7. The use of measures that have questionable or unreported reliability and validity.
8. The absence of a conceptual system within which complex findings can be systematically organized and interpreted.

In addressing the last issue, Kurdek (1981) already suggested a comprehensive theoretical framework within which available data on variables affecting children's reactions to parental divorce might be fitted and reorganized. To this end, Kurdek offered to conceptualize and order the widely scattered findings that deal with the subjects, within the framework of Bronfenbrenner's four-systems schema.

1. The Macrosystem: This includes a wide range of social beliefs, values, and attitudes that bear on the family. Among the issues relevant to family life are marriage, divorce, role division within the family, women's status, and the norms that determine the methods of relating to, nurturing, and raising children. The assumption is that a person's development, behavior, and reactions are parallel to and influenced by the social, political, and cultural milieu of a given time.
2. The Exosystem: This consists of the social factors affecting the environment within which a person lives. These include the various support systems available to single-parent families, and the extent of environmental change associated with the divorce.

3. The Microsystem: This comprises the variables associated with the interpersonal relationships among the family members. With regard to divorce, microsystem analysis focuses on the changes in these relationships following the divorce, and on the level of individual functioning and adjustment that intrafamilial relations and is in turn affected by them.

4. The Ontogenic System: The concern here is with the child's competencies in dealing with the family's crisis. Thus, the area of ontogenic system analysis comprises the various personal characteristics that put the individual child in an advantageous or disadvantageous position for successfully negotiating the crisis of parental divorce.

In his review article, Kurdek (1981) classified the relevant studies under the headings of these four systems, and proposes that

> a child's positive or negative divorce adjustment is influenced by hierarchically embedded sets of factors regarding overarching ideologies about family life (the macrosystem), the stability of the post-divorce environment and the availability of social supports to the single-parent family (the exosystem), reciprocal changes in parent–child roles in the post-divorce period (the microsystem), and the child's competencies for dealing with stress (the ontogenic system). (p. 863)

He pointed out that it is necessary to look beyond the particular system that has been singled out, and to consider the enormous number of possible interactions between them in order to get a clearer understanding of the reasons behind an individual child's reaction to his or her parents' divorce.

In this particular context, a major problem with Kurdek's attempt to fit a vast body of existing research into a well-defined theory is that this requires the imposition of the data onto the theory. Such a proceeding sometimes blurs the distinctions among the four systems of the theory, so that the resultant groupings of the research studies may not always be the most meaningful. For example, the macrosystem and exosystem, as presented by Kurdek, include social factors that have no direct effect on the person. Effects are exerted only through the environment, either immediate or remote, in which the person lives. Factors such as beliefs and attitudes toward the family (the macrosystem) have no effect whatsoever on the person, unless they are part of the more immediate exosystem, or the "setting within which that person is contained."

Another problem with Kurdek's approach is the absence of concern with developmental aspects. This is particularly noticeable when we consider that age and developmental stage are the most important factors in determining the nature of a child's response to the divorce of parents. Many studies show significant qualitative differences between how preschool, latency-aged, and adolescent children respond to parental divorce (e.g., Kalter & Plunkett, 1984; Lowery & Settle, 1985; Wallerstein & Kelly, 1980b).

There seem also to be inconsistencies arising from classifying some of the research under the general descriptive categories of the four systems in order to match Bronfenbrenner's ecological approach to the data on children of divorced parents. For example, Kurdek spoke of the exosystem as representing "environmental stability and external social support." This subheading does not seem to be in direct line with the general description of this system. Still, the conceptual framework of Kurdek et al. is unique in its comprehensiveness, and therefore deserves careful consideration by researchers. A better conceptual framework seems to be that of children's sociocognitive developmental sequence. As is explained in the next chapter, the sociocognitive framework better fits the available data and better incorporates the father-absence, economic deprivation, and family dynamics perspectives.

7   Parental Divorce and the Reaction of Children

More than 1 million children a year experience parental divorce or separation. Having become increasingly aware of children's reactions to divorce, social scientists have made many attempts since the 1960s to study the impact of divorce on children (for recent reviews see Chase-Lansdale & Hetherington, 1990; Emery, 1988; Hetherington, 1989). It can be stated with some certainty that when compared to children of intact families, children of divorced parents function on a lower level on various psychological, social, and cognitive measures (see Amato & Keith, 1991, for a recent review). Still, it cannot be stated with certainty that divorce has any single, broad-reaching and long-lasting effect on children. It is also uncertain what factors associated with the divorce experience account for the divorce effects. Findings to date remain inconsistent, often contradicting, and overall equivocal. Situational variables such as socioeconomic, support systems, parenting, and family relationships account for some of the variables; others are accounted for by the personal characteristics of age, gender, and temperament. A child's developmental stage appears to be the most significant single factor (Amato & Keith, 1991) among all these variables in determining the nature of much of his or her response to parental divorce. Therefore, as other writers have done before (e.g., Kaslow & Schwartz, 1987; Roseby, 1985), this chapter examines the major findings in the research literature in the context of children's developmental stages.

Although there are cross-sectional studies of children who experienced divorce several years prior to testing, few of these investigations have systematically compared the effects of separation and divorce on children of different ages at specific junctions in the divorce process. Thus, much of the data gathered in these studies is colored by memory and confused with the child's current level of development (Kulka & Weingarten, 1979; Kurdek & Siesky, 1980; Luepnitz, 1979; Parish & Nunn, 1981; Pope & Mueller, 1976; Rosen, 1977, 1979). A small number of longitudinal studies have been carried out with children of different ages or at different stages of development (Hetherington, 1989; Hetherington, Cox, & Cox, 1985; Reznick, Mednick, Baker, & Hocevar, 1986; Wallerstein, 1984; Wallerstein & Kelly, 1980b). There has been some investigation of the responses of children of a specific age at the time of the divorce, without, however, comparing their responses with cross-sections of children of different ages (Blanchard & Biller, 1971; Hetherington et al., 1978, 1979b; McDermott, 1970; Raschke & Raschke, 1979; Santrock, 1975). In studies of the effect of divorce on children, the issue of measurement is also critical. Findings suggest that significant differences occur when comparing parents' and children's perceptions of the children's functioning and adjustment to a divorce (Hingst, 1981; Kurdek & Siesky, 1980). Parents' measures as well as the children's evaluations are insufficient indices of the child's level of adjustment. Cognitive dissonance as social desirability may affect their responses. To the extent that parents perceive themselves as being responsible and feel guilty for the pain of divorce, they may overstate their children's positive outcome. Children also may appear to one or both parents as angry, withdrawn, or unresponsive because they have the capacity to "layer" their responses over deeper feelings of sadness and loss (Roseby, 1985).

Teachers' reports are subject to criticism as well, especially as the sole measure of children's outcomes. There is some evidence that teachers maintain stereotypes that affect the objectivity of their judgment (Cooper, Holman, & Braithwaite, 1983; Guttmann & Broudo, 1988–1989; Guttmann, Geva, & Gefen, 1988; Santrock & Tracy, 1978). There are indications to show that when provided with real schoolwork, teachers' evaluations are not effected by the children's family background (Guttmann & Broudo, 1988). Teachers, however, may be the targets of the displaced anger of latency-aged children, a situation that can reasonably be expected to affect teachers' evaluations.

The independent variable (divorce, separation, or parent absence) is also often poorly defined in the literature, making it difficult to predict the interaction between the specific aspects of the single-parent experience and the child's level of development. But the child's level of development appears to be the single most consistent variable predicting children's reaction to divorce. Amato and Keith (1991) recently conducted a meta-analysis of 92 studies of children of divorced parents. They report that age at the time of divorce has a significant effect on the children's psychological and social adjustments and on their relationship with both parents.

Therefore, this chapter is structured along children's developmental lines and focuses on the studies that clearly identify children's age or developmental stage at the time of divorce (i.e., preschool, latency-age, and adolescence).

THE PRESCHOOL CHILD

Wallerstein and Kelly (1980b) noted that preschool children were relatively vulnerable to the short-term crisis effects of divorce, and demonstrated more acute and global reactions than did the older children in their sample. Preschool boys were described as particularly vulnerable as compared with their female counterparts, who over the course of a year regained their developmental equilibrium more rapidly.

Fear, sadness, and anger manifested by regression, emotional neediness, dependency, clinging, and increased aggression would appear to describe the response of preschool children to the divorce of their parents. In general, the clinical and quantitative studies discussed here do not differ in their reports of almost all young children's responses during the decision and early mourning period.

Three specific vulnerability factors emerge with striking consistency within this developmental stage (Roseby, 1985). The first factor is gender. In many reports, preschool boys showed more developmental disruptions and for longer periods (up to 2 years and beyond) than did girls (Emery, 1982; Hetherington et al., 1978, 1979a; Hodges & Bloom, 1984; Kurdek & Berg, 1983; Wallerstein & Kelly, 1980b; Westman et al., 1970). There are other studies that report no such gender difference (e.g., Pett, 1982; Reinhard, 1977). An analysis of more than 90 studies led Amato and Keith (1991) to conclude that their data show that "boys and girls did not differ in the extent to which parental divorce was associated with problems, with the exception that boys from divorced families exhibited more difficulty adjusting socially than did girls" (p. 33). The fact that when divorce occurs it is the father who most often leaves may, from the psychoanalytic perspective, explain some of this specific gender difference. "Compensatory masculinity" and the fearful dependency of preschool boys who experience parental divorce may be explained by the mergence of egocentric thought, fear of Oedipal triumph, and the subsequent attempts to defend against an overly enmeshed relationship with the custodial parent (Roseby, 1985).

A second factor is the stress experienced at home in the predivorce stage, in consequence of which children are vulnerable to more severe and longer term effects (McDermott, 1968; Wallerstein & Kelly, 1974). And third, the lack of adequate parenting may negatively effect children's sense of trust and autonomy (Westman, 1972) and put them at psychological risk. Also consistent with behavioral manifestations of mistrust, shame, and doubt, the children become needy, dependent, and behaviorally problematic. Finally, the children's own cognitive developmental limitations and emotional immaturity exacerbate their reaction to the situation.

SHORT-TERM EFFECTS

Behavioral Reactions

Clinical studies (e.g., McDermott, 1970; Wallerstein & Kelly, 1980b) of children's behavior describe preschoolers as coping characteristically by means of regression during the periods of the decision to divorce and of early mourning following the separation.

Children of divorce were described as regressed by teachers, parents, and naive independent raters in a longitudinal multimethod analysis of the response of preschool children to the divorce of their parents (Hetherington et al., 1978). Specifically, it was reported that these children engaged in more noncompliant, dependent, and aggressive behavior than did the control group at home as well as in the classroom and lab. This was true for a period of 1 year. After 2 years, however, although the differences between subjects and controls were still significant, some improvement in the former was noted.

Hetherington et al. (1979b) reported similar differences for boys and girls in a specific analysis of the social interaction and play of children from divorced families. All children from such homes were described in the first year following divorce as being more constricted and cognitively immature in their play than were children from intact families, as well as generally more immature, ineffective, and negative in their social interactions. At the end of 2 years, these differences were found only for boys.

Hetherington et al. (1978, 1979a) noted that financial, social, and interparental support systems can significantly affect parenting, which in turn shapes the young child's experience. However, they agreed with clinicians in identifying the relationship of the mother (or custodial parent) and the child as the most critical variable affecting children's ability to adjust. At least for preschool boys, the finding of increased dependency is consistent with other reports of children in the decision and mourning stages (Hetherington et al., 1978, 1979a; McDermott, 1968; Wallerstein & Kelly, 1974, 1980b). This would suggest that dependency and emotional neediness may be a long-term effect. Decreased aggression is not consistent with these reports.

Kalter and Rembar's (1981) study of the effects of a child's age at the time of divorce shows a consistency with these findings. The study revealed significantly lower incidences of aggression toward parents and peers in latency and adolescence among boys who had experienced separation or divorce before the age of 3. In latency, however, boys experiencing early separation showed more problems of overdependency and entanglement with parents than did boys who experienced separation in later preschool years. These findings replicate Santrock's (1977) data regarding boys who had experienced separation or divorce by their third year, except that mothers in his study reported that boys showed extreme dependency and lowered aggression even before latency, if the experience of parental separation occurred very early. On the other hand, the responses of older, Oedipal-stage preschoolers who displayed aggressive as well as dependent reactions has been described by Wallerstein and Kelly (1974), Hetherington et al. (1978), and McDermott (1968).

Emotional Reactions

Thirty-four children between the ages of 2½ and 6 were the subjects of Wallerstein and Kelly's (1975) sample. The first set of interviews with these children took place in the early mourning period, close to the time that their parents had announced their final decision to separate or divorce. The emotional responses of these young children were chiefly fear, anxiety, and sadness; these being manifested behaviorally by regression in toilet training, irritability, whining, acute separation anxiety, sleep problems, cognitive confusion, increased autoerotic activities, return to transitional objects, escalation of aggressive behavior, and tantrums. According to Wallerstein and Kelly, these responses could partially be attributed to the children's immature grasp of the events, their confusion in differentiating between fantasy and reality, and their awareness of dependency on their parents for care and protection. Boys were less able than girls to deny the father's departure, and widespread fantasy and denial were reported among this sample of preschoolers. The children were intensely fearful, which was compounded by the failure of their parents to furnish them with suitable explanations and assurances. As a consequence, the children were led to rely on their own fantasy explanations, which included self-blame and the belief that they too were discardable or replaceable, in the same way as were husbands and wives.

These responses appeared as characteristic of almost all preschoolers in the sample in the decision and early mourning stages. Wallerstein and Kelly (1975) specifically noted that rather than being psychologically disturbed, the preschoolers as a group appeared to be children responding to severe life stress.

An evaluation was made again 1 year after separation. The regression, aggression, and fear disappeared in most children. Preschoolers who continued to be affected beyond the initial crisis seemed to be reacting to factors other than the divorce itself. That is, mainly continued parental conflicts and inadequate parenting. A deterioration was found in 15 of the 34 children; that is, among almost half the group. The more severely disturbed preschoolers manifested symptoms of sleeplessness, inhibition, constriction in play and fantasy, aggression, and an urgent need for physical contact with adults and for adult attention. No correlation was found between the intensity or number of initial symptoms and later psychological health or developmental progress. This would suggest that for most young children, crisis reactions to the decision and early mourning stages of divorce may be normal. The predivorce period appeared to have increased the vulnerability of 6 of the sample's children who had deteriorated because each had fathers with neurotic illnesses or problems of alcoholism, and as a result had been exposed for years to harsh and irrational discipline.

Wallerstein and Kelly concluded that the quality of the parent–child relationship was the most significant determinant of a young child's experience in the first year following divorce. Mother's employment, their results show, was not predictive of the quality of that relationship.

Rosenthal's (1979) clinical report sheds further light on the preschoolers who are vulnerable to the trauma of parental divorce. His subjects were children who were referred to a child psychiatry clinic less than 1 year after the divorce of their parents. The reasons for the referrals were much the same as described in Wallerstein and Kelly's study. The children showed severe symptoms of regression, aggression, and excessive dependence on objects and adults. These children, however, had become symptomatic only after their mothers themselves became depressed and unable to respond positively to the children's needs. Rosenthal, like Wallerstein and Kelly, concluded that the children's reactions were due more to the deterioration of the parent–child relationship and lack of cognitive understanding of the situation than to the loss of one parent.

In a later study by Rosenthal, Leigh, and Elardo (1985/1986), however, home environment and mother–child relationship were not different between single- and two-parent families. The conflicting results between this and earlier studies by Rosenthal and by Wallerstein may be explained by the fact that in the latter Rosenthal study the sample of the preschool children and their mothers was a nonclinical one.

Children's predivorce adjustment was found to determine their reaction to divorce in McDermott (1968). He examined nonclinical samples of children in a preschool setting before and immediately after parent separation. The before and after comparison indicated that children who were well adjusted before the separation showed no disruptions in their developmental achievements after the separation. These children had good relationships with their parents and were actively attempting to overcome the difficulties associated with divorce. In direct contrast, children who showed the most severe regression (ultimately requiring referral for clinical treatment) were those who, before the separation, had experienced long-lasting parental conflicts and had limited resources with which to cope with the additional stresses associated with the separation. The girls in McDermott's study, as in the Wallerstein and Kelly study, were generally less severely affected than boys.

LONG-TERM EFFECTS

Contrary to her earlier findings, Wallerstein (1984), in her 10-year follow-up study, found that younger children were considerably less burdened emotionally by divorce than older children. She attributed this to the fact that preschool children seemed to remember less of parental conflicts before and immediately after the separation or of their own painful feelings at that time.

Boys' Gender Identification

At first, researchers have taken the dependency regression reactions of boys who experience very early divorce as evidence of weakened gender identification and of disruptive trust and autonomy (Biller, 1970; Santrock, 1970; Westman, 1972). In the discussion of short-term effects, it was suggested that boys who experience divorce during the Oedipal stage of psychosexual development show more aggressive behaviors than do boys who undergo parental divorce before the age of 3.

In his study of 11-year-old boys who had experienced divorce or separation at ages 0–2, 3–5, and 6–9, respectively, Santrock (1970) reported that the earlier the divorce occurred, the lower the level of aggression. Kalter and Rembar (1981) reported that the lowered aggression and increased dependency evinced by boys over the short term also continued through latency. For latency-aged boys, parental separation or divorce before age 3 was significantly associated with a higher incidence of nonaggressive overdependency on parents. Santrock found that nonaggression was associated with overdependency rather than higher levels of disobedience. It may be that because Kalter and Rembar's sample was middle class and clinical, whereas Santrock's was lower class and nonclinical, disobedience in this case was an adaptive defense against overdependency. This could also be more characteristic of low socioeconomic status (SES) children in school settings (Roseby, 1985).

Compensatory masculinity is the definition given to increased aggression during the Oedipal period by researchers and clinicians within the psycho-analytic framework that typically underlies father-absence studies. It is a defense against an enmeshed, eroticized relationship with the female parent and the feared consequences of attaining Oedipal fantasies (Anthony, 1974; Gardner, 1977; Toomin, 1974; Westman et al., 1970). Others have pro-posed that the more negative, less supportive attitudes of parents and teachers toward the needs of young boys (as opposed to girls) result in a primarily aggressive response (Hetherington et al., 1978; Santrock, 1975; Santrock & Tracy, 1978; Wallerstein & Kelly, 1980b). Although the causes continue to be debated, a critical concern in assessing the seriousness of this outcome is whether these effects continue in the long term.

Girls' Gender Behavior

In their study of the relationship between children's ages, Kalter and Rembar (1981) reported that adolescent females who had experienced separation and/or divorce between the ages of 3 and 5 showed higher levels of aggression toward parents and peers, as well as more academic problems than did all boys of all ages as well as girls who had experienced divorce at other stages in their development. The researchers suggested that for these girls, the rage over a divorce experienced during the Oedipal phase was well internalized until puberty. At that point, when sexual issues are reawa-kened, there was a "time bomb" effect.

Latency-aged boys (Kalter & Rembar, 1981) tended to experience fewer subjective feelings of distress than did girls. Instead, there were more behavioral expressions of conflict. This would suggest that preschool boys express conflict more overtly, not that they are more vulnerable. Girls appear equally vulnerable when the analysis extends to long-term effects, but at a later point in their development.

Hetherington (1972), in her comparison of 13- to 17-year-old girls from intact, divorced, and widowed families, hypothesized that latent effects in preschool girls would be manifested as disturbances in self-esteem and heterosexual behavior during adolescence. This was confirmed by her findings. All the daughters from divorced families showed more hetero-sexual patterns and lower self-esteem than did the daughters of widows. More inappropriate receptiveness and seductiveness toward males (naive interviewers), and earlier and more frequent dating and sexual intercourse were shown by girls who experienced parental divorce before age 5 than by girls experiencing divorce after age 5. Taking a father-absence perspective, Hetherington concluded that for girls, the effects of the loss of a male parent during the Oedipal period appeared during adolescence, and were manifested mainly as an inability to interact appropriately with males.

The data are equivocal regarding the conclusion that preschool girls internalize their responses to divorce, the disturbances becoming manifest only in adolescence. In two separate studies, Hainline and Feig (1978) and Young and Parish (1977) failed to replicate Hetherington's findings. In Hainline and Feig's work, 17- to 23-year-old female college students who had experienced early and late parental divorce (before age 5 and ages 5–11, respectively), were compared with daughters from intact and widowed homes. Daughters experiencing early father absence were reported as being more accepting in their attitudes toward sexual intercourse. They were also more traditional than late father-absent girls on a measure of gender-role traditionalism; and they revealed attitudes of dependency toward personal relationships, marriage, and sexual intercourse, and in their behavior toward male interviewers. There were no differences in self-esteem; nor were there differences in observed or reported behavior with males. Overall, these researchers reported that they had failed to replicate Hetherington's (1972) major findings. They offered a sociopolitical interpretation of their failure to replicate, noting that Hetherington's subjects were of a lower SES than those in their own sample. They suggested that reduced income, pressure on the mother, and family stress may more directly influence the developing child than does the absence of a father. It is understandable that Hetherington found significant differences and Hainline and Feig did not because these stresses would be expected in a lower SES sample.

Also important from a developmental perspective is the greater youthfulness of Hetherington's sample as compared to that of Hainline and Feig (ages 13–17 as opposed to 18–23). It may be that the new developmental tasks associated with early adolescence create conflict and anxiety in the father-absent preschool girl who has put these issues aside during latency; so that the period of early adolescence may require a "working through" of the effects of early parental divorce. As Hainline and Feig noted, this working through may have been accomplished among their sample of older girls who had also managed to get to college.

Hetherington had reported lower self-esteem for adolescents from divorced homes only, whereas Hainline and Feig (1978) found no differences between the three groups on this measure. In a study of 98 college females ages 17–22, Young and Parish (1977) compared college-aged daughters from divorced, widowed, and intact homes on measures of self-esteem, insecurity, and willingness to associate with the opposite gender. They reported that daughters of the two father-absent groups had lower self-esteem than the intact group. This confirmed their specific hypothesis that the social and emotional difficulties of young father-absent adolescent females would be attenuated by age and interaction with peers. This finding differed from the findings of Hetherington and of Hainline and Feig. Young and Parish also failed to find differences between the groups on the subjects' stated willingness to associate with the opposite gender. Finally,

Young and Parish found no main effect of age at time of separation with regard to Kalter and Rembar (1981) and Hetherington's (1972) time bomb effects of parental divorce during preschool years.

Young and Parish also pointed to the different SES of their own and Hetherington's sample. They suggested that this difference may be a more powerful determinant of children's subsequent development than the age at which the separation from father occurred. They concluded that the passage of time may indeed weaken the heterosexual difficulties found by Hetherington in adolescent daughters from divorced families.

The long-term effects of divorce on preschool girls offered in these studies are somewhat contradictory and clearly incomplete. Conclusions, therefore, must be tentative and are presented for heuristic rather than diagnostic or prescriptive purposes.

From the evaluations of Hetherington and of Kalter and Rembar (1981) regarding girls within similar age (ages 12–17, and 13–18, respectively), it would appear that preschool girls who experience separation or divorce may indeed manifest disturbances in heterosexual and peer interactions in their early adolescence. Increased rates of peer aggression in females who had experienced early separation were found by Kalter and Rembar. Hainline and Feig (1978) reported more acceptance of sexual intercourse in early separation adolescent females than in other groups. Precocious heterosexuality and social aggression appearing in early adolescence may be the form taken by the latent effects of divorce on the preschool development of females. However, as indicated by the work of Hainline and Feig (1978) and Young and Parish (1977), these disturbances may be worked through in the course of adolescence.

The finding is inconclusive regarding lowered self-esteem in female adolescents being a product of parental divorce in early childhood. The cause of low self-esteem may reside in sociopolitical and economic factors rather than absence of father because lower self-esteem was found in adolescents from divorced families only in Hetherington's low SES sample (with no father in the home after the divorce), and among Young and Parish's adolescents from widowed and divorced families with no father substitute.

Behavioral and Academic Consequences

As reported by Kalter and Rembar (1981), boys who were of Oedipal age when their parents separated showed significantly higher levels of school behavior problems, exhibiting a tendency to act out. The researchers concluded that the short-term effect of heightened aggression in boys experiencing divorce or separation during the Oedipal period continues into latency. In the Santrock (1970) sample, the boys were 11 at the time of the study and the category of the oldest age at divorce was 6 to 9 years. Santrock did not specifically identify increasingly higher rates of aggression that he found as being a product of the Oedipal period as the age of children at the time of divorce increased. His conclusions are difficult to interpret. Considering the ages of the subjects in his study, Santrock's failure to distinguish specific effects of the Oedipal stage may have reflected the recentness of the divorce for many boys, thereby confounding short- and long-term effects.

Hetherington (1979) also noted the connection of school-related problems and aggression in latency-aged boys who had experienced separation during their preschool years. Finding significant lags in these boys' cognitive development 2 years following divorce, Hetherington hypothesized that the tendency of boys to act out their feelings during preschool years interfered with their ability to focus on academic achievement. Blanchard and Biller (1971), studying the academic achievement of third-grade boys from high and low father-present homes, also found considerably more underachievement in latency-aged boys experiencing parental divorce before the age of 5 than among other groups.

As these data suggest, the development of a sense of "industry" that is the central psychosocial task of latency is significantly interfered with in the aggressive acting-out that marks the behavior of boys who were Oedipal age at the time of divorce or separation. Unfortunately, Kalter and Rembar's (1981) reported that adolescent boys experiencing separation during their Oedipal years revealed significantly lower levels of aggression and school problems than all other male and adolescent female subjects in their sample is inconsistent with the preceding findings. It is possible, these researchers suggested, that their findings may be the result of revived fantasies of Oedipal victories, accompanied by guilt and anxiety. The consequence would be to increase pressure on adolescent boys to maintain a tighter rein on their aggressive impulses, and to expend less energy on acting out and more on academic achievement. Can puberty have so dramatically affected the boys who displayed significantly high rates of aggressive behavior and academic problems in latency? Further research is needed for the answers, because Kalter and Rembar's sample was clinical and other data on long-term effects of Oedipal stage divorce in adolescent boys are not available.

To conclude, therefore, the latent effects of parental divorce in early childhood, accompanied perhaps by feelings of low self-esteem (aggravated or produced by low SES), may be expected to appear in females at the onset of adolescence, when issues of sexuality, heterosexual behavior, and attitudes toward males must be confronted and resolved. The available data, although taking into account that the passage of time may attenuate these difficulties for those not hampered by socioeconomic factors, hold no such promise for children who must cope with developmental and sociopolitical stressors when they reach adolescence.

LATENCY-AGED CHILDREN

Social awareness and self-awareness increase significantly during the latency stage of development. But the expanding awareness of behaviors and feelings of others develops before the ability to fully interpret their meanings (Longfellow, 1979; Neal, 1983). Consequently, children experiencing divorce in early latency may be aware of their anger but may fail to integrate it with their feelings of loyalty and fear. Both clinical and quantitative reports on the short-term effects of parental divorce highlight the latency-aged child's conflict between anger and loyalty. These findings may be partially explained by the gains in social cognition and the limitations in interpersonal reasoning that are characteristic of latency.

Nor does the ability to integrate conflicting feelings increase in later latency, although the understanding of these feelings does become greater. Neal (1983) reported that a belief in absolutes and willful intentionality of behavior continue to impede an interpretation of the feelings and behavior of others. In considering the issue from a psychosexual perspective, Westman (1972) noted that because the latency-aged child is actively involved in identifying with parents, the hurt experienced from a sense of rejection by the departing parent is all the more intense. The departure of a parent is felt as a personal rebuff. The targets for directed anger that emerge out of these conflict-provoking developmental capacities are deprivation of a "normal family" structure; being pushed out of center stage; the perceived willful behavior of one or both parents; and the experience of shame arising from a growing ability to view the behavior of parents from what is perceived to be the standpoint of society.

Characteristically, the preschool child shows extreme dependency on a primary parent; not so the latency-aged child, who has developed beyond this stage. Wallerstein and Kelly (1980b), Hess and Camara (1979), and Young (1983) reported an increased responsiveness to broader family dynamics and a willingness to actively manipulate postdivorce relationships so as to achieve the firm familial identity that is necessary to differentiate the self from the peer group. Latency-aged children are vulnerable to isolation and/or alignment with one parent and alienation from the other, as a result of their capacity for directed anger and active involvement in family dynamics. Hess and Camara (1979) and Cooper et al. (1983) reported that the children who are most severely vulnerable to loss of self-esteem, depression, and impaired behavior and performance at school are those who are isolated.

In light of these developmental characteristics, the presence of interpersonal conflict emerges as a powerful factor in latency-aged children's vulnerability to the consolidation of negative, short-term effects during all stages of divorce. This is particularly true if the divorce is attended by the denigration of one parent by another and/or the child's loss of contact with one parent (Blanchard & Biller, 1971; Hess & Camara, 1979; Wallerstein & Kelly, 1980b).

Wallerstein and Kelly (1980b) and Santrock (1975, 1977) observed that, as in the case of preschool children, gender appears to affect the latency-aged child's relative vulnerability to parental separation. Boys were consistently reported, particularly by teachers, to act out in ways that were perceived as aggressive and aversive. These behaviors in boys were explained from a psychosexual perspective as an all-consuming drive to prove masculinity after the father's departure (Anthony, 1974).

The interaction of cognitive and psychosexual developmental agendas of a latency-aged boy whose father leaves, following parental separation, appears to exacerbate the boy's vulnerability, particularly to disruptions in gender identification and in the development of a sense of industry. Psychosocially, the boy's perception of his father's rejection may tip the balance between "industry" and "inferiority" in the direction of the latter. Further evidence of this is furnished by reports that behavioral manifestations of anxiety, anger, sadness, and cognitive confusion (more pronounced in boys) encroach on academic performance and/or the teacher's ability to teach. Additionally, Wallerstein and Kelly (1980b) as well as Jacobson (1978) and Shinn (1978) found that lack of information, communication, and understanding regarding the causes of divorce will increase the likelihood of negative short-term and, possibly, of negative long-term effects.

SHORT-TERM EFFECTS

Behavioral Reactions

In the few studies that specifically identified a latency-aged population, boys were reported to express (like their preschool brothers) a greater degree of anger and stress than did girls. On the other hand, neither the children's vulnerability to alignments nor their blame and withdrawal in their relationships with divorcing parents were documented as predictable by gender in the literature reviewed thus far. In a study that differentiated the responses of younger and older latency-aged children, Wallerstein and Kelly (1980b) described the younger group as overwhelmed by sadness and anxiety, against which they could muster no defense; but they also found a subgroup of young latency-aged boys able to mobilize and express their anger. Most boys displaced their anger onto teachers and siblings, although some of them directly and overtly blamed their mothers for making the father leave. It is possible that for young latency-aged children, fears of abandonment and feelings of vulnerability would be increased by direct expression of anger.

Several other studies (Camara & Resnick, 1989; Santrock & Warshak, 1979; Zill, 1978) also dealt with displaced anger. In studying gender-typed behaviors among latency-aged boys from separated and divorced families, Santrock (1977) used doll-play interviews and teacher evaluations to make assessments. Higher levels of aggression were reported on both measures for boys who had experienced parental separation or divorce in early latency than for boys who had experienced separation or divorce during their preschool years. In both measures, the targets of aggression were extrafamilial.

Kalter and Rembar's (1981) study appears to contradict the findings of the studies that suggest that young latency-aged boys experiencing separation and divorce may defensively inhibit expressions of anger within the family, while venting their feelings in less-threatening environments. Kalter and Rembar studied the effects of anger at divorce in a group of latency-aged boys who had experienced separation at age 6 or 7. The researchers found significantly lower levels of aggression toward inanimate objects in this group than among children who had experienced separation or divorce at other points in their development, and significantly higher rates of nonaggressive overdependence on peers. No significant findings were reported for girls.

Kalter and Rembar's sample was drawn from a clinical population, which is an important factor to keep in mind in attempting to reconcile the conclusions of the three studies. Among young latency-aged boys, pathology may be exhibited in the form of highly anxious overinhibition of aggression, so that anger remains internalized in all settings and toward all objects.

It was McDermott's (1968) findings, based on his work with younger children, that suggested this hypothesis. The children who were ultimately referred for treatment were those who did not act out. McDermott found that boys from separated or divorced families who expressed their anger in a school setting, recovered their equilibrium within a brief period, whereas the more severely disturbed children were those who passively regressed.

Unlike younger children, who feared their own anger and questioned their ability to control it, older latency children used anger as a defense against underlying feelings of helplessness. According to Wallerstein and Kelly, older latency-aged children responded to their feelings of anger with less anxiety. Attempts to put the divorce in perspective, or at least to achieve a sense of intellectual control, may be a reason for attributing blame to one or both parents.

In their study of postdivorce family relationships, Hess and Camara (1979) found that levels of aggression were more reliably predicted by family conflict than by divorce. They reported higher levels of aggression in preadolescent children who had experienced divorce within the previous 2 or 3 years. These researchers found, as had Wallerstein and Kelly (1980b), that teachers and parents were aware of significantly higher levels of aggression in boys than in girls. The findings may suggest that latency-aged children are vulnerable to familial alignments, as well as being sensitive to broader family dynamics. This trait contrasts with the more egocentric sensitivity of preschoolers to changes in the relationship with whichever parent assumes care and control of the child after marital separation.

Santrock (1975), in a study of the moral development of preadolescent boys, reported that teachers rated boys from separated and divorced families as less considerate of others, less accepting of blame, and more likely to get into trouble in and out of school. Just as the anger of early latency-aged children may be expressed in overinhibition, so may the intense rage of later latency be expressed in more passive forms.

The anger of younger latency-aged boys was attributed by Wallerstein and Kelly to fears of Oedipal regression. They further hypothesized that the stark anger of older children was the result of failed attempts to achieve a sense of control by comprehending the interpersonal meaning of divorce. In younger children, anger was vented as a defense against regression; and in those who were older at the time of the divorce, against powerlessness and cognitive confusion.

Santrock (1975) defined anger in terms similar to those of Hetherington's analysis of the meaning of aggressive behavior in preschool boys of divorce. Increased levels of aggression in boys were defined as a response to the increased use of power and assertion by the divorced mother, as she attempted to assume the role of disciplinarian in her family.

Emotional Reactions

Sadness and grief that could not be fended off by fantasy or denial were the most pervasive response by 6- to 8-year-olds (Wallerstein & Kelly, 1975, 1980b). These researchers studied 57 children between the ages of 6 and 12. They were unable theoretically to account for the striking difference they found in the responses of the 6- to 8-year-olds and those of the older latency groups. Being without either the primitive defenses available to younger children or the more sophisticated cognitive and behavioral defenses that emerge in later years, these early latency children were described by Wallerstein and Kelly as being fully conscious of their grief and therefore more vulnerable. Sadness appeared to be associated with a marked longing for the absent parent that was unique to this age group in Wallerstein and Kelly's sample. This was expressed in fantasies of deprivation of toys or food, so that some children compulsively overate or sought to acquire toys and other objects. The researchers hypothesized that this yearning, particularly in boys who had newly resolved Oedipal conflicts, resulted from acute fears of regression. Aggression was directed toward the custodial mother, as the children's longing for their father expressed itself by an inhibition of aggression toward him. Typically, children attempted to remain loyal to both the parents, although the tendency of both parents actively to enlist their children as allies against their spouse intensified the children's sadness and lowered their ability to confide in and be supported by either parent. Nonetheless, unlike the preschool children, neither early nor late latency children reported feeling responsible for their parents' divorce.

Wallerstein and Kelly described the late latency-age group's reactions to the early stages of divorce as a "layering of responses." At the time of divorce, children in this age group were able to mobilize passive defenses such as denial and coping, as well as more active strategies, such as seeking support from others. By vigorously endeavoring not to think about the divorce or understand it, this group provided so effective a cover that only after several clinical interviews were the researchers able to gain access to their feelings of loss, rejection, and helplessness. Feelings of anger, on the other hand, were clearly directed and articulately expressed. Wallerstein and Kelly described this coping response as the most pervasive and unique characteristic of late latency children.

Finally, a noticeable decline in both school performance and the ability to relate to peers was shown by half of the late latency children. In a follow-up done after 1 year, more than half of the early latency children had improved or maintained earlier developmental achievements. Symptoms of severe depression were shown by the children who failed to recover from their early responses, and by those who had deteriorated.

Almost all latency-aged children recovered from their initial academic decline. Half had lost their initial feelings of fear and worry, and the remaining effect was anger. Among latency-aged children, vulnerability to deterioration after 1 year was associated with continued interparent hostility, inadequate parenting from the remaining parent, and insufficient contact with the custodial parent. The group of late latency children who had deteriorated at the end of 1 year showed depression (as had the younger deteriorated group), and loss of self-esteem.

Family Relationships

For latency-aged children, an alignment may be a particularly attractive way to reestablish their equilibrium because their conception of their own identity in this developmental stage is closely tied to the external family structure (Gardner, 1977; Lamb, 1977; Wallerstein & Kelly, 1980b). As Wallerstein and Kelly (1980b) noted, latency-aged children are more vulnerable to the demands of their parents for loyalty than are either preschoolers or adolescents. The tendency of parents to view a child of this age as being old enough to serve as an ally and young enough to be manipulated in this way may be partially accountable for this.

Wallerstein and Kelly (1980b) and Adams (1982) reported that adolescents who experience divorce or separation typically seek support outside of family relationships. This is particularly true for those children who are developmentally prepared to individuate; which would suggest that both latency-aged children and adolescents are consciously aware of their vulnerability. However, latency-aged children are developmentally unprepared to individuate from the family system, and are therefore limited to seeking support within the family wherever and however they may find it. The coping value for latency-aged children of finding an ally within the family, has been suggested by nonclinical reports; although it would seem reasonable to expect that familial alignment is too subtle an issue to be reported outside of clinical interviews.

Working with 7- to 11-year-olds participating in a postfiling workshop that had been mandated by the court, Young (1983) conducted a study of self-reported blame styles. He found that children reported anticipating greater difficulty in coping with the divorce when blaming their mother (the custodial parent) or both parents, and thus aligning themselves with their noncustodial father or neither parent, than did children who blamed their noncustodial father but not the custodial mother. Young also reported that children said they anticipated few problems or no problems in coping with the divorce when neither parent was blamed. The issue of denial must be considered here, as it must in all highly positive single-source and self-report samples.

Possibly, the children who blame neither parent are early latency children who seek to avoid alignment by keeping their thoughts and feelings to themselves. If this is so, a further indication of their effort to remain neutral may be their reports of fewer anticipated difficulties. This explanation remains conjectural because Young (1983) did not evaluate the effect of age within his sample. It is also surprising that future problems were not anticipated nor either parent blamed by older latency children whose principal response in Wallerstein and Kelly's (1980b) sample was anger. Unlike the children in Wallerstein and Kelly's sample, those in Young's group may have been exceptionally well informed and understood the divorce so clearly as to feel no blame toward their parents; although this explanation seems doubtful because of Young's finding that more than one third of the sample reported receiving no explanation at all before joining the workshop.

Among latency-aged children, there remains a clear correlation between blaming the custodial parent (or mother) and anticipated difficulty in coping with divorce. This finding tends to support the view that children see alignment with the custodial parent as a source of support.

Parish and Dostal (1980) also reported identification with the custodial parent; although this process was found to occur more gradually than did the professions of loyalty and attributions of blame that were found in the decision and the early mourning stages of divorce both by Young (1983) and by Wallerstein and Kelly (1980b). These researchers found that the self-concepts of children in intact families were significantly correlated with their evaluation of each of their parents. For children who were between the ages of 8 and 11 at the time of divorce (2 years prior to the study), their self-concepts were as significantly correlated with their mothers (with whom they lived) as among children from intact families. Although the finding was less robust than in correlation with mothers, the children's self-concepts were also significantly correlated with their evaluations of their fathers. Those children who had experienced divorce more than 2 years prior to the investigation maintained a strong identification with their mother, but showed no significant correlation between their self-concept and their evaluation of their father.

These clinical and quantitative reports suggest that at least late latency children view alignment with one parent as adaptive when faced with parental divorce. Parish and Dostal (1980) concluded that children from divorced families rapidly identified with their remaining parent, in this case the mother. This, they hypothesized, represented an attempt to reestablish parent–child stability, as defense against uncertainty. Alignment may help children to secure themselves against their own feelings of helplessness and anxiety by providing them with an acceptable target, in the form of the other parent, against whom they can vent their feelings of anger. Unfortunately, it is unclear whether these short-term gains produce negative side effects.

In a study of Australian 10- and 11-year-olds, Cooper et al. (1983) compared the effect of different types of family cohesion on children's self-esteem. This study was conducted across family structures in both divorced and intact families. Their findings suggest that when divorce has the effect of isolating children from their parents, the result may be a significant diminution of children's self-esteem. Feelings of intense anger, helplessness, and insignificance, fostered by perceptions of being thrust aside by parents who were involved in concerns and conflicts of their own, were reported by Wallerstein and Kelly (1980b) in late latency children.

It may be that parents who are preoccupied with their own needs during the early stages of divorce feel isolated from their children because of the defensive neutrality of young latency-aged children, and of the masked responses of older children. Because alignment requires a degree of dissembling in aligned children's interaction with both parents, the isolation and loss of genuine communication may be true for children in aligned relationships as well as for children who hold back from both parents (Roseby, 1985). In comparing responses of latency-aged children to a questionnaire regarding their adjustment to divorce with the parents' responses to the same questionnaire, Young (1983) found some support for this hypothesis. He noted that, except for the items measuring academic and school behavior problems (which were likely to be reported to parents by the school), there were no significant similarities in the reports of parents and children.

Hingst (1981) interviewed latency-aged children, and subsequently their custodial mothers, on the question of the children's perception of and adjustment to parental divorce. In comparing the results of interviews, Hingst reported that mothers were unaware of young latency-aged children's longing for their absent father. In general, mothers described the adjustment of their children in considerably more positive terms than did the children themselves. There is a suggestion here that these children may indeed have been concealing their feelings from their parents. The various ways in which latency-aged children attempt to maintain the support of at least one parent may paradoxically result in the loss of parental involvement in resolving their true feelings and increased sense of isolation.

School Performance

The conclusion reached by Hetherington, Camara, and Featherman (1981), in an analysis of 58 studies of parental absence and academic achievement, was that children in single-parent families receive lower grades and lower achievement ratings from teachers. Several studies have reported that diffuse expression of various forms of anger is consistently manifested in school settings, especially by boys. It is possible that the failure of these children to separate out their feelings may subsequently interfere with their academic performance. However these researchers hypothesized that "teachers' reports of depressed achievement among children from one-parent households may be based on their reactions to disruptive classroom behaviors that do not conform to school expectations rather than on the actual academic performance of these children" (Hetherington et al., 1981, p. 112).

In evaluating specifically the academic performance of latency-aged children experiencing separation or divorce, studies have tended to confirm the view that children from divorced families may receive lower grades from their teachers. Low grades, however, may be attributed to factors other than definitive intellectual deficits.

The academic performances of third-grade boys from early and late divorce homes and from low and high father-available intact homes was studied by Blanchard and Biller (1971). They found that teachers' grades, pointed to marginal academic performance for boys who had experienced parental divorce recently (within the prior 2 years) and for boys experiencing low father availability. The academic achievement test scores of these boys were 3 to 5 months below grade level; whereas boys from intact homes with high father availability scored significantly better on both measures. The teacher-rated measures were only significantly correlated with IQ for high father-available boys. Blanchard and Biller, therefore, concluded that boys from divorced and low father-available families were less likely to actualize their potential because of the lack of an achieving male model.

It is important to keep in mind, however, that low father availability also implies increased maternal power assertion associated with boys' aggression (Hetherington et al., 1978; Santrock, 1977); isolated or aligned family relationships associated with children's low self-esteem (Cooper et al., 1983); and increased family conflict associated with children's increased stress and aggression (Raschke & Raschke, 1979; Rickard et al., 1982; Whitehead, 1979). Similar behavioral deficits, affecting academic achievements and teachers' ratings may therefore be equally credible in boys from low father-available and divorced homes.

In studies of latency-aged children carried out by Stolberg and Anker (1983) and Hess and Camara (1979), a domino effect is suggested of divorce and/or family conflict that produces behavioral and intellectual deficits. Less productive work styles in school were noted in children who had recently experienced divorce and children who were in conflict with one or both parents. The degree of parental attention and permission to discuss the divorce openly was found to be significantly related to the degree of impairment in children's academic functioning in a study by Jacobson (1978) of latency-aged children 1 year following divorce.

These data suggest that children's success in other cognitive areas can be impaired by cognitive preoccupation resulting from limited understanding. Santrock and Tracy (1978) asked two groups to rate the behavior of an 8-year-old boy. One group was told that the boy was from a divorced family; the second group was told that he was from an intact family. The first group rated the child from the divorced family as significantly more negative in his level of happiness, overall emotional adjustment, and ability to cope with stress. The researchers suggested that behavioral deficits in children of divorce interfere less with their academic performance than do the stereotypes of their teachers.

The conclusions of Wallerstein and Kelly (1980b) suggest that not only are teachers' attitudes shaped by the behavior of children, but that their attitudes may in turn also negatively affect children by lowering self-esteem and inhibiting the desire to achieve. Wallerstein and Kelly's descriptions — together with those of Santrock (1977) and Hess and Camara (1979) — of the tendency to displace anger in young latency-aged children, and of the intense and enduring rage that overlays the confusion and helplessness of older latency-aged children, combine with findings of behavioral deficits in school settings to suggest that these children either displace rage onto school or experience responses to parental divorce that are too powerful to be contained. In either case, children's school performance is adversely affected by their increased agitation, aggression, and preoccupation with understanding the divorce; and the effects of this appear to spill over into the school setting.

LONG-TERM EFFECTS

The historical predominance of psychoanalytic views of divorce, according to which the father's absence is expected to disrupt gender role development only during the preschool years, producing long-term effects during adolescence, may partially explain the scant attention that has been paid to the long-term effects of divorce experienced during latency. Yet Wallerstein (1985, 1986a, 1986b) and Wallerstein and Kelly (1980b) presented a grim picture of the long-term outcomes for children who were overtly angry with both divorcing parents during late latency.

A distinct subgroup of intensely angry adolescents was identified by Wallerstein and Kelly (1980b) in their 5-year follow-up. This group consisted of 9- to 12-year-old males who had been described as almost characteristically angry during the decision and early mourning stages. Even worse, the researchers reported that children who had been only moderately angry during latency grew even angrier as they moved into adolescence. They hypothesized that the earlier anger was heightened by "the characteristic rebelliousness of adolescence."

Almost all children who had been involved in parent–child alignments during the early stages of divorce were no longer involved in such relationships and had regained normal functioning. By contrast, the behavior of the angry adolescent males was antisocial and self-destructive. Their conduct consisted of explosive outbursts of temper, rejection of parents, delinquencies, school failure, and truancy. The most severe acting-out occurred among boys who had initially been angry with both parents, as was to be expected from the severity of the short-term effects of blaming both parents, and the subsequent isolation and withdrawal from the family.

Among this group of adolescents, significantly fewer females than males were found by Wallerstein to still be disturbed and angry 5 years following parental divorce. Also, increased sexual activity and promiscuity were the predominant behavioral manifestations among the girls. It may be that females perceive this type of acting-out as more hostile and more rejecting of parents than failure at school.

Kalter and Rembar (1981) reported that if girls experienced divorce during latency, rather than at any point earlier in their development, they had fewer academic problems. On the other hand, there were long-term negative effects on school performance in adolescent males who had experienced separation or divorce during latency. Specifically, they found higher rates of school refusal and truancy for this group in their clinical sample.

Not all latency-aged children were angry and rejecting at the time of the divorce; nor did all latency-aged children become acting-out adolescents. But Wallerstein and Kelly's (1980b) findings describe long-term outcomes for the subgroup of children who were most angry and rejecting of their parents in the early stages of divorce. Because the Kalter and Rembar (1981) sample was clinical, they also described outcomes in the most severely affected group.

In a study of 10-year-olds who had experienced divorce during latency, Kurdek and Berg (1983) found that the children's divorce adjustment was significantly related to internal locus of control and a high level of interpersonal understanding. Girls were significantly better adjusted than boys. Kurdek and Berg also reported in this study that, in addition to being related to locus of control and interpersonal understanding, divorce adjustment was positively related to the custodial mother's adjustment, time spent alone with the noncustodial parent, and low interparent conflict. The degree of environmental change, social status, frequency or regularity of visitation or phone contact with the noncustodial parent were not related to divorce adjustment.

In an earlier study of the correlates of latency-aged children's long-term adjustment at 4 and 6 years following divorce, Kurdek et al. (1981) hypothesized that the children's level of interpersonal knowledge and degree of internality in their locus of control would be the most powerful predictors of long-term adjustment. Their hypothesis was confirmed. In addition, girls were found to be significantly more accepting of the divorce than were boys, and to feel less negatively about its effects in the way of loss of contact with the father and disruption of the peer group.

Hess and Camara (1979), Shinn (1978), Wallerstein and Kelly (1980b), and Jacobson (1978) reported these findings as being consistent with reports that negative short-term effects are related to the child's ability to understand the divorce and the behavior of the other parent.

These findings suggest that boys may indeed be more vulnerable to the negative effects of parental separation and the subsequent disruption of interpersonal relationships, in consequence of possibly having less well-developed capacities for interpersonal reasoning than do girls. The data further suggest that children with the most highly developed capacity for interpersonal understanding will feel less externally controlled, and will consequently feel less anger and harbor less blame than those having limited interpersonal knowledge. Increased interpersonal knowledge coming with maturity seems incapable of mitigating anger and blame in the face of the apparently enduring quality of such attitudes in children who are the angriest and most blaming in the early stages of divorce. It is as though the absolute and judgmental explanation for the divorce developed during latency had become the child's entrenched defense against helplessness and confusion. The resulting cognitive rigidity appears in turn to impair cognitive development, as measured by academic performance.

The long-term outcomes of parental divorce experienced during latency by girls are less clear. Concerning her sample of low-income adolescent females, Hetherington (1972) reported that disturbances in heterosexual behavior (increased anxiety and seductiveness in interaction with males) were more severe in girls who had experienced parental divorce during their preschool years than in girls experiencing divorce during latency. The few girls who continued to be angry into adolescence tended to increased sexual activity and promiscuity. Wallerstein and Kelly (1980b) reported similar findings for girls whose anger continued into adolescence. In two studies subsequent to Hetherington's, Young and Parish (1977) and Hainline and Feig (1978) failed to replicate her results. They found no effects of age at the time of divorce.

As indicated by these sparce findings, fewer females than males are vulnerable to long-term effects. When reported, negative effects in females are most likely to be manifested as sexual acting out. Hetherington (1972) proposed that disturbances in heterosexual behavior were due to the lack of opportunity of females to interact with adult males. Wallerstein and Kelly (1980b), on the other hand, described this behavior as being a manifestation of anger.

ADOLESCENTS

One step that is necessary in achieving a healthy integrated identity is a gradual loosening of ties to the family. The difficulty of this step toward autonomy depends in large measure on the nature of the adolescent–parent relationship.

Adolescents' autonomy develops in three areas: emotions, behaviors, and values (Douvan & Adelson, 1966). Emotional autonomy occurs when people have resolved their infantile attachment to parents and have someone outside the home to satisfy some of their needs for affection and intimacy. Behavioral autonomy comes gradually as people are given, or demand and win, the right to make decisions about personal behavior. Value autonomy occurs when people have constructed their own set of values, a sense of right and wrong, or a commitment or lack of it to a given lifestyle, that are not simply borrowed from or reaction against those of their parents, but developed out of their own inner sense of themselves.

The strive for autonomy clearly involves difficult times for both parents and children. Deep feelings have already been generated in the earlier years of childhood, and neither parents nor adolescents can be expected to react dispassionately to the quest for independence. This quest, however, is the overriding task of adolescents. The drive for independence has motivated the child in many previous stages of development, but now in adolescence it is finally achieved. Whereas at one point the most pressing developmental task was to become part of the family, now the task at hand is to separate oneself from the family successfully. It may be more difficult for adolescents of divorced families than for others to accomplish this task.

The most rapid increase in the divorce rate seems to be in those families with adolescents—in 1982, 14 million 10- to 18-year-olds lived in single parent families (Select Committee on Children, 1983). Whereas one of four children of any age in the United States lives with one parent (U.S. Bureau of the Census, 1983), by the age of 16 one of three White and almost two of three Black adolescents lived for some period with one parent due to divorce (Bumpass & Rindfuss, 1979).

The studies that have specifically evaluated short-term responses of adolescents to divorce are affected, for the most part, by methodological shortcomings. Divorce, being as complex a phenomenon as it is, effects adolescents in a variety of ways depending on multiple factors. Typically, researchers investigating the effect of divorce on adolescents have compared those of divorced parents with those from intact families. By doing so they have disregarded many of the intervening and important factors. Therefore, any generalization and conclusions drawn from the following review must be done with great care.

The subjects of sexual behavior and intergenerational transmission of divorce have been the central issues for studies investigating long-term effects of parental divorce. Other long-term effects of divorce as experienced during adolescence were not found in most studies.

SHORT-TERM EFFECTS

Behavioral Reactions

Behavioral problems of adolescents were found to be associated with parental divorce (e.g., Allison & Furstenberg, 1989). Data on the behavioral reactions of boys do not, however, support the idea that father absence leads to masculinity deficiencies. On the contrary. Father-absent boys were found to behave in a more traditionally masculine way than boys from intact families (Patterson, 1982). Santrock (1977), for example, found his 10- to 12-year-old subjects from divorced families to be significantly more masculine, disobedient, aggressive, and likely take risks than were those from intact families.

The adolescents in Wallerstein & Kelly's (1980b) and Schwartzberg's (1980) studies responded to their parents' divorce in two distinct ways. One group regressed, spending time with younger children. Disruptions in school attendance and performance reflected their preoccupation with the divorce and their need for the reassurances of home. The second group transferred their dependency needs to peers. They attempted to become independent even when not ready. For the boys, this resulted in antisocial behavior and delinquencies. Among females, increased dependency on peers was expressed by early involvement in sexual relationships.

There are other studies as well (e.g., Hainline & Feig, 1978; Hetherington, 1972; Hetherington et al., 1979a; Wallerstein & Kelly, 1976) that report that parental divorce effects the sexual behavior of adolescents girls. These girls began dating earlier, were more sexually active, married younger, and were more likely to be pregnant at the time of their marriage. Their relationships with adults and female friends, however, were not different than girls from intact families (Hetherington, 1972). Both studies also report that when parents continued their support of gradual growth, those adolescents who had displayed temporary regressions were able to resume normal functioning (Schwartzberg, 1980; Wallerstein & Kelly, 1980b).

Weiss (1979) described changes in family structure and role functions in an anecdotal report on the experiences of single parents and their adolescent children. These changes created maturity demands for which only some adolescents were prepared. Particularly when the custodial parent was working outside the home, single parents in the early stages of divorce tended to share managerial responsibilities with their adolescent children. Household chores were taken more seriously after divorce, because the obligation now reflected a more genuine need, as did the responsibility for caring for younger siblings. And, in financial matters and social relationships, adolescents were also expected to function in the role of friend and confidant to their parents.

Delinquency was often related and explained by the "broken home" background of the male (Monahan, 1957, 1960a) as well as female offenders (Austin, 1978). More recent reviews of the relevant studies (Bane, 1976; Herzog & Sudia, 1973; Raschke & Raschke, 1979) conclude that the father-absence–delinquency relationship is far more complicated. They found that other (although related) factors such as the emotional atmosphere and climate at home and the frequent, overt conflict between the parents may be more important than the absence of a father as such.

Emotional Reactions

Research and clinical reports indicate a severe emotional response of adolescents to their parents divorce. In fact, in a recent meta-analysis of the relevant literature, Amato and Keith (1991) reported that parental divorce has the most detrimental effect for children at the primary and high school age. Although there appears to be no difference between adolescents from divorced and intact homes in the rate of referrals to mental health clinics, the reasons for the referrals are different (Bedi, 1981; Schoettle & Cantwell, 1980). In general, adolescents from intact families are referred for developmental and medical reasons. Those from divorced families for behavioral reasons, such as drug abuse, sexually acting out, delinquency, and acting-out behavior (Kalter, 1977; Offord, Abrams, Allen, & Poushinsky, 1979; Schoettle & Cantwell, 1980; Sullivan & Fleshman, 1975–1976).

The majority of adolescents in Wallerstein and Kelly's (1980b) sample of 21 adolescents, the smallest group in their study, were described as angry and grieving in the decision stage. Yet one third of the adolescents were catalyzed into psychological independence. This was reflected in their ability to detach from the family conflict and to demonstrate a high degree of interpersonal understanding in their clinical interviews. The remaining adolescents exhibited signs of psychological distress.

Adolescents experiencing parental divorce may be expected to respond as friends and helpmates to their distressed parents. The extent to which they are able to do so without being enmeshed in the family, depends on their prior developmental achievements, and may shape the course of subsequent adjustment.

Eighteen months after the separation, the adolescents who had become involved in "parenting" one of their parents, so that they were enmeshed in familial relationships with no opportunity to individuate successfully, were those who were also vulnerable to developmental delay. Equilibrium was also not regained by the prematurely detached group; in a downward spiral that could not contribute to the achievement of successful autonomy, they continued their detrimental peer involvement (Wallerstein & Kelly, 1980b).

Clinical reports (Kalter, 1977; Wallerstein & Kelly, 1980b) indicate that among adolescents the most vulnerable to regression and premature disengagement from the family are those who fail to achieve a sense of personal identity or individual strength prior to the divorce, and those who fail to perceive support within the family from either parent. Their failure to achieve autonomy may in fact reflect a history of poor parenting and lack of familial support. These, then, may be the most vulnerable adolescents.

Adolescents who had achieved a psychologically "strategic withdrawal" from the family were functioning well, as were the majority of adolescents who had temporarily regressed. Young (1983) hypothesized that, for adolescents, "leaving the coalition of the family in a kind of 'strategic withdrawal' " (p. 64) was the cause of the weakened prediction value of anger and blame toward parents in the adjustment of adolescents. The parents interviewed by Weiss (1979) thought that the new maturity demands were, in fact, beneficial for the development of independence for their adolescent children. The adolescents seemed to concur. When interviewed, they described themselves as unusually competent and independent. But for others, the increased knowledge of their parents' financial and personal concerns had prompted increased feelings of insecurity. Schlesinger (1982a) reported similarly mixed responses.

In a discussion of the psychological effects of divorce on adolescents, Sorosky (1977) hypothesized that those who are catalyzed into ego-enhancing maturity have an "innate temperament of adaptability." These are adolescents who have a minimum of residual separation anxiety, and have successfully resolved the Oedipal conflict. Previous losses, Sorosky noted, tend to be cumulative, and reactions intensify with each experience. Adolescents who had experienced parental divorce as a loss of generational boundaries before they themselves had ceased to be children, responded angrily with premature detachment. From this perspective, sexual and delinquent acting out were viewed as attempts to force parents back into their parental roles.

The most powerful determinants of adjustment among vulnerable adolescents appear to be the cumulative and current stress of family relationships (McLanahan, 1983; Rutter, 1983). The custodial parent's prior and present ability to provide information, support, and guidance while encouraging increased autonomy have been consistently identified as the most powerful predictor of an adolescent's adjustment (Schlesinger, 1982a; Schwartzberg, 1980; Sorosky, 1977; Wallerstein & Kelly, 1980b).

Farber, Primavera, and Felner's (1983) results of regression analysis also led them to the conclusion that adolescents' perception and experience of the family relationship were the most powerful predictors of their emotional reaction to divorce. Their findings suggest that the experience of prolonged living in a conflicted family may produce more negative long-term effects than does parental divorce followed by a return to equilibrium. Forehand et al.'s (1991) summation of the results of their recent study expresses well the same idea. They wrote: "as family stressors increased, adolescent functioning deteriorated. Furthermore, a positive parent–adolescent relationship as perceived by the adolescent was associated with less deterioration in all areas of functioning" (p. 316). This, however, may be true with regard to the custodial parent–adolescent relationship only. Furstenberg, Morgan, and Allison (1987) reported that the noncustodial fathers' involvement with 11- to 16-year-old children made no specific positive effect on the children's psychological well-being.

School Behavior and Performance

The results of studies investigating the relationship between school behavior and performance and parental divorce do not permit an unequivocal conclusion. For one, many of the studies do not define clearly their independent variable and use the ambiguous *father-absent* term (for detailed review see Adams et al., 1984). Also, although many studies report lower academic and cognitive performance of adolescents from divorced families (e.g., Allison & Furstenberg, 1989; Hunt & Hunt, 1975; Rosenthal & Hansen, 1980; Santrock, 1972), other studies show that family structure is unrelated or only slightly related to intellectual performance (Burchinal, 1964; Mednick, Baker, Reznick, & Hocevar, 1990).

Shinn (1978) reviewed the literature on cognitive performance and father absence and concluded that: (a) children of intact families score higher on achievement and IQ tests than children of father-absent families, (b) father absence due to divorce has more detrimental effects than father absence due to death, and (c) parental conflict has more detrimental effects on children's cognitive performance than the mere fact of father absence.

Several possible explanations are possible for these results. First, adolescents of single-parent families are absent from school more than others. They are more likely to drop out of school and have higher rates of truancy, suspension, and expulsion (Brown, 1980; Conyers, 1977). Second, in single-parent families, adolescents may have less parental attention, authority, and expressed concern over school behavior and work (Zajonc, 1976). It should be noted, however, that these results exclude the noncustodial parent. The noncustodial father's degree of involvement was found to have no effect on adolescents' academic performance (Furstenberg et al., 1987). Third, adolescents' academic performance is hindered by higher test anxiety (Guttmann, 1987). Finally, the result of Guttmann, Amir, and Katz (1987) suggest that when confronted with difficult and frustrating schoolwork, adolescents of divorced parents tend to withdraw earlier than those from intact families.

LONG-TERM EFFECTS

Intergenerational Transmission of Divorce

The possibility that marriages of children of divorced parents are more likely to end in divorce has been the subject of several studies. Although since the 1980s, researchers have begun to study the question of "intergenerational transmission" of marital instability, the effect of age at divorce has unfortunately not been assessed in these studies. The focus has been on whether those who experience parental divorce or separation during childhood or adolescence have different attitudes toward marriage and divorce and are more vulnerable to disruption of their own marriages.

The propensity for early marriage among females from separated or divorced homes was noted, in the attitudes of adolescent females toward marriage, as reported by Ganong, Coleman, & Brown (1981) and Mott and Moore (1979). Because women, to a greater extent than men, look upon marriage as the essential framework of their adult life and self-worth (Glenn, 1975), it was hypothesized that females are more favorable toward marriage, regardless of parental marital status. Females were indeed found to have significantly more positive attitudes toward marriage than did males in a study of attitudes of young adolescents toward marriage and divorce. Ganong, Coleman, and Brown (1981) found a nonsignificant attitudinal difference between their subjects' family structures. Females, however, were found to express more favorable attitudes toward marriage than male adolescents. Investigating Israeli male soldiers, Guttmann (1988–1989) also found no effect of parental divorce on these young adults' attitudes about and expectations of marriage.

In consequence, it seems that even if the conception of marriage presented to them by their parents was a negative image, adolescents of divorced parents revealed themselves as being highly motivated to reject that image. Paradoxically, however, the probability of marital instability to be ultimately recycled is still higher for those with divorced parents.

Pope and Mueller (1976), in a study of "intergenerational instability," hypothesized that "the appropriateness of the sex and marital roles learned in the family by the child determines his or her marital success, the child in an unhappy or broken home will not learn marital roles as appropriately as one in an intact happy home" (p. 52). Pope and Mueller's conclusions of "intergenerational transmission of divorce" is based on their analysis of five large sociological surveys and the differences they found in the frequency of divorce between adults from intact and disrupted families.

Pope and Mueller reported a "transmission effect" for Whites of both genders and for Black females. Significant transitional effects were found, however, for White females only in Glenn and Kramer's (1987) analysis of

11 national large surveys. Living with their fathers after divorce and/or in remarried families seems to reduce the propensity to divorce (Pope & Mueller, 1976).

The researchers concluded that transmission effects may be mediated by economic, social control, and parenting style factors, and that these ultimately offer the most adequate explanation of such effects.

Hetherington (1972) and Kalter and Rembar (1981) found that low SES and clinical samples of females who experienced divorce during their preschool years showed more immature and precocious heterosexual behavior than did controls; whereas the college-educated samples did not (Hainline & Feig, 1978; Young & Parish, 1977). Increased sexual acting-out in adolescent females who were in their latency age at divorce was also reported by Wallerstein and Kelly (1980b). This behavior was associated in particular with failed parent–child relationships and isolation from the family. Similar behavioral symptoms for adolescent females with poor predivorce adjustment were found in many other studies (Schlesinger, 1982b; Schwartzberg, 1980; Sorosky, 1977; Wallerstein & Kelly, 1980b). The age at which the parental divorce occurred, however, seems not to effect the quantity and quality of dating behavior of college students (Booth, Brinkerhoff, & White, 1984). These were effected by the degree of parental hostility during and after the divorce. Those students whose parents' divorce was accompanied by much acrimony, whose custodial parent remained single, and who had a poor relationship with the custodial parent, dated more and perceived their courtship relationship less satisfying. No differences in any of these results were found between males and females.

Although Pope and Mueller (1976) found support for the hypothesis that parental divorce does increase children's vulnerability to divorce in their own marriages, they found little support for the role model rationale. Girls from remarried families showed the highest transmission effects, and marriages of males as well as females who lived with their mothers only showed equally high rates of instability.

Although the simplistic role model may not explain the recycling of divorce, adapting a low "threshold of withdrawal" mode of responses in face of difficulties (Guttmann et al., 1987), may account for some of phenomenon. In a study investigating the threshold of withdrawal from schoolwork of children of divorced parents, Guttmann et al. (1987) found that in comparison to adolescents from intact families, those of divorced parents withdraw sooner from difficult and frustrating tasks. Although generalizing these results to the domain of interpersonal relationships is still difficult, the idea deserves further investigation.

Using data from one of the five samples in their 1976 study, Mueller and Pope (1977) undertook a second study to evaluate their transmission hypothesis specifically in the case of females. They concluded that women from intact homes tend to marry older, higher status males who have not been previously married. These women are generally older and better educated; they are also less often pregnant at the time of marriage. The researchers concluded that the individuals involved in early marriages are those who are less socially and emotionally mature, and subject to greater economic hardship and enjoy less social support than are those who marry later.

Employing a sample from a national survey considered representative of a full cross-section of U.S. women, Mott and Moore (1979) studied the causes of marital disruption in young women. They found that age at marriage and level of education were significant determinants of divorce and separation. Both factors correlated negatively with the incidence of divorce. But like Pope and Mueller (1976), Mott and Moore reported that being raised in a broken home was positively associated with marital disruption.

Yet, in a more recent study of 1,979 married people, Booth and Edwards (1989), reported that marital unhappiness more than divorce in the parents' generation is associated with offsprings' divorce. Thus, although much evidence is accumulated to support the intergenerational transmission hypothesis, it is still not conclusive.

CONCLUSIONS

Research on the effect of parental divorce on children has become increasingly sophisticated in its conceptualization of divorce, since Herzog and Sudia's (1973) classic critique of the early research. Herzog and Sudia argued against what then was the prevailing notion, that "divorce is a unitary event that has uniform effect on all children" (p. 194). Such a conceptualization, they noted, leads researchers to ignore critical intervening factors that may better explain the effect of divorce on children. This challenge has since been taken by most researchers and the importance of identifying the multiple mediating variables has since been acknowledged.

The results of two teams of investigators (Hetherington and her colleagues and Wallerstein and Kelly) have pioneered and dominated much of the earlier research in the field. Since then, many other researchers and numerous studies have investigated the effect of divorce on children. Children of divorced parents were compared to children of intact families on numerous variables such as their relationship with parents, psychological and behavioral adjustment, and scholastic and cognitive achievement. The results of many of the studies indicated lower levels of functioning of the former group on these dependent variables. Not all studies, however, concurred. Disagreements are also found among the conclusions of several quantitative reviews of the literature. Thus, for example, Krantz (1988) concluded that most children of divorced parents are at risk with regard to their psychosocial development. Edwards (1987), on the other hand, found that the results of studies indicate that, in due time, most of these children do adjust and function well. Other researchers interpreted the results of their reviews as an indication of some developmental difficulties associated with parental divorce, but even these do not permit unequivocal conclusion (Demo & Acock, 1988; Emery, 1988). A good example of the dubiousness of the data is the result of Amato and Keith's meta-analysis. It led the researchers to conclude, on the basis of statistical generalizations across studies, that although children of divorce scored lower on most dependent measures, the effect is small, with a median effect size of 0.14 of a standard deviation.

Two intervening variables attracted researchers' particular attention; children's age and gender. The early studies of Hetherington et al. (1978) and Wallerstein and Kelly (1980b) suggested that: (a) parental divorce was more detrimental for boys than for girls, and (b) parental divorce was more detrimental the younger the children were at the time of the divorce. These results have triggered many attempts to replicate and generalize them. Some have found that boys are indeed more vulnerable than girls (e.g., Guidubaldi et al., 1983; Hetherington, 1982). Others found no gender differences (e.g., Amato, 1987; Amato & Ochiltree, 1987; Furstenberg et al., Allison, 1987), and yet some even found that girls are more vulnerable than boys (e.g., Allison & Furstenberg, 1989; Cherlin, et al., 1991; Slater, Stewart, & Linn, 1983). In their recent study, for example, Cherlin and his colleagues (1991) compared pre- and postdivorce functioning of children in Great Britain and the United States. The effect of parental divorce on girls was more pronounced than for boys when "preexisting conditions were considered" (p. 1386). Yet, after an extensive review of the literature, Zaslow (1987) concluded that the differential effect (if any) of divorce on boys and girls is still unclear. And with the exception of social adjustment, Amato and Keith (1991) found no indication in the literature of gender differences.

As for variable of children's age at time of divorce, there are similar inconsistencies. Confounding variables such as parents' age and time since the divorce may have made the interpretation of the studies' results difficult. Furthermore, only a few studies (e.g., Amato, 1987; Brady, Bray, & Zeeb, 1986) have made direct comparisons between children of different ages. After reviewing the literature, Emery (1988) concluded that no clear conclusion can be made with regard to differential effects of parental divorce on children of various ages. Three years later, however, Amato and Keith (1991) concluded that "Age [of the child] was significantly associated with effect size for psychological adjustment, social adjustment, mother-child relations, and father-child relations" (p. 33). The most detrimental effect of parents' divorce was found for children in the middle age group (i.e., children in primary and high schools). For preschoolers and college-age students, the effect sizes "rarely achieved significance." Allison and Furstenberg (1989), however, did find that "effects sizes are larger for children who are very young at the time of the [family] dissolution" (p. 540). The confusion thus, goes on and makes swiping conclusions impossible.

Three theoretical perspectives served as frameworks to explain why the divorce of parents may negatively effect children: (a) family structure, (b) family process, and (c) economic disadvantage. (For detailed discussions see Amato & Keith, 1991; Kalter, Kloner, Schreier, & Okla, 1989).

The family structure perspective's premise is that children of divorce exhibit problems because of inadequate socialization that results from growing up in a single-parent family. The idea is that because both parents are principle models and sources of support and guidance for the children, the absence of one parent must have a detrimental effect on the development and functioning of the children. (See Amato, 1987; and Furstenberg & Nord, 1985, for examples of studies supporting this perspective.)

The family process perspective's premise is that the negative effect of divorce on children is due to the major breakdown in the family's relationships. The assumption is that parental conflict before and after the divorce creates a major stress on the children and they respond negatively to the aversive home environment. Intense and long conflicts between parents make them less effective in their parental roles; may draw the children into a Solomonian dilemma; and further damage the child–parent relationship. (See Amato, 1986; and Wallerstein & Kelly, 1980b, for examples of studies supporting this perspective.)

The economic disadvantage perspective's premise is that the negative effect of divorce on children is due mainly to the economic hardship that is often associated with divorce. The severe decline in the family's standard of living may have several ramifications all of which may have negative effects on children. For one, the family may have to move to a poorer neighborhood that offers poorly financed schools and services. Second, the single-parent is less financially able to provide the children with the necessary substitutions and outside support in case of need. Third, living in poverty is often associated with social stigma that may engulf the children into a developmentally hazardous lifestyle. (See McLanahan, 1989; and Weitzman, 1985, for studies supporting this perspective.)

Supporters of any one of these three perspectives can cite many studies that corroborate a particular perspective. But, in their sophisticated comparison of 92 studies, Amato and Keith (1991) reported that although "some support was found for theoretical perspectives emphasizing parental absence and economic disadvantage, the most consistent support was found for a family conflict perspective" (Amato & Keith, 1991, p. 26). Kalter et al.'s (1989) results may also be considered as somewhat supporting of the family dynamic perspective. Kalter and his colleagues tested six different hypotheses and found that their data support most the "parental adjustment hypothesis." That is, the custodial parent's adjustment is the best predictor of children's adjustment.

From research and clinical points of view, all three theoretical frameworks are useful. They offer simple and intuitively sound plausible explanations for some children's reactions to divorce. For researchers and theoreticians of family life and family functioning this, however, is not enough. It should be clear that just as the multiple facets of the child's development (psychosocial, psychosexual, and sociocognitive processes) cannot be separated, neither can any single theory account for the already large body of research and too often contradicting results. No single theoretical perspective can by itself advance the ability to predict the short- and long-term effects of divorce on children at different developmental stages.

Until recently, researchers and clinicians who have attempted to account for differences in children's responses at different developmental levels have drawn largely upon a single theoretical framework. At present, this approach seems to be nearly exhausted. Now it seems the need is to go one step further. To do that we must try and integrate theoretically the three perspectives and extract research questions and hypotheses that go beyond a single theoretical approach.

REFERENCES

Abarbanel, A. (1979). Shared parenting after separation and divorce: A study of joint custody. *American Journal of Orthopsychiatry, 49*(2), 320–329.

Adams, G. R. (1982). The effects of divorce on adolescents. *The High School Journal, 65,* 205–211.

Adams, P. L., Milner, J. R., & Scherpf, N. A. (1984). *Fatherless children.* New York: Wiley.

Ahrons, C. (1979). The binuclear family: Two households, one family. *Alternative Lifestyles, 2,* 499–515.

Ahrons, C. (1980a). Divorce: A crisis of family transition and change. *Family Relations, 29,* 533–540.

Ahrons, C. (1980b). Joint custody arrangements in the postdivorce family. *Journal of Divorce, 3*(3), 189–205.

Ahrons, C. (1980c). Redefining the divorced family: A conceptual framework for postdivorce family systems reorganization. *Social Work, 25,* 437–441.

Ahrons, C., & Rodgers, R. H. (1987). *Divorced families.* New York: Norton.

Albrecht, S. L., Bahr, H. M., & Goodman, K. L. (1983). *Divorce and remarriage: Problems, adaptations, and adjustments.* Westport, CT: Greenwood Press.

Albrecht, S. L., & Kunz, P. R. (1980). The decision to divorce: A social exchange perspective. *Journal of Divorce, 3,* 319–337.

Aldous, J. (1977). Family interaction patterns. *Annual Review of Sociology, 3,* 105–136.

Allison, P. D., & Furstenberg, F. F. (1989). How marital dissolution affects children: Variations by age and sex. *Developmental Psychology, 25*(4), 540–549.

Alloy, L. B. (1982). The role of perception and attribution for response–outcome noncontingencies in learned helplessness: A commentary and discussion. *Journal of Personality, 50,* 443–479.

Amato, P. R. (1986). Marital conflict, the parent–child relationship, and child self-esteem. *Family Relations, 35,* 103–110.

Amato, P. R. (1987). Family process in one-parent, stepparent, and intact families: The child's point of view. *Journal of Marriage and the Family, 40,* 327-337.

Amato, P. R., & Keith, B. (1991). Parental divorce and the well-being of children: A meta-analysis. *Psychological Bulletin, 110*(1), 26-46.

Amato, P. R., & Ochiltree, G. (1987). Child and adolescent competence in intact, one-parent, and stepfamilies: An Australian study. *Journal of Divorce, 10,* 75-96.

Ambert, A-M. (1982, February). Differences in children's behavior toward custodial mothers and custodial fathers. *Journal of Marriage and the Family,* 73-86.

Ambrose, P., Harper, J., & Pemberton, R. (1983). *Surviving divorce.* Brighton: Wheatsheaf Books.

Anderson-Khleif, S. (1982). *Divorced but not disastrous: How to improve the ties between single-parent mothers, divorced fathers and the children.* Englewood Cliffs, NJ: Prentice-Hall.

Anspach, D. F. (1976). Kinship and divorce. *Journal of Marriage and the Family, 38,* 343-350.

Anthony, E. J. (1974). Children at risk from divorce: A review. In E. Anthony & C. Koupenick (Eds.), *The child in his family: Children at psychiatric risk* (Vol. 3, pp. 142-173). New York: Wiley.

Aries, P. (1962). *Centuries of childhood.* London: Jonathan Cape.

Aronson, E. (1968). Dissonance theory: Progress and problems. In R. P. Ableson, E. Aronson, W. J. McGuire, T. M. Newcomb, M. J. Rosenberg, & P. H. Tannenbaum (Eds.), *Theories of cognitive consistency: A sourcebook* (pp. 5-27). Chicago: Rand McNally.

Ashenhurst, H. S. (1984). *Divorce and beyond.* Independence, MO: Herald Publishing House.

Asher, S. J., & Bloom, B. L. (1983). Geographic mobility as a factor in adjustment to divorce. *Journal of Divorce, 6,* 69-84.

Atkeson, B. M., Forehand, R. L., & Rickard, K. M. (1982). The effects of divorce on children. In B. Lahey (Ed.), *Advances in clinical child psychology* (pp. 255-281). New York: Academic Press.

Atkin, E., & Rubin, E. (1976). *Part-time father: A guide for the divorced father.* New York: Vanguard.

Atkins, R. N., & Cath, S. H. (1989). Divorce and fathers: Some intrapsychic factors affecting outcome; afterword. In S. H. Cath, A. Gurwitt, & L. Gunsberg (Eds.), *Fathers and their families* (pp. 173-203). Hillsdale, NJ: The Analytic Press.

Atlas, S. L. (1984). *The parents without partners sourcebook.* Philadelphia: Running Press.

Austin, R. L. (1978). Race, father-absence, and female delinquency. *Criminology: An Interdisciplinary Journal, 15*(4), 487-504.

Ausubel, D. P., Montemayor, R., & Svajian, P. (1977). *Theories and problems of adolescent development.* New York: Grune & Stratton.

Bachrach, L. L. (1973). *Marital status of discharges from psychiatric inpatient units of general hospitals, United States 1970-1971: I. Analysis by age, color and sex* (Statistical Note 82, NIMH). Washington, DC: U.S. Government Printing Office.

Bachrach, L. L. (1975). *Marital status and mental disorder: An analytical review* (DHEW Publication No. ADM 75-217). Washington, DC: U.S. Government Printing Office.

Badinter, E. (1981). *L'amour en plus* [And also love]. Paris: Flammarion.

Bahr, S. J. (1979). The effects of welfare on marital stability and remarriage. *Journal of Marriage and the Family, 41,* 553-560.

Bahr, S. J. (1982). The pains and joys of divorce: A survey of Mormons. *Family Perspective, 16,* 191-200.

Bahr, S. J. (1986). Impact of recent changes in divorce laws for women. *Family Perspective, 20,* 95-103.

Bahr, S. J., & Galligan, R. J. (1984). Teenage marriage and marital stability. *Youth and Society, 15,* 387-400.

Bain, C. (1973). Lone fathers: An unnoticed group. *Australian Social Welfare, 3,* 14-17.

Bane, M. J. (1976). Marital disruption and the lives of children. *Journal of Social Issues, 32*(1), 103-117.

Bane, M. J., & Weiss, R. (1980). Alone together the world of single-parent families. *American Demographics, 2*(5), 11-15.

Bardwick, J. M. (1979). *In transition: How feminism, sexual liberation, and the search for self-fulfillment have altered America*. New York: Holt, Rinehart & Winston.

Bartz, K. W., & Witcher, W. C. (1978). When father gets custody. *Children Today, 7*, 2-6.

Baucom, D. H. (1986). Attributions in distressed relationships: How can we explain them? In S. Duck & D. Perlman (Eds.), *Heterosexual relations, marriage and divorce* (pp. 102-132). London: Sage.

Beal, E. W. (1979). Children of divorce: A family systems perspective. *Journal of Social Issues, 35*(4), 140-154.

Becker, G. S. (1981). *A treatise on the family*. Cambridge, MA: Harvard University Press.

Bedi, A. R. (1981). The demographic correlates of admissions to the child and adolescent inpatient clinic at a midwestern metropolitan mental health complex. *Journal of Youth and Adolescence, 10*, 339-351.

Bell, C., & Newby, H. (1976). Husbands and wives: The dynamics of the deferential dialectic. In S. Allen & D. Barker (Eds.), *Dependence and exploitation in work and marriage* (pp. 152-168). London: Longmans.

Bellah, R. N., Madsen, R., Sullivan, W. M., Swidler, A., & Tipton, S. M. (1985). *Habits of the heart*. Berkeley: University of California Press.

Benedek, E. P., & Benedek, R. S. (1979). Joint custody: Solution or illusion? *American Journal of Psychiatry, 136*(12), 1540-1544.

Benson, L. (1968). *Fatherhood: A sociological perspective*. New York: Random House.

Berg, B., & Kelly, R. (1979). The measured self-esteem of children from broken, rejected, and accepted families. *Journal of Divorce, 2*, 363-369.

Berkman, P. (1969). Spouseless motherhood, psychological stress and physical morbidity. *Journal of Health and Social Behavior, 10*, 323-334.

Berman, W. H., & Turk, D. C. (1981). Adaptation to divorce: Problems and coping strategies. *Journal of Marriage and the Family, 43*(2), 179-189.

Bernard, J. C. (1971). *Remarriage: A study of marriage*. Tampa, FL: Russel.

Bernard, J. C. (1975). *The future of motherhood*. Baltimore: Penguin.

Bernard, J. C. (1979). Foreward. In G. Levinger & O. C. Moles (Eds.), *Divorce and separation: Context, causes and consequences* (pp. ix-xv). New York: Basic Books.

Bernard, J. C. (1986). The good-provider role: Its rise and fall. In A. S. Skolnick & J. H. Skolnick (Eds.), *Family in transition* (pp. 125-143). Boston: Little, Brown.

Bernstein, B. E. (1977). Lawyer and counselor as an interdisciplinary team: Preparing the father for custody. *Journal of Marital and Family Therapy, 3*(3), 29-40.

Bettelheim, B. (1956, October). Fathers shouldn't try to be mothers. *Parents' Magazine*, pp. 124-125.

Bianchi, S. M., & Farley, R. (1979). Racial differences in family living arrangements and economic well-being: An analysis of recent trends. *Journal of Marriage and the Family, 41*, 537-557.

Biller, H. B. (1970). Father absence and the personality development of the male child. *Developmental Psychology, 2*(2), 181-201.

Billingsley, A., & Giovannoni, J. M. (1971). Family, one-parent. *Encyclopedia of Social Work, 16*(1), 362-373.

Billy, J. O. G., Landale, N. S., & McLaughlin, S. D. (1986). The effect of marital status at first birth on marital dissolution among adolescent mothers. *Demography, 23*(3), 329-349.

Bird, C. (1971). *The two-paycheck marriage*. New York: Rawson, Wade.

Bishop, J. (1980). Jobs cash transfers, and marital instability: A review and synthesis of the evidence. *Journal of Human Resources, 15,* 301–334.

Bisnaire, L. M., Firestone, P., & Rynard, D. (1990). Factors associated with academic achievement in children following parental separation. *American Journal of Orthopsychiatry, 60*(1), 67–76.

Blackburn, R. M., & Mann, M. (1979). *The working class in the labour market.* London: Macmillan.

Blair, M. (1970). Divorces' adjustment and attitudinal changes about life. *Dissertation Abstracts, 30,* 5541–5542.

Blanchard, R. W., & Biller, H. B. (1971). Father availability and academic performance among third-grade boys. *Developmental Psychology, 4,* 301–305.

Blechman, E. A. (1982). Are children with one parent at psychological risk? A methodological review. *Journal of Marriage and the Family, 44*(1), 179–195.

Blechman, E. A., & Manning, M. (1976). A reward–cost analysis of the single-parent family. In E. J. Mah, L. A. Hamerlynck, & L. C. Handy (Eds.), *Behavior modification and families* (pp. 87–112). New York: Brunner/Mazel.

Block, J., Block, J-H., & Gjerde, P-F. (1989). Parental functioning and the home environment in families of divorce: Prospective and concurrent analyses. *Annual Progress in Child Psychiatry and Child Development,* 192–207.

Bloom, B. L., Asher, S. J., & White, S. W. (1978). Marital disruption as a stressor: A review and analysis. *Psychological Bulletin, 85*(4), 867–894.

Bloom, B. L., & Hodges, W. F. (1981). The predicament of the newly separated. *Community Mental Health Journal, 17*(4), 277–293.

Bloom, B. L., Hodges, W. F., & Caldwell, R. A. (1977). Marital separation: A community survey. *Journal of Divorce, 1*(1), 7–19.

Blumstein, P., & Schwartz, P. (1983). *American couples.* New York: William Morrow.

Bohannan, P. J. (1968). *Divorce and after.* New York: Doubleday.

Bohannan, P. J. (1985). *All the happy families: Exploring the varieties of family life.* New York: McGraw-Hill.

Bolton, F. G., Laner, R. H., & Kane, S. P. (1980). Child maltreatment risk among adolescent mothers: A study of reported cases. *American Journal of Orthopsychiatry, 50,* 489–504.

Bond, M. H. (1983). A proposal for cross-cultural studies of attribution. In M. Hewstone (Ed.), *Attribution theory* (pp. 144–157). Oxford, England: Basil Blackwell.

Booth, A., Brinkerhoff, D. B., & White, L. K. (1984). The impact of parental divorce on courtship. *Journal of Marriage and the Family, 46*(1), 85–94.

Booth, A., & Edwards, J. N. (1989). Transmission of marital and family quality over the generations: The effect of parental divorce and unhappiness. *Journal of Divorce, 13*(2), 41–58.

Booth, A., Johnson, D. R., & Edwards, J. N. (1983). Measuring marital instability. *Journal of Marriage and the Family, 45,* 387–394.

Booth, A., Johnson, D. R., White, L., & Edwards, J. N. (1986). Divorce and marital instability over the life course. *Journal of Family Issues, 7,* 421–447.

Booth, A., & White, L. (1980). Thinking about divorce. *Journal of Marriage and the Family, 42,* 605–616.

Boss, P. (1977). A clarification of the concept of psychological father presence in families experiencing ambiguity of boundary. *Journal of Marriage and the Family, 39*(1), 141–151.

Boss, P. (1980). The relationship of psychological father presence, wife's personal qualities and wife/family dysfunction in families of missing fathers. *Journal of Marriage and the Family, 42*(3), 541–549.

Boszormenyi-Nagy, I., & Spark, G. M. (1973). *Invisible loyalties.* New York: Harper & Row.

Bowen, M. (1978). *Family therapy and clinical practice: Collected papers of Murray Bowen.* New York: Aronson.

Bowlby, J. (1958). The nature of the child's tie to the mother. *International Journal of Psycho-Analysis, 39,* 350–373.

Bowlby, J. (1969). *Attachment and loss (Vol. 1). Attachment.* New York: Basic Books.

Bowskill, D. (1980). *Single parents.* London: Futura.

Bradbury, K., Danziger, S., Smolensky, E., & Smolensky, P. (1979). Public assistance, female headship, and economic well-being. *Journal of Marriage and the Family, 41,* 519–535.

Brandt, A. (1982, November). Father love. *Esquire,* pp. 81–89.

Brady, C. P., Bray, J. H., & Zeeb, L. (1986). Behavior problems of clinic children: Relation to parental marital status, age and sex of child. *American Journal of Orthopsychiatry, 56,* 399–411.

Brandwein, R. A., Brown, C. A., & Fox, E. M. (1974). Women and children last: The social situation of divorced mothers and their families. *Journal of Marriage and the Family, 36*(3), 498–514.

Breault, K. D., & Kposowa, A. J. (1987). Explaining divorce in the United States: A study of 3,111 counties, 1980. *Journal of Marriage and the Family, 49,* 549–558.

Briggs, B. A., & Walters, C. M. (1985). Single-father families: Implications for early childhood educators. *Young Children, 40*(3), 23–27.

Briscoe, C. W., & Smith, J. B. (1973). Depression and marital turmoil. *Archives of General Psychiatry, 29*(6), 811–817.

Briscoe, C. W., & Smith, J. B. (1974). Psychiatric illness: Marital units and divorce. *Journal of Nervous and Mental Disease, 158*(6), 440–445.

Briscoe, C. W., & Smith, J. B. (1975). Depression in bereavement and divorce: Relationship to primary depressive illness: A study of 128 subjects. *Archives of General Psychiatry, 32*(4), 439–443.

Briscoe, C. W., Smith, J. B., Robins, E., Marten, S., & Gaskin, F. (1973). Divorce and psychiatric disease. *Archives of General Psychiatry, 29,* 119–125.

Brodbar-Nemzer, J. K. (1986). Divorce and group commitment: The case of the Jews. *Journal of Marriage and the Family, 48*(2), 329–340.

Brown, A., & Stones, C. (1979). A group for lone fathers. *Social Work Today, 47*(10), 3–7.

Brown, B. F. (1980). A study of the school needs of children from one-parent families. *Phi Delta Kappan, 61,* 537–540.

Brown, C. A., Feldberg, R., Fox, E. M., & Kohen, J. (1976). Divorce: Chance of a new lifetime. *Journal of Social Issues, 32*(1), 119–133.

Brown, E. M. (1976). Divorce counseling. In D. H. Olson (Ed.), *Treating relationships* (pp. 212–257). Lake Mills, IA: Graphic.

Brown, M. D. (1985). The comprehensive divorce treatment center: The divorce and marital stress model clinic. In D. H. Sprenkle (Ed.), *Divorce therapy* (pp. 159–170). New York: Haworth.

Brown, P., & Manela, R. (1978). Changing family roles: Women and Divorce. *Journal of Divorce, 1,* 315–327.

Buehler, C. A., Hogan, M. J., Robinson, B. E., & Levy, R. J. (1985/1986). The parental divorce transition: Divorce-related stressors and well-being. *Journal of Divorce, 9*(2), 61–82.

Bumpass, L. L. (1984). Children and marital disruption: A replication and update. *Demography, 21,* 71–82.

Bumpass, L. L., & Rindfuss, R. R. (1979). Children's experience of marital disruption. *American Journal of Sociology, 85,* 49–65.

Bumpass, L. L., & Sweet, J. (1972). Differentials in marital instability: 1970. *American Sociological Review, 37,* 754–766.

Burchinal, L. G. (1964). Characteristics of adolescents from unbroken, broken, and reconstituted families. *Journal of Marriage and the Family, 26,* 44–51.

Burchinal, L. G., & Chancellor, L. E. (1962). Survival rates among religiously homogamous and interreligious marriages. *Iowa Agricultural and Home Economics Experiment Station Bulletin, 512,* 743–770.

Burgess, E. W., & Locke, H. J. (1953). *The family: From institution to companionship* (2nd ed.). New York: American Books.

Burgess, J. K. (1970). The single-parent family: A social and sociological problem. *Family Coordinator, 19*(2), 137–144.

Burgoyne, J. (1984). *Breaking even: Divorce, your children and you.* Harmondsworth: Penguin.

Burgoyne, J., & Clark, D. (1984). *Making a go of it: A study of step-families in Sheffield.* London: Routledge & Kegan Paul.

Burgoyne, J., Ormrod, R., & Richards, M. (1987). *Divorce matters.* New York: Penguin Books.

Burr, W. R. (1973). *Theory construction and the sociology of the family.* New York: Wiley.

Camara, K. A., & Resnick, G. (1989). Styles of conflict resolution and cooperation between divorced parents: Effects on child behavior and adjustment. *American Journal of Orthopsychiatry, 59*(4), 560–575.

Cantor, D. W., & Drake, E. A. (1983). *Divorced parents and their children.* New York: Springer.

Carter, H., & Glick, P. C. (1976). *Marriage and divorce: A social and economic study* (rev. ed.). Cambridge, MA: Harvard University Press.

Chan, L. Y., & Heaton, T. B. (1989). Demographic determinants of delayed divorce. *Journal of Divorce, 13*(1), 97–112.

Chang, P., & Deinard, A. S. (1982). Single-father caretakers: Demographic characteristics and adjustment processes. *American Journal of Orthopsychiatry, 52*(2), 236–243.

Chase-Lansdale, P. L., & Hetherington, E. M. (1990). The impact of divorce on life-span development: Short- and long-term effects. In D. L. Featherman & R. M. Lerner (Eds.), *Life-span development and behavior* (Vol. 10, pp. 118–135). Hillsdale, NJ: Lawrence Earlbaum Associates.

Cherlin, A. (1979). Work life and marital dissolution. In G. Levinger & O. C. Moles (Eds.), *Divorce and separation: Context, causes and consequences* (pp. 151–166). New York: Basic Books.

Cherlin, A. (1981). *Marriage, divorce, remarriage: Social trends in the United States.* Cambridge, MA: Harvard University Press.

Cherlin, A. J., Furstenberg, F. F., Chase-Lansdale, P. L., & Kiernan, K. E. (1991). Longitudinal studies of effects of divorce on children in Great Britain and the United States. *Science, 252,* 1386–1589.

Chester, R. (1971). Health and marriage breakdown: Experience of a sample of divorced women. *British Journal of Preventive and Social Medicine, 25*(4), 231–244.

Chiriboga, D. A., Coho, A., Stein, J. A., & Roberts, J. (1979). Divorce, stress and social supports: A study of help-seeking behaviour. *Journal of Divorce, 3*(2), 121–135.

Chiriboga, D. A., & Cutler, L. (1977). Stress responses among divorcing men and women. *Journal of Divorce, 1,* 95–106.

Chiriboga, D. A., Roberts, J., & Stein, J. A. (1978). Psychological well-being during marital separation. *Journal of Divorce, 2*(1), 21–36.

Christensen, H. T. (1963). Timing of first pregnancy as a factor in divorce: A cross-cultural analysis. *Eugenics Quarterly, 10,* 119–130.

Christensen, H. T., & Meissner, H. H. (1953). Studies in child spacing: Premarital pregnancy as a factor in divorce. *American Sociological Review, 18,* 641–644.

Clark, H. (1968). *The law of domestic relations in the United States.* St. Paul, MN: West.

Cline, D., & Westman, J. (1971). The impact of divorce in the family. *Child Psychiatry and Human Development, 2,* 78–83.

Cogswell, B., & Sussman, M. (1972). Changing family and marriage forms: Complications for human service systems. *Family Coordinator, 21,* 505–515.

Colletta, N. D. (1979a). Support systems after divorce: Incidence and impact. *Journal of Marriage and the Family, 41,* 837–846.

Colletta, N. D. (1979b). The impact of divorce: Father absence or poverty? *Journal of Divorce, 3*(1), 27–35.

Conyers, M. G. (1977). Comparing school success of students from conventional and broken homes. *Phi Delta Kappan, 58,* 647.

Coombs, L. C., & Zumeta, Z. (1970). Correlates of marital dissolution in a perspective fertility study: A research note. *Social Problems, 18,* 92–102.

Cooper, J. E., Holman, J., & Braithwaite, V. A. (1983). Self-esteem and family cohesion: The child's perspective and adjustment. *Journal of Marriage and the Family, 45,* 153–159.

Corcoran, M. (1976). *The economic consequences of marital dissolution for women in the middle years.* Paper presented at the Conference on Women in Mid-life Crises, Cornell University, Ithaca, NY.

Crosby, J. F., Gage, B. A., & Raymond, M. C. (1983). The grief resolution process in divorce. *Journal of Divorce, 7,* 3–18.

Cutright, P. (1971). Income and family events: Marital stability. *Journal of Marriage and the Family, 33,* 291–306.

Dager, E. Z. (1967). Socialization and personality development in the child. In H. T. Christensen (Ed.), *Handbook of marriage and the family* (pp. 308–329). Chicago: Rand McNally and Co.

Dally, A. (1982). *Inventing motherhood.* London: Burnett.

Daniels-Mohring, D., & Berger, M. (1984). Social network changes and the adjustment to divorce. *Journal of Divorce, 8,* 17–32.

Darity, W. A., & Myers, S. J. (1984). Does welfare dependency cause female headship? The case of the Black family. *Journal of Marriage and the Family, 46,* 765–779.

Davenport, D. S. (1981). A closer look at the "healthy" grieving process. *Personnel and Guidance Journal, 59*(6), 332–335.

DeFazio, V. J., & Klenbort, I. (1975). A note on the dynamics of psychotherapy during marital dissolution. *Psychotherapy Theory, Research and Practice, 12*(1), 101–104.

DeFrain, J., & Eirick, R. (1981). Coping as divorced single parents: A comparative study of fathers and mothers. *Family Relations, 30*(2), 265–274.

Degler, C. N. (1980). *At odds: Women and the family in America from the revolution to the present.* New York: Oxford University Press.

Dell, P., & Applebaum, A. (1977). Trigenerational enmeshment: Unresolved ties of single parents to family of origin. *American Journal of Orthopsychiatry, 47,* 52–59.

Demo, D. H., & Acock, A. C. (1988). The impact of divorce on children. *Journal of Marriage and the Family, 50,* 619–648.

Derdeyn, A. P. (1976). Child custody contests in historical perspective. *American Journal of Psychiatry, 133*(12), 1369–1376.

Derdeyn, A. P., & Scott, E. (1984). Joint custody. *American Journal of Orthopsychiatry, 54,* 199–209.

DeSimone-Luis, J., O'Mahoney, K., & Hunt, D. (1979). Children of separation and divorce: Factors influencing adjustment. *Journal of Divorce, 3*(1), 37–42.

Dill, D., Feld, E., Martin, J., Beukema, S., & Belle, D. (1980). The impact of the environment on the coping efforts of low-income mothers. *Family Relations, 29,* 503–509.

Dinerman, M. (1977). Catch 23: Women, work and welfare. *Social Work, 22,* 472–477.

Dixon, R. B., & Weitzman, L. J. (1982). When husbands file for divorce. *Journal of Marriage and the Family, 44*(1), 103–115.

Doherty, W. J. (1978). *Cognitive processes in intimate conflict: Applications of attribution theory and social learning theory.* Paper presented at the meeting of the National Council of Family Relations, Boston.

Doherty, W. J. (1981). Cognitive processes in intimate conflict: I. Extending attribution theory. *American Journal of Family Therapy, 9*(1), 3–13.

Doherty, W. J. (1982). Attribution style and negative problem-solving in marriage. *Family Relations, 31,* 23–27.

Dominic, K. T., & Schlesinger, B. (1980). Weekend fathers: Family shadows. *Journal of Divorce, 3*(3), 241–247.

Doudna, C. (1982, October 3). The weekend mother. *The New York Times Magazine,* pp. 72–75, 84–88.

Douvan, E., & Adelson, J. (1966). *The adolescent experience.* New York: Wiley.

Duncan, G. J., & Hoffman, S. D. (1985). A reconsideration of the economic consequences of marital dissolution. *Demography, 22,* 485–498.

Duncan, G. J., & Morgan, J. N. (1975). *Five thousand American families: Patterns of economic progress* (Vol. 3). Ann Arbor, MI: Institute for Social Research.

Duncan, G. J., & Morgan, J. N. (1981). *Five thousand American families: Patterns of economic progress* (Vol. 9.) Ann Arbor, MI: University of Michigan.

Earl, L., & Lohmann, N. (1978). Absent fathers and Black male children. *Social Work, 23,* 413–415.

Earls, F., & Siegel, B. (1980). Precocious fathers. *American Journal of Orthopsychiatry, 50*(3), 469–480.

Edwards, J. N. (1987). Changing family structure and youthful well-being: Assessing the future. *Journal of Family Issues, 8,* 355–372.

Ellwood, M. S., & Stolberg, A. L. (1991). A preliminary investigation of family systems' influences on individual divorce adjustments. Special Issue: Marital instability and divorce outcomes: Issues for therapists and educators. *Journal of Divorce and Remarriage, 15*(1–2), 157–174.

Emery, R. E. (1982). Interparental conflict and the children of discord and divorce. *Psychological Bulletin, 92*(2), 310–330.

Emery, R. E. (1988). *Marriage, divorce, and children's adjustment.* Beverly Hills, CA: Sage.

Erikson, E. H. (1963). *Childhood and society.* New York: Norton.

Eshleman, J. R. (1985). *The family: An introduction.* Boston: Allyn & Bacon.

Espenshade, T. J. (1979). The economic consequences of divorce. *The Journal of Marriage and the Family, 41,* 615–627.

Espenshade, T. J. (1985). Marriage trends in America: Estimates, implications and underlying causes. *Population and Development Review, 11,* 193–245.

Everly, K. (1978). *Leisure network and role strains: A study of divorced women with custody.* Unpublished doctoral dissertation, Syracuse University, Syracuse, NY.

Falek, A., & Britton, S. (1974). Phases in coping: The hypothesis and its implications. *Social Biology, 21*(1), 1–7.

Farber, S. S., Primavera, J., & Felner, R. D. (1983). Older adolescents and parental divorce: Adjustment problems and mediators of coping. *Journal of Divorce, 7,* 59–76.

Farnworth, M. (1984). Family structure, family attributes, and delinquency in a sample of low-income, minority males and females. *Journal of Youth and Adolescence, 13*(4), 349–364.

Farson, R. (1978). Parental divorce: A growth experience for children? [Letter to the editor]. *American Journal of Orthopsychiatry, 48*(1), 183–185.

Federico, J. (1979). The marital termination period of the divorce adjustment process. *Journal of Divorce, 3*(2), 93–106.

Feldberg, R., & Kohen, J. A. (1980). Family life in an anti-family setting: A critique of marriage and divorce. In J. M. Henslin (Ed.), *Marriage and family in a changing society* (pp. 415–427). New York: The Free Press.

Felner, R. D., & Farber, S. S. (1980). Social policy for child custody: A multidisciplinary framework. *American Journal of Ortho-psychiatry, 50*(2), 341–347.

Fergusson, D. M., Horwood, L. J., & Shannon, F. T. (1984). A proportional hazards model of family breakdown. *Journal of Marriage and the Family, 46,* 539–549.

Ferri, E. (1976). *Growing up in a one-parent family: A long-term study of child development.* London: NFER Publishing.

Festinger, L. (1957). *A theory of cognitive dissonance.* Stanford, CA: Stanford University Press.

Fincham, F. D., Beach, S. R., & Baucom, D. H. (1987). Attribution processes in distressed and nondistressed couples: 4. Self-partner attribution differences. *Journal of Personality and Social Psychology, 52,* 739–748.

Fischer, J. (1983). Mothers living apart from their children. *Family Relations, 32,* 351–357.

Fischer, J., & Cardea, J. M. (1981). Mothers living apart from their children. *Alternative Lifestyles, 4*(2), 218–227.

Ford, K. (1981). *Socioeconomic differentials and trends in the timing of births* (National Center for Health Statistics, Series 23, 6). Washington, DC: Government Printing Office.

Forehand, R., McCombs, A., Long, N., Brody, G. H., & Fauber, R. (1988). Early adolescent adjustment to recent parental divorce: The role of interparental conflict and adolescent sex as mediating variables. *Journal of Consulting and Clinical Psychology, 56*(4), 624–627.

Forehand, R., Wierson, M., McCombs Thomas, A., Armistead, L., Kempton, T., & Neighbors, B. (1991). The role of family stressors and parent relationships on adolescent functioning. *Journal of the American Academy of Child and Adolescent Psychiatry, 30*(2), 316–322.

Foster, H. H., & Freed, D. J. (1974). Marital property reform in New York: Partnership of co-equals? *Family Law Quarterly, 8,* 169–205.

Francke, L. B. (1983). *Growing up divorced.* New York: Simon & Schuster.

Frazier, E. F. (1939). *The negro family in the United States.* Chicago: University of Chicago Press.

Free, M. D. (1991). Clarifying the relationship between the broken home and juvenile delinquency: A critique of the current literature. *Deviant Behavior, 12*(2), 109–167.

Freund, J. (1974). Divorce and grief. *Journal of Family Counseling, 2*(2), 40–43.

Friedman, B. (1971). *The feminine mystique.* London: Gollancz.

Frisbie, P. W. (1986). Variations in pattern of marital instability among Hispanics. *Journal of Marriage and the Family, 48,* 99–106.

Froiland, D. J., & Hozman, T. L. (1977). Counseling for constructive divorce. *Personnel and Guidance Journal, 55,* 525–529.

Fromm, E. (1974). *The art of loving.* New York: Harper & Row.

Fulton, J. A. (1979). Parental reports of children's post-divorce adjustment. *Journal of Social Issues, 35,* 126–139.

Furstenberg, F. F. (1976a). Premarital pregnancy and marital instability. *The Journal of Social Issues, 32*(1), 67–86.

Furstenberg, F. F. (1976b). *Unplanned parenthood: The social consequences of teenage childbearing.* New York: The Free Press.

Furstenberg, F. F. (1982). *Childcare after divorce and remarriage.* Paper presented at the MacArthur Foundation Conference on Child Care, Chicago, IL.

Furstenberg, F. F. (1983). *Marital disruption and childcare.* Working paper for the Family Impact Seminar, National Center for Family Studies, Catholic University, Washington, DC.

Furstenberg, F. F., Morgan, S. P., & Allison, P. D. (1987). Paternal participation and children's well-being after marital dissolution. *American Sociological Review, 52,* 695–701.

Furstenberg, F. F., & Nord, C. W. (1985). Parenting apart: Patterns of childrearing after marital disruption. *Journal of Marriage and the Family, 47,* 893–904.

Furstenberg, F. F., Nord, C. W., Peterson, J. L., & Zill, N. (1983). The life course of children of divorce: Marital disruption and parental contact. *American Sociological Review, 48*(5), 656–668.

Furstenberg, F. F., & Spanier, G. B. (1984). *Recycling the family: Remarriage after divorce.* Beverly Hills, CA: Sage.

Furstenberg, F. F., & Talvitie, K. G. (1980). Children's names and paternal claims: Bonds between unmarried fathers and their children. *Journal of Family Issues, 1,* 31–58.

Galligan, R. J., & Bahr, S. J. (1978). Economic well-being and marital stability: Implications for income maintenance programs. *Journal of Marriage and the Family, 40,* 283–290.

Galper, M. (1978). *Co-parenting: A source book for the separated or divorced family.* Philadelphia: Running Press.

Ganong, L., Coleman, M., & Brown, G. (1981). Effect of family structure on marital attitudes of adolescents. *Adolescence, 16,* 281–288.

Gardner, R. A. (1974). Psychological aspects of divorce. In S. Arieti (Ed.), *American handbook of psychiatry* (Vol. 1, 2nd ed., pp. 496–512). New York: Basic Books.

Gardner, R. A. (1977). Children of divorce: Some legal and psychological considerations. *Journal of Clinical Child Psychology, 6*(2), 3–6.

Gardner, R. A. (1978). Social, legal, and therapeutic changes that should lessen the traumatic effects of divorce on children. *Journal of the American Academy of Psychoanalysis, 6*(2), 231–247.

Gasser, R. D., & Taylor, C. M. (1976). Role adjustment of single parent fathers with dependent children. *Family Coordinator, 25*(4), 397–401.

George, L. K. (1980). *Role transitions in later life.* Monterey, CA: Brooks/Cole.

George, V., & Wilding, P. (1972). *Motherless families.* London: Routledge & Kegan Paul.

Gershansky, I. S., Hainline, I., & Goldstein, H. S. (1978). Maternal differentiation, onset and type of father's absence and psychological differentiation in children. *Perceptual and Motor Skills, 46,* 1147–1152.

Gersick, K. E. (1979). Fathers by choice: Divorced men who receive custody of their children. In G. Levinger & O. C. Moles (Eds.), *Divorce and separation* (pp. 307–323). New York: Basic Books.

Gerstel, N., Riessman, C. K., & Rosenfield, S. (1985). Explaining the symptomatology of separated and divorced women and men: The role of material conditions and social networks. *Social Forces, 64*(1), 84–101.

Gibbs, J. P. (1969). Marital status and suicide in the United States: A special test of the status integration theory. *American Journal of Sociology, 14,* 521–533.

Gibson, J. A., Range, L. M., & Anderson, H. N. (1986). Adolescents' attitudes toward suicide: Does knowledge that the parents are divorced make a difference? Special Issue: The divorce process: A handbook for clinicians. *Journal of Divorce, 10*(1-2), 163–167.

Ginott, H. (1975). *Between parent and child.* New York: Macmillan.

Girdner, L. K. (1985). Adjudication and mediation: A comparison of custody decision-making processes involving third parties. *Journal of Divorce, 8*(3/4), 33–47.

Glasser, P., & Navarre, E. (1965). Structural problems of the one-parent family. *Journal of Social Issues, 21,* 98–109.

Glenn, N. D. (1975). The contribution of marriage to the psychological well-being of males and females. *Journal of Marriage and the Family, 37,* 594–600.

Glenn, N. D. (1981). The well being of persons remarried after divorce. *Journal of Family Issues, 2,* 61–75.

Glenn, N. D. (1982). Interreligious marriage in the United States: Patterns and recent trends. *Journal of Marriage and the Family, 44,* 555–566.

Glenn, N. D. (1987). Social trends in the United States: Evidence from sample surveys. *Public Opinion Quarterly, 51*(2), S109–S126.

Glenn, N. D., & Kramer, K. B. (1987). The marriage and divorces of the children of divorce. *Journal of Marriage and the Family, 49*(4), 811–825.

Glenn, N. D., & Shelton, B. A. (1983). Pre-adult background variables and divorce: A note of caution about over-reliance on explained variance. *Journal of Marriage and the Family, 45,* 405–410.

Glenn, N. D., & Shelton, B. A. (1985). Regional differences in divorce in the U.S. *Journal of Marriage and the Family, 47,* 641–652.

Glenn, N. D., & Supancic, M. (1984). The social and demographic correlates of divorce and separation in the United States: An update and reconsideration. *Journal of Marriage and Family, 46,* 563–575.

Glenn, N. D., & Weaver, C. N. (1977). The marital happiness of remarried divorced persons. *Journal of Marriage and the Family, 39,* 331–337.

Glick, P. C. (1957). *American families.* New York: Wiley.

Glick, P. C. (1979). Children of divorced parents in demographic perspective. *Journal of Social Issues, 35*(4), 170–182.

Glick, P. C. (1980). Remarriage: Some recent changes and variations. *Journal of Family Issues, 1,* 455–478.

Glick, P. C. (1984). Marriage, divorce, and living arrangements: Prospective changes. *Journal of Family Issues, 5,* 7–26.

Glick, P. C., & Lin, S-L. (1986). Recent changes in divorce and remarriage. *Journal of Marriage and the Family, 48,* 737–747.

Glick, P. C., & Norton, A. J. (1973). Perspectives on the recent upturn in divorce and remarriage. *Demography, 10,* 301–314.

Goetting, A. (1979). Some societal-level explanations for the rising divorce rate. *Family Therapy, 6*(2), 71–87.

Goldberg, S. (1976). The inevitability of patriarchy. *Journal of the American Academy of Psychiatry and Neurology, 1*(1), 21–24.

Goldsmith, J. (1980). Relationships between former spouses: Descriptive findings. *Journal of Divorce, 4,* 1–19.

Goldstein, J., Freud, A., & Solnit, A. J. (1973). *Beyond the best interest of the child.* New York: The Free Press.

Gongla, P. A. (1982). Single parent families: A look at families of mothers and children. *Marriage & Family Review, 5,* 5–27.

Goode, W. J. (1956a). *After divorce.* Glencoe, IL: The Free Press.

Goode, W. J. (1956b). *Women in divorce.* New York: The Free Press.

Goode, W. J. (1963). *World revolution and family patterns.* New York: The Free Press.

Goode, W. J. (1980). The resistance of family forces to industrialization. In J. M. Eekelaar & S. N. Katz (Eds.), *Marriage and cohabitation in contemporary societies: Areas of legal, social, and ethical change* (pp. 35–52). Toronto: Butterworth.

Goslin, D. A. (Ed.). (1969). *Handbook of socialization theory and research.* Chicago: Rand McNally.

Gove, W. R. (1972). Sex, marital status, and suicide. *Journal of Health and Social Behavior, 13,* 204–213.

Gove, W. R., & Geerken, M. (1977). The effect of children and employment on the mental health of married men and women. *Social Forces, 56,* 66–76.

Gray, G. M. (1978). The nature of the psychological impact of divorce upon the individual.

Journal of Divorce, 1, 289–301.

Green, D. (1983). Joint custody and the emerging two-parent family. *Conciliation Courts Review, 21*(1), 65–75.

Green, M. (1977). *Fathering.* St. Louis: McGraw-Hill.

Green, R. G., & Sporakowski, M. J. (1983). The dynamics of divorce: Marital quality, alternative attractions and external pressures. *Journal of Divorce, 7,* 77–88.

Greenberg, J. B. (1979). Single-parenting and intimacy: A comparison of fathers and mothers. *Alternative Lifestyles, 2*(3), 308–329.

Greenstein, T. N. (1985). Occupation and divorce. *Journal of Family Issues, 6,* 347–357.

Greif, G. L. (1984). Custodial dads and their ex-wives. *The Single Parent, 27*(1).

Greif, G. L. (1985). *Single fathers.* Lexington, MA: Heath.

Greif, G. L. (1986). Mothers without custody and child support. *Family Relations, 35,* 87–93.

Greif, G. L. (1987). Mothers without custody. *Social Work, 32*(1), 11–16.

Greif, J. B. (1979). Fathers, children, and joint custody. *American Journal of Orthopsychiatry, 49*(2), 311–319.

Greif, J. B. (1982). Therapy with remarriage families: IV. The father–child relationship subsequent to divorce. *Family Therapy Collections, 2,* 47–57.

Guidubaldi, J., Cleminshaw, H. K., Perry, J. D., & Mcloughlin, C. S. (1983). The impact of parental divorce on children: Report of the nationwide NASP study. *School Psychology Review, 12*(3), 300–323.

Gurin, G., Veroff, J., & Feld, S. (1960). *Americans view their mental health.* New York: Basic Books.

Guttentag, M., Salasin, S., & Belle, D. (1980). *The mental health of women.* New York: Academic Press.

Guttentag, M., & Secord, P. F. (1983). *Too many women? The sex ratio.* Beverly Hills. CA: Sage.

Guttmann, J. (1982). *Children's social functioning in school: A comparison of children in mother's and father's custody.* Unpublished manuscript, Tel-Aviv University, Tel-Aviv.

Guttmann, J. (1987). Test anxiety and performance of adolescent children of divorced parents. *Educational Psychology, 7*(3), 225–229.

Guttmann, J. (1988–1989). Intimacy in young adult males' relationships as a function of divorced and non-divorced family of origin structure. In Children of divorce: developmental and clinical issues [Special Issue]. *Journal of Divorce, 12*(2–3), 253–261.

Guttmann, J., Amir, T., & Katz, M. (1987). Threshold of withdrawal from schoolwork among children of divorced parents. *Educational Psychology, 7*(4), 295–302.

Guttmann, J., & Broudo, M. (1988). Teachers' evaluations of pupils' performance as a function of pupils' sex, family type and past school performance. *Educational Review, 40*(1), 105–113.

Guttmann, J., & Broudo, M. (1988–1989). The effect of children's family type on teachers' stereotypes. In Children of divorce: Developmental and clinical issues [Special issue]. *Journal of Divorce, 12*(2–3), 315–328.

Guttmann, J., Geva, N., & Gefen, S. (1988). Teachers' and school children's stereotypic perception of "the child of divorce." *American Educational Research Journal, 25*(4), 555–571.

Hainline, L., & Feig, E. (1978). The correlates of childhood father absence on college age women. *Child Development, 49*(1), 37–42.

Halem, L. C. (1982). *Separated and divorced women.* Westport, CT: Greenwood Press.

Halem, L. C. (1989). *Divorce reform: Changing legal and social perspectives.* New York: The Free Press.

Hampton, R. L. (1975). Marital disruption: Some social and economic consequences. In J. N.

Morgan (Ed.), *Five thousand American families* (Vol. 3, pp. 579–593). Ann Arbor, MI: Institute for Social Research.

Hancock, E. (1980). The dimensions of meaning and belonging in the process of divorce. *American Journal of Orthopsychiatry, 50,* 18–27.

Hancock, E. (1981). The power of the attorney in divorce. *Journal of Family Law, 19*(2), 235–245.

Hannan, M. J., Tuma, N. B., & Groenevold, L. P. (1977). Income and marital events: Evidence from an income-maintenance experiment. *American Journal of Sociology, 82,* 1186–1211.

Hannan, M. J., Tuma, N. B., & Groenevold, L. P. (1978). Income and independence effects on marital dissolution: Results from the Seattle and Denver income-maintenance experiments. *American Journal of Sociology, 84,* 611–633.

Hansen, D. A., & Johnson, V. A. (1979). Rethinking family stress theory: Definitional aspects. In W. R. Burr, R. Hill, F. I. Nye, & I. L. Reiss (Eds.), *Contemporary theories about the family* (pp. 582–603). New York: The Free Press.

Hanson, S. (1981). Single custodial fathers and the parent–child relationship. *Nursing Research, 30,* 202–204.

Hanson, S. (1985). Fatherhood: Contextual variations. *American Behavioral Scientist, 29*(1), 55–78.

Hanson, S. (1986a). Father–child relationships: Beyond Kramer vs. Kramer. In R. S. Lewis & M. B. Sussman (Eds.), *Men's changing roles in families* (pp. 135–150). New York: Haworth.

Hanson, S. (1986b). Parent–child relationships in single father families. In R. Lewis & B. Salts (Eds.), *Men in families* (pp. 181–196). Beverly Hills, CA: Sage.

Hanson, S. (1986c). Healthy single parent families. *Family Relations, 35*(1), 125–132.

Hanson, S. (1988). Divorced fathers with custody. In P. Bronstein & C. P. Cowan (Eds.), *Fatherhood today* (pp. 166–194). New York: Wiley.

Hanson, S., & Bozett, F. W. (Eds.). (1985). *Dimensions of fatherhood.* Beverly Hills, CA: Sage.

Hanson, S., & Trilling, J. A. (1983). A proposed study of the characteristics of the healthy single-parent family. *Family Perspective, 17,* 79–88.

Hanson, S., & Tuch, S. A. (1984). The determinants of marital instability: Some methodological issues. *Journal of Marriage and the Family, 46,* 631–642.

Hare-Mustin, R. T., Bennett, S. K., & Broderick, P. C. (1983). Attitude toward motherhood: Gender, generational, and religious comparisons. *Sex Roles, 9*(5), 643–661.

Harper, J. F., & Ryder, J. M. (1986). Parental bonding, self-esteem and peer acceptance in father-absent male adolescents. *Australian Journal of Sex, Marriage and Family, 7*(1), 17–26.

Havighurst, R. J. (1961, Spring). Early marriage and the schools. *The School Review,* 36–47.

Hawkins, L. (1979). The impact of policy decisions on families. *Family Coordinator, 28,* 264–272.

Heaton, T. B. (1984). Religious homogamy and marital satisfaction reconsidered. *Journal of Marriage and the Family, 46,* 729–733.

Heer, D. M., & Grossbard-Shechtman, A. (1981). The impact of the female marriage squeeze and the contraceptive revolution on sex roles and the women's liberation movement in the United States, 1960–1975. *Journal of Marriage and the Family, 43,* 49–65.

Heider, F. (1958). *The psychology of interpersonal relations.* New York: Wiley.

Hernandez, D. J. (1988). Demographic trends and the living arrangements of children. In M. E. Hetherington & J. D. Arasteh (Eds.), *Impact of divorce, single parenting and stepparenting on children* (pp. 3–22). Hillsdale, NJ: Lawrence Erlbaum Associates.

Herzog, E., & Sudia, C. E. (1968). Fatherless homes: A review of research. *Children, 15*(5), 177–182.

Herzog, E., & Sudia, C. E. (1973). Children in fatherless families. In B. M. Caldwell & H. N. Riciuti (Eds.), *Review of child development research* (Vol. 3, pp. 141–232). Chicago: University of Chicago Press.

Hess, R. D., & Camara, K. A. (1979). Post-divorce family relationships as mediating factors in the consequences of divorce for children. *Journal of Social Issues, 35,* 79–96.

Hetherington, E. M. (1972). Effects of father absence on personality development in adolescent daughters. *Developmental Psychology, 7*(3), 313–326.

Hetherington, E. M. (1979). Divorce: A child's perspective. *American Psychologist, 34*(10), 851–858.

Hetherington, E. M. (1982). Effects of divorce on parents and children. In M. E. Lamb (Ed.), *Nontraditional families: Parenting and child development* (pp. 233–288). Hillsdale, NJ: Lawrence Erlbaum Associates.

Hetherington, E. M. (1989). Coping with family transitions: Winners, losers, and survivors. *Child Development, 60,* 1–14.

Hetherington, E. M., Camara, K. A., & Featherman, D. L. (1981). *Cognitive performance, school behavior and achievement of children of one-parent families.* Medford, MA: Child and Family Study, Tufts University.

Hetherington, E. M., Cox, M., & Cox, R. (1976). Divorced fathers. *The Family Coordinator, 25*(4), 417–428.

Hetherington, E. M., Cox, M., & Cox, R. (1978). The aftermath of divorce. In J. H. Stevens & M. Matthews (Eds.), *Mother–child, father–child relations* (pp. 149–176). Washington, DC: National Association for the Education of Young Children.

Hetherington, E. M., Cox, M., & Cox, R. (1979a). Family interaction and the social, emotional and cognitive development of children following divorce. In V. Vaughn & T. B. Brazelton (Eds.), *The family* (pp. 49–93). New York: Science Medicine.

Hetherington, E. M., Cox, M., & Cox, R. (1979b). Play and social interaction in children following divorce. *Journal of Social Issues, 35*(4), 26–49.

Hetherington, E. M., Cox, M., & Cox, R. (1985). Long-term effects of divorce and remarriage on the adjustment of children. *Journal of the American Academy of Child Psychiatry, 24*(5), 518–530.

Hetzel, A. M., & Capetta, M. (1973). Teenagers: Marriages, divorces, parenthood, and mortality. *Vital and Health Statistics: U.S. Dept. of Health, Education, and Welfare,* Series 21:23. Hyattsville, MD: Public Health Service.

Hill, C. T., Rubin, Z., & Peplau, L. A. (1976). Breakups before marriage: The end of 103 affairs. *Journal of Social Issues, 32,* 147–168.

Hiller, D. V., & Philliber, W. W. (1980). Necessity, compatibility, and status attainment as factors in the labor-force participation of married women. *Journal of Marriage and the Family, 42,* 103–110.

Hiller, D. V., & Philliber, W. W. (1982). Predicting marital and career success among dual-worker couples. *Journal of Marriage and the Family, 44,* 53–62.

Hingst, A. G. (1981). Children and divorce: The child's view. *Journal of Clinical Child Psychology, 10,* 161–164.

Hodges, W. F. (1986). *Interventions for children of divorce: Custody, access and psychotherapy.* New York: Wiley.

Hodges, W. F., & Bloom, B. L. (1984). Parent's report of children's adjustment to marital separation: A longitudinal study. *Journal of Divorce, 8*(1), 33–50.

Hoffman, M. L. (1971). Father absence and conscience development. *Developmental Psychology, 4*(3), 400–406.

Holtzworth-Munroe, A., & Jacobson, N. S. (1985). Causal attributions of married couples: When do they search for causes? What do they conclude when they do? *Journal of Personality and Social Psychology, 48,* 1398–1412.

Horowitz, J., & Perdue, B. (1977). Single-parent families. *Nursing Clinics of North America, 12,* 503-511.

Houseeknecht, S. K., & Spanier, G. B. (1980). Marital disruption and higher education among women in the United States. *Sociological Quarterly, 21,* 375-389.

Howell, M. C. (1973). Employed mothers and their families. *Pediatrics, 52*(2), 7.

Hozman, T. L., & Froiland, D. J. (1976). Families in divorce: A proposed model for counseling the children. *Family Coordinator, 25*(3), 271-276.

Huber, J., & Spitze, G. (1980). Considering divorce: An expansion of Becker's theory of marital instability. *American Journal of Sociology, 86,* 75-89.

Hulme, T. (1976). Health concerns of the single-parent family. In S. Burden, P. Houston, E. Kriple, R. Simpson, & W. Stultz (Eds.), *Proceedings of the changing family conference V: The single-parent family* (pp. 147-199). Iowa City: University of Iowa.

Hunt, L. L., & Hunt, J. G. (1975). Race and the father–son connection: The conditional relevance of father absence for the orientation and identities of adolescent boys. *Social Problems, 23,* 35-52.

Hunt, M. (1966). *The world of the formerly married.* New York: Fawcett World Library.

Hunt, M., & Hunt, B. (1977). *The divorce experience.* New York: McGraw-Hill.

Hurowitz, N. (1981). *Divorce: Your fault, my fault, no fault.* Bridgeport, PA: LawTrac Press.

Israel, B. (1982). Social networks and health status: Linking theory, research, and practice. *Patient Counseling and Health Education, 4,* 65-79.

Jacobs, J. W. (1982). The effect of divorce on fathers: An overview of the literature. *American Journal of Psychiatry, 139*(10), 1235-1241.

Jacobs, J. W. (1983). Treatment of divorcing fathers: Social and psychotherapeutic considerations. *American Journal of Psychiatry, 140*(10), 1294-1299.

Jacobs, J. W. (1986). Divorce and child custody resolution: Conflicting legal and psychological paradigms. *American Journal of Psychiatry, 143*(2), 192-197.

Jacobson, D. S. (1978). The impact of marital separation/divorce on children. II: Interparent hostility and child adjustment. *Journal of Divorce, 2,* 3-19.

Johnson, W. D. (1977). Establishing a national center for the study of divorce. *The Family Coordinator, 26*(3), 263-268.

Johnston, J. R., & Campbell, L. E. (1986). Tribal warfare: The involvement of extended kin and significant others in custody and access disputes. *Conciliation Courts Review, 24*(1), 1-16.

Kalter, N. (1977). Children of divorce in an outpatient psychiatric population. *American Journal of Orthopsychiatry, 47,* 40-51.

Kalter, N., Kloner, A., Schreier, S., & Okla, K. (1989). Predictors of children's postdivorce adjustment. *American Journal of Orthopsychiatry, 59,* 605-620.

Kalter, N., & Plunkett, J. W. (1984). Children's perceptions of the causes and consequences of divorce. *Journal of the American Academy of Child Psychiatry, 23*(3), 326-334.

Kalter, N., & Rembar, J. (1981). The significance of a child's age at the time of parental divorce. *American Journal of Orthopsychiatry, 51,* 85-100.

Kantor, D., & Lehr, W. (1975). *Inside the family.* San Francisco, CA: Jossey-Bass.

Kaplan, S. L. (1977). Structural family therapy for children of divorce: Case reports. *Family Process, 16,* 75-83.

Kaslow, F. W. (1981). Divorce and divorce therapy. In A. S. Gurman & D. P. Kniskern (Eds.), *Handbook of family therapy* (pp. 662-698). New York: Brunner/Mazel.

Kaslow, F. W. (1983). Stages and techniques of divorce therapy. In P. A. Keller & L. G. Ritt
· (Eds.), *Innovations in clinical practice: A sourcebook* (Vol. 2, pp. 5-16). Sarasota, FL: Professional Resource Exchange.

Kaslow, F. W., & Schwartz, L. L. (1987). *The dynamics of divorce: A life cycle perspective.* New York: Brunner/Mazel.

Katz, A. (1979). Lone fathers: Perspectives and implications for family policy. *The Family Coordinator, 28*(4), 521–528.

Kay, H. H. (1970). A family court: The California proposal. In P. Bohannan (Ed.), *Divorce and after* (pp. 215–248). New York: Doubleday.

Kelly, C. (1980). Assessment of potential single parent family units for child custody purposes. *Conciliation Courts Review, 18,* 21–26.

Kelly, J. B. (1982). Divorce: The adult perspective. In B. B. Wolman (Ed.), *Handbook of developmental psychology* (pp. 734–750). Englewood Cliffs, NJ: Prentice-Hall.

Kelly, J. B., & Wallerstein, J. S. (1977). Part-time parent, part-time child: Visiting after divorce. *Journal of Clinical Child Psychology, 6*(2), 51–54.

Kerpelman, L. (1983). *Divorce: A guide for men.* South Bend, IN: Icarus.

Keshet, H. F. (1980). From separation to stepfamily: A subsystem analysis. *Journal of Family Issues, 1,* 517–532.

Keshet, H. F., & Rosenthal, K. M. (1978). Fathering after marital separation. *Social Work, 23,* 11–18.

Keshet, J. K. (1980). From separation to stepfamily: A subsystem analysis. *Journal of Family Issues, 1,* 517–532.

Kessler, S. (1975). *The American way of divorce: Prescription for change.* Nelson Hall: Chicago.

Kieffer, C. (1977). New depths of intimacy. In R. Libby & R. Whitehurst (Eds.), *Marriage and its alternatives: Exploring intimate relationships* (pp. 267–293). Glenview, IL: Scotts, Foresman.

Kitson, G. C. (1982). Attachment to the spouse in divorce: A scale and its application. *Journal of Marriage and the Family, 44,* 379–398.

Kitson, G. C., Babri, K. B., & Roach, M. J. (1985). Who divorces and why. A review. *Journal of Family Issues, 6,* 255–293.

Kitson, G. C., Holmes, W. M., & Sussman, M. B. (1983). Withdrawing divorce petitions: A predictive test of the exchange model of divorce. *Journal of Divorce, 7,* 51–66.

Kitson, G. C., Lopata, H. Z., Holmes, W. M., & Meyering, S. M. (1980). Divorcees and widows: Similarities and differences. *American Journal of Orthopsychiatry, 50,* 291–301.

Kitson, G. C., & Raschke, H. J. (1981). Divorce research: What we know, what we need to know. *Journal of Divorce, 4,* 1–37.

Kitson, G. C., & Sussman, M. B. (1982). Marital complaints, demographic characteristics, and symptoms of mental distress in divorce. *Journal of Marriage and the Family, 44,* 87–102.

Klebanow, S. (1976). Parenting in the single parent family. *Journal of American Psychoanalysis, 4*(1), 37–48.

Klein, N. (1981). *Breaking up.* New York: Avon.

Koch, M. A., & Lowery, C. R. (1984). Visitation and the noncustodial father. *Journal of Divorce, 8*(2), 47–65.

Koehler, J. M. (1982). Mothers without custody. *Children Today, 11,* 12–15.

Kohen, J. A., Brown, C. A., & Feldberg, R. (1979). Divorced mothers: The costs and benefits of female family control. In G. Levinger & O. C. Moles (Eds.), *Divorce and separation: Context, causes and consequences* (pp. 228–245). New York: Basic Books.

Koziey, P. W., & Davies, L. (1982). Broken homes: Impact on adolescents. *The Alberta Journal of Educational Research, 28*(2), 95–99.

Krantz, S. L. (1988). Divorce and children. In S. M. Dornbusch & N. H. Strober (Eds.), *Feminism, children, and the new families* (pp. 249–273). New York: Guilford.

Krantzler, M. (1975). *Creative divorce: A new opportunity for personal growth.* New York: New American Library.

Kraus, S. (1979). The crisis of divorce: Growth promoting or pathogenic? *Journal of Divorce, 3,* 107–119.

Kressel, K., & Deutsch, M. (1977). Divorce therapy: An in-depth survey of therapists' views. *Family Process, 16*, 413–444.

Kruglanski, A. W. (1989). *Lay epistemics and human knowledge: Cognitive and motivational bases.* New York: Plenum.

Kruglanski, A. W., Baldwin, M. W., & Shelagh, M. J. (1983). The lay-epistemic process in attribution-making. In M. Hewstone (Ed.), *Attribution theory* (pp. 81–95). Oxford, England: Basil Blackwell.

Kubler-Ross, E. (1969). *On death and dying.* London: Macmillan.

Kulka, R. A., & Weingarten, H. (1979). The long-term effects of parental divorce in childhood on adult adjustment. *The Journal of Social Issues, 35*(4), 50–78.

Kunz, P., & Albrecht, S. L. (1977). Religion, marital happiness and divorce. *International Journal of Sociology of the Family, 7*, 227–232.

Kurdek, L. A. (1981). An integrative perspective on children's divorce adjustment. *American Psychologist, 36*, 856–866.

Kurdek, L. A. (1986). *Children's adjustment to parental divorce.* Unpublished manuscript, Wright State University, Dayton, OH.

Kurdek, L. A., & Berg, B. (1983). Correlates of children's adjustment to their parents' divorces. *New Directions for Child Development, 19*, 47–60.

Kurdek, L. A., & Blisk, D. (1983). Dimensions and correlates of mothers' divorce experiences. *Journal of Divorce, 6*(4), 1–24.

Kurdek, L. A., Blisk, D., & Siesky, A. E. (1981). Correlates of children's long-term adjustment to their parents' divorce. *Developmental Psychology, 17*, 565–579.

Kurdek, L. A., & Siesky, A. E. (1979). An interview study of parents' perceptions of their children's reactions and adjustment to divorce. *Journal of Divorce, 3*(1), 5–17.

Kurdek, L. A., & Siesky, A. E. (1980). Effects of divorce on children: The relationship between parent and child perspectives. *Journal of Divorce, 4*(2), 85–99.

Kurdek, L. A., & Sinclair, R. J. (1988). Adjustment of young adolescents in two-parent nuclear, stepfather, and mother-custody families. *Journal of Consulting and Clinical Psychology, 56*(1), 91–96.

L'Hommedieu, T. (1984). *The divorce experience of working and middle class women.* Ann Arbor, MI: UMI Research Press.

LaBarre, W. (1954). *The human animal.* Chicago: University of Chicago Press.

Lamb, M. E. (Ed.). (1976). *The role of the father in child development.* New York: Wiley.

Lamb, M. E. (1977). Infant social cognition and "second-order" effects. *Infant Behaviour and Development, 1*(1), 1–10.

Landis, J. (1960). The trauma of children when parents divorce. *Marriage and Family Living, 22*, 7–13.

Laws, J. (1975). A feminist view of the marital adjustment. In A. Gurmin & D. Rice (Eds.), *Couples in conflict* (pp. 62–83). New York: Jason Aronson.

LeMasters, E. E. (1974). *Parents in modern America.* (rev. ed.). Homewood, IL: Dorsey Press.

LeMasters, E. E., & DeFrain, J. (1983). *Parents in contemporary America: A sympathetic view.* Homewood, IL: Dorsey Press.

Lenthall, G. (1977). Marital satisfaction and marital stability. *Journal of Marriage and Family Counseling, 3*, 25–32.

Lenz, E., & Myerhoff, B. (1985). *The feminization of America: How women's values are changing our public and privates lives.* Los Angeles, CA: J. P. Tarcher.

Leslie, G. R., & Korman, S. K. (1985). *The family in social context* (6th ed.). New York: Oxford University Press.

Leslie, L. A., & Grady, K. (1988). Social support for divorcing mothers: What seems to help? *Journal of Divorce, 11*(3–4), 147–165.

Levine, J. A. (1976). *Who will raise the children: New options for fathers (and mothers)*. New York: Lippincott.

Levinger, G. (1965). Marital cohesiveness and dissolution: An integrative review. *Journal of Marriage and the Family, 27,* 19–28.

Levinger, G. (1976). A social perspective on divorce. *Journal of Social Issues, 32,* 21–47.

Levinger, G. (1979a). A social psychological perspective on marital dissolution. In G. Levinger & O. C. Moles (Eds.), *Divorce and separation* (pp. 37–60). New York: Basic Books.

Levinger, G. (1979b). *Social exchange in developing relationships*. New York: Academic Press.

Levinger, G., & Moles, O. C. (Eds.). (1979). *Divorce and separation: Context, causes and consequences*. New York: Basic Books.

Levitan, S. A., & Belous, R. S. (1981). *What's happening to the American family?* Baltimore, MD: Johns Hopkins University Press.

Levitan, T. E. (1979). Children of divorce. *The Journal of Social Issues, 35*(4), 1–25.

Lewin, K. (1951). *Field theory in social science*. New York: Harper.

Lewis, K. (1978). Single-father families: Who they are and how they fare. *Child Welfare, 57,* 643–652.

Lewis, P. H. (1983). Innovative divorce rituals: Their psycho-social functions. *Journal of Divorce, 6,* 71–81.

Libby, R. W., & Whitehurs, R. N. (1977). *Marriage and alternatives: Exploring intimate relationships*. Glenview, IL: Scott, Foresman.

Lindahl, A. (1979). An Evaluation of Divorced Single Parents' Views of Local Church Ministries. *Dissertation Abstracts, 40*(A), 1708.

Little, M. (1982). *Family breakup*. San Francisco: Jossey-Bass.

Locksley, A. (1982). Social class and marital attitudes and behavior. *Journal of Marriage and the Family, 44,* 427–440.

Loewen, J. W. (1988). Visitation fatherhood. In P. Bronstein & C. P. Cowan (Eds.), *Fatherhood today* (pp. 214–235). New York: Wiley.

Longabaugh, R. (1973). Mother behavior as a variable moderating the effects of father absence. *Ethos, 1*(4), 456–465.

Longfellow, C. (1979). Divorce in context: Its impact on children. In G. Levinger & O. C. Moles (Eds.), *Divorce and separation* (pp. 287–306). New York: Basic Books.

Lopata, H. Z. (1979). *Women as widows*. New York: Elsevier.

Lowe, N. V. (1982). The legal status of fathers: Past and present. In L. McKee & M. O'Brien (Eds.), *The father figure* (pp. 26–42). London: Tavistock.

Lowenstein, J. S., & Koopman, E. J. (1978). A comparison of the self-esteem between boys living with single-parent mothers and single-parent fathers. *Journal of Divorce, 2,* 195–208.

Lowenthal, M. F., & Haven, C. (1968). Interaction and adaptation: Intimacy as a critical variable. In B. L. Neugarten (Ed.), *Middle age and aging* (pp. 121–139). Chicago: University of Chicago Press.

Lowery, C. R., & Settle, S. A. (1985). Effects of divorce on children: Differential impact of custody and visitation patterns. *Family Relations Journal of Applied Family and Child Studies, 34*(4), 455–463.

Luepnitz, D. A. (1979). Which aspects of divorce affect children. *Family Coordinator, 28,* 79–85.

Luepnitz, D. A. (1982). *Child custody: A study of families after divorce*. Lexington, MA: Lexington Books.

Lynn, D. B. (1974). *The father: His role in child development*. Monterey: Brooks Cole.

MacBride, A. B. (1973). *The growth and development of mothers*. New York: Harper & Row.

Maccoby, E. E., Depner, C. E., & Mnookin, R. H. (1990). Coparenting in the second year after divorce. *Journal of Marriage and the Family, 52,* 141–155.

Maccoby, E. E., & Jacklin, C. N. (1975). *The psychology of sex differences.* Palo Alto: Stanford University Press.

MacKinnon, C. E., Brody, G. H., & Stoneman, Z. (1982). The effect of divorce and maternal employment on the home environments of preschool children. *Child Development, 53*(5), 1392–1399.

MacKinnon, C. E., Brody, G. H., & Stoneman, Z. (1986). The longitudinal effects of divorce and maternal employment on the home environments of preschool children. *Journal of Divorce, 9,* 65–78.

Magrab, P. R. (1978). For the sake of the children: A review of the psychological effects of divorce. *Journal of Divorce, 1,* 233–245.

Maidment, S. (1984). *Child custody and divorce: The law in social context.* London: Croom Helm.

Malinowski, B. (1974). Parenthood, the basis of social structure. In V. F. Calverton & S. Schmalhausen (Eds.), *The new generation* (pp. 57–83). New York: Citadel Press. (Original work published 1930)

Malzberg, G. (1964). Marital status and the incidence of mental disease. *International Journal of Social Psychiatry, 10,* 19–26.

Maneker, J. S., & Rankin, R. P. (1991). Religious affiliation and marital duration among those who file for divorce in california, 1966–1971. *Journal of Divorce and Remarriage, 15*(3–4), 205–218.

Marsden, D. (1969). *Mothers alone.* Harmondsworth: Penguin.

Martin, T. C., & Bumpass, L. L. (1989). Recent trends in marital disruption. *Demography, 26*(1), 37–51.

Mason, K. O., Czajka, J. L., & Arber, S. (1976). Change in U.S. women's sex-role attitudes, 1964–1974. *American Sociological Review, 41,* 573–596.

Matusow, A. J. (1984). *The unraveling of America: A history of liberalism in the 1960s.* New York: Harper & Row.

McCarthy, J. (1979). Religious commitment, affiliation, and marital dissolution. In R. Wuthnow (Ed.), *The religious dimension: New directions in qualitative research* (pp. 177–198). New York: Academic Press.

McCubbin, H. I., Joy, C. B., Cauble, A. E., Comeau, J. K., Patterson, J. M., & Needle, R. H. (1980). Family stress and coping decade review. *Journal of Marriage & the Family, 42,* 855–871.

McDermott, J. F. (1968). Parental divorce in early childhood. *American Journal of Psychiatry, 124,* 1424–1432.

McDermott, J. F. (1970). Divorce and its psychiatric sequelae in children. *Archives of General Psychiatry, 23,* 421–427.

McKee, L., & O'Brien, M. (Eds.). (1982). *The father figure.* London: Tavistock.

McLanahan, S. S. (1983, May). Family structure and stress: A longitudinal comparison of two-parent and female-headed families. *Journal of Marriage and the Family,* 347–357.

McLanahan, S. S. (1989). Mother-only families: Problems, reproduction and politics. *Journal of Marriage and the Family, 51,* 557–580.

McLanahan, S. S., & Bumpass, L. (1988). Intergenerational consequences of family disruption. *American Journal of Sociology, 94*(1), 130–152.

McLanahan, S. S., Wedemeyer, N. V., & Adelberg, T. (1981). Network structure, social support, and psychological well-being in the single-parent family. *Journal of Marriage and the Family, 43,* 601–612.

McPhee, J. T. (1984). Ambiguity and change in the post-divorce family: Towards a model of divorce adjustment. *Journal of Divorce, 8*(2), 1–15.

Mead, M. (1964). Some theoretical considerations on the problem of mother–child separation. *American Journal of Orthopsychiatry, 24*(3), 480.

Mednick, B. R., Baker, R. L., Reznick, C., & Hocevar, D. (1990). Long-term effects of divorce on adolescent academic achievement. *Journal of Divorce, 13*(4), 69-88.

Melichar, J. F., & Chiriboga, D. A. (1988). Significance of time in adjustment to marital separation. *American Journal of Orthopsychiatry, 58*(2), 221-227.

Mendes, H. A. (1976). Single fathers. *The Family Coordinator, 25,* 439-444.

Mendes, H. A. (1979). Single parent families: A typology of life styles. *Social Work, 24,* 193-200.

Miller, A. A. (1970). Reactions of friends to divorce. In P. Bohannan (Ed.), *Divorce and after: An analysis of the emotional and social problems of divorce* (pp. 56-80). New York: Doubleday.

Miller, D. R., & Swanson, G. E. (1958). *The changing American parent.* New York: Wiley.

Miller, J. B. (1982). Psychological recovery in low-income single parents. *American Journal of Orthopsychiatry, 52,* 346-352.

Mintz, S., & Kellogg, S. (1988). *Domestic revolutions.* New York: The Free Press.

Minuchin, S. (1974). *Families and family therapy.* Cambridge, MA: Harvard University Press.

Mitchell, G. (1969). Paternalistic behavior in primates. *Psychological Bulletin, 71,* 399-417.

Mitchell, G., Redican, W. K., & Gomber, J. (1974, April). Lesson from a primate: Males can raise babies. *Psychology Today,* p. 67.

Mnookin, R. H., & Kornhauser, L. (1979). Bargaining in the shadow of the law: The case of divorce. *Yale Law Journal 88,* 8950-997.

Moltz, H., Lubin, M., Leon, M., & Numan, M. (1970). Hormonal induction of maternal behavior in the ovariectomized rat. *Physiology and Behavior, 5,* 1373-1377.

Monahan, T. P. (1957). Family status and the delinquent child: A reappraisal and some new findings. *Social Forces, 35,* 250-258.

Monahan, T. P. (1960a). Broken homes by age of delinquent children. *Journal of Social Psychology, 51,* 387-397.

Monahan, T. P. (1960b). Premarital pregnancy in the United States. *Eugenics Quarterly, 7,* 140.

Montemayor, R. (1982). The relationship between parent–adolescent conflict and the amount of time adolescents spend with parents, peers, and alone. *Child Development, 53,* 1512-1519.

Morawetz, A., & Walker, G. (1983). *Brief therapy with single-parent families.* New York: Brunner-Mazel.

Morgan, S. P., & Rindfuss, R. R. (1985). Marital disruption: Structural and temporal dimensions. *American Journal of Sociology, 90,* 1055-1077.

Moroney, R. (1980). *Families, social services, and social policy: The issue of shared responsibility* (DHHS Publication No. ADM 80-846). Washington, DC: U.S. Department of Health and Human Services.

Mott, F. L. (1990). When is a father really gone: Paternal–child contact in father absent homes. *Demography, 27*(4), 499-517.

Mott, F. L., & Moore, S. F. (1979). The causes of marital disruption among young American women: An interdisciplinary perspective. *Journal of Marriage and the Family, 41,* 355-365.

Moynihan, D. P. (1965). *The negro family: The case for national action* (U.S. Department of Labor, Office of Policy Planning and Research). Washington, DC: U.S. Government Printing Office.

Moynihan, D. P. (1986). *Family and nation: The Godkin lectures, Harvard University.* San Diego, CA: Harcourt Brace Javanovich.

Mueller, C. W., & Pope, H. (1977). Marital instability: A study of its transmission between generations. *Journal of Marriage and the Family, 39,* 83-93.

Murch, M. (1980). *Justice and welfare in divorce.* London: Sweet & Maxwell.

Murray, C. (1986). No, welfare isn't really the problem. *Public Interest, 84,* 5-6.

Napier, A. Y. (1978, January). The rejection-intrusion pattern: A central family dynamic. *Journal of Marriage and Family Counseling*, 5-12.

National Center for Health Statistics. (1980). *Advanced Data from Vital and Health Statistics*, February 14(58), Washington, DC: U.S. Government Printing Office.

National Center for Health Statistics. (1984). *Births, marriages, divorces, and deaths, United States 1983* (DHHS Publications No. PHS 84-1120). Hyattsville, MD: Public Health Service.

National Center for Health Statistics. (1985). Advance report of final divorce statistics. *Monthly Vital Statistics Reports, 34*(9), Suppl. DHHS Pub. No. PHS 85-1120. Washington, DC: U.S. Government Printing Office.

National Center for Health Statistics. (1989). Advance report of final marriage statistics. *Monthly Vital Statistics Reports, 38*(3), Suppl. 2. Hyattsville, MD: Public Health Service.

Neal, J. H. (1983). Children's understanding of their parents' divorces. *New Directions for Child Development, 19,* 3-14.

Nelson, G. (1981). Moderators of women's and children's adjustment following parental divorce. *Journal of Divorce, 4,* 71-83.

Nelson, G. (1982). Coping with the loss of father: Family reaction to death and divorce. *Journal of Family Issues, 3,* 41-60.

Nimkoff, M. F. (Ed.). (1965). *Comparative family systems.* Boston: Houghton Mifflin.

Nock, S. L. (1981). Family life-cycle transitions: Longitudinal effects on family members. *Journal of Marriage and the Family, 43,* 703-714.

Norton, A. J. (1983). Family life cycle: 1980. *Journal of Marriage and the Family, 45*(2), 267-275.

Norton, A. J., & Glick, P. C. (1976). Marital instability: Past, present, and future. *The Journal of Social Issues, 32*(1), 5-20.

Nye, F. I. (1957). Child adjustment in broken and unhappy unbroken homes. *Marriage and Family Living, 19,* 356-360.

Nye, F. I. (1967). Values, family, and a changing society. *Journal of Marriage and the Family, 29,* 241-248.

Nye, F. I. (1979). Choice, exchange, and the family. In W. Burr, R. Hill, F. I. Nye, & I. Russ (Eds.), *Contemporary theories about the family* (Vol. 2, pp. 1-41). New York: The Free Press.

Nye, F. I., & Berardo, F. M. (1973). *The family: Its structure and interaction.* New York: Macmillan.

Offord, D. R., Abrams, N., Allen, N., & Poushinsky, M. (1979). Broken homes, parental psychiatric illness, and female delinquency. *American Journal of Orthopsychiatry, 49,* 252-264.

Ogburn, W. F., & Thomas, D. S. (1922). The influence of the business cycle on certain social conditions. *Journal of the American Statistical Association, 18,* 324-340.

Ogburn, W. F., & Nimkoff, M. F. (1955). *Technology and the changing family.* Cambridge: Houghton Mifflin.

Orthner, D. K., & Bowen, G. L. (1983). *Families in blue: Opportunities for ministry.* Washington, DC: Department of the Air Force.

Orthner, D. K., Brown, T., & Ferguson, D. (1976). Single-parent fatherhood: An emerging family life style. *Family Coordinator, 25*(4), 429-437.

Parish, T. S. (1980). The relationship between factors associated with father loss and individual's level of moral judgement, *Adolescence, 15*(59), 535-541.

Parish, T. S., & Dostal, J. W. (1980). Relationships between evaluations of self and parents by children from intact and divorced families. *Journal of Psychology, 104,* 35-38.

Parish, T. S., & Nunn, G. D. (1981). Children's self-concepts and evaluations of parents as a function of family structure and process. *Journal of Psychology, 107*(1), 105-108.

Parke, R. D. (1981). *Fathers*. Cambridge, MA: Harvard University Press.

Parsons, T., & Bales, R. F. (1955). *Family, socialization, and interaction processes*. Glencoe, IL: The Free Press.

Partridge, S., & Kotler, T. (1987). Self-esteem and adjustment in adolescents from bereaved, divorced, and intact families: Family type versus family environment. *Australian Journal of Psychology, 39*(2), 223-234.

Paskowicz, P. (1984). *Absentee mothers*. New York: Universe Books.

Patterson, G. R. (1982). *Coercive family process*. Eugene, OR: Castalia.

Pearlin, L. I., & Johnson, J. S. (1977). Marital status, life strains and depression. *American Sociological Review, 42,* 704-715.

Pederson, F. A., & Robson, K. S. (1969). Father participation in infancy. *American Journal of Orthopsychiatry, 39*(3), 467-468.

Perlman, J. L. (1982). Divorce—A psychological and legal process. *Journal of Divorce, 6,* 99-114.

Pett, M. G. (1982). Correlates of children's social adjustment following divorce. *Journal of Divorce, 5,* 25-39.

Pett, M. A., & Vaughan-Cole, B. (1986). The impact of income issues and social status on post-divorce adjustment of custodial parents. In The single parent family [Special issue] *Family Relations Journal of Applied Family and Child Studies, 35*(1), 103-111.

Philliber, W. W., & Hiller, D. V. (1983). Relative occupational attainments of spouses and later changes in marriage and wife's work experience. *Journal of Marriage and the Family, 45,* 161-170.

Pihl, R. O., & Caron, M. (1980). The relationship between geographic mobility, adjustment, and personality. *Journal of Clinical Psychology, 36,* 190-194.

Plateris, A. A. (1969). *Divorce statistics and analysis: United States 1964 and 1965* (National Center for Health Statistics, Vital and Health Statistics, Series 21, No. 17). Washington, DC: U.S. Government Printing Office.

Pope, H., & Mueller, C. W. (1976). The intergenerational transmission of marital instability: Comparisons by race and sex. *The Journal of Social Issues, 32*(1), 49-66.

Popenoe, D. (1988). *Disturbing the nest: Family change and decline in modern societies*. New York: Aldine De Gruyter.

Preston, S. H., & McDonald, J. (1979). The incidence of divorce within cohorts of American marriages contracted since the Civil War. *Demography, 16,* 1-25.

Price-Bonham, S., & Balswick, J. O. (1980). The noninstitutions: Divorce, desertion, and remarriage. *Journal of Marriage and the Family, 42,* 959-972.

Propst, L. R., Pardington, A., Ostrom, R., & Watkins, P. (1986). Predictors of coping in divorced single mothers. *Journal of Divorce, 9*(3), 33-53.

Radloff, L. (1975). Sex differences in depression: The effects of occupation and marital status. *Sex Roles: A Journal of Research, 1,* 249-265.

Rapoport, R. (1965). *The study of marriage as a critical transition for personality and family development*. Unpublished manuscript, Harvard Medical School, Cambridge, MA.

Raschke, H. J. (1977). The role of social participation in postseparation and postdivorce adjustment. *Journal of Divorce, 1,* 129-139.

Raschke, H. J., & Raschke, V. J. (1979). Family conflict and children's self-concepts: A comparison of intact and single-parent families. *Journal of Marriage and the Family, 41,* 367-374.

Rasmussen, P. K., & Ferraro, K. J. (1979). The divorce process. *Alternative Lifestyles, 2*(4), 443-460.

Redican, W. K. (1976). Adult male–infant interactions in nonhuman primates. In M. E. Lamb (Ed.), *The role of the father in child development* (pp. 345-386). New York: Wiley.

Redick, R. W., & Johnson, C. (1974). *Marital status, living arrangements and family characteristics of admission to state and county mental hospitals and outpatient psychiatric clinics, United States, 1970* (Statistical note 100, National Institute of Mental Health). Washington, DC: U.S. Government Printing Office.

Reinhard, D. W. (1977). The reaction of adolescent boys and girls to the divorce of their parents. *Journal of Clinical Child Psychology, 6,* 15-20.

Reiss, I. L., & Lee, G. R. (1988). *Family systems in America* (4th ed.). New York: Holt, Rinehart & Winston.

Reuter, M. W., & Biller, H. B. (1973). Perceived paternal nurturance-availability and personality adjustment among college males. *Journal of Consulting and Clinical Psychology, 40,* 339-352.

Reznick, C., Mednick, B., Baker, R., & Hocevar, D. (1986). *Comparison of stresses and resources in divorced and intact homes.* Paper presented at the conference of the American Psychological Association, Washington, DC.

Rice, J. K., & Anderson, N. C. (1982). Attitudes of women active in the community regarding the women's liberation movement. *Journal of the National Association of Women Deans, Administrators, and Counselors, 46,* 9-16.

Rice, J. K., & Rice, D. G. (1986). *Living through divorce: A developmental approach to divorce therapy.* New York: Guilford.

Richards, M., & Dyson, M. P. M. (1982). *Separation, divorce and the development of children: A review.* Cambridge, MA: University of Cambridge.

Rickard, K., Forehand, R., Atkeson, B., & Lopez, C. (1982). An examination of the relationship of marital satisfaction and divorce with parent–child interactions. *Journal of Clinical Psychology, 11*(1), 61-65.

Rindfuss, R., & MacDonald, M. (1980). *Earnings, relative income, and family formation, Part II: Fertility.* Madison: University of Wisconsin Madison, Institute for Research on Poverty Discussion Paper.

Risman, B. J. (1986). Can men "mother?" Life as a single father. *Family Relations, 35*(1), 95-102.

Robinson, B. E., & Barrett, R. L. (1986). *The developing father: Emerging roles in contemporary society.* New York: Guilford.

Roman, M. (1977). The disposable parent. *Conciliation Courts Review, 15,* 1-10.

Roman, M., & Haddad, W. (1978). *The disposable parent: The case of joint custody.* New York: Holt.

Rorris, J. T. (1971). *Separation agreements—support for the spouse and minor children: Minnesota family law. Minnesota Practice Manual.* Minneapolis: University of Minnesota.

Rose, V. L., & Price-Bonham, S. (1973). Divorce adjustment: A woman's problem? *Family Coordinator, 22,* 291-297.

Roseby, V. (1985). *Divorce: Short- and long-term consequences for children and adolescents.* Unpublished manuscript, University of Wisconsin, Madison.

Rosen, R. (1977). Children of divorce: What they feel about access and other aspects of the divorce experience. *Journal of Clinical Child Psychology, 6,* 15-20.

Rosen, R. (1979). Some crucial issues concerning children of divorce. *Journal of Divorce, 3,* 19-25.

Rosenblatt, J. S. (1969). The development of maternal responsiveness in the rat. *American Journal of Orthopsychiatry, 39,* 36-56.

Rosenfeld, J. M., Rosenstein, E., & Raab, M. (1973). Sailor families: The nature and effects of one kind of father absence. *Child Welfare, 52*(1), 33-44.

Rosenthal, D., & Hansen, J. (1980). Comparison of adolescents' perceptions and behaviors in single- and two-parent families. *Journal of Youth and Adolescence, 9,* 407-417.

Rosenthal, D., Leigh, G. K., & Elardo, R. (1985/1986). Home environment of three- to six-year-old children from father-absent and two-parent families. *Journal of Divorce, 9*(2), 41-48.

Rosenthal, K. M., & Keshet, H. F. (1981). *Fathers without partners: A study of fathers and the family after marital separation.* Totowa, NJ: Rowan & Littlefield.

Rosenthal, P. A. (1979). Sudden disappearance of one parent with separation and divorce: The grief and treatment of preschool children. *Journal of Divorce, 3,* 43–54.

Rosow, I., & Daniel, R. K. (1972). Divorce among doctors. *Journal of Marriage and the Family, 32*(4), 587–599.

Ross, H. L., & Sawhill, I. V. (1975). *Time of transition: The growth of families headed by women.* Washington, DC: Urban Institute Press.

Rossi, A. S. (1980). Life span theories and women's lives. *Signs, 6,* 4–32.

Rossi, A. S. (1984). Gender and parenthood. *American Sociological Review, 49,* 1–10.

Roussel, L., & Thery, I. (1988). France: Demographic change and family policy since World War II. *Journal of Family Issues, 9*(3), 336–353.

Russo, N. F. (1979). Overview: Sex roles, fertility and the motherhood mandate. *Psychology of Women Quarterly, 4,* 7–15.

Rutter, M. (1983). Stress, coping, and development: Some issues and some questions. In N. Garmezy & M. Rutter (Eds.), *Stress, coping, and development in children* (pp. 1–42). New York: McGraw-Hill.

Sager, C. J., Brown, H. S., Crohn, H., Engel, T., Rodstein, E., & Walker, L. (1983). *Treating the remarried family.* New York: Brunner/Mazel.

Salts, C. J. (1979). Divorce process: Integration of theory. *Journal of Divorce, 2*(3), 233–240.

Sanik, M. M., & Mauldin, T. (1986). Single versus two parent families: A comparison of mothers' time. Special Issue: The single parent family. *Family Relations Journal of Applied Family and Child Studies, 35*(1), 53–56.

Santrock, J. W. (1970). Paternal absence, self typing and identification. *Developmental Psychology, 2,* 264–272.

Santrock, J. W. (1972). Relation of type and onset of father absence to cognitive development. *Child Development, 43,* 455–469.

Santrock, J. W. (1975). Father absence, perceived maternal behavior, and moral development in boys. *Child Development, 46,* 753–757.

Santrock, J. W. (1977). Effects of father absence on sex-typed behaviors in male children: Reason for the absence and age of onset of the absence. *Journal of Genetic Psychology, 130*(1), 3–10.

Santrock, J. W., & Tracy, R. L. (1978). The effects of children's family structure status on the development of stereotypes by teachers. *Journal of Educational Psychology, 70,* 754–757.

Santrock, J. W., & Warshak, R. (1979). Father custody and social development in boys and girls. *Journal of Social Issues, 35,* 112–125.

Saposnek, D. T. (1983). *Mediating child custody disputes.* San Francisco: Jossey-Bass.

Sawhill, I. (1976). Discrimination and poverty among women who head households. *Signs, 1,* 301–321.

Scanzoni, J., & Szincovacz, M. E. (1980). *Family decision-making: A developmental sex role model.* Beverly Hills, CA: Sage.

Schaffer, H. R. (1977). *Mothering.* London: Fontana.

Schlesinger, B. (1978). Single parent fathers: A research review. *Children Today, 7,* 12, 18–19.

Schlesinger, B. (1980). One parent families in Australia. *Conciliation Courts Review, 18,* 27–29.

Schlesinger, B. (1982a). Children's viewpoints of living in a one-parent family. *Journal of Divorce, 5*(4), 1–23.

Schlesinger, B. (1982b). One-parent families in Britain: A review. *Conciliation Courts Review, 20,* 71–80.

Schoettle, U. C., & Cantwell, D. P. (1980). Children of divorce: Demographic variables, symptoms, and diagnoses. *Journal of American Academy of Child Psychiatry, 19,* 453–475.

Schorr, A. L., & Moen, P. (1979). The single parent and public policy. *Social Policy, 9,* 15–21.

Schwartzberg, A. Z. (1980). Adolescent reactions to divorce. *Adolescent Psychiatry, 8,* 379–392.

Sears, R. (1957). Identification as a form of behavior development. In P. B. Harris (Ed.), *The concept of development* (pp. 149–161). Minneapolis: University of Minnesota Press.

Secord, P. F. (1983). Imbalanced sex ratios: The social consequences. *Personality and Social Psychology Bulletin, 9*(4), 525–543.

Select Committee on Children, U.S. House of Representatives. (1983). *U.S. children and their families* (98th Congress, 1st session). Washington, DC: Author.

Selman, R. L. (1980). *The growth of interpersonal understanding.* New York: Academic Press.

Seltzer, J. A., & Bianchi, S. M. (1988). Children's contact with absent parents. *Journal of Marriage and the Family, 50,* 663–677.

Seltzer, J. A., & Garfinkel, I. (1990). Inequality in divorce settlements: An investigation of property settlements and child support awards. *Social Science Research, 19,* 82–111.

Seward, R. (1978). *The American family: A demographic history.* Beverly Hills, CA: Sage.

Shaver, K. G. (1975). *An introduction to attribution processes.* Cambridge, MA: Winthrop.

Shaw, C. R., & McKay, J. D. (1932). Are broken homes a causative factor in juvenile delinquency? *Social Forces, 10*(4), 514–525.

Shinn, M. (1978). Father absence and children's cognitive development. *Psychological Bulletin, 85,* 295–324.

Shulman, J., & Pitt, V. (1982). Second thoughts on joint custody: Analysis of legislation and its implications for women and children. *Golden Gate University Law Review, 12,* 539–577.

Silver, G. A., & Silver, M. (1981). *Weekend father: For divorced fathers, second wives and grandparents: Solutions to the problems of child custody, child support, alimony and property settlements.* Los Angeles: Stratford Press.

Singer, L. J. (1975). Divorce and the single life: Divorce as development. *Journal of Sex and Marital Therapy, 1,* 54–262.

Skolnick, A. S., & Skolnick, J. H. (1986). *Family in transition.* Boston: Little, Brown.

Slater, E. J., Stewart, K., & Linn, M. (1983). The effects of family disruption on adolescent males and females. *Adolescence, 18,* 933–942.

Smart, L. S. (1977). An application of Erikson's theory to the recovery-from-divorce process. *Journal of Divorce, 1*(1), 67–79.

Smith, A. W., & Meitz, J. E. G. (1983). Life-course effects on marital disruption. *Social Indicators Research, 13*(4), 395–417.

Smith, M. J. (1980). The social consequences of single parenthood: A longitudinal perspective. *Family Relations, 29,* 75–81.

Smith, R. M. (1976). *Single-parent fathers: An application of role transitions* (ERIC Document Reproduction Service No. ED 151 719). Tuscon, AZ: The University of Arizona.

Smith, R. M., & Smith, C. W. (1981). Child-rearing and single parent fathers. *Family Relations, 30*(3), 411–417.

Sorosky, A. D. (1977). The psychological effects of divorce on adolescents. *Adolescence, 12,* 123–136.

South, S. J. (1985). Economic conditions and the divorce rate: A time-series analysis of the post-war United States. *Journal of Marriage and the Family, 47,* 31–41.

South, S. J., & Spitze, G. (1986). Determinants of divorce over the marital life course. *American Sociological Review, 51,* 583–590.

Spanier, G. B., & Casto, R. F. (1979). Adjustment to separation and divorce: An analysis of 50 case studies. *Journal of Divorce, 2,* 241–253.

Spanier, G. B., & Glick, P. C. (1980). Paths to remarriage. *Journal of Divorce, 3,* 283–298.

Spanier, G. B., & Hanson, S. (1981). The role of extended kin in the adjustment to marital separation. *Journal of Divorce, 5,* 33–48.

Spanier, G. B., & Thompson, L. (1984). *Parting: The aftermath of separation and divorce.*

Beverly Hills, CA: Sage.

Spicer, J. W., & Hampe, G. D. (1975). Kinship interaction after divorce. *Journal of Marriage and the Family, 37,* 113–119.

Spitze, G. D., & South, S. J. (1985). Women's employment, time expenditure, and divorce. *Journal of Family Issues, 6,* 307–329.

Sprey, J. (1967). The study of single-parenthood: Some methodological considerations. *The Family Life Coordinator, 16,* 29–34.

Sprey, J. (1979). Conflict theory and the study of marriage and the family. In W. R. Burr, R. Hill, F. I. Nye, & I. L. Reiss (Eds.), *Contemporary theories about the family* (Vol. 2, pp. 130–159). New York: Macmillan.

Stack, C. B. (1974). *All our kin: Strategies for survival in a Black community.* New York: Harper & Row.

Staff. (1970). Editorial. *Women: A Journal of Liberation, 3*(1), 1.

Staples, R. (1985). Changes in Black family structure: The conflict between family ideology and structural conditions. *Journal of Marriage and the Family, 47,* 1005–1013.

Stewart, J. R., Schwebel, A. I., & Fine, M. A. (1986). The impact of custodial arrangement on the adjustment of recently divorced families. *Journal of Divorce, 9*(3), 55–66.

Stirling, K. J. (1987). *The road to financial security for divorced women: Who succeeds, who doesn't.* Unpublished doctoral dissertation, University of Notre Dame, IN.

Stolberg, A. L., & Anker, J. M. (1983). Cognitive and behavioral changes in children resulting from parental divorce and consequent environmental changes. *Journal of Divorce, 7*(2), 23–41.

Stolberg, A. L., Camplair, C. W., Currier, K., & Wells, M-J. (1987). Individual, familial and environmental determinants of children's post-divorce adjustment and maladjustment. *Journal of Divorce, 11*(1), 51–70.

Stolberg, A. L., & Garrison, K. M. (1985). Evaluating a primary prevention program for children of divorce. *American Journal of Community Psychology, 13*(2), 111–124.

Strube, M. J., & Barbour, L. S. (1983). The decision to leave an abusive relationship: Economic dependence and psychological commitment. *Journal of Marriage and the Family, 45,* 785–793.

Sturner, W. (1983). *Love loops: A divorced father's personal journey.* New York: Libra Publishers.

Sullivan, N. D., & Fleshman, R. P. (1975–1976). Paternal deprivation in male heroin addicts. *Drug Forum, 5*(1), 75–79.

Sweet, J. A., & Bumpass, L. L. (1988). *American families and households.* New York: Russell Sage.

Taibbi, R. (1979). Transitional relationships after divorce. *Journal of Divorce, 2,* 263–269.

Teachman, J. D. (1983). Early marriage, premarital fertility, and marital dissolution. *Journal of Family Issues, 4,* 105–126.

Teachman, J. D. (1986). First and second marital dissolution: A decomposition exercise for Blacks and Whites. *Sociological Quarterly, 27,* 571–590.

Theodorson, G. A. (1965). Romanticism and motivation to marry in the United States, Singapore, Burma, and India. *Social Forces, 44,* 17–28.

Thibaut, J. W., & Kelly, H. H. (1959). *The social psychology of groups.* New York: Wiley.

Thoits, P. (1982). Conceptual, methodological, and theoretical problems in studying social support as a buffer against life stress. *Journal of Health and Social Behavior, 23,* 145–159.

Thomas, G. P. (1982). After divorce: Personality factors related to the process of adjustment. *Journal of Divorce, 5,* 19–36.

Thompson, E. H., & Gonzola, P. A. (1983). Single parent families: In the mainstream of American society. In E. M. Macklin & R. R. Rubin (Eds.), *Contemporary families and alternative lifestyles* (pp. 87–109). Beverly Hills, CA: Sage.

Thornes, B., & Collard, J. (1979). *Who divorces?* London: Routledge & Kegan Paul.

Thornton, A. (1978). Marital instability differentials and interactions: Insights from multivariate contingency table analysis. *Sociology and Social Research, 62,* 572–595.

Thornton, A. (1985). Changing attitudes toward separation and divorce: Causes and consequences. *American Journal of Sociology, 90*(4), 856–872.

Thornton, A., & Freedman, D. S. (1983). The changing American family. *Population Bulletin, 38*(4).

Tietjen, A-M. (1985). The social networks and social support of married and single mothers in Sweden. *Journal of Marriage and the Family, 47,* 489–496.

Todres, R. (1978). Runaway wives: An increasing North-American phenomenon. *Family Coordinator, 27,* 17–21.

Toomin, M. K. (1974). The child of divorce. In R. E. Hardy & J. C. Cull (Eds.), *Therapeutic needs of the family: Problems, descriptions, and therapeutic approaches* (pp. 56–90). Springfield, IL: Charles C. Thomas.

Trafford, A. (1982). *Crazy time.* New York: Harper & Row.

Trent, K., & South, S. J. (1989). Structural determinants of the divorce rate: A cross-societal analysis. *Journal of Marriage and the Family, 51,* 391–404.

Udry, J. R. (1966). Marital instability by race, sex, education, and occupation, using 1960 census data. *American Journal of Sociology, 72,* 203–209.

Udry, J. R. (1974). *The social context of marriage* (3rd ed.). Philadelphia: Lippincott.

U.S. Bureau of the Census. (1980). Population profile of the United States. *Current Population Reports* (Series P-20, No. 350). Washington, DC: U.S. Government Printing Office.

U.S. Bureau of the Census. (1983). Marital status and living arrangements: March, 1982. *Current Population Reports* (Series P-20, No. 380). Washington, DC: U.S. Government Printing Office.

U.S. Bureau of the Census. (1984). *Statistical abstract of the United States: 1985.* Washington, DC: U.S. Government Printing Office.

U.S. Bureau of the Census. (1985). Population characteristics: Households, families, marital status, and living arrangements: March, 1985 (Advance Report). *Current Population Reports* (Series P-20, No. 402). Washington, DC: U.S. Government Printing Office.

U.S. Bureau of the Census. (1986). Marital status and living arrangement: March, 1986. *Current Population Reports* (Series P-20, No. 418). Washington, DC: U.S. Government Printing Office.

U.S. Bureau of the Census. (1987). Population characteristics: Households, families, marital status, and living arrangements: November, 1987. *Current Population Reports*, Series P-23, No. 417. Washington, DC: U.S. Government Printing Office.

U.S. Bureau of the Census. (1988). *Statistical abstract of the United States: 1988.* Washington, DC: U.S. Government Printing Office.

U.S. Bureau of the Census. (1989). *Statistical abstract of the United States: 1989.* Washington, DC: U.S. Government Printing Office.

U.S. Bureau of the Census. (1990). *Statistical abstract of the United States: 1990.* Washington, DC: U.S. Government Printing Office.

United Nations (1984). *United Nations Statistical Yearbook, Vol. 35.* New York, NY: United Nations.

Vanderlinden, J., & Vandereycken, W. (1991). Guidelines for the family therapeutic approach to eating disorders. *Psychotherapy and Psychosomatics, 56*(1–2), 36–42.

Vigderhous, G., & Fishman, G. (1978). Social indicators of marital instability, USA, 1920–1969. *Social Indicators Research, 5,* 325–344.

Voelker, R. M., & McMillan, S. L. (1983). Children and divorce: An approach for the pediatrician. *Journal of Developmental and Behavioral Pediatrics, 4*(4), 272–277.

Vogel, E. F. (1968). The family and kinship. In T. Parsons (Ed.), *American sociology: Perspectives, problems, methods* (pp. 121–130). New York: Basic Books.

Walker, K. N., & Messinger, L. (1979). Remarriage after divorce: Dissolution and reconstruction of family boundaries. *Family Process, 18,* 185–192.

Waller, W. (1958). *The old love and the new* (2nd ed.). Carbondale, IL: Southern Illinois University Press.

Wallerstein, J. S. (1983). Children of divorce: The psychological tasks of the child. *American Journal of Orthopsychiatry, 53*(2), 230–243.

Wallerstein, J. S. (1984). Children of divorce: The psychological tasks of the child. *Annual Progress in Child Psychiatry and Child Development,* 263–280.

Wallerstein, J. S. (1985). The overburdened child: Some long-term consequences of divorce. *Social Work, 30*(2), 116–123.

Wallerstein, J. S. (1986a). Child of divorce: An overview. *Behavioral Sciences and the Law, 4*(2), 105–118.

Wallerstein, J. S. (1986b). Children of divorce: Preliminary report of a ten-year follow-up of older children and adolescents. *Annual Progress in Child Psychiatry and Child Development,* 430–447.

Wallerstein, J. S., & Kelly, J. B. (1974). The effects of parental divorce: The adolescent experience. In E. J. Anthony & C. Koupernik (Eds.), *The child in his family* (Vol. 3, pp. 211–236). New York: Wiley.

Wallerstein, J. S., & Kelly, J. B. (1975). The effects of parental divorce: Experiences of the preschool child. *Journal of the American Academy of Child Psychiatry, 14,* 600–616.

Wallerstein, J. S., & Kelly, J. B. (1976). The effects of parental divorce: Experiences of the child in later latency. *American Journal of Orthopsychiatry, 46,* 256–269.

Wallerstein, J. S., & Kelly, J. B. (1980a). Effects of divorce on the father–child relationship. *American Journal of Psychiatry, 137,* 1534–1539.

Wallerstein, J. S., & Kelly, J. B. (1980b). *Surviving the breakup: How children and parents cope with divorce.* New York: Basic Books.

Warheit, G. J., Holzer, C. E., III, Bell, R. A., & Arey, S. A. (1976). Sex, marital status and mental health: A reappraisal. *Social Forces, 55,* 459–470.

Warshak, R. A., & Santrock, J. S. (1983). The impact of divorce in father-custody and mother-custody homes: The child's perspective. *New Directions for Child Development, 19,* 29–46.

Webster's New World Dictionary of American Language. (1984). New York: Simon and Schuster.

Wedermeyer, N. (1984). Child custody. In T. Oakland (Ed.), *Divorced fathers: Reconstructing a quality life* (pp. 218–262). New York: Human Sciences Press.

Wedemeyer, N., & Johnson, J. M. (1982). Learning the single-parent-role: Overcoming traditional marital-role influences. *Journal of Divorce, 5,* 41–53.

Weiner, B. (1980). A cognitive (attribution)-emotion-action model of motivated behavior: An analysis of judgments of help-giving. *Journal of Personality and Social Psychology, 39,* 186–200.

Weiner, B. (1986). *An attributional theory of motivation and emotion.* New York: Springer-Verlag.

Weiner, B., Russel, D., & Lerman, D. (1978). Affective consequences of causal ascriptions. In J. H. Harvey, W. J. Ickes, & R. F. Kidd (Eds.), *New directions in attributions research* (Vol. 2, pp. 59–90). Hillsdale, NJ: Lawrence Erlbaum Associates.

Weiss, R. S. (1973). The contributions of an organization of single parents to the well-being of the members. *The Family Coordinator, 22,* 321–326.

Weiss, R. S. (1975). *Marital separation.* New York: Basic Books.

Weiss, R. S. (1976). The emotional impact of marital separation. *Journal of Social Issues, 32*(1), 135–145.

Weiss, R. S. (1979). Growing up a little faster: The experience of growing up in a single-parent household. *The Journal of Social Issues, 35*(4), 97–111.

Weiss, R. S. (1980). Growing up a little faster: The experience of children in a single-parent household. In C. Baden (Ed.), *Children of divorce* (pp. 56–72). Boston: Wheelock College.

Weiss, R. S. (1984). The impact of marital dissolution on income and consumption in single-parent households. *Journal of Marriage and the Family, 46*(1), 115–127.

Weitzman, L. J. (1981). *The marriage contract: Spouses, lovers, and the law.* New York: The Free Press.

Weitzman, L. J. (1985). *The divorce revolution: The unexpected social and economic consequences for women and children in America.* New York: The Free Press.

Weitzman, L. J., & Dixon, R. (1986). The transformation of legal marriage through no-fault divorce. In A. Skolnick & J. Skolnock (Eds.), *Family in transition* (pp. 338–350). Boston: Little, Brown.

Westman, J. C. (1972). Effects of divorce on child's personality development. *Medical Aspects of Human Sexuality, 6,* 38–55.

Westman, J. C., & Cline, D. W. (1971). Divorce is a family affair. *Family Law Quarterly, 5,* 1–10.

Westman, J. C., Cline, D. W., Swift, W. J., & Kramer, D. A. (1970). Role of child psychiatry in divorce. *Archives of General Psychiatry, 23,* 416–421.

White, S. W., & Asher, S. J. (1976). *Separation and divorce: A study of the male perspective.* Unpublished manuscript, University of Colorado, Denver.

White, S. W., & Bloom, B. L. (1981). Factors related to the adjustment of divorcing men. *Family Relations, 30,* 349–360.

White, S. W., & Mika, K. (1983). Family divorce and separation: Theory and research. *Marriage and Family Review, 6,* 175–192.

Whitehead, L. (1979). Sex differences in children's responses to family stress: A re-evaluation. *Journal of Child Psychology and Psychiatry and Allied Disciplines, 20,* 247–254.

Whiteside, M. F. (1983). Families of remarriage: The weaving of many life cycle threads. In J. C. Hansen & H. A. Liddle (Eds.), *Clinical implications of the family life cycle* (pp. 100–119). Rockville, MD: Aspen.

Wilcox, B. L. (1981). Social support in adjusting to marital disruption: A network analysis. In B. H. Gottlieb (Ed.), *Social networks and social support* (pp. 97–115). Beverly Hills, CA: Sage.

Wilk, J. (1979). Assessing single-parent needs. *Journal of Psychiatric Nursing, 17*(6), 21–22.

Wilkinson, K. (1974). The broken family and juvenile delinquency: Scientific explanation or ideology? *Social Problems, 21,* 726–739.

Wineberg, H. (1988). Duration between marriage and first birth and marital instability. *Social Biology, 35*(1–2), 91–102.

Wise, M. S. (1980). The aftermath of divorce. *American Journal of Psychoanalysis, 40,* 149–158.

Wiseman, R. S. (1975). Crisis theory and the process of divorce. *Social Casework, 56*(4), 205–212.

Wolff, K. (1950). *The sociology of George Simmel.* New York: Macmillan.

Woody, R. H. (1977). Behavioral science criteria in child custody determinations. *Journal of Marriage and Family Counseling, 3*(1), 11–17.

Woolley, P. (1979). *The custody handbook.* New York: Summit Books.

Woolsey, S. (1977). Pied Piper and the child care debate. *Daedalus, 106,* 127–145.

Wright, D. (1988). Revitalizing exchange models of divorce. *Journal of Divorce, 12*(1), 1–19.

Wright, G. C., & Stetson, D. M. (1978). The impact of no-fault divorce law reform on divorce in American states. *Journal of Marriage and the Family, 40,* 575–580.

Yorburg, B. (1973). *The changing family.* New York: Columbia University Press.

Young, D. M. (1983). Two studies of children of divorce. *New Directions for Child Development, 19,* 61–69.

Young, E. R., & Parish, T. S. (1977). Impact of father absence during childhood on the psychological adjustment of college females. *Sex Roles, 3,* 217–227.

Zajonc, R. B. (1976). Family configuration and intelligence. *Science, 192,* 227–236.

Zartman, I. W. (1979). The analysis of negotiation. In I. W. Zartman (Ed.), *The fifty percent solution* (pp. 1–42). New York: Anchor Books.

Zaslow, M. J. (1987). *Sex differences in children's response to parental divorce.* Paper presented at the Symposium on Sex Differences in Children's Responses to Psychosocial Stress, Woods Hole, MA.

Zeiss, A., Zeiss, R., & Johnson, S. (1980). Sex differences in initiation of and adjustment to divorce. *Journal of Divorce, 4*(2), 21–33.

Zill, N. (1978). *Divorce, marital happiness, and the mental health of children: Findings from the Foundation for Child Development National Survey of Children.* Paper prepared for National Institute of Mental Health Workshop on Divorce and Children, Bethesda, MD.

Author Index

Page numbers in *italics* denotes full bibliographical reference.

A

Abarbanel, A., 88, 89, *202*
Abrams, N., 193, *222*
Acock, A. C., 199, *208*
Adams, G. R., 184, *202*
Adams, P. L., 94, 114, 148, 195, *202*
Adelberg, T., 74, 78, 96, 97, 98, 99, 102, *220*
Adelson, J., 191, *209*
Ahrons, C., 51, 61, 62, 65, 67, 68, 72, 73, 84, 88, 89, 102, *202*
Albrecht, S. L., 21, 52, 60, 61, 64, 67, 70, 119, *202, 218*
Aldous, J., 94, *202*
Allen, N., 193, *222*
Allison, P. D., 92, 192, 195, 199, 200, *202, 211*
Alloy, L. B., 54, *202*
Amato, P. R., 168, 169, 170, 193, 199, 200, *202, 203*
Ambert, A. M., 92, 132, 135, 160, *203*
Ambrose, P., 128, *203*
Amir, T., 195, 197, *213*
Anderson, H. N., 98, *211*
Anderson, N. C., 77, *224*
Anderson-Khleif, S., 127, 128, 129, *203*
Anker, J. M., 187, *227*
Anspach, D. F., 96, *203*

Anthony, E. J., 85, 151, 153, 155, 159, 175, 180, *203*
Applebaum, A., 96, *208*
Arber, S., 77, *220*
Arey, S. A., 67, 99, *229*
Aries, P., 22, *203*
Armistead, L., 195, *210*
Aronson, E., 52, 54, *203*
Asher, S. J., 62, 77, 95, 98, 122, 123, 163, *203, 205, 230*
Atkeson, B. M., 145, 164, 165, 187, *203, 224*
Atkin, E., 74, 88, 89, 126, 127, *203*
Atkins, R. N., 120, *203*
Atlas, S. L., 161, *203*
Austin, R. L., 193, *203*
Ausubel, D. P., 91, *203*

B

Babri, K. B., 11, 12, 16, 17, 25, 67, *217*
Bachrach, L. L., 120, 121, 123, *203*
Badinter, E., 105, *203*
Bahr, H. M., 64, 67, 70, 119, *202*
Bahr, S. J., 16, 21, 25, 27, 68, *203, 211*
Bain, C., 133, *203*
Baker, R. L., 169, 195, *221, 224*

Baldwin, M. W., 54, *218*
Bales, R. F., 118, *223*
Balswick, J. O., 17, *223*
Bane, M. J., 87, 100, 101, 102, 159, 161, 193, *204*
Barbour, L. S., 15, *227*
Bardwick, J. M., 24, *204*
Barrett, R. L., 118, *224*
Bartz, K. W., 134, 137, *204*
Baucom, D. H., 54, *204, 210*
Beach, S. R., 54, *210*
Beal, E. W., 154, *204*
Becker, G. S., 25, *204*
Bedi, A. R., 193, *204*
Bell, C., 68, *204*
Bell, R. A., 67, 99, *229*
Bellah, R. N., 22, *204*
Belle, D., 74, 94, 96, 99, *208, 213*
Belous, R. S., 23, 85, *219*
Benedek, E. P., 89, *204*
Benedek, R. S., 89, *204*
Bennett, S. K., 107, *214*
Benson, L., 82, 112, *204*
Berardo, F. M., 21, *222*
Berg, B., 94, 149, 153, 163, 170, 189, *204, 218*
Berger, M., 70, *208*
Berkman, P., 95, *204*
Berman, W. H., 79, *204*
Bernard, J. C., 23, 59, 67, 85, 106, 115, 118, *204*
Bernstein, B. E., 124, *204*
Bettelheim, B., 116, *204*
Beukema, S., 96, *208*
Bianchi, S. M., 100, 101, 125, 126, *204, 226*
Biller, H. B., 94, 95, 141, 146, 147, 148, 169, 174, 178, 180, 187, *204, 205, 224*
Billingsley, A., 84, 94, *204*
Billy, J. O. G., 27, *204*
Bird, C., 24, *204*
Bishop, J., 25, *204*
Bisnaire, L. M., 94, 95, *205*
Blackburn, R. M., 64, *205*
Blair, M., 121, *205*
Blanchard, R. W., 95, 147, 148, 169, 178, 180, 187, *205*
Blechman, E. A., 83, 86, 87, 90, 91, 93, 94, 165, *205*
Blisk, D., 70, 73, 79, 149, 153, 156, 189, *218*
Block, J., 95, *205*

Bloom, B. L., 62, 67, 77, 95, 98, 121, 122, 123, 163, 170, *203, 205, 215, 230*
Blumstein, P., 119, *205*
Bohannan, P. J., 36, 37, 38, 49, 51, 54, 63, 69, 70, 97, 98, 129, *205*
Bolton, F. G., 27, *205*
Bond, M. H., 53, *205*
Booth, A., 5, 12, 16, 197, 198, *205*
Boss, P., 84, 88, 89, 95, *205*
Boszormenyi-Nagy, I., 92, *205*
Bowen, G. L., 134, *222*
Bowen, M., 92, *205*
Bowlby, J., 117, *206*
Bowskill, D., 131, *206*
Bozett, F. W., 118, *214*
Bradbury, K., 87, 100, *206*
Brady, C. P., 199, *206*
Braithwaite, V. A., 169, 179, 185, 187, *208*
Brandt, A., 130, *206*
Brandwein, R. A., 68, 70, 73, 74, 87, 163, *206*
Bray, J. H., 199, *206*
Breault, K. D., 18, *206*
Briggs, B. A., 137, *206*
Brinkerhoff, D. B., 197, *205*
Briscoe, C. W., 67, 99, 120, *206*
Birtton, S., 121, *209*
Brodbar-Nemzer, J. K., 22, *206*
Broderick, P. C., 107, *214*
Brody, G. H., 95, 145, 160, 161, *210, 220*
Broudo, M., 169, *213*
Brown, A., 131, *206*
Brown, B. F., 195, *206*
Brown, C. A., 68, 70, 71, 73, 74, 85, 87, 97, 125, 163, *206, 217*
Brown, E. M., 63, 98, *206*
Brown, G., 196, *211*
Brown, H. S., 72, *225*
Brown, M. D., 131, *206*
Brown, P., 121, *206*
Brown, T., 103, 121, 124, 134, 137, *222*
Buehler, C. A., 72, 74, *206*
Bumpass, L. L., 3, 15, 17, 21, 24, 27, 28, 142, 146, 191, *206, 220, 227*
Burchinal, L. G., 21, 195, *206, 207*
Burden, D., *207*
Burgess, E. W., 22, *207*
Burgess, J. K., 83, 85, 90, 93, 97, *207*
Burgoyne, J., 17, 62, 69, *207*
Burr, W. R., 21, 65, *207*

C

Caldwell, R. A., 67, *205*
Camara, K. A., 90, 95, 144, 163, 179, 180,181, 182, 186, 187, 188, 190, *207, 215*
Campbell, L. E., 96, *216*
Camplair, C. W., 94, *227*
Cantor, D. W., 77, *207*
Cantwell, D. P., 193, *225*
Capetta, M., 27, *215*
Cardea, J. M., 88, 89, 104, 105, 107, 108, 109, 110, *210*
Caron, M., 123, *223*
Carter, H., 17, 119, *207*
Castro, R. F., 67, 71, 98, 121, *226*
Cath, S. H., 120, *203*
Cauble, A. E., 57, 71, 96, *220*
Chan, L. Y., 20, 21, 24, 25, *207*
Chancellor, L. E., 21, *207*
Chang, P., 123, 132, 133, 134, 135, 137, 138, *207*
Chase-Lansdale, P. L., 153, 155, 168, 199, *207*
Cherlin, A. J., 11, 12, 13, 14, 16, 23, 25, 64, 68, 153, 155, 199, *207*
Chester, R., 122, *207*
Chiriboga, D. A., 61, 76, 98, 121, 122, 163, *207, 221*
Christensen, H. T., 27, *207*
Clark, D., 62, 69, *207*
Clark, H., 5, *207*
Cleminshaw, H. K., 164, 199, *213*
Cline, D. W., 89, 144, 155, 170, 175, *207, 230*
Cogswell, B., 86, 87, *208*
Coho, A., 76, 98, 163, *207*
Coleman, M., 196, *211*
Collard, J., 27, *228*
Colletta, N. D., 71, 78, 96, 100, 102, *208*
Comeau, J. K., 57, 71, 96, *220*
Conyers, M. G., 195, *208*
Coombs, L. C., 27, *208*
Cooper, J. E., 169, 179, 185, 187, *208*
Corcoran, M., 100, *208*
Cox, M., 70, 71, 72, 73, 74, 92, 96, 121, 122, 123, 125, 129, 154, 155, 159, 160, 161, 163, 169, 170, 171, 172, 175, 187, 192, 199, *215*

Cox, R., 70, 71, 72, 73, 74, 92, 96, 121, 122, 123, 125, 129, 154, 155, 159, 160, 161, 163, 169, 170, 171, 172, 175, 187, 192, 199, *215*
Crohn, H., 72, *225*
Crosby, J. F., 62, 63, 79, *208*
Currier, K., 94, *227*
Cutler, L., 121, 122, *207*
Cutright, P., 14, 15, 16, *208*
Czajka, J. L., 77, *220*

D

Dager, E. Z., 24, *208*
Dally, A., 105, *208*
Daniel, R. K., 16, *225*
Daniels-Mohring, D., 70, *208*
Danziger, S., 87, 100, *206*
Darity, W. A., 25, *208*
Davenport, D. S., 81, 109, *208*
Davies, L., 146, 147, *217*
DeFazio, V. J., 67, *208*
DeFrain, J., 121, 135, *208, 218*
Degler, C. N., 11, *208*
Deinard, A. S., 123, 132, 133, 134, 135, 137, 138, *207*
Dell, P., 96, *208*
Demo, D. H., 199, *208*
Depner, C. E., 126, *219*
Derdeyn, A. P., 124, 165, *208*
DeSimone-Luis, J., 159, *208*
Deutsch, M., 62, 73, 153, 154, 155, 158, *218*
Dill, D., 96, *208*
Dinerman, M., 100, 101, *208*
Dixon, R. B., 6, 7, 8, 52, *208, 230*
Doherty, w. J., 54, *209*
Dominic, K. T., 74, 126, *209*
Dostal, J. W., 185, *222*
Doudna, C., 103, 104, 108, *209*
Douvan, E., 191, *209*
Drake, E. A., 77, *207*
Duncan, G. J., 101, *209*
Dyson, M. P. M., 139, *224*

E

Earl, L., 88, *209*
Earls, F., 88, *209*

Edwards, J. N., 5, 16, 198, 199, *205, 209*
Eirick, R., 135, *208*
Elardo, R., 173, *224*
Ellwood, M. S., 95, *209*
Emery, R. E., 155, 168, 170, 199, *209*
Engel, T., 72, *225*
Erikson, E. H., 44, 150, *209*
Eshleman, J. R., 5, *209*
Espenshade, T. J., 66, 100, 101, *209*
Everly, K., 77, *209*

F

Falek, A., 121, *209*
Farber, S. S., 153, 164, 194, *209, 210*
Farley, R., 100, 101, *204*
Farnworth, M., 22, *209*
Farson, R., 162, *209*
Fauber, R., 145, *210*
Featherman, D. L., 186, *215*
Federico, J., 48, 51, 56, 59, 60, *209*
Feig, E., 147, 176, 177, 190, 192, 197, *213*
Feld, E., 96, *208*
Feld, S., 99, *213*
Feldberg, R., 2, 71, 85, 97, 125, *206, 209, 217*
Felner, R. D., 153, 164, 194, *209, 210*
Ferguson, D., 103, 121, 124, 134, 137, *222*
Fergusson, D. M., 15, 20, *210*
Ferraro, K. J., 70, 72, *223*
Ferri, E., 136, *210*
Festinger, L., 52, 54, *210*
Fincham, F. D., 54, *210*
Fine, M. A., 74, *227*
Firestone, P., 94, 95, *205*
Fischer, J., 88, 89, 104, 105, 107, 108, 109, 110, *210*
Fishman, G., 13, *228*
Fleshman, R. P., 193, *227*
Ford, K., 28, *210*
Forehand, R. L., 145, 164, 165, 187, 195, *203, 210, 224*
Foster, H. H., 8, *210*
Fox, E. M., 68, 70, 73, 74, 85, 87, 163, *206*
Francke, L. B., 126, 129, *210*
Frazier, E. F., 25, *210*
Free, M. D., 22, *210*
Freed, D. J., 8, *210*
Freedman, D. S., 21, *228*
Freud, A., 85, 127, *212*

Freund, J., 123, *210*
Friedman, B., 24, *210*
Frisbie, P. W., 48, 57, 156, *210, 216*
Fromm, E., 80, *210*
Fulton, J. A., 88, 89, 126, 127, 152, 164, *210*
Furstenberg, F. F., 27, 28, 88, 92, 126, 127, 128, 142, 153, 155, 192, 195, 199, 200, *202, 207, 210, 211*

G

Gage, B. A., 62, 63, 79, *208*
Galligan, R. J., 16, 27, *203, 211*
Galper, M., 88, *211*
Ganong, L., 196, *211*
Gardner, R. A., 98, 127, 151, 175, 184, *211*
Garfinkel, I., 100, *226*
Garrison, K. M., 94, *227*
Gaskin, F., 120, *206*
Gasser, R. D., 111, 133, *211*
Geerken, M., 99, *212*
Gefen, S., 169, *213*
George, L. K., 57, *211*
George, V., 111, 133, *211*
Gershansky, I. S., 147, *211*
Gersick, K. E., 103, 132, 134, 137, *211*
Gerstel, N., 71, *211*
Geva, N., 169, *213*
Gibbs, J. P., 99, *211*
Gibson, J. A., 98, *211*
Ginott, H., 112, 116, *211*
Giovannoni, J. M., 84, 94, *204*
Girdner, L. K., 112, *211*
Gjerde, P. F., 95, *205*
Glasser, P., 84, *211*
Glenn, N. D., 4, 15, 16, 17, 20, 21, 22, 24, 67, 196, *211, 212*
Glick, P. C., 13, 17, 25, 29, 58, 82, 86, 199, 121, 142, *207, 212, 222, 226*
Goetting, A., 94, *212*
Goldberg, S., 119, *212*
Goldsmith, J., 89, 102, 127, 128, *212*
Goldstein, H. S., 147, *211*
Goldstein, J., 85, 127, *212*
Gomber, J., 117, *221*
Gongla, P. A., 96, *212*
Gonzola, P. A., 23, *227*
Goode, W. J., 11, 13, 16, 21, 22, 61, 62, 65, 71, 80, 97, 98, 100, *212*

Goodman, K. L., 64, 67, 70, 119, *202*
Goslin, D. A., 113, *212*
Gove, W. R., 99, *212*
Grady, K., 96, *218*
Gray, G. M., 121, *212*
Green, D., 66, *213*
Green, M., 116, 133, *213*
Green, R. G., 58, *213*
Greenberg, J. B., 84, 91, 96, *213*
Greenstein, T. N., 15, 16, *213*
Greif, G. L., 73, 88, 107, 108, 109, 110, 111, 121, 126, 129, 131, 132, 133, 134, 135, 137, 138, *213*
Greif, J. B., 73, 122, 125, 129, 132, *213*
Groenevold, L. P., 12, 16, *214*
Grossbard-Shechtman, A., 26, *214*
Guidubaldi, J., 164, 199, *213*
Gurin, G., 99, *213*
Guttentag, M., 26, 27, 74, 94, 99, *213*
Guttmann, J., 135, 169, 195, 196, 197, *213*

H

Haddad, W., 88, 121, *224*
Hainline, I., 147, *211*
Hainline, L., 147, 176, 177, 190, 192, 197, *213*
Halem, L. C., 2, 6, 8, 9, 10, 65, *213*
Hampe, G. D., 96, *227*
Hampton, R. L., 15, 25, 100, *213*
Hancock, E., 63, 69, *214*
Hannan, M. J., 12, 16, *214*
Hansen, D. A., 95, *214*
Hansen, J., 195, *224*
Hanson, S., 12, 55, 71, 118, 132, 133, 134, 135, 137, 138, 162, *214, 226*
Hare-Mustin, R. T., 107, *214*
Harper, J. F., 128, 148, *203, 214*
Haven, C., 68, *219*
Havighurst, R. J., 91, *214*
Hawkins, L., 86, 87, *214*
Heaton, T. B., 20, 21, 24, 25, *207, 214*
Heer, D. M., 26, *214*
Heider, F., 52, 53, 54, 55, *214*
Hernandez, D. J., 4, 142, *214*
Herzog, E., 94, 95, 141, 146, 193, 198, *214, 215*
Hess, R. D., 90, 95, 144, 163, 179, 180, 182, 187, 188, 190, *215*

Hetherington, E. M., 70, 71, 72, 73, 74, 92, 94, 96, 121, 122, 123, 125, 126, 128, 129, 146, 147, 153, 154, 155, 159, 160, 161, 163, 168, 169, 170, 171, 172, 175, 176, 177, 178, 186, 187, 190, 192, 197, 199, *207, 215*
Hetzel, A. M., 27, *215*
Hill, C. T., 59, 60, 119, *215*
Hiller, D. V., 12, *215, 223*
Hingst, A. G., 169, 186, *215*
Hocevar, D., 169, 195, *221, 224*
Hodges, W. F., 67, 77, 120, 155, 170, *205, 215*
Hoffman, M. L., 94, *215*
Hoffman, S. D., 101, *209*
Hogan, M. J., 72, 74, *206*
Holman, J., 169, 179, 185, 187, *208*
Holmes, W. M., 11, 52, 90, 96, *217*
Holtzworth-Munroe, A., 54, *215*
Holzer, C. E., III, 67, 99, *229*
Horowitz, J., 86, 87, *216*
Horwood, L. J., 15, 20, *210*
Houseeknecht, S. K., 16, 17, *216*
Howell, M. C., 105, 118, *216*
Hozman, T. L., 48, 57, 156, *210, 216*
Huber, J., 12, *216*
Hulme, T., 86, 87, *216*
Hunt, B., 63, *216*
Hunt, D., 159, *208*
Hunt, J. G., 195, *216*
Hunt, L. L., 195, *216*
Hunt, M., 63, 79, 80, 122, *216*
Hurowitz, N., 80, *216*

I

Israel, B., 77, *216*

J

Jacklin, C. N., 117, *220*
Jacobs, J. W., 111, 122, 125, *216*
Jacobson, D. S., 153, 155, 158, 163, 180, 187, 190, *216*
Jacobson, N. S., 54, *215*
Johnson, C., 67, *223*
Johnson, D. R., 5, 16, *205*
Johnson, J. M., 74, *229*

Johnson, M. S., 62, 67, 99, 164, *223*
Johnson, V. A., 95, *214*
Johnson, W. D., 72, 123, *216*
Johnston, J. R., 96, *216*
Joy, C. B., 57, 71, 96, *220*

K

Kalter, N., 94, 167, 171, 174, 175, 177, 178, 181, 189, 193, 197, 200, *216*
Kane, S. P., 27, *205*
Kantor, D., 88, *216*
Kaplan, S. L., 77, *216*
Kaslow, F. W., 59, 60, 61, 65, 66, 71, 77, 98, 168, *216*
Katz, A., 84, 111, 132, 133, 137, 138, *217*
Katz, M., 195, 197, *213*
Kay, H. H., 69, *217*
Keith, B., 168, 169, 170, 193, 199, 200, *203*
Kellogg, S., 6, 8, 23, *221*
Kelly, C., 158, *217*
Kelly, H. H., 52, 53, *227*
Kelly, J. B., 61, 63, 72, 73, 74, 77, 80, 88, 89, 90, 91, 92, 93, 95, 102, 126, 128, 129, 150, 152, 153, 154, 155, 158, 159, 160, 161, 163, 164, 167, 169, 170, 171, 172, 175, 179, 180, 182, 184, 185, 186, 187, 189, 190, 192, 193, 194, 197, 199, 200, *217, 229*
Kelly, R., 94, *204*
Kempton, T., 195, *210*
Kerpelman, L., 128, *217*
Keshet, H. F., 73, 74, 88, 89, 90, 94, 96, 102, 115, 121, 122, 129, 134, 137, 138, *217, 225*
Keshet, J. K., 89, 90, *217*
Kessler, S., 9, 39, 41, 42, 44, 49, 51, 56, 62, 67, 122, *217*
Kieffer, C., 91, *217*
Kiernan, K. E., 153, 155, 199, *207*
Kitson, G. C., 11, 12, 16, 17, 25, 52, 67, 70, 76, 79, 80, 90, 96, *217*
Klebanow, S., 152, *217*
Klein, N., 90, *217*
Klenbort, I., 67, *208*
Kloner, A., 200, *216*
Koch, M. A., 128, *217*
Koehler, J. M., 104, *217*

Kohen, J. A., 2, 71, 85, 97, 125, *206, 209, 217*
Koopman, E. J., 135, 163, *219*
Korman, S. K., 4, *218*
Kornhauser, L., 100, *221*
Kotler, T., 145, *223*
Koziey, P. W., 146, 147, *217*
Kposowa, A. J., 18, *206*
Kramer, D. A., 144, 155, 170, 175, *230*
Kramer, K. B., 196, *212*
Krantz, S. L., 199, *217*
Krantzler, M., 48, 51, 61, 122, 131, *217*
Kraus, S., 57, 61, *217*
Kressel, K., 62, 73, 153, 154, 155, 158, *218*
Kruglanski, A. W., 53, 54, *218*
Kubler-Ross, E., 32, 156, *218*
Kulka, R. A., 95, 169, *218*
Kunz, P. R., 21, 52, 60, 61, *202, 218*
Kurdek, L. A., 69, 70, 73, 148, 149, 153, 155, 156, 158, 161, 163, 164, 165, 166, 169, 170, 189, *218*

L

LaBarre, W., 118, *218*
Lamb, M. E., 94, 117, 151, 184, *218*
Landis, J., 98, *218*
Laner, R. H., 27, *205*
Lansdale, N. S., 27, *204*
Laws, J., 66, *218*
Lee, G. R., 11, 12, 13, 20, 21, *224*
Lehr, W., 88, *216*
Leigh, G. K., 173, *224*
LeMasters, E. E., 113, 115, 121, *218*
Lenthall, G., 58, *218*
Lenz, E., 24, *218*
Leon, M., 117, *221*
Lerman, D., 52, *229*
Leslie, G. R., 4, *218*
Leslie, L. A., 96, *218*
Levine, J. A., 111, 113, 138, *219*
Levinger, G., 52, 53, 57, 65, 69, 79, 123, *219*
Levitan, S. A., 23, 85, *219*
Levitan, T. E., 83, 95, 150, *219*
Levy, R. J., 72, 74, *206*
Lewin, K., 53, 131, *219*
Lewin, P. H., 71, 72, *219*

L'Hommedieu, T., 64, *218*
Libby, R. W., 91, *219*
Lin, S. L., 13, *212*
Lindahl, A., 86, *219*
Linn, M., 199, *226*
Little, M., 129, *219*
Locke, H. J., 22, *207*
Locksley, A., 16, *219*
Loewen, J. W., 127, 130, *219*
Lohmann, N., 88, *209*
Long, N., 145, *210*
Longabaugh, R., 94, *219*
Longfellow, C., 146, 149, 150, 179, *219*
Lopata, H. Z., 89, 90, 96, *217, 219*
Lopez, C., 145, 164, 187, *224*
Lowe, N. V., 124, *219*
Lowenstein, J. S., 135, 163, *219*
Lowenthal, M. F., 68, *219*
Lowery, C. R., 128, 167, *217, 219*
Lubin, M., 117, *221*
Luepnitz, D. A., 95, 126, 154, 155, 169, *219*
Lynn, D. B., 85, *219*

M

MacBride, A. B., 105, *219*
Maccoby, E. E., 117, 126, *219, 220*
MacDonald, M., 28, 29, *224*
MacKinnon, C. E., 95, 160, 161, *220*
Madsen, R., 22, *204*
Magrab, P. R., 152, *220*
Maidment, S., 126, 127, 129, *220*
Malinowski, B., 83, *220*
Malzberg, G., 99, *220*
Maneker, J. S., 21, *220*
Manela, R., 121, *206*
Mann, M., 64, *205*
Manning, M., 83, 86, 87, 90, 91, 93, 94, *205*
Marsden, D., 18, 97, 98, 164, *220*
Marten, S., 120, *206*
Martin, J., 96, *208*
Martin, T. C., 15, 17, 24, 28, *220*
Mason, K. O., 77, *220*
Matusow, A. J., 22, *220*
Mauldin, T., 94, *225*
McCarthy, J., 20, *220*
McCombs, A., 145, *210*

McCombs Thomas, A., 195, *210*
McCubbin, H. I., 57, 71, 96, *220*
McDermott, J. F., 152, 162, 169, 170, 172, 173, 181, *220*
McDonald, J., 14, *223*
McKay, J. D., 102, *226*
McKee, L., 88, 124, 132, 134, 136, 137, 139, *220*
McLanahan, S. S., 74, 78, 95, 96, 97, 98, 99, 102, 146, 194, 200, *220*
McLaughlin, S. D., 27, *204*
McLoughlin, C. S., 164, 199, *213*
McMillan, S. L., 165, *228*
McPhee, J. T., 49, *220*
Mead, M., 112, 118, *220*
Mednick, B. R., 169, 195, *221, 224*
Meissner, H. H., 27, *207*
Meitz, J. E. G., 12, *226*
Melichar, J. F., 61, *221*
Mendes, H. A., 73, 84, 88, 93, 111, 132, 133, 137, 138, *221*
Messinger, L., 93, *229*
Meyering, S. M., 90, 96, *217*
Mika, K., 55, *230*
Miller, A. A., 97, *221*
Miller, D. R., 113, *221*
Miller, J. B., 121, *221*
Milner, J. R., 94, 114, 148, 195, *202*
Mintz, S., 6, 8, 23, *221*
Minuchin, S., 88, 89, 95, *221*
Mitchell, G., 117, *221*
Mnookin, R. H., 100, 126, *219, 221*
Moen, P., 23, 84, 85, 86, 87, 93, 101, 102, *225*
Moles, O. C., 123, *219*
Moltz, H., 117, *221*
Monahan, T. P., 27, 193, *221*
Montemayor, R., 91, *203, 221*
Moore, S. F., 12, 14, 16, 196, 198, *221*
Morawetz, A., 72, *221*
Morgan, J. N., 101, *209*
Morgan, S. P., 28, 195, 199, *211, 221*
Moroney, R., 86, 87, *221*
Mott, F. L., 12, 14, 16, 126, 196, 198, *221*
Moynihan, D. P., 24, 25, *221*
Mueller, C. W., 146, 147, 169, 196, 197, 198, *221, 223*
Murch, M., 69, *221*
Murray, C., 25, *221*
Myerhoff, B., 24, *218*
Myers, S. J., 25, *208*

N

Napier, A. Y., 78, 80, *222*
Navarre, E., 84, *211*
Neal, J. H., 149, 179, *222*
Needle, R. H., 57, 71, 96, *220*
Neighbors, B., 195, *210*
Nelson, G., 75, 152, 153, 163, *222*
Newby, H., 68, *204*
Nimkoff, M. F., 10, 13, 14, *222*
Nock, S. L., 84, *222*
Nord, C. W., 142, 200, *211*
Norton, A. J., 13, 15, 25, 58, 82, 121, *212*, *222*
Numan, M., 117, *221*
Nunn, G. D., 169, *222*
Nye, F. I., 21, 24, 52, 95, 141, 143, 144, *222*

O

O'Brien, M., 88, 124, 132, 134, 136, 137, 139, *220*
Ochiltree, G., 199, *203*
Offord, D. R., 193, *222*
Ogburn, W. F., 13, 14, *222*
Okla, K., 200, *216*
O'Mahoney, K., 159, *208*
Ormrod, R., 17, 69, *207*
Orther, D. K., 103, 121, 124, 134, 137, *222*
Ostrom, R., 75, *223*

P

Pardington, A., 75, *223*
Parish, T. S., 146, 147, 169, 176, 177, 185, 190, *222, 231*
Parke, R. D., 118, *223*
Parsons, T., 118, *223*
Partridge, S., 145, *223*
Paskowicz, P., 103, 104, 105, 108, *223*
Patterson, G. R., 192, *223*
Patterson, J. M., 57, 71, 96, *220*
Pearlin, L. I., 62, 67, 99, 164, *223*
Pederson, F. A., 114, *223*
Pemberton, R., 128, *203*
Peplau, L. A., 59, 60, 119, *215*

Perdue, B., 86, 87, *216*
Perlman, J. L., 68, *223*
Perry, J. D., 164, 199, *213*
Peterson, J. L., 142, *211*
Pett, M. A., 15, *223*
Pett, M. G., 75, 163, 170, *223*
Philliber, W. W., 12, *215, 223*
Pihl, R. O., 123, *223*
Pitt, V., 104, *226*
Plateris, A. A., 82, *223*
Plunkett, J. W., 167, *216*
Pope, H., 146, 147, 169, 196, 197, 198, 221, *223*
Popenoe, D., 2, 9, 22, *223*
Poushinsky, M., 193, *222*
Preston, S. H., 14, *223*
Price-Bonham, S., 17, 66, *223, 224*
Primavera, J., 153, 194, *209*
Propst, L. R., 75, *223*

R

Raab, M., 84, *224*
Radloff, L., 67, *223*
Range, L. M., 98, *211*
Rankin, R. P., 21, *220*
Rapoport, R., 32, *223*
Raschke, H. J., 70, 71, 76, 78, 95, 102, 145, 169, 187, 193, *217, 223*
Raschke, V. J., 95, 102, 145, 169, 187, 193, *223*
Rasmussen, P. K., 70, 72, *223*
Raymond, M. C., 62, 63, 79, *208*
Redican, W. K., 117, *221, 223*
Redick, R. W., 67, *223*
Reinhard, D. W., 170, *224*
Reiss, I. L., 11, 12, 13, 20, 21, *224*
Rembar, J., 171, 174, 175, 177, 178, 181, 189, 197, *216*
Resnick, G., 181, *207*
Reuter, M. W., 95, *224*
Reznick, C., 169, 195, *221, 224*
Rice, D. G., 22, 48, 51, 58, 62, 64, 69, *224*
Rice, J. K., 22, 48, 51, 58, 62, 64, 69, 77, *224*
Richard, K. M., 145, 164, 165, 187, *203, 224*
Richards, M., 17, 69, 139, *207, 224*
Riessman, C. K., 71, *211*
Rindfuss, R. R., 28, 29, 191, *206, 221, 224*

Risman, B. J., 133, 134, 137, 138, *224*
Roach, M. J., 11, 12, 16, 17, 25, 67, *217*
Roberts, J., 76, 98, 121, 163, *207*
Robins, E., 120, *206*
Robinson, B. E., 72, 74, 118, *206, 224*
Robson, K. S., 114, *223*
Rodgers, R. H., 51, 65, 67, 73, *202*
Rodstein, E., 72, *225*
Roman, M., 88, 121, *224*
Rorris, J. T., 112, *224*
Rose, V. L., 66, *224*
Roseby, V., 168, 169, 170, 174, 186, *224*
Rosen, R., 169, *224*
Rosenblatt, J. S., 117, *224*
Rosenfeld, J. M., 84, *224*
Rosenfield, S., 71, *211*
Rosenstein, E., 84, *224*
Rosenthal, D., 173, 195, *224*
Rosenthal, K. M., 73, 74, 88, 90, 93, 96, 115, 121, 122, 129, 134, 137, 138, *217, 225*
Rosenthal, P. A., 173, *225*
Rosow, I., 16, *225*
Ross, H. L., 12, 15, 16, 102, *225*
Rossi, A. S., 58, 87, *225*
Roussel, L., 22, *225*
Rubin, E., 74, 88, 89, 126, 127, *203*
Rubin, Z., 59, 60, 119, *215*
Russel, D., 52, *229*
Russo, N. F., 106, *225*
Rutter, M., 194, *225*
Ryder, J. M., 148, *214*
Rynard, D., 94, 95, *205*

S

Sager, C. J., 72, *225*
Salasin, S., 74, 94, 99, *213*
Salts, C. J., 49, *225*
Sanik, M. M., 94, *225*
Santrock, J. S., 135, 136, *229*
Santrock, J. W., 132, 135, 136, 146, 147, 169, 172, 174, 175, 177, 180, 181, 182, 187, 188, 192, 195, *225*
Saposnek, D. T., 104, *225*
Sawhill, I. V., 12, 15, 16, 68, 87, 101, 102, *225*
Scanzoni, J., 57, 58, 64, *225*
Schaffer, H. R., 106, *225*
Scherpf, N. A., 94, 114, 148, 195, *202*

Schlesinger, B., 74, 111, 126, 133, 135, 151, 194, 197, *209, 225*
Schoettle, U. C., 193, *225*
Schorr, A. L., 23, 84, 85, 86, 87, 93, 101, 102, *225*
Schreier, S., 200, *216*
Schwartz, L. L., 59, 60, 61, 65, 66, 77, 168, *216*
Schwartz, P., 119, *205*
Schwartzberg, A. Z., 192, 194, 197, *226*
Schwebel, A. I., 74, *227*
Scott, E., 165, *208*
Sears, R., 113, *226*
Secord, P. F., 26, 27, *213, 226*
Selman, R. L., 149, *226*
Seltzer, J. A., 100, 125, 126, *226*
Settle, S. A., 167, *219*
Seward, R., 83, *226*
Shannon, F. T., 15, 20, *210*
Shaver, K. G., 54, *226*
Shaw, C. R., 102, *226*
Shelagh, M. J., 54, *218*
Shelton, B. A., 4, *212*
Shinn, M., 147, 180, 190, 195, *226*
Shulman, J., 104, *226*
Siegel, B., 88, *209*
Siesky, A. E., 149, 153, 156, 158, 161, 169, 189, *218*
Silver, G. A., 121, *226*
Silver, M., 121, *226*
Sinclair, R. J., 148, *218*
Singer, L. J., 22, *226*
Skolnick, A. S., 64, 72, *226*
Skolnick, J. H., 64, 72, *226*
Slater, E. J., 199, *226*
Smart, L. S., 44, 47, 48, 50, 51, 75, *226*
Smith, A. W., 12, *226*
Smith, C. W., 121, *226*
Smith, J. B., 67, 99, 120, *206*
Smith, M. J., 84, 90, 96, *226*
Smith, R. M., 121, 134, *226*
Smolensky, E., 87, 100, *206*
Smolensky, P., 87, 100, *206*
Solnit, A. J., 85, 127, *212*
Sorosky, A. D., 151, 194, 197, *226*
South, S. J., 11, 12, 13, 14, 15, 17, 18, 21, 26, *226, 227, 228*
Spanier, G. B., 16, 17, 29, 31, 55, 67, 71, 98, 121, 126, *211, 216, 226*
Spark, G. M., 92, *205*
Spicer, J. W., 96, *226*
Spitze, G. D., 12, 15, 17, 26, *216, 226, 227*

Sporakowski, M. J., 58, *213*
Sprey, J., 84, 86, 89, 94, *227*
Stack, C. B., 25, *227*
Staples, R., 85, 93, *227*
Stein, J. A., 76, 98, 121, 163, *207*
Stetson, D. M., 9, *231*
Stewart, J. R., 74, *227*
Stewart, K., 199, *226*
Stirling, K. J., 100, *227*
Stolberg, A. L., 94, 95, 187, *209, 227*
Stoneman, Z., 95, 160, 161, *220*
Stones, C., 131, *206*
Strube, M. J., 15, *227*
Sturner, W., 127, *227*
Sudia, C. E., 94, 95, 141, 146, 193, 198, *214, 215*
Sullivan, N. D., 193, *227*
Sullivan, W. M., 22, *204*
Supancic, M., 15, 16, 17, 20, 21, 24, *212*
Sussman, M. B., 11, 52, 80, 86, 87, *208, 217*
Svajian, P., 91, *203*
Swanson, G. E., 113, *221*
Sweet, J. A., 3, 21, 27, 28, *206, 227*
Swidler, A., 22, *204*
Swift, W. J., 144, 155, 170, 175, *230*
Szincovacz, M. E., 57, 58, 64, *225*

T

Taibbi, R., 78, *227*
Talvitie, K. G., 88, *211*
Taylor, C. M., 111, 133, *211*
Teachman, J. D., 24, 27, 28, *227*
Theodorson, G. A., 2, *227*
Thery, I., 22, *225*
Thibaut, J. W., 52, 53, *227*
Thoits, P., 77, *227*
Thomas, D. S., 13, *222*
Thomas, G. P., 75, 77, 123, *227*
Thompson, E. H., 23, *227*
Thompson, L., 31, *226*
Thornes, B., 27, *228*
Thornton, A., 9, 21, 23, *228*
Tiejen, A. M., 98, *228*
Tipton, S. M., 22, *204*
Todres, R., 108, 109, *228*
Toomin, M. K., 122, 151, 159, 175, *228*
Tracy, R. L., 169, 175, 187, *225*

Trafford, A., 62, *228*
Trent, K., 11, 18, 21, 26, *228*
Trilling, J. A., 132, 162, *214*
Tuch, S. A., 12, *214*
Tuma, N. B., 12, 16, *214*
Turk, D. C., 79, *204*

U

Udry, J. R., 14, *228*

V

Vandereycken, W., 22, *228*
Vanderlinden, J., 22, *228*
Vaughan-Cole, B., 15, *223*
Veroff, J., 99, *213*
Vigderhous, G., 13, *228*
Voelker, R. M., 165, *228*
Vogel, E. F., 11, *229*

W

Walker, G., 72, *221*
Walker, K. N., 93, *229*
Walker, L., 72, *225*
Waller, W., 48, *229*
Wallerstein, J. S., 61, 72, 73, 74, 77, 88, 89, 90, 91, 92, 93, 95, 102, 126, 128, 129, 150, 152, 153, 154, 155, 156, 158, 159, 160, 161, 163, 164, 167, 169, 170, 171, 172, 175, 179, 180, 182, 184, 185, 186, 187, 189, 190, 192, 193, 194, 197, 199, 200, *217, 229*
Walters, C. M., 137, *206*
Warheit, G. J., 67, 99, *229*
Warshak, R. A., 132, 135, 136, 181, *225, 229*
Watkins, P., 75, *223*
Weaver, C. N., 21, *212*
Wedemeyer, N. V., 74, 78, 96, 97, 98, 99, 102, 127, 128, *220, 229*
Weiner, B., 52, 54, 78, 80, *229*
Weingarten, H., 95, 169, *218*

Weiss, R. S., 15, 48, 51, 60, 61, 63, 64, 67, 70, 71, 73, 74, 79, 84, 85, 87, 89, 90, 91, 92, 93, 96, 97, 98, 100, 102, 121, 122, 162, 192, 194, *204, 229, 230*

Weitzman, L. J., 6, 7, 8, 9, 10, 18, 22, 52, 58, 66, 70, 74, 76, 84, 100, 101, 104, 131, 159, 200, *208, 230*

Wells, M. J., 94, *227*

Westman, J. C., 89, 144, 151, 155, 170, 174, 175, 179, *207, 230*

White, L. K., 12, 16, 197, *205*

White, S. W., 55, 62, 77, 95, 98, 121, 122, 123, 163, *205, 230*

Whitehead, L., 145, 187, *230*

Whitehurs, R. N., 91, *219*

Whiteside, M. F., 159, *230*

Wierson, M., 195, *210*

Wilcox, B. L., 77, 98, *230*

Wilding, P., 111, 133, *211*

Wilk, J., 86, 87, *230*

Wilkinson, K., 22, *230*

Wineberg, H., 28, *230*

Wise, M. S., 68, *230*

Wiseman, R. S., 32, 35, 50, 51, 54, 57, 61, 75, *230*

Witcher, W. C., 134, 137, *204*

Wolff, K., 86, 90, *230*

Woody, R. H., 112, *230*

Woolley, P., 74, *230*

Woolsey, S., 87, *230*

Wright, D., 52, 53, 55, 57, 66, 67, *230*

Wright, G. C., 9, *231*

Y

Yorburg, B., 2, *231*

Young, D. M., 179, 184, 185, 186, 194, 197, *231*

Young, E. R., 146, 147, 176, 177, 190, *231*

Z

Zajonc, R. B., 195, *231*

Zartman, I. W., 58, *231*

Zaslow, M. J., 199, *231*

Zeeb, L., 199, *206*

Zeiss, A., 119, *231*

Zeiss, R., 119, *231*

Zill, N., 142, 181, *211, 231*

Zumeta, Z., 27, *208*

Subject Index

A

Academic achievement, 144
  adolescence and, 195
  latency-aged children and, 186–188
  paternal absence and, 186–188, 195
  preschool children and, 177–179
Acceptance, 35–36, 156
Active spouse, 62–63
Adjustment to divorce
  of adolescents
    stress of family relationship and,
      194–195
  building new social networks, 70–72
  of children, 145, 155–157
    five stages in, 156
    quality of predivorce family and,
      153–154
    six developmental tasks to master,
      156–157
  of fathers
    being apart from children, 125–126
    mobility after divorce, 123
    visitation and, 129–130
  length of time following divorce and, 122
  measurement of, 55
  to parenting in divorced families, 72–75
  speed of passage through stages of di-
    vorce and, 61–62
  variables associated with, 121–123

and winning, 75–76
Adolescents, 190–191
  conflicts with parents, 91–92
  development of autonomy in, 190–191,
    194
  early sexual activity in, 175–177
  effects of paternal absence on, 147
  increase in divorce rate and, 191
  long-term effects of divorce
    intergenerational transmission of
      divorce, 196–198
  seeking support outside the family, 184
  short-term effects of divorce
    behavioral reactions, 192–193
    emotional reactions, 193–195
    school behavior and performance, 195
Age
  of child
    and problems in parent–child relation-
      ships, 91–92
    and reaction to divorce, 168–201
    at time of divorce, 171–172, 197, 198,
      199
  effects of, on divorce, 4–5
  at time of marriage, 17
Aggression, 144, 174, 175, 177–178,
  181–182, 183
Aid to Families with Dependent Children
  (AFDC), 101–102
Alignment, 184–186

Alimony, 10
  judges' considerations for, 8–9
Anger, 33–34, 43, 67, 183, 188, 193
  in latency-aged children, 180–182
Anger stage, 156
Animal research
  problems with generalizing results to
    human behavior, 117
Antisocial behavior. *See Behavioral prob-
    lems*
Anxiety, 42, 62
Argentina
  divorce laws in, 10
Attributions
  and cognitive consistency, 80
Attribution theory, 52, 54
Authoritarian parenting style, 136
Authoritative parenting style, 136
Authority structure
  in single-parent family, 90–92
Autonomy, 39
  adolescents' development of, 190–191,
    194
Autonomy versus shame stage, 45, 151

B

Bargaining stage, 156
Behavioral autonomy, 191
Behavioral reactions/problems, 145
  of adolescents, 192–193
  of latency-aged children, 180–182
  of preschool children, 171–172,
    177–179
Best interest of the child standard, 104
Binuclear family, 72, 88
Births
  divorce and premarital, 27–30
    explanations for strong relationship
      regarding, 28–29
    three interrelated dimensions to con-
      sider, 28
Blacks. *See Race/ethnicity*
Blame styles, 184–185
Boundary redefinition, 90
Broken family. *See Single-parent families*
Bronfenbrenner's four-system schema,
    165–167

C

Causal attribution, 78
Child development
  and divorce, 152–155
    adjustment to, 155–157
    psychosocial and psychosexual develop-
      mental theory, 150–152
    social cognitive developmental theory,
      149–150
  psychological theories concerning, 114
Children of divorce, 141–142, 149–155,
    158–159
  adjustment of, 155–157
    and age of, at time of divorce, 171–172
    and fathers being apart from, 125–126
    five stages of, 156
    and quality of family before divorce
      for, 153–154
  age and reaction to divorce, 168–170,
    198–201
    adolescents, 190–198
    latency-aged, 179–190
    preschool, 170–179
    problems in parent–child relationships
      and, 91–92
    regarding social interaction and play
      of, 171
  parents recieving custody of, 37–38, 47,
    134–137
  economic situation of, 159–162
  exhibiting negative behavior, 161
  family dynamics of, 143–148
  family relationships of, 162–164
  father's absence and, 146–148
  fathers visiting, 124–130
    mothers preventing, 127, 128–129
  feelings on income loss and maternal em-
    ployment, 161
  negative effects of divorce on, 200–201
  overprotected, 92
  parents jelous of, 92
  parents reestablishing relationship with,
    72–73, 74–75
  privileges of, in single-parent family, 162
  rejecting mothers, 160
  research on, 164–167
  in single-father families, 134–137
  six developmental tasks to master,
    156–157
  statistics for, 142–143

status of, in family hierarchy, 162
support sources for, 163
Child's best interest guideline, 9
Child support, 9, 10
Church. *See Religion*
Coercion, cycle of, 161
Cognitive consistency, 66, 69, 70, 78, 80
    attributions and, 80–81
    theory of, 52, 54–55
Cognitive development
    effects of paternal absence on, 147–148
Cognitive dissonance
    strategies used in resolving, 59
    theory of, 54
Community divorce, 38, 70–71
Compensatory masculinity, 174–175
Conflicts, 57, 153, 187
    approach–avoidance, 59, 66
    between adolescents and parents, 91–92
    causal dimensions of, 54
    family, 194–195
    interparental, 89, 153–154
    regarding economic settlements, 70
Co-parental divorce, 37–38
Co-parenting, 75, 88
Coping mechanisms, 35
Couple identity, 20
Crisis theory, 32, 35
Crude rate, 3–4, 82
Culture
    biases about fathers' visitation, 127
    and determining maternal behavior,
        105–107
    and determining roles in child care and
        family, 118
    values and attitudes of, on divorce,
        22–24, 72
Custodial parents, *see also Fathers,*
        divorced; Mothers, divorced; Non-
        custodial parents
    children identifying with, 185
    conflict with, 128–129
    courts' preference for, 37–38
    fathers, 73–74, 130–138
    mothers, 73–74, 83–103
        voluntary noncustodial, 105, 108
Custody, 73, 88–89
    historical perspective on granting,
        124–125
    joint, 88, 131
    legal standards for decisions involving,
        104–105, 124–125

child's best interest guideline, 9
parent granted, 37–38, 47
    fathers, 111, 132–133, 134–137
    same- vs. opposite-gender, 134–137
    sole, 131
    split, 131

D

Deciding stage, 56–57, 153
    personal and social resources involved in,
        57–58
    weighing psychological/social attractions
        and barriers, 58–61
Delinquency, 192, 193
    paternal absence and, 193
Denial, 33, 57, 172
    stage of, 156
Dependency on parent, 174, 179
Depression, 43, 137
    divorce and number of children concern-
        ing, 99
    fathers being apart from children and,
        125–126
    loss and, 33
    separated and divorced individuals and,
        99
Depression stage, 156
Detachment, 47
    stage of, 41–42
Development
    divorce as a process of, 152–155
    psychosocial and psychosexual theories
        on, 150–151
Discrimination
    against single-parent families, 86–88
Disillusionment stage, 40
Divorce, *see also Adjustment to divorce;*
        Gender differences
    and adolescents, 190–198
    children
        age at time of, 197, 198, 199
        experience of, 157–164
        latency-aged, 179–190
        measuring its effects on, 169
        negative effects of, on, 200–201
        preschool, 170–179
    cost of, 14, 15
    as a developmental process, 152–155
    dynamic vs. structural view of, 143–144

economic conditions of family after,
　　10–18, 100–102, 159–162
effects of, on friendships, 38, 64–65,
　　70–72, 96–98
effects of industrialization and urbaniza-
　　tion on, 4, 11–13, 18
effects on men vs. women, 120–121
family dynamics of, 143–148
fathers' moving away after, 123
four main aspects of formal, 68–75
intergenerational transmission of, 147
　　and adolescents, 196–198
as a matter of mistaken choice, 2
mental health problems and, 120–121,
　　125–126, 193–194
　　for fathers, 119–121
　　for mothers, 98–100
opportunities for personal growth from,
　　75
past views on, 2–3
positive vs. negative outcomes of, 143
relationship of family after, 162–164
social interaction to reduce stress during,
　　78
from a social perspective
　　cultural values and attitudes, 22–24
　　economic conditions, 10–18
　　gender-ratio theory, 26–27
　　individualistic vs. social explanations,
　　　1–3
　　legal procedure, 5–10
　　premarital pregnancy and birth, 27–30
　　race and ethnicity, 24–25
　　religion, 18–21
　　statistics, 3–5
two unique characteristics of, 32
weighing psychological/social attractions
　　and barriers to, 17–18, 52–54, 58–61,
　　65–67, 78–80
Divorce crisis, 59, 158–159
definitions of, 55–56
Divorced family. See Single-parent families
Divorced fathers. See Fathers, divorced
Divorced mothers. See Mothers, divorced
Divorce process
adjustment and speed of passage through
　　stages of, 61–62
application of crisis theory to, 32, 35
stages of, 153–155
various models of, 31–50, 51–81
Divorce rates. See Rates, divorce
Divorce settlements, 37, 65, 70

based on equality, 8–9
Dynamic analysis, 143–146

E

Earnings. See Income
Economic conditions, 29–30, 200, see also
　　Income
divorce and, 10
　　industrialization and urbanization con-
　　　cerning, 11–13
　　prosperity and depression concerning,
　　　13–15
　　socioeconomic levels in relation to,
　　　15–18
of divorced mothers and families, 10,
　　100–102, 159–162
Economic divorce, 37
Economic transition, 69–70
Education
adjustment to divorce and, 76–77
divorce rate and, 16–18
　　three types of relationships between,
　　　16–17
of single father, 133
Egocentric pre-Oedipal stage, 149
Ego integrity versus despair stage, 48
Emotional autonomy, 191
Emotional divorce, 36, 50
Emotional reactions to divorce
of adolescents to divorce, 193–195
of latency-aged children to divorce,
　　182–183
of preschool children to divorce, 172–174
Employment, maternal, 15, 11–12, 160,
　　161, 173
Erikson's theory
of personality development, 44–48
Erosion stage, 40–41
Ethnicity. See Race/ethnicity
Exchange model, 52–53
Exosystem, 165, 166, 167
Exploration and hard work stage, 43–44

F

Failure, feelings of, 42
Family, 64–65

binuclear, 72, 88
child's status in, 162
culture determining roles in child care
    and, 118
dynamic view of divorce regarding,
    143–148
economic conditions of divorced, 10,
    100–102, 159–162
relationship of, after divorce, 162–164
    adolescents' adjustment and stress of,
        194–195
    latency-aged children and, 184–186
support of, 70–71, 98
Family, single-father. See Single-parent
    families
Family, single-parent. See Single-parent
    families
Family cohesion
    effects of, on self-esteem, 185–186
Family deficit (FD) model, 145
Family environment (FE) model, 145, 152
Family process perspective, 200
Family structure, 200
    changes in, 73, 192
    changing women's roles and, 23–24
Father–child relationships, 88–89
Fatherhood
    historical perspective on, 112–113
    scientific perspective on, 113–115
Fathers, role of, 114–115, 115–119
Fathers, divorced, see also Custodial par-
    ents; Parents; Noncustodial parents
    absence of, 146–148, 175, 186, 192
        and academic achievement of child,
            186–188, 195
        and delinquency, 193
        effects on daughters, 175–176
        and gender role development, 188
        long-term effect of, 145
    custodial, 73–74, 111, 130–138
        interfering in mother–child relation-
            ship, 109
    custody decisions favoring, 124–125
    impact of divorce on, 119–121
    improvement in economic status of,
        100–101
    moving away after divorce, 123
    noncustodial, 74
    research on, 138–140
        limitations on, 138–139
        new directions for, 139–140
    and single-parent families

as heads of, 130–138
involvement in their life, 88–89
variables associated with adjustment of,
    121–123
visitation
    adjusting to divorce and, 129–130
    artificiality in, 128
    conflict with custodial parent, 128–129
    cultural biases, 127
    effects of being apart from the chil-
        dren, 125–126
    effects of other commitments on, 128
    emotionally difficult, 127–128
    frequency of, 125, 126–127, 129–130
    historical perspective on, 124–125
    mothers preventing, 127, 128–129
Financial settlements, 37, 65, 70
    based on equality, 8–9
Friendships
    divorce and, 64–65
    establishing new, 38, 70–72, 96–98
    single mothers' problems with, 97
    three phases in, 71

G

Gender
    age at time of marriage and divorce re-
        garding, 4–5
Gender differences
    in adolescent behavioral problems,
        188–190, 192–193
    of children
        in custody of fathers vs. mothers,
            134–137
        in interpersonal reasoning, 190
        latency-aged, regarding anger and
            stress, 180–182
        and paternal absence, 147
        preschool, reacting to divorce, 170
        preschool, regarding relationship to
            mothers, 171
        related to divorce, 199
    concerning importance of marriage,
        119–120
    regarding divorce, 60
        adjusting to, 71–72
        educational levels and rate of, 17
        laws in Islamic countries, 10
        risks for, 24–25

regarding problems with parent–child relationship, 91–92
regarding stress from separation, 67–78
Gender identification, 151
    boys', 174–175
    girls', 175–177
Gender-ratio theory, 26–27
Gender role, *see also Roles*
    development, effects of paternal absence on, 146
    division, 113
        natural, 117–118
Generativity versus stagnation stage, 47–48
Glick effect, 17
Grief, 158, 182–183
Guilt, feelings of, 42, 46

H

Health, *see also Mental health problems; Psychological consequences/ problems*
    adjustment to divorce and, 77
    fathers being apart from children and declining, 125–126
Health professionals
    discrimination against single-parent families and, 87

I

Identification
    gender
        boys', 174–175
        girls', 175–177
    with parent, 179
        absent, 152
        custodial, 185
        same-gender, 151
Identity, 151, 194
    couple, 20
    reorientation of lifestyle and, 34–35
Identity versus role confusion stage, 46–47
Idiosyncratic reaction stage, 71
Income, *see also Economic conditions*
    as a deciding factor in custody decisions, 104–105, 108, 125

divorce and, 15–16
    effects of, 76, 161, 190
    increase in wife's, 12
    of single father, 133, 137
Industrialization, 29
    divorce and, 11–13, 18
        effects of economic independence, 11–12
        selection of spouse regarding, 12–13
Industry
    interference with development in sense of, 178
Industry versus inferiority stage, 46, 151
Inferiority, 46
Initiative versus guilt stage, 45–46
In-laws
    diminishing interaction with, 96
Interfaith marriages, 21
Intergenerational transmission of divorce, 147
    and adolescents, 196–198
Interparental relationship, 144–145
Interpersonal reasoning, 149–150, 190
Intimacy versus isolation stage, 47
Irreconcilable differences, 6, 7
Islamic countries
    divorce laws in, 10
    industrialization's effect on divorce rate in, 11
Isolation, 47
Italy
    divorce laws in, 10

J

Japan
    industrialization's effect on divorce rate in, 11
Joint custody, 88, 131

L

Laissez-faire parenting style, 136
Latency, 151
Latency-aged children, 179–180
    aligning with parent, 184–186
    blame styles of, 184–185

long-term effects of divorce, 188–190
seeking support inside the family, 184
short-term effects of divorce
  behavioral reactions, 180–182
  emotional reactions, 182–183
  family relationships, 184–186
  school performance, 186–188
Laws, divorce, 5–10
  effects of social trends and changes on,
    6–7
  international, 10
  no-fault, 6–10, 68–69
  older and traditional, 5–6
  purposes served by reforming, 7
Lawyers
  as being supportive to clients, 69
Legal divorce, 36–37, 50
Legal transition, 68–69
Lifestyle
  reorientation of identity and, 34–35
Loneliness, feelings of, 42, 121, 122, 137

M

Macrosystem, 165, 166
Marital status
  change in, 121
  and suicide, 99
Marriages
  age at time of, 17
  arranged, 11
  effects of length of, on divorce, 5
  effects of number of, on divorce, 4
  gender differences in importance of,
    119–120
  interfaith, 21
  intergenerational transmission of unsta-
    ble, 147, 196–198
  pregnancy and birth before, 17, 27–30
  rate of, 1–2
  second, 35
    attractiveness of, 79
    effects on visitation, 128
    median time interval between divorce
      and, 86
  self-fulfillment and love as basis for, 22
  as a social resource, 64
  weighing psychological/social attractions
    and barriers in, 17–18, 52–54, 58–61,
    65–67, 78–80

Masculinity, compensatory, 174–175
Maternal behavior
  as innate vs. culturally determined,
    105–107
Maternal employment, 160, 161, 173
Mental health problems, *see also Health;*
    Psychological consequences/
    problems
  of adolescents from divorced families,
    193–194
  divorced vs. married individuals,
    120–121
  fathers being apart from children and
    developing, 125–126
  single individuals and, 99
Microsystem, 166
Models of divorce process, 31–32, 48–50
  comparison of, 49–50, 51
  problems with, 49–50
  psychological, 39–44
  psychosocial, 51–81
  regarding Erikson's personality develop-
    ment theory, 44–48
  six stations of divorce, 36–39
  Wiseman's model, 32–36
Mother–child relationships, 171
  father's interference in, 109
  of noncustodial mothers, 109–110
  in single-parent families, 90–93
Mothers, divorced, 82–83, *see also Custo-*
    dial parents; Parents; Noncustodial
    parents
  child exhibiting negative behavior in pres-
    ence of, 161
  child's rejection of, 160–161
  custodial, 73–74, 83–103
  custody decisions favoring, 124–125
  dating of, 93
  economic situation of, 10, 101, 159–162
  employment of, 160, 161
  innate vs. culturally determined behavior
    of, 105–107
  kin support of, in Japan, 11
  noncustodial, 103–110
  parentification and dependent, 92
  preventing fathers from visiting children,
    127, 128–129
Mourning
  divorce as a process of, 32–36
  stage of, 42–43, 154
Mutual withdrawal stage, 71

N

Neighbors
  supportive of single mothers, 98
No-fault divorce law, 6-10
  effects of, 9-10
  four most important characteristics of,
    7-9
No-fault divorce laws, 68-69
  criticism of, 68-69
Noncustodial parents, 88-89, *see also Custodial parents; Fathers, divorced; Mothers, divorced; Parents*
  fathers, 74
  mothers, 103
    characteristics of, 107-108
    father's interference in relationship with child, 109
    mother-child relationships of, 109-110
    psychological consequences for, 108-109
    stigma and guilt of, 103-104
    stressful status of, 105, 107, 108-110
    viewed as deviant, 103-107
    voluntary, 105, 108

O

Occupation
  divorce rate and type of, 16
Oedipal stage, 151, 174, 175, 177-178, 182, 194
Ontogenic system, 166

P

Parental transition, 72-75
Parent-child relationships, 88-89, 144-145, 152, 163-164
  age of child and problems with, 91-92
  of custodial vs. noncustodial parents, 47-48, 109-110
  divorce and changes in, 163
  father-child, 88-89
  mother-child, 171
    father's interference in, 109
    of noncustodial mothers, 109-110
    in single-parent families, 90-93

quality of, 173
reestablishment of, 72-73, 74-75
in single-parent families, 90-93
Parenthood
  in single-father families, 137-138
Parentification, 193
  of sons and daughters, 92
Parenting
  behavior of animals, 117
  culture determining roles in family and, 118
  overprotecting children, 92
  quality of
    preschool children and, 170-171
    single-fathers and, 136-137
  three styles of, 136
Parents, *see also Custodial parents; Fathers, divorced; Mothers, divorced; Noncustodial parents*
  children aligning with, 184-186
  fathers as auxiliary, 88
  granted custody, 37-38, 124-125
  jealous of children, 92
  measuring the effects of divorce on children, 169
Partial family. *See Single-parent families*
Passive spouse, 62-63
Paternal absence, 146-148, 175, 186, 192
  and academic achievement of child, 186-188, 195
  and delinquency, 193
  effects of, on daughters, 175-176
  and gender role development, 188
  long-term effect of, 145
Personality development
  Erikson's theory of, 44-48
Personal resources, 57-58, 63-65, 76-78
Physical separation stage, 42
Poverty, 101, 159
Predecision period, 153
Pregnancy
  divorce and premarital, 17, 27-30
    explanations for strong relationship regarding, 28-29
    three interrelated dimensions to consider, 28
Preschool children, 170-171
  long-term effects of divorce on behavioral and academic consequences, 177-179
  boy's gender identification, 174-175
  girls' gender behavior, 175-177

short-term effects of divorce on
  behavioral reactions, 171–172
  emotional reactions, 172–174
Promiscuity. *See Sexual intercourse*
Property settlements, 37, 65, 70
  based on equality, 8–9
Psychic divorce, 39, 153
Psychoanalytic theory, 114
Psychological attractions/barriers
  weighing of, 58–61, 65–67, 78–80
Psychological consequences/problems, *see
  also Health; Mental health problems*
  of divorce for mothers, 98–100
  for noncustodial mothers, 108–109
Psychosexual development
  effects of paternal absence on, 146
  theories of, 150–151
Psychosocial model of divorce process,
    51–52
  stages of, 55–56
    deciding, 56–61
    separating, 61–67
    struggling, 67–75
    winning, 75–81
  theoretical orientation and principles re-
    garding, 52–55, 150–151

R

Race/ethnicity
  divorce and, 24–25
  gender-ratio theory and, 27
  intergenerational transmission of divorce
    and, 196–197
  premarital pregnancy and birth regarding,
    28, 29
Rallying around stage, 71
Rates, divorce, 1–2
  economic independence of women and,
    17, 18
  effects of industrialization and urbaniza-
    tion on, 11–13
  factors influencing, 4–5
  increase in, 82
    families with adolescents, 191
  no-fault divorce laws and, 68
  techniques for calculation of, 3–4
Rationalization, 57
Reasoning, interpersonal, 149–150
Reconciliation, 63, 67, 79

Re-equilibration, 155
Regression, 44, 46, 171, 174, 183, 194
Relationships, building new, 70–72
Relatives, support of, 96, 98
Religion, 18–21
  categories of, 19–20
  discrimination against single-parent fami-
    lies and, 86
  divorce and degree of involvement in, 10,
    20–21
  effects of, on divorce, 5
  interfaith marriages, 21
  of single father, 134
Remarriage, 35
  attractiveness of, 79
  effects of, on visitation, 128
  median time interval between divorce
    and, 86
Research
  on children of divorce, 164–167
  intact vs. divorced families, 143–144
  problems with generalizing animal
    research to human, 117
  on single-father families, 131–132
    limitations for, 138–139
    new directions for, 139–140
  on single-parent families, 102–103
    family systems approach for, 95
    importance of, 94–95
    new directions for, 95–96, 103
Resources, personal and social, 57–58,
    63–65, 76–78
Role confusion, 46–47, 151
Roles
  changes in, 192
  family structure and changing women's,
    23–24
  of fathers, 114–115, 115–117
    as changing, 118–119
    natural gender role division and, 113,
      117–118
  redefinition of parental, 73–74
  reversal of, 92
  society and defining, 123
  theories concerning, 49, 114, 120
Rural areas
  divorce rate in, 4, 11

S

School performance. *See Academic achievement*

Second adolescence stage, 43
Selectivity theory, 120
Self-actualization, 48
Self-affirmation, 80–81
Self-concept, 145
Self-esteem, 175, 176, 177
    effects of different types of family cohesion on, 185–186
Self-fulfillment, 22
Self-reflective late latency stage, 150
Separating stage
    active and passive spouses in, 62–63
    impact of, 61–62
    weighing social/psychological attractions and barriers during, 63–65, 65–67
Separation, 42
    not deciding about permanency of, 65
    social interaction to reduce stress during, 78
    spouse initiating, 42, 64
Settlements, divorce, 37, 65, 70
    based on equality, 8–9
    judges' considerations for, 8–9
Sexual intercourse
    divorced individuals and, 35
    early adolescent, 175–177, 189–190
Sibling rivalry, 92–93
Single-parent families, 82, 83–110, see also
        Mothers, divorced
    adjustment and redefining roles in, 72–75
    authority structure in, 90–92
    characteristics of, 84
    child's status and privileges in, 162
    as deviant, 85–88
    double, 72
    economic consequences of divorce for, 100–102
    factors associated with success of, 102
    family systems approach to studying, 95
    father's involvement in, 88–89
    fathers as heads of
        background and statistics on, 130–131
        characteristics of father in, 133–134
        children in, 134–137
        limited research on, 131–132
        managing life and parenthood in, 137–138
        reasons for receiving custody in, 132–133
    mother–child relationships in, 90–93
    psychological consequences of divorce for, 98–100

quality of life in, 93–96
research studies on, 94–96
seeking help with problems, 94
society and, 84–88, 93–94
stigma attached to, 22–23
support networks and social life for, 96–98
as a temporary condition, 85–86
three spheres of life for, 84
Social attractions/barriers
    weighing of, 58–61, 65–67, 78–80
Social class
    effects of, on divorce, 4
Social cognitive developmental theory, 149–150
Social exchange theory, 52–54
    testing of, at deciding stage, 60
Social isolation, 47, 121
Socialization
    for single-parent families, 96–98
Social resources, 57–58, 63–65, 76–78
Social status
    of being married, 64
Social support networks, 123
    adjustment to divorce and, 70–72, 77–78
    for adolescents, 184
    for single fathers, 136–137, 138
    for single-parent families, 96–98
    sources for children, 163
Social transition, 70–72
Social trends
    effects of, on divorce laws, 6–7
Society
    and defining roles for divorced men, 123
    divorce and, 1–3, 72
    noncustodial mothers and, 104–107
    and single-parent families, 84–88
    values and attitudes of, on divorce, 22–24
    views on maternal behavior, 105–107
Socioeconomic status, 29, 160–161, 174, 176
    divorce and
        education, 16–18
        income, 15–16
        occupation, 16
    and divorce rate, 25
    intergenerational transmission of divorce and, 197
    of single father, 133
Sole custody, 131
Soviet Union
    divorce laws in, 10

Spain
  divorce laws in, 10
Split custody, 131
Spouses
  active vs. passive, 62–63
  industrialization and selection of, 12–13
  quality of relationship between former,
    163
  reestablishing of relationship after
    divorce, 73
  wives preventing fathers from visiting
    children, 127
Statistics, divorce, 1–2, 3–5, 82
  for children of divorced parents, 142–143
  difficulty interpreting, 3
  factors influencing, 4–5
  on single-father families, 131
  techniques for calculating, 3–4
Stigma
  diminishing, on divorce, 85
  regarding noncustodial mothers, 103–104
Strategic withdrawal, 194
Stress, 33, 89, 121, 122, 144, 155, 180
  during struggling stage, 67–68
  economic, 69–70, 159–161
  experienced before divorce and preschool
    children, 170
  of family relationship and adolescents'
    adjustment, 194–195
  of noncustodial mothers, 105, 107,
    108–110
  from separation, 62
  social interaction to reduce, 78
Stress theory, 120
Structural analysis, 143–144
Struggling stage
  economic transition in, 69–70
  emotional stress felt, 67–68
  legal transition in, 68–69
  parental transition during, 72–75
  social transition in, 70–72
Subjective early latency stage, 149
Suicide and marital status, 99
Superego, 151
Support
  for adolescents, 184
  of family and friends regarding visitation,
    130
  from lawyers, 69
  for single-fathers, 136–137, 138
  for single-parent families, 96–98
  sources for children, 163

T

Teachers
  evaluating children of divorce, 169,
    186–188
  supporting single fathers, 136–137
Tender years doctrine, 104, 124–125
Theoretical models
  of divorce process, 31–50
Third-person reasoning adolescence stage,
  150
Trust versus mistrust stage, 45, 151

U

Unemployment, 13
  of single mothers, 101
United States
  industrialization's effect on divorce rate,
    11
  rates of divorce and marriage in, 1–2
Urbanization, 29
  divorce and, 4, 11–13, 18

V

Value autonomy, 191
Visitation
  adjusting to divorce and, 129–130
  arrangements for, 73
  artificiality in, 128
  conflict with custodial parent and,
    128–129
  cultural biases, 127
  effects of being apart from the children
    on, 125–126
  effects of other commitments on, 128
  effects of remarriage on, 128
  emotionally difficult, 127–128
  fathers decreasing visits, 125
  frequency of, 125, 126–127, 129–130
  historical perspectives on, 124–125
  mothers preventing, 127, 128–129

W

War
  effects of, on divorce rate, 14–15
Welfare system
  Aid to Families with Dependent Children
    (AFDC), 101–102
  encouraging divorce, 25
Whites. *See Race/ethnicity*
Winning stage
  adjustment during, 75–76
  attributions and cognitive consistency
    during, 80–81
  personal and social resources involved in,
    76–78

weighing psychological/social attractions
  and barriers in, 78–80
Wiseman's model, 32–36
Withdrawal, 145
  strategic, 194
  threshold of, 197
Women
  building a new identity after divorce,
    34–35
  economic independence of, 11–12, 17,
    18
  intergenerational transmission of divorce
    and, 197–198
Women's liberation movement, 23–24,
  124